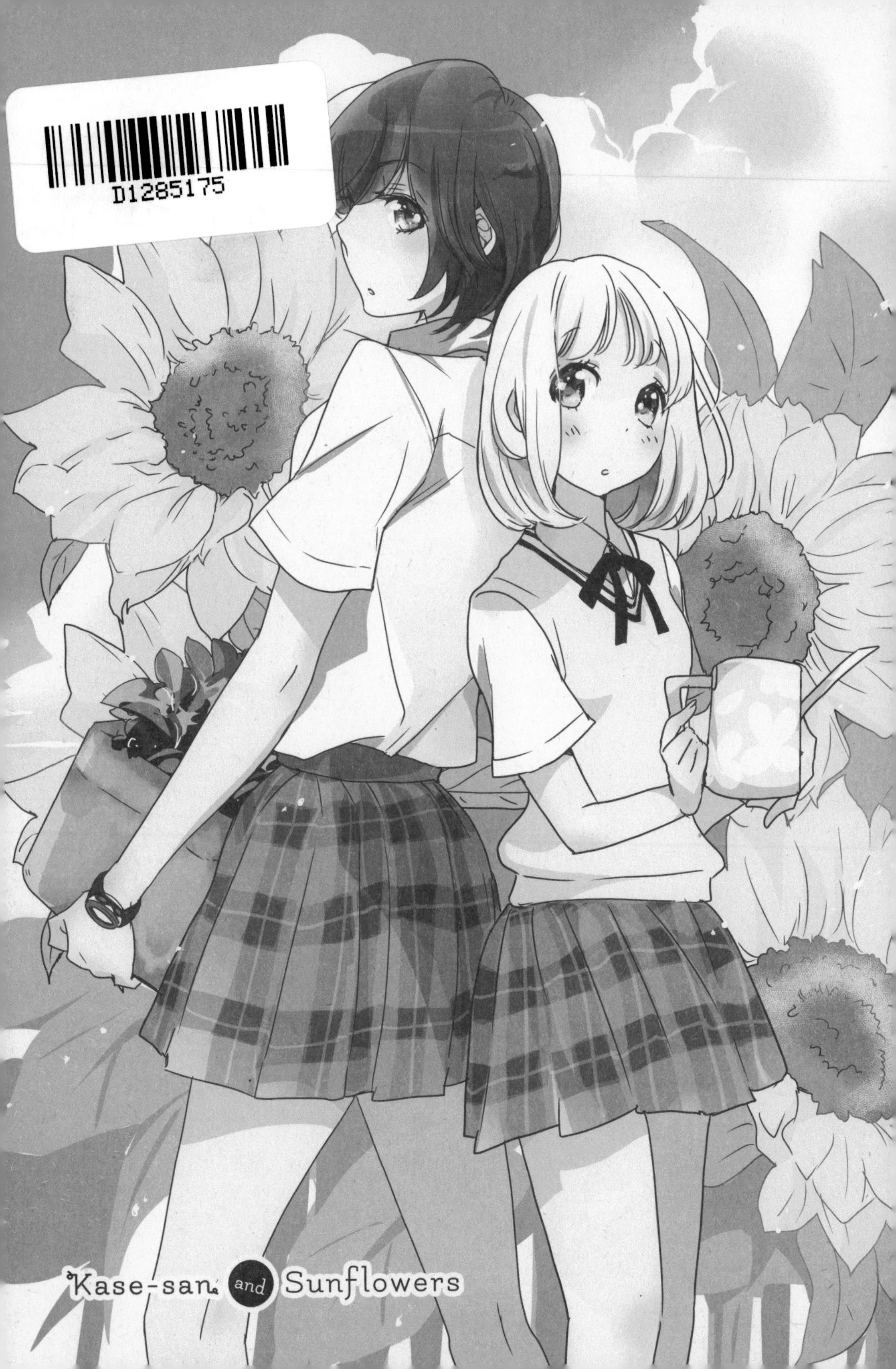
Kase-san and Sunflowers

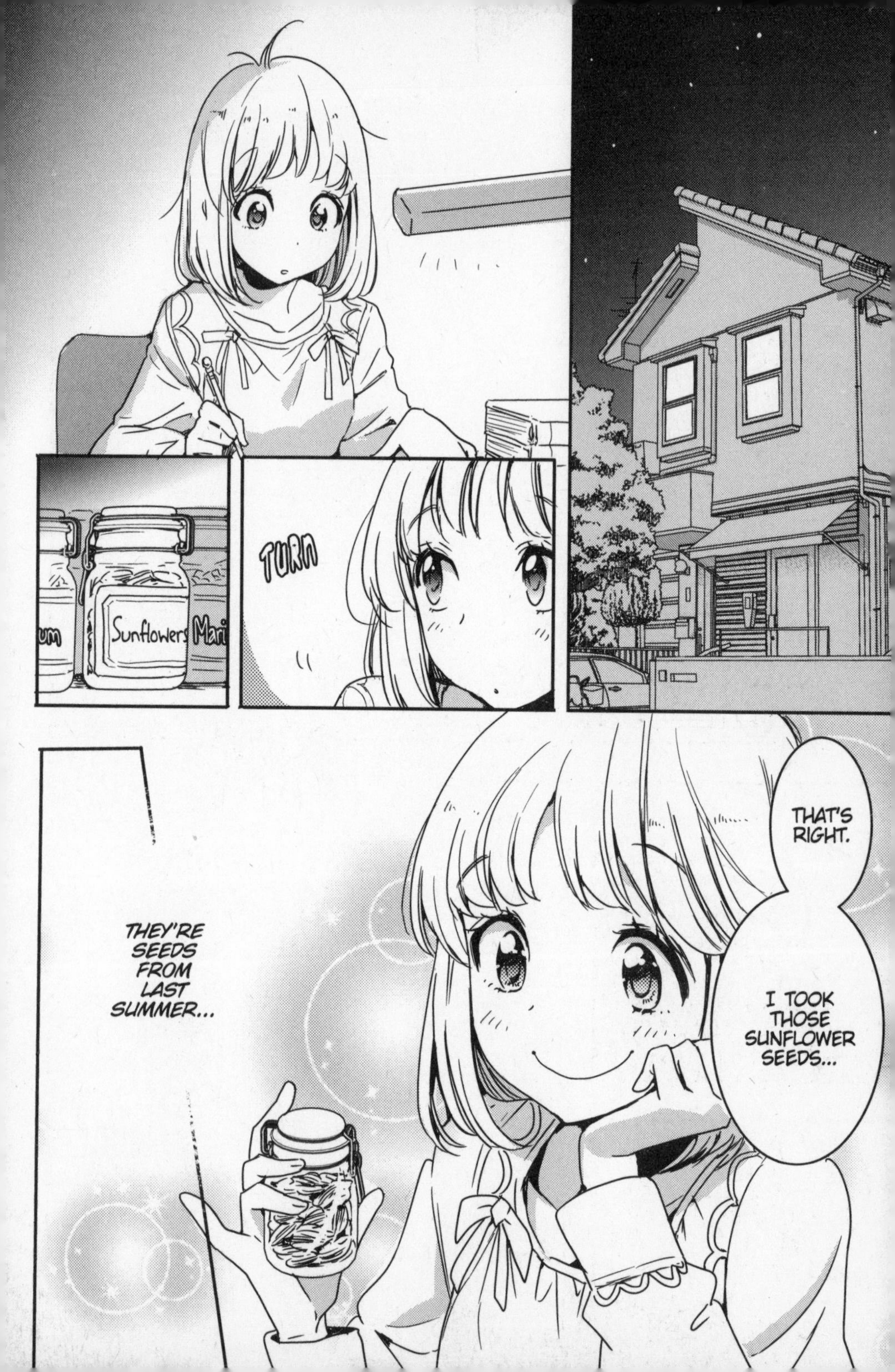
TURN
Sunflowers
THAT'S RIGHT.
I TOOK THOSE SUNFLOWER SEEDS...
THEY'RE SEEDS FROM LAST SUMMER...

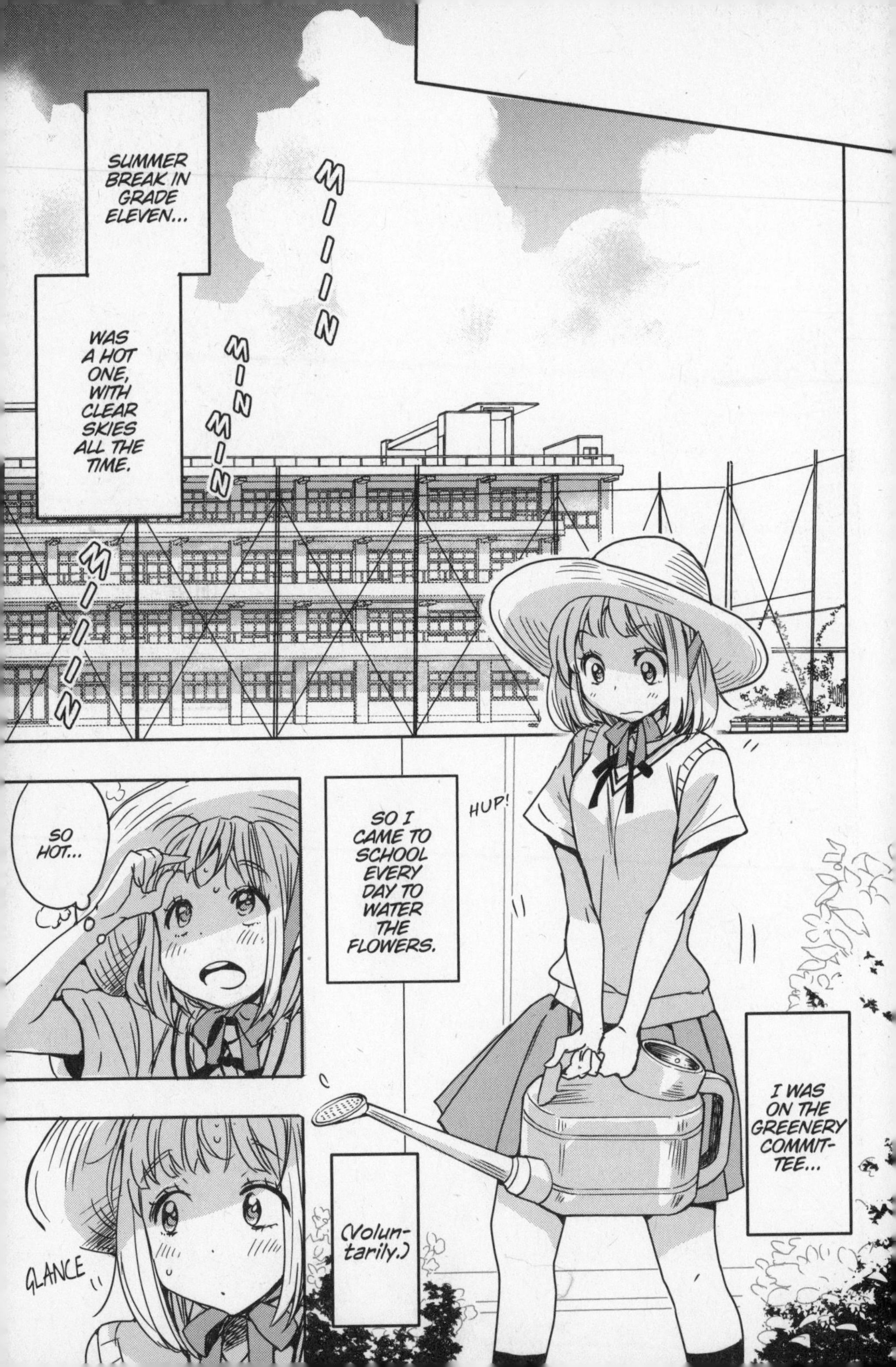
SUMMER BREAK IN GRADE ELEVEN...
WAS A HOT ONE, WITH CLEAR SKIES ALL THE TIME.
MIIIN
MIN MIN
MIIIIN
HUP!
I WAS ON THE GREENERY COMMIT-TEE...
SO I CAME TO SCHOOL EVERY DAY TO WATER THE FLOWERS.
(Volun-tarily.)
SO HOT...
GLANCE

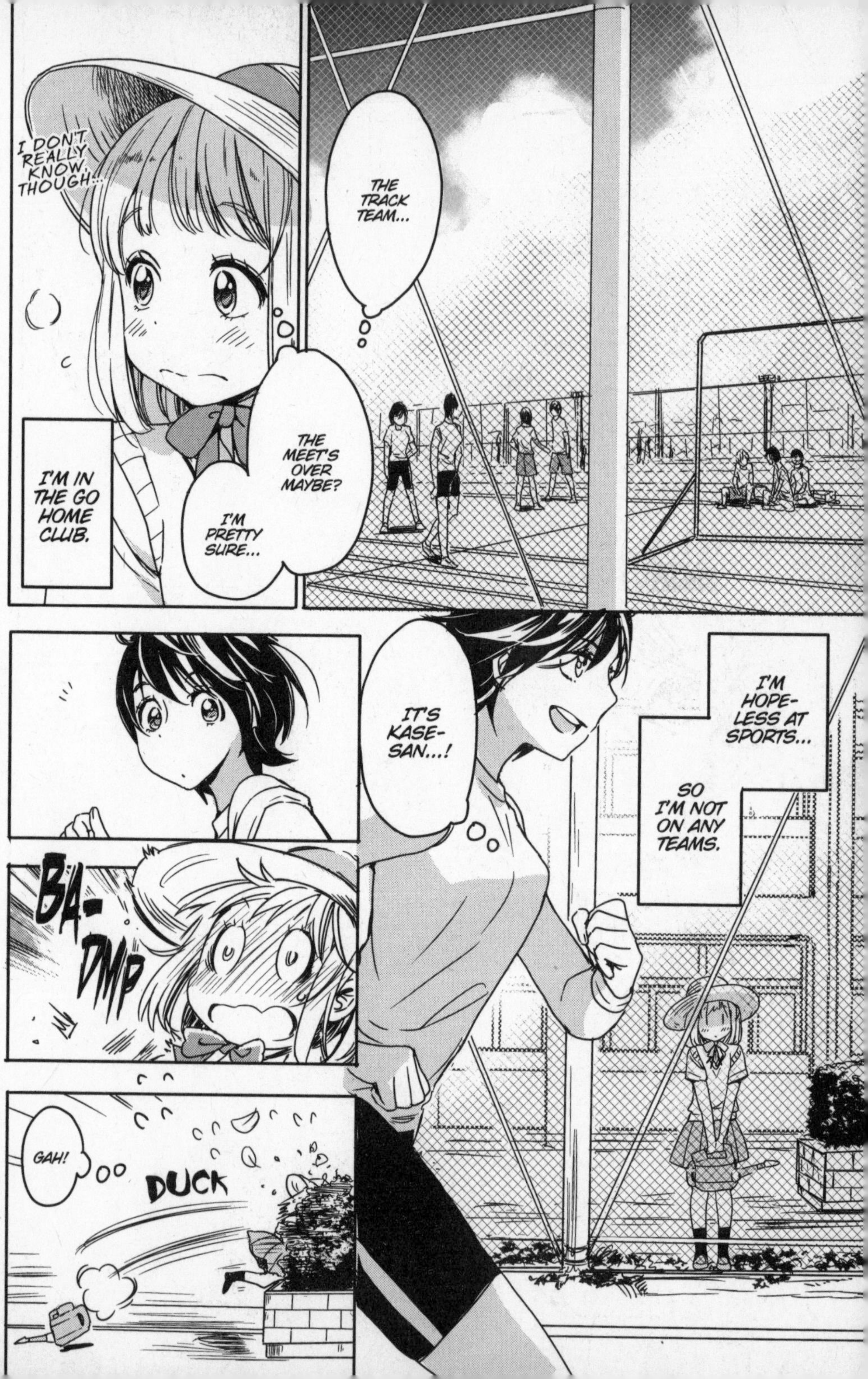
THE TRACK TEAM...
THE MEET'S OVER MAYBE?
I'M PRETTY SURE...
I DON'T REALLY KNOW, THOUGH...
I'M IN THE GO HOME CLUB.
I'M HOPELESS AT SPORTS...
SO I'M NOT ON ANY TEAMS.
IT'S KASE-SAN...!
BA-DMP
GAH!
DUCK

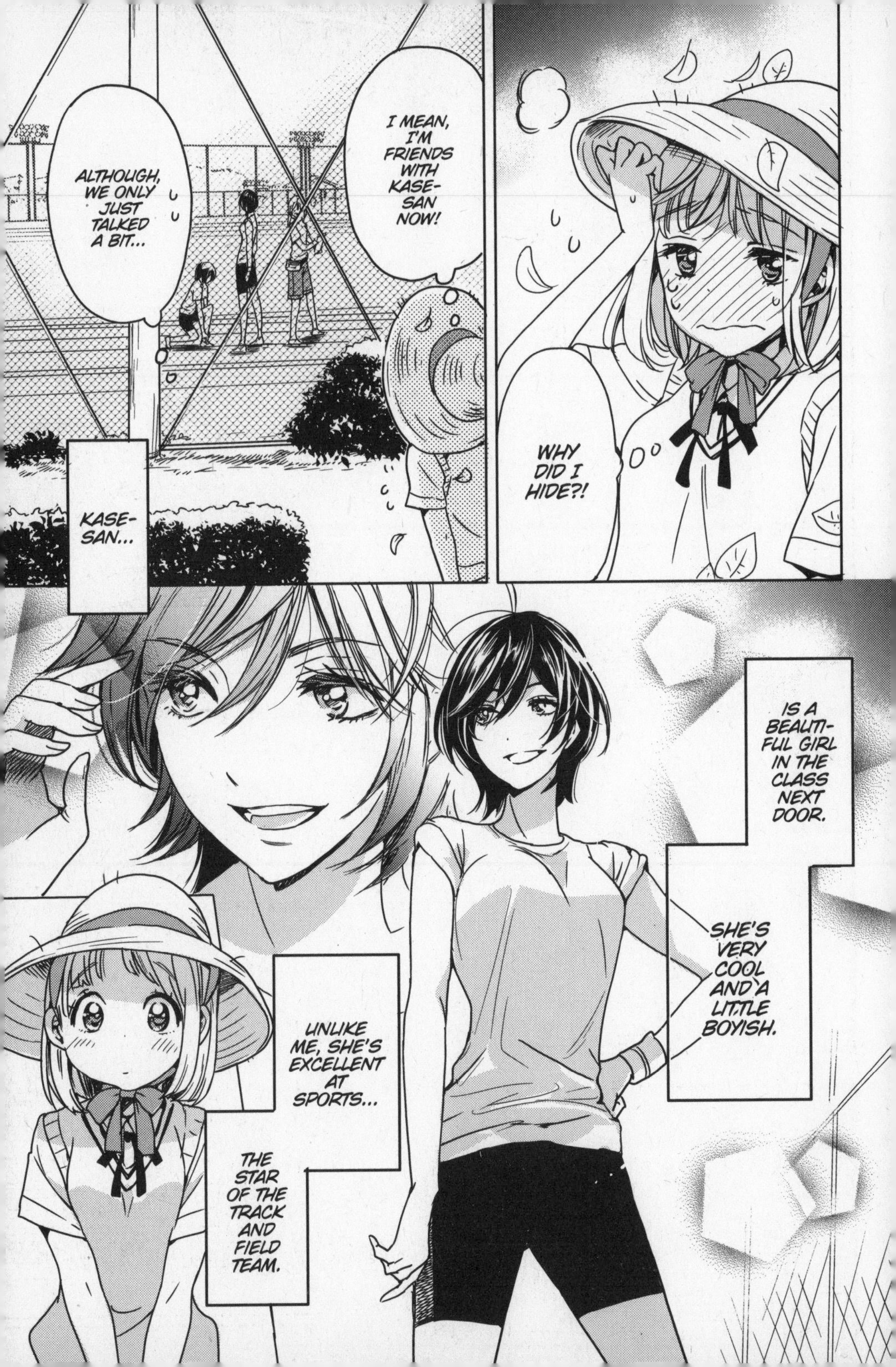
WHY DID I HIDE?!
I MEAN, I'M FRIENDS WITH KASE-SAN NOW!
ALTHOUGH, WE ONLY JUST TALKED A BIT...
KASE-SAN...
IS A BEAUTIFUL GIRL IN THE CLASS NEXT DOOR.
SHE'S VERY COOL AND A LITTLE BOYISH.
UNLIKE ME, SHE'S EXCELLENT AT SPORTS...
THE STAR OF THE TRACK AND FIELD TEAM.

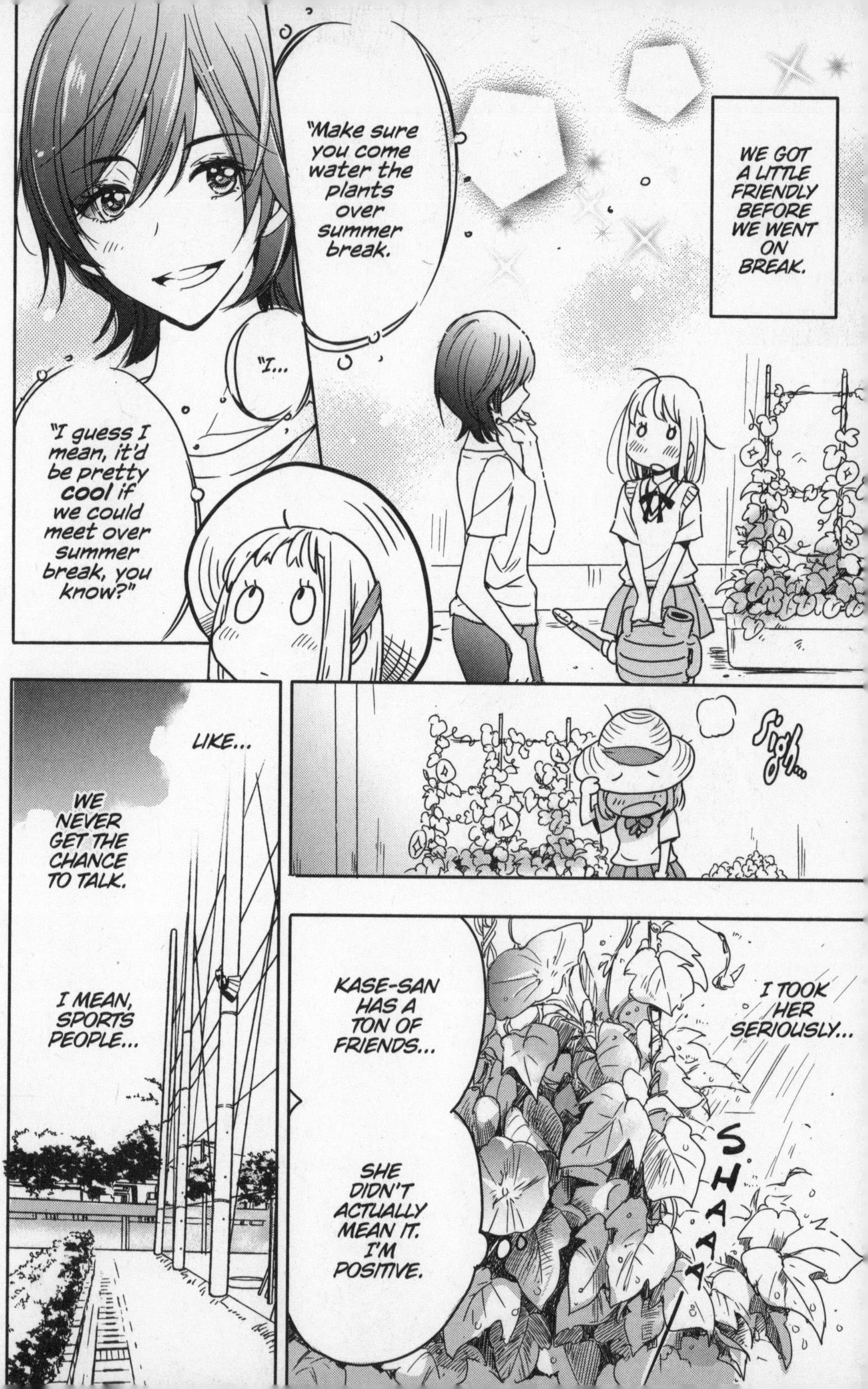
WE GOT A LITTLE FRIENDLY BEFORE WE WENT ON BREAK.
"Make sure you come water the plants over summer break.
"I...
"I guess I mean, it'd be pretty cool if we could meet over summer break, you know?"
Sigh...
I TOOK HER SERIOUSLY...
KASE-SAN HAS A TON OF FRIENDS...
SHE DIDN'T ACTUALLY MEAN IT. I'M POSITIVE.
SHAAA
LIKE...
WE NEVER GET THE CHANCE TO TALK.
I MEAN, SPORTS PEOPLE...

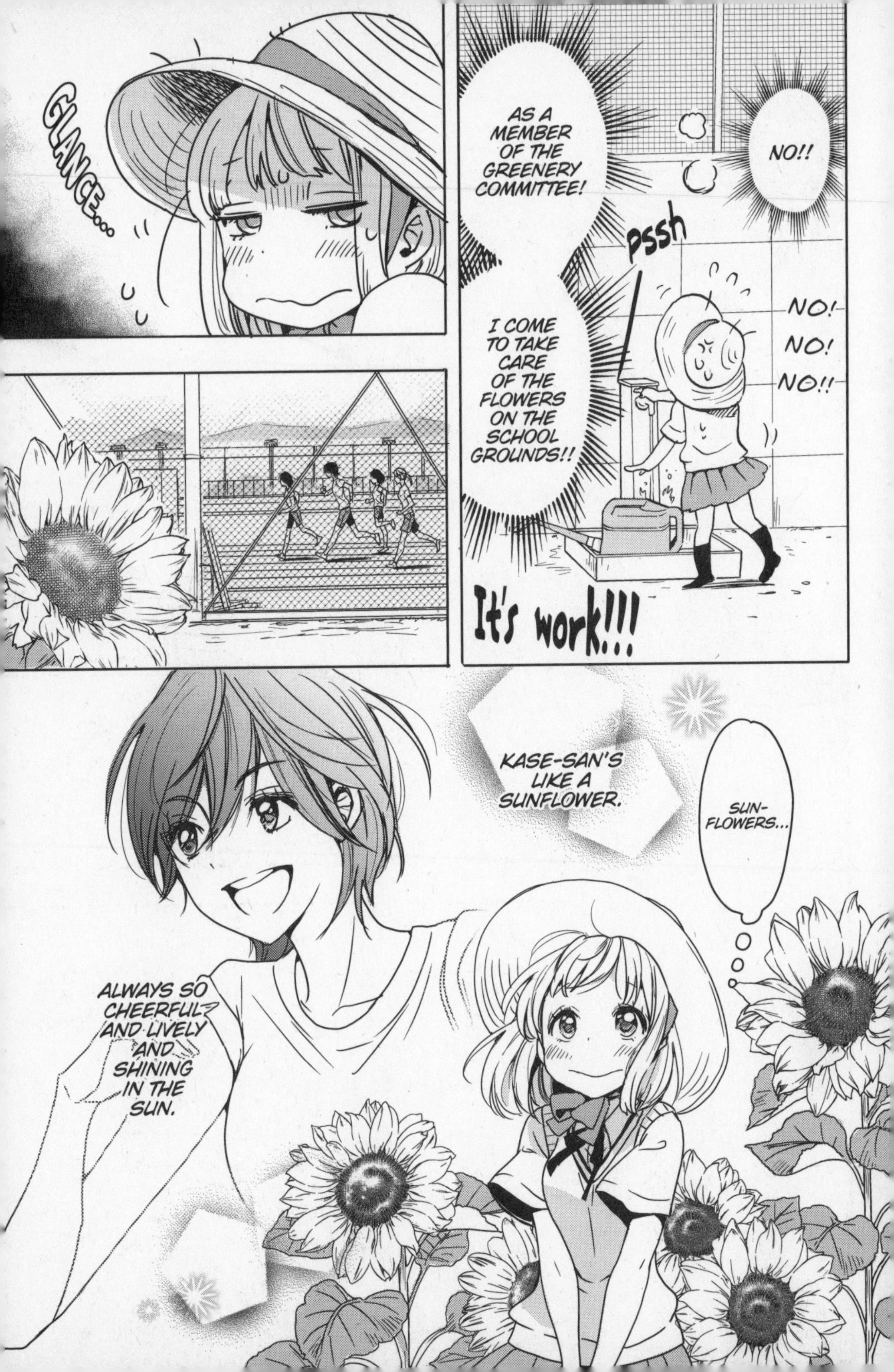
NO!!
AS A MEMBER OF THE GREENERY COMMITTEE!
Pssh
NO! NO! NO!!
I COME TO TAKE CARE OF THE FLOWERS ON THE SCHOOL GROUNDS!!
It's work!!!
GLANCE...
SUN-FLOWERS...
KASE-SAN'S LIKE A SUNFLOWER.
ALWAYS SO CHEERFUL AND LIVELY AND SHINING IN THE SUN.

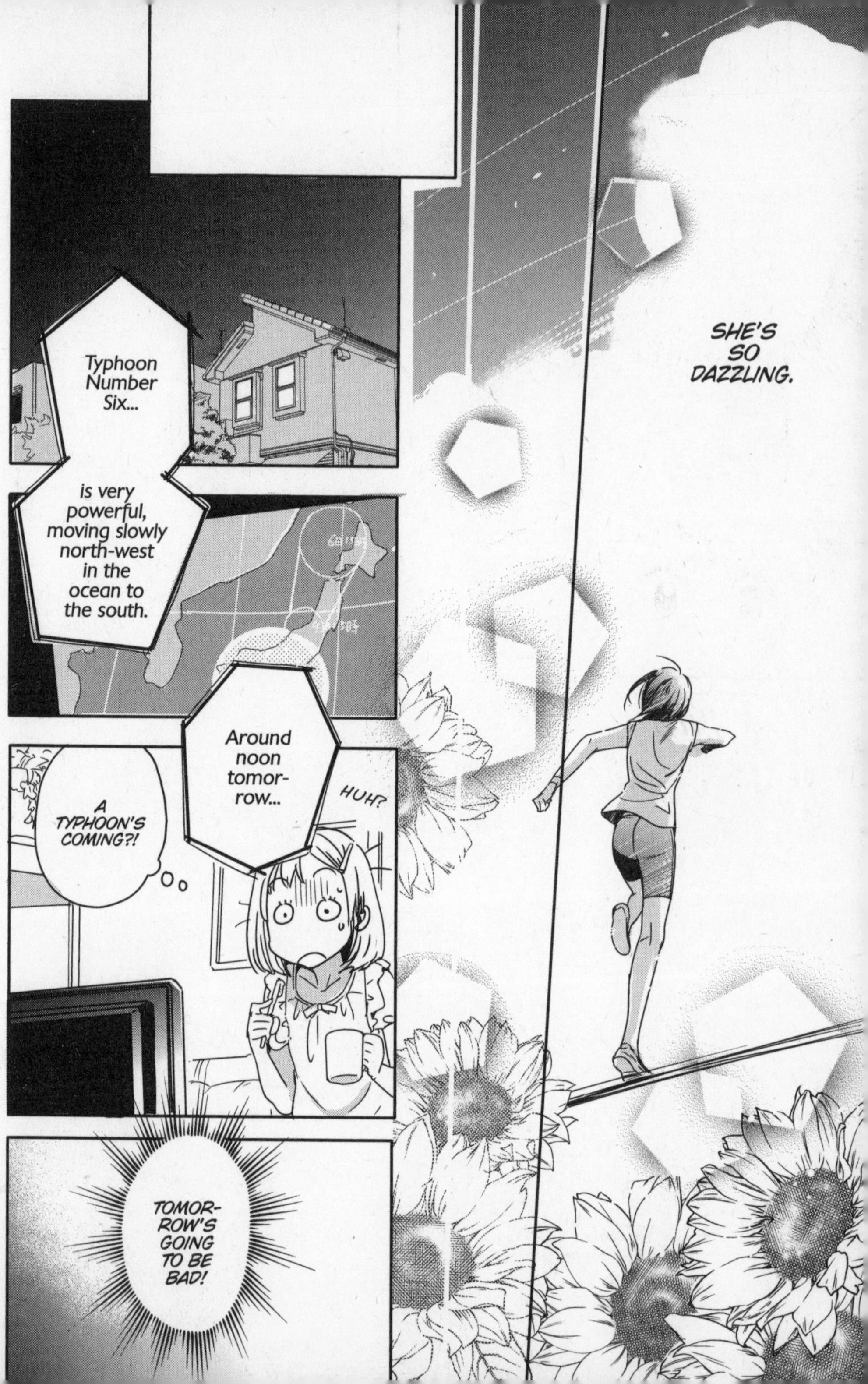
SHE'S SO DAZZLING.
Typhoon Number Six...
is very powerful, moving slowly north-west in the ocean to the south.
Around noon tomorrow...
HUH?
A TYPHOON'S COMING?!
TOMORROW'S GOING TO BE BAD!

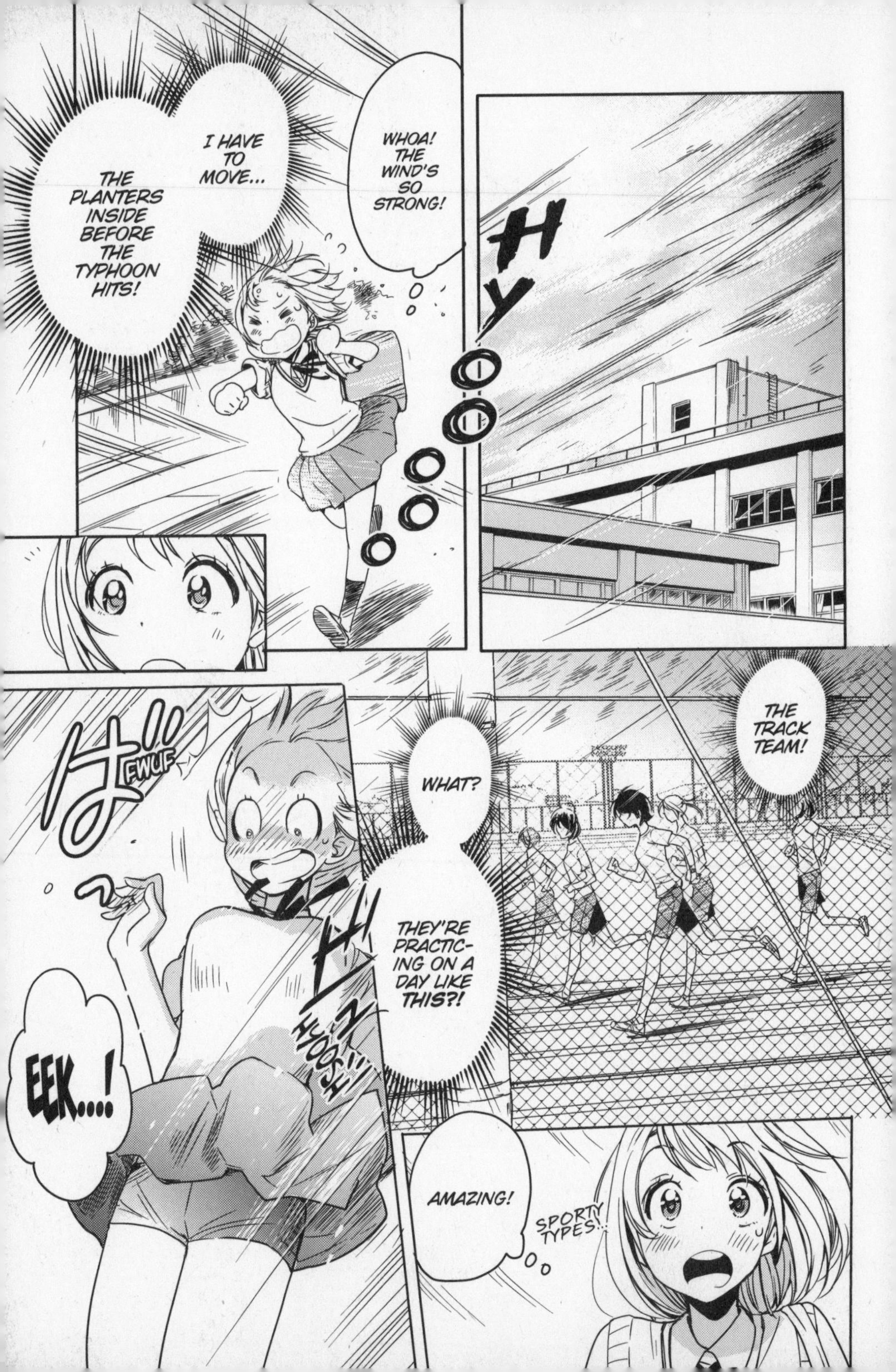

WHOA! THE WIND'S SO STRONG!
HYOOOOOO
I HAVE TO MOVE... THE PLANTERS INSIDE BEFORE THE TYPHOON HITS!
THE TRACK TEAM!
WHAT?
THEY'RE PRACTIC-ING ON A DAY LIKE THIS?!
FWUF
HYOOSH
EEK...!
AMAZING!
SPORTY TYPES...

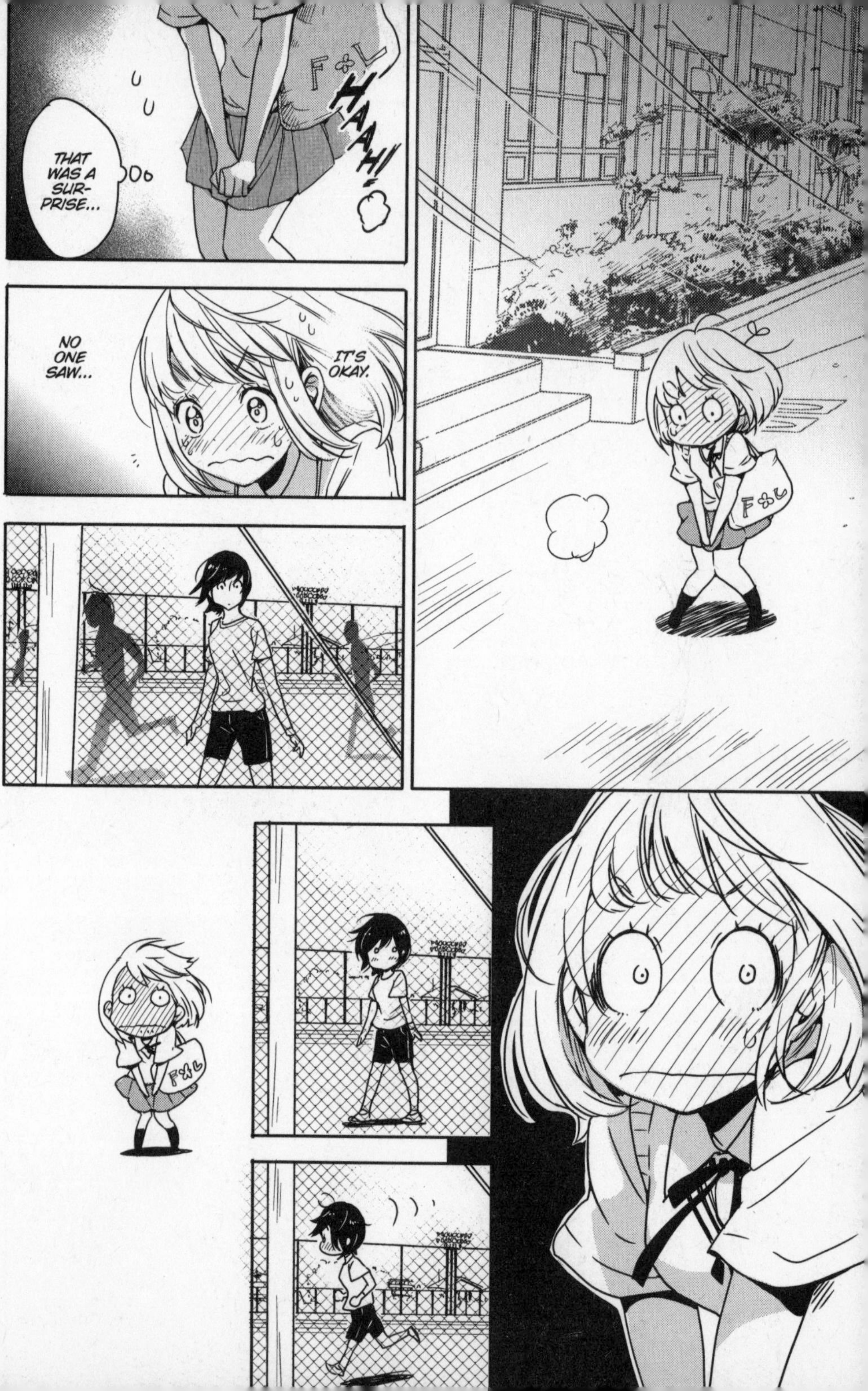

HAAAH!
THAT WAS A SUR-PRISE...
IT'S OKAY.
NO ONE SAW...

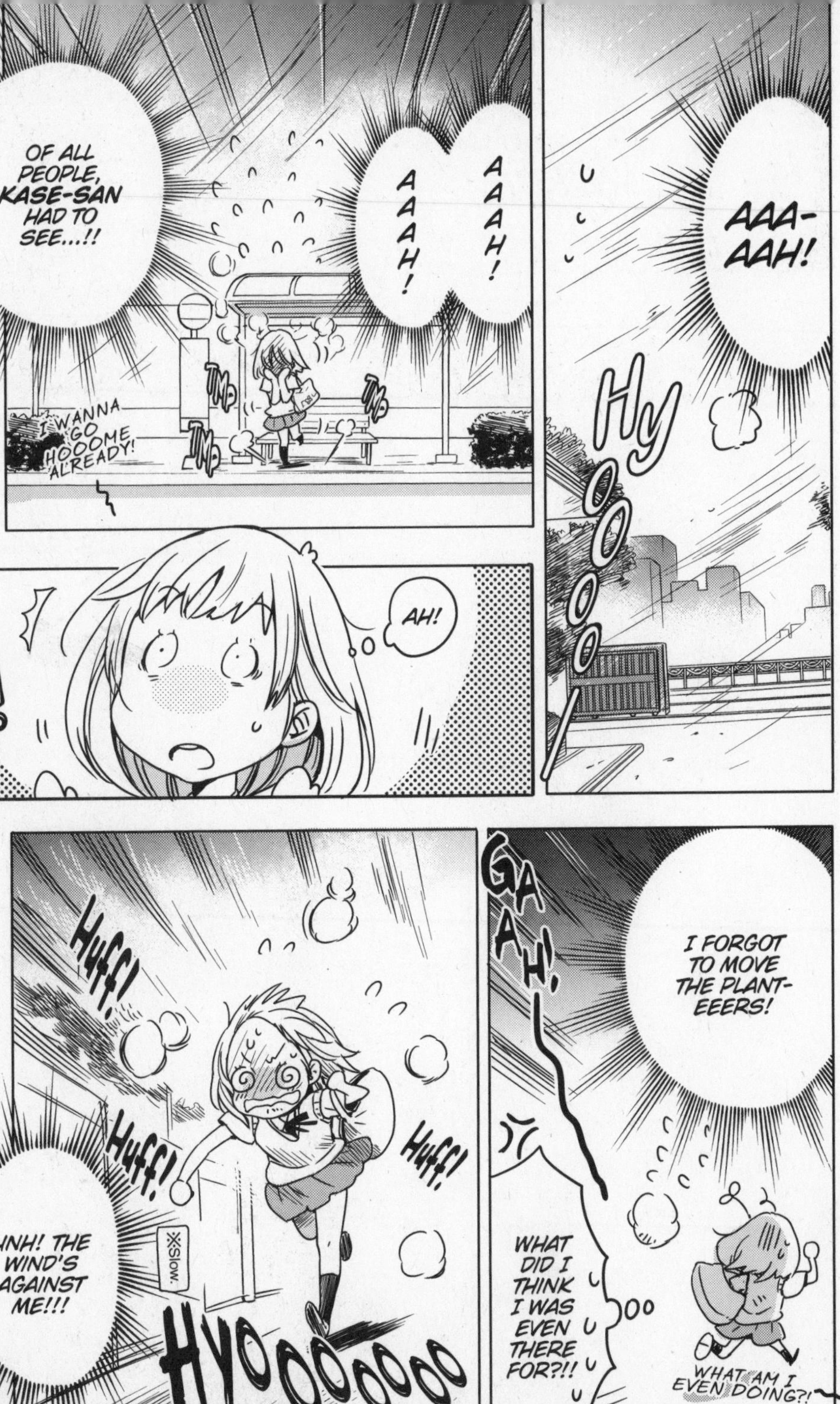
AAA-AAH!
Hyooooo
AAAAH! AAAAH!
OF ALL PEOPLE, KASE-SAN HAD TO SEE...!!
TMP TMP TMP
I WANNA GO HOOOME ALREADY!
AH!
I FORGOT TO MOVE THE PLANT-EEERS!
GAAAH!
WHAT DID I THINK I WAS EVEN THERE FOR?!!
WHAT AM I EVEN DOING?!
Huff! Huff! Huff!
UNH! THE WIND'S AGAINST ME!!!
※Slow.
HYOOOOOOO

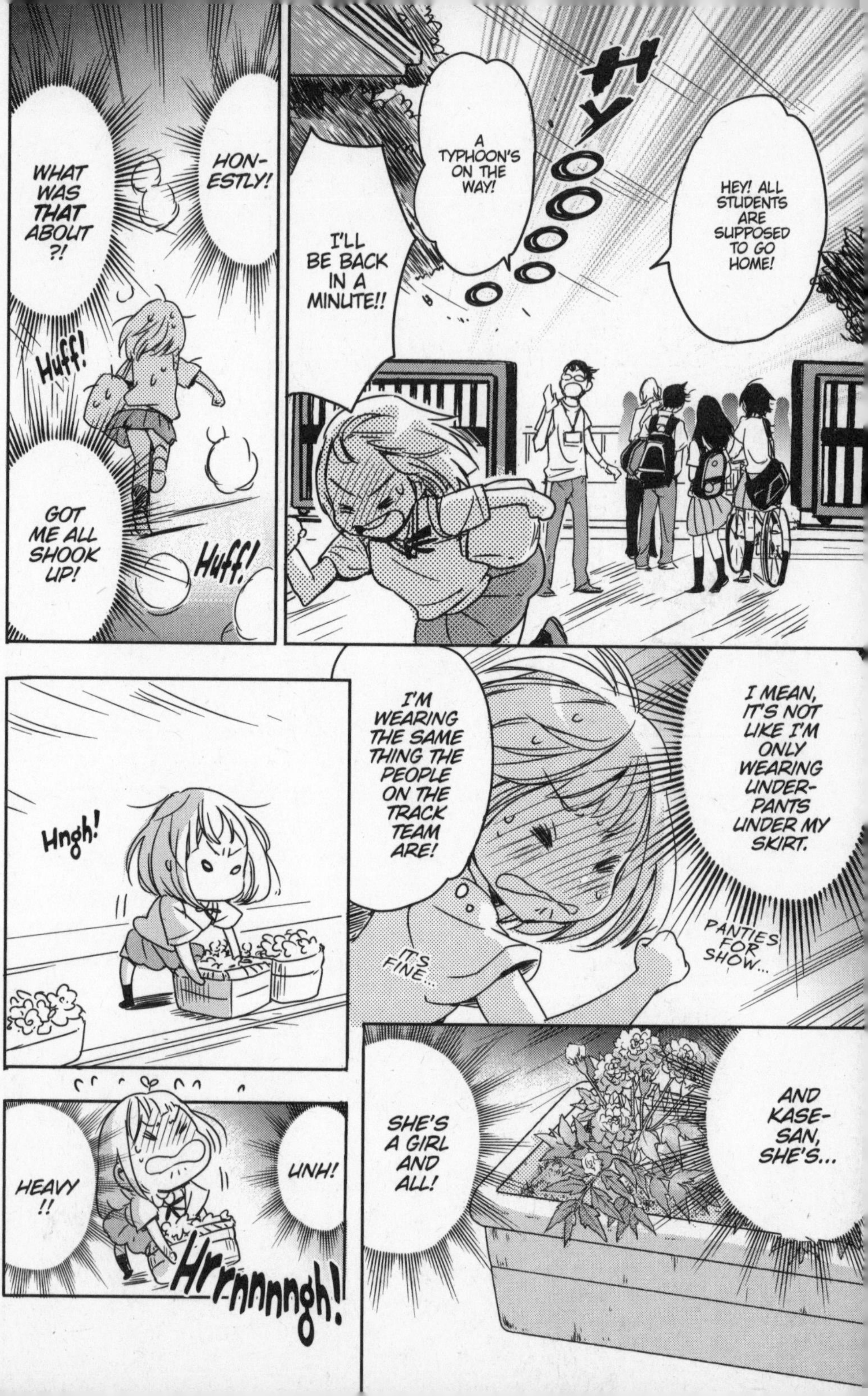
HEY! ALL STUDENTS ARE SUPPOSED TO GO HOME!
HYOOOOOOOO
A TYPHOON'S ON THE WAY!
I'LL BE BACK IN A MINUTE!!
HON-ESTLY!
WHAT WAS THAT ABOUT?!
Huff!
GOT ME ALL SHOOK UP!
Huff!
I MEAN, IT'S NOT LIKE I'M ONLY WEARING UNDER-PANTS UNDER MY SKIRT.
I'M WEARING THE SAME THING THE PEOPLE ON THE TRACK TEAM ARE!
PANTIES FOR SHOW...
IT'S FINE...
Hngh!
AND KASE-SAN, SHE'S...
SHE'S A GIRL AND ALL!
UNH!
HEAVY!!
Hrrnnnngh!

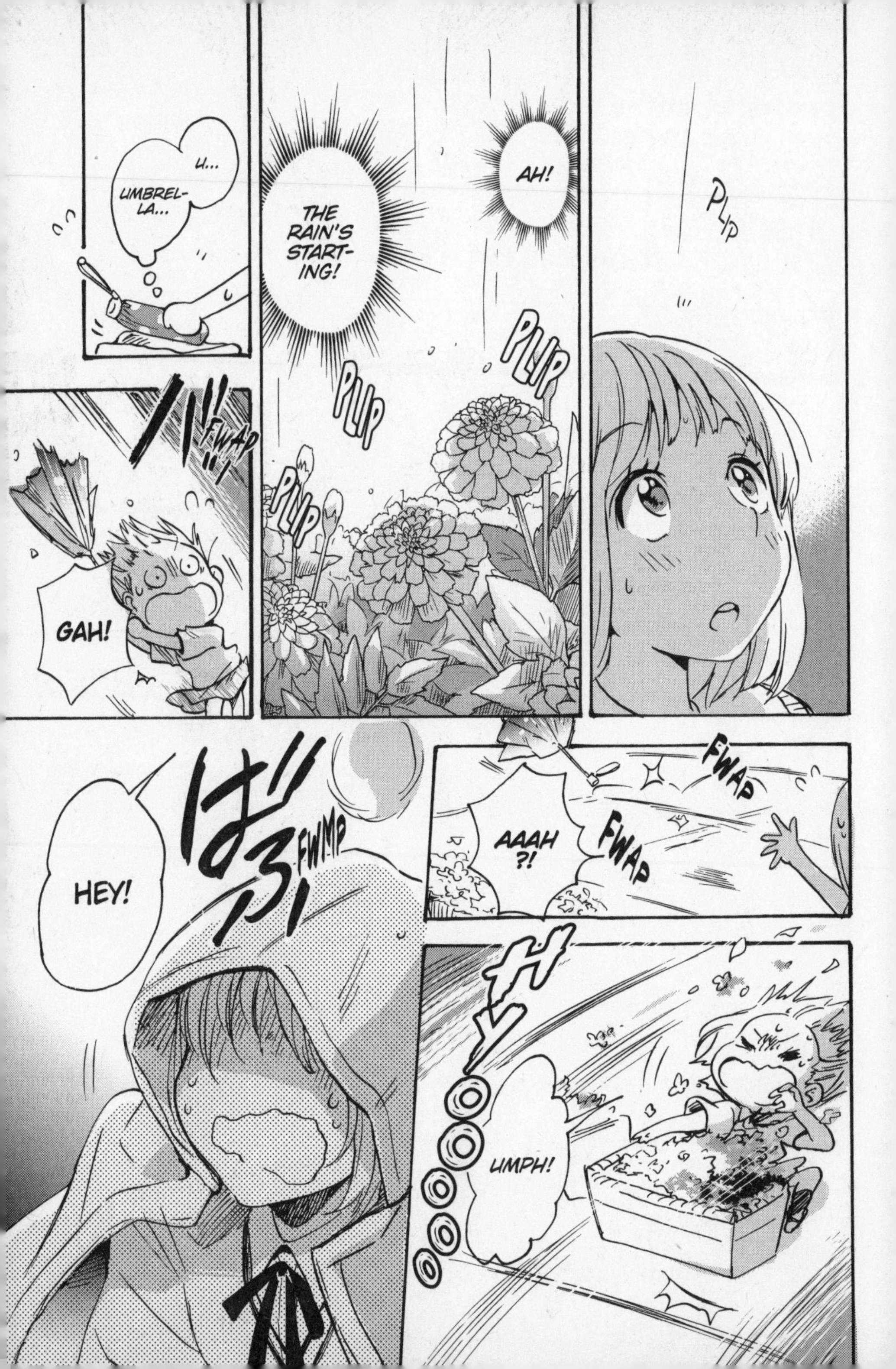
PLIP
AH!
THE RAIN'S START-ING!
PLIP
PLIP
PLIP
U...
UMBREL-LA...
FWAP
GAH!
FWAP
FWAP
AAAH ?!
UMPH!
FWMP
HEY!

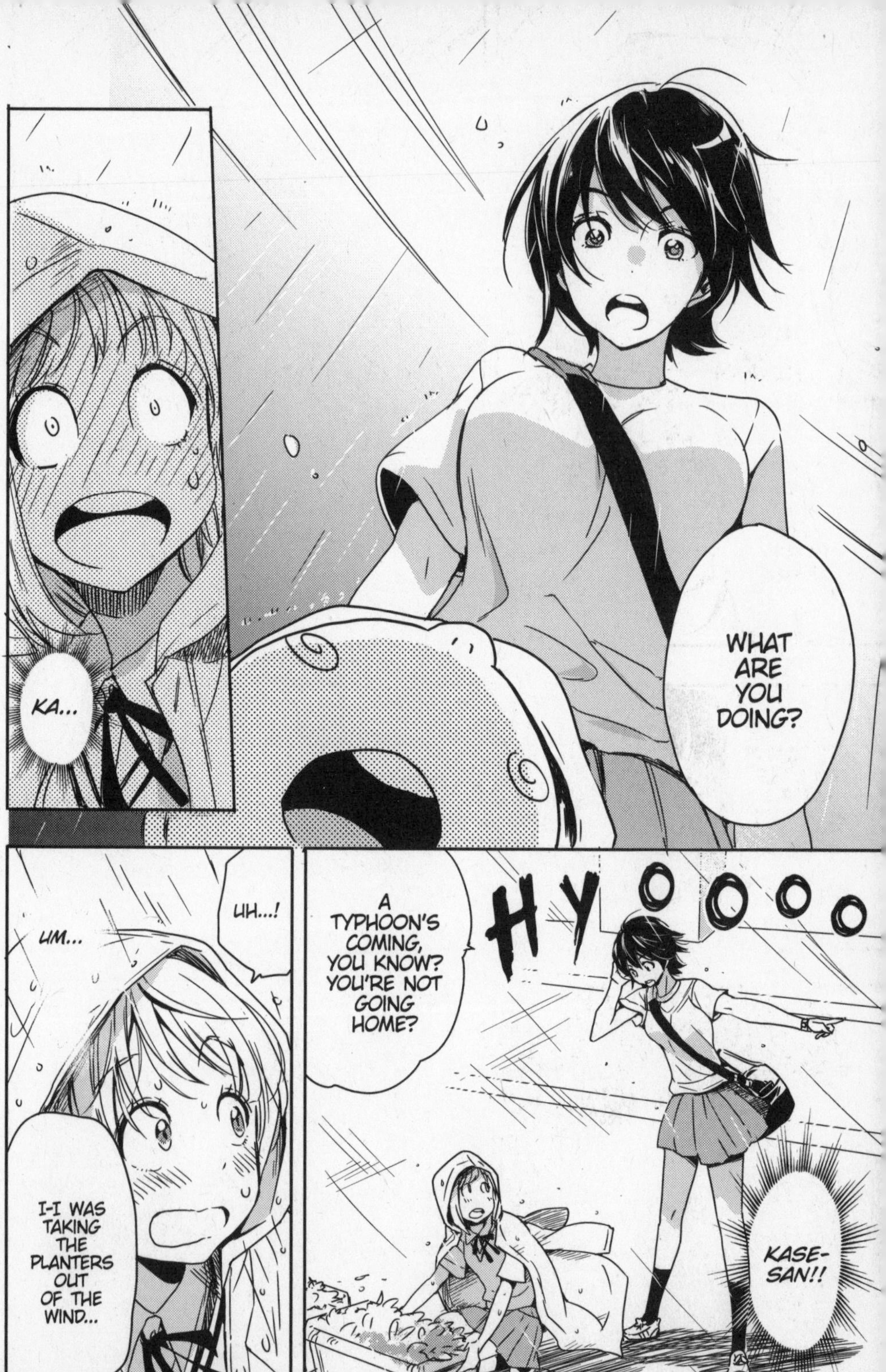
WHAT ARE YOU DOING?
KA...
HYOOOO
KASE-SAN!!
A TYPHOON'S COMING, YOU KNOW? YOU'RE NOT GOING HOME?
UH...!
UM...
I-I WAS TAKING THE PLANTERS OUT OF THE WIND...

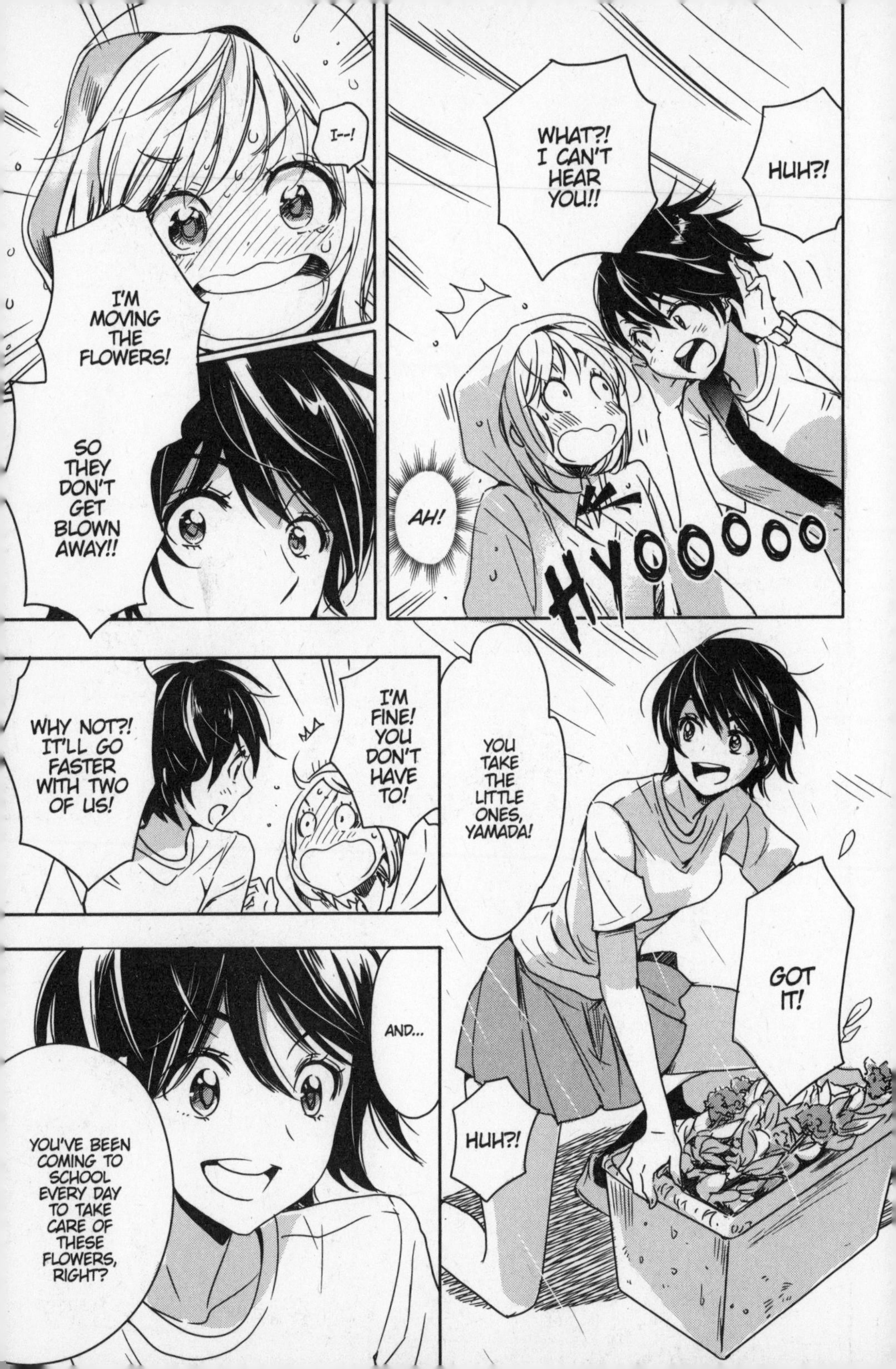
HUH?!
WHAT?! I CAN'T HEAR YOU!!
AH!
HYOOOOOO
I--!
I'M MOVING THE FLOWERS!
SO THEY DON'T GET BLOWN AWAY!!
YOU TAKE THE LITTLE ONES, YAMADA!
GOT IT!
HUH?!
I'M FINE! YOU DON'T HAVE TO!
WHY NOT?! IT'LL GO FASTER WITH TWO OF US!
AND...
YOU'VE BEEN COMING TO SCHOOL EVERY DAY TO TAKE CARE OF THESE FLOWERS, RIGHT?

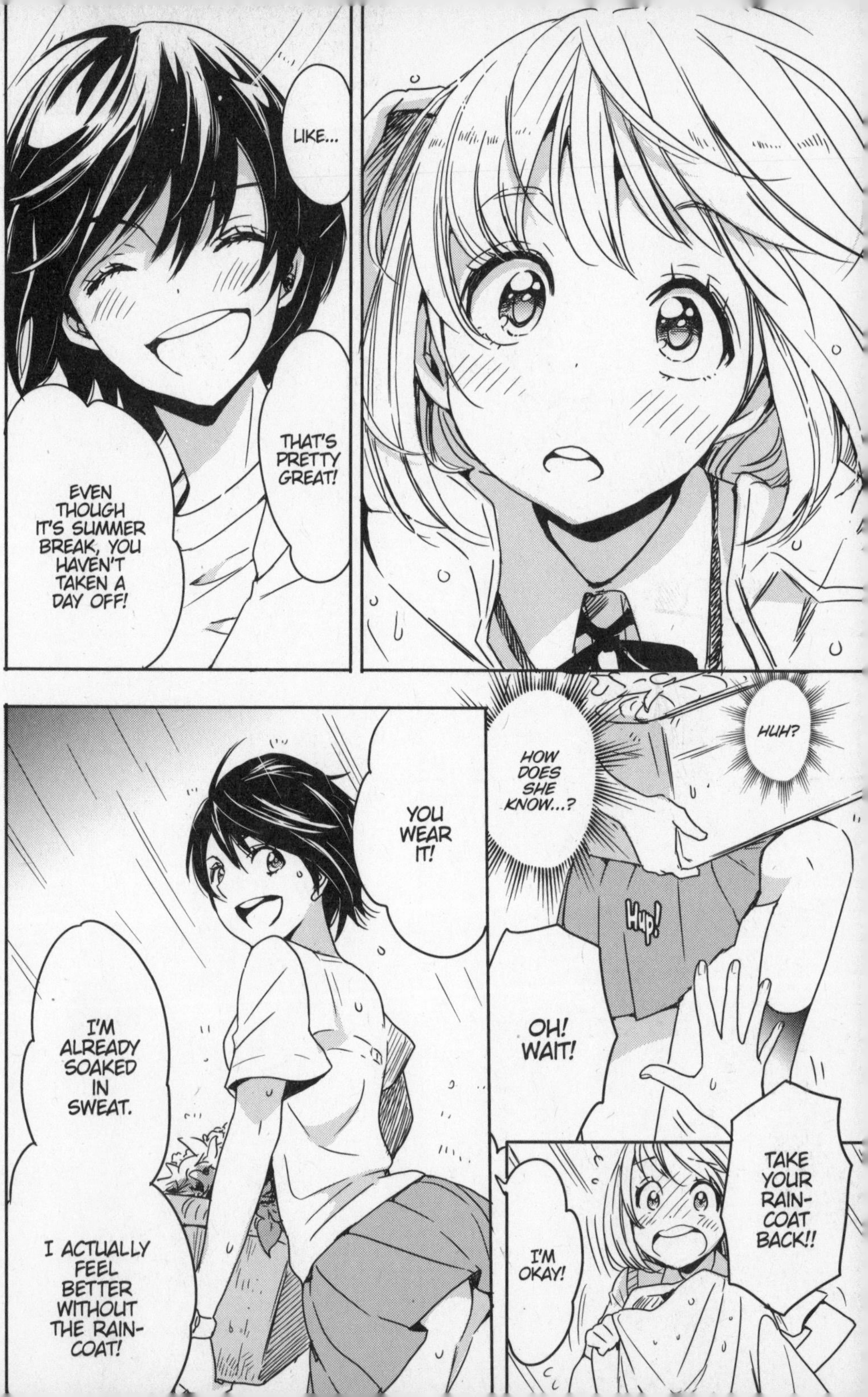
LIKE...
THAT'S PRETTY GREAT!
EVEN THOUGH IT'S SUMMER BREAK, YOU HAVEN'T TAKEN A DAY OFF!
HUH?
HOW DOES SHE KNOW...?
Hup!
OH! WAIT!
TAKE YOUR RAIN-COAT BACK!!
I'M OKAY!
YOU WEAR IT!
I'M ALREADY SOAKED IN SWEAT.
I ACTUALLY FEEL BETTER WITHOUT THE RAIN-COAT!

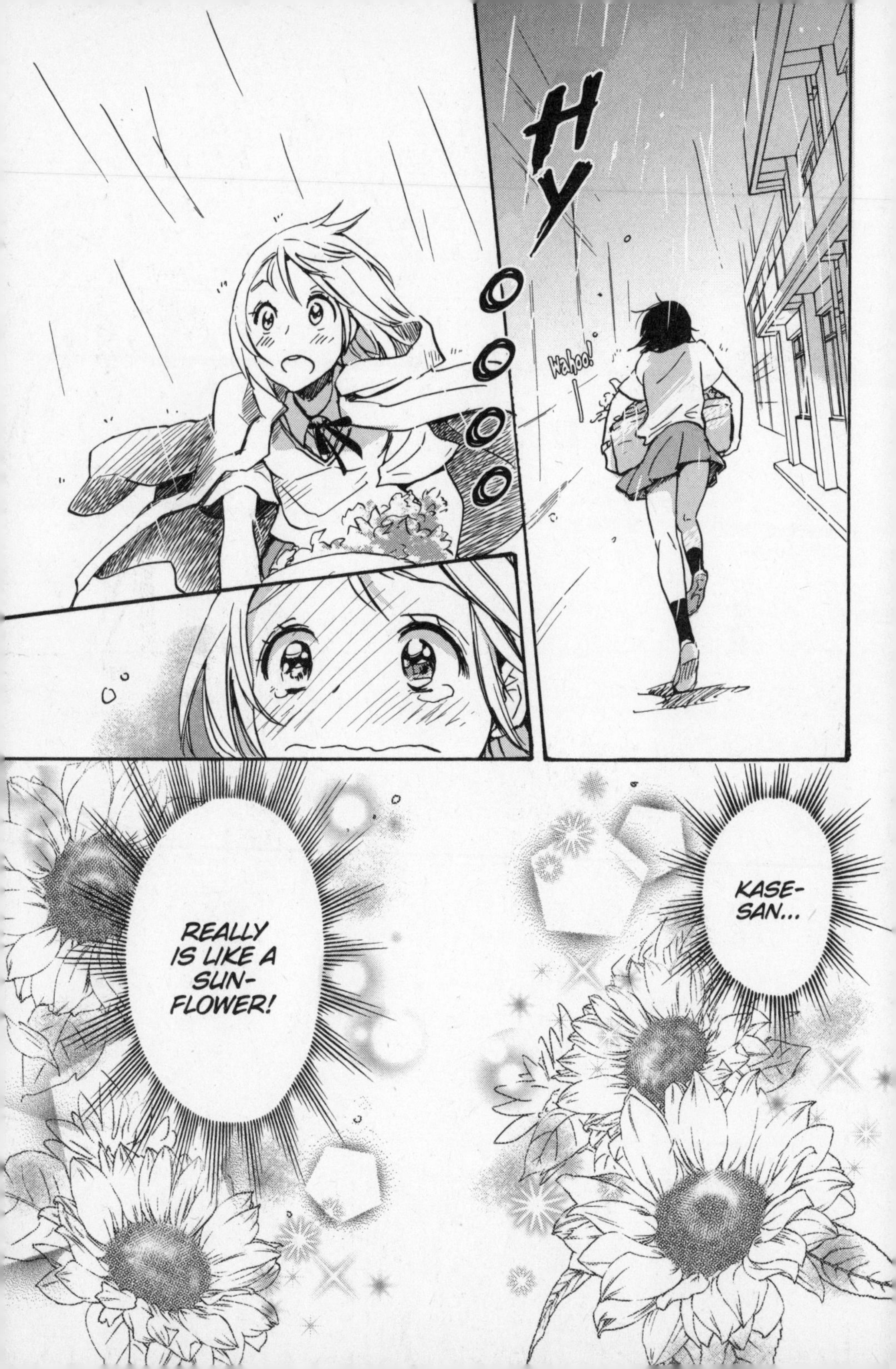
HYOOOO
Wahoo!
KASE-SAN...
REALLY IS LIKE A SUN-FLOWER!

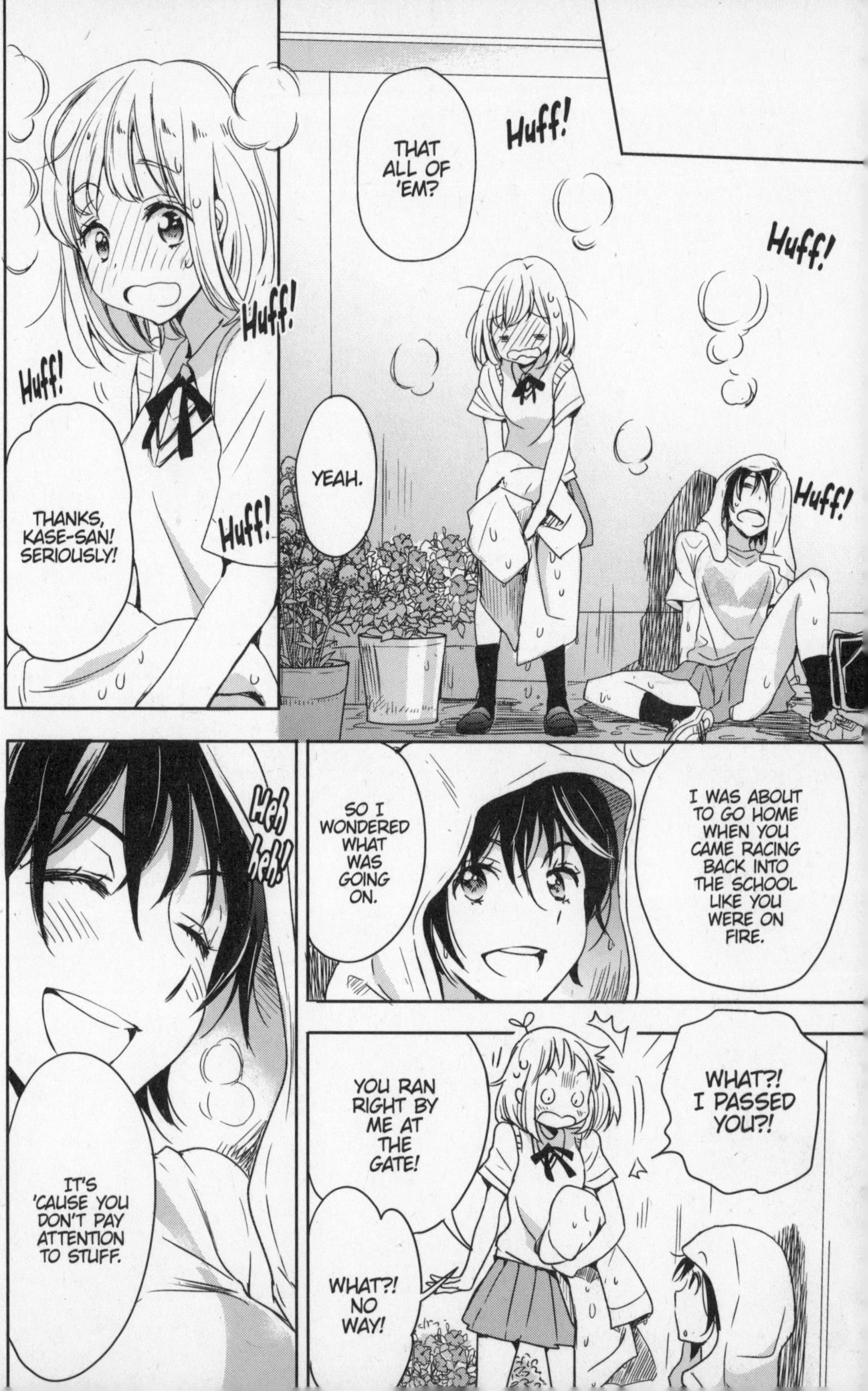
Huff!
THAT ALL OF 'EM?
Huff!
YEAH.
Huff!
Huff!
Huff!
Huff!
THANKS, KASE-SAN! SERIOUSLY!
I WAS ABOUT TO GO HOME WHEN YOU CAME RACING BACK INTO THE SCHOOL LIKE YOU WERE ON FIRE.
SO I WONDERED WHAT WAS GOING ON.
WHAT?! I PASSED YOU?!
YOU RAN RIGHT BY ME AT THE GATE!
WHAT?! NO WAY!
Heh heh!
IT'S 'CAUSE YOU DON'T PAY ATTENTION TO STUFF.

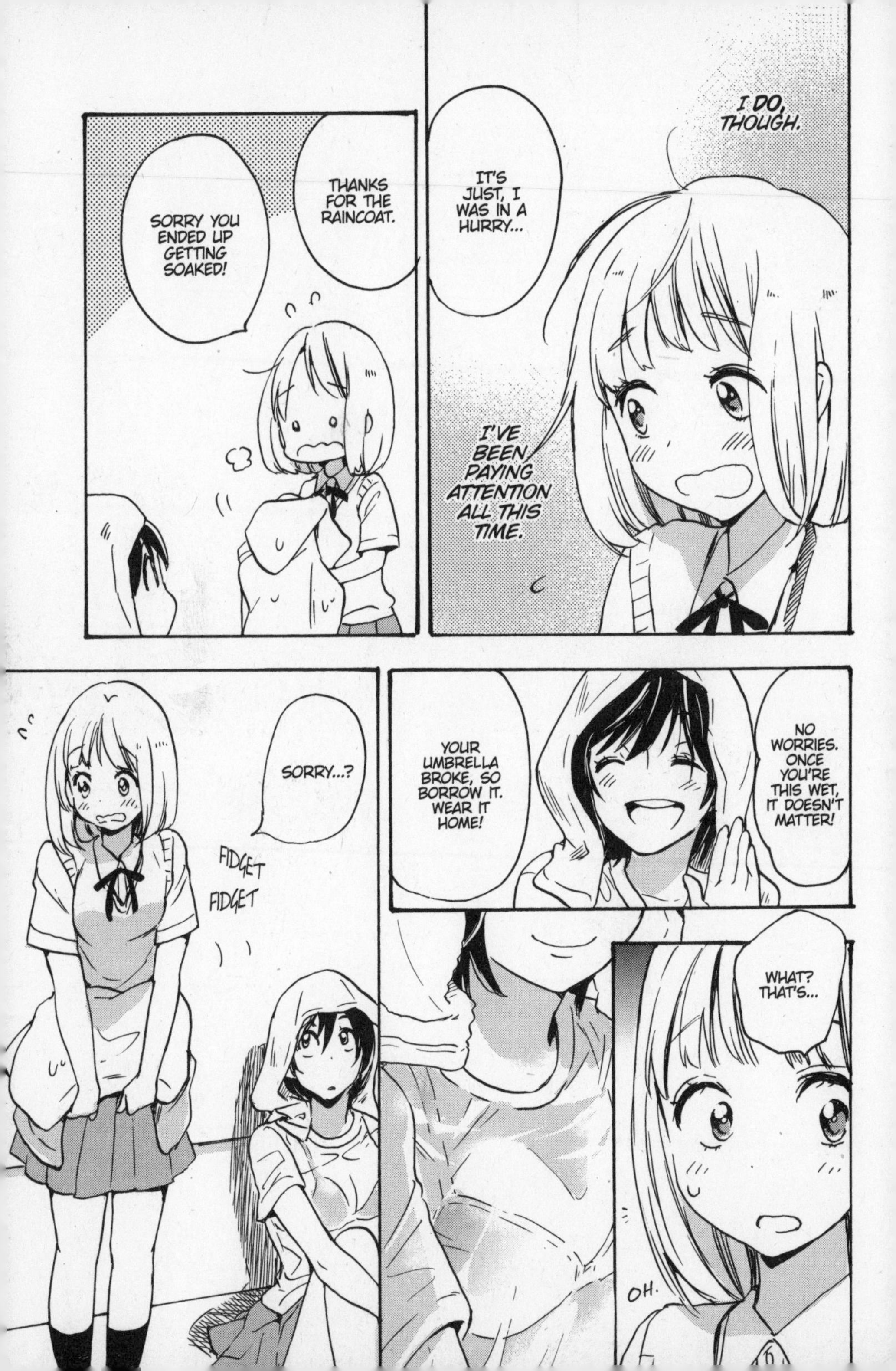
I DO, THOUGH.
IT'S JUST, I WAS IN A HURRY...
I'VE BEEN PAYING ATTENTION ALL THIS TIME.
THANKS FOR THE RAINCOAT.
SORRY YOU ENDED UP GETTING SOAKED!
NO WORRIES. ONCE YOU'RE THIS WET, IT DOESN'T MATTER!
YOUR UMBRELLA BROKE, SO BORROW IT. WEAR IT HOME!
WHAT? THAT'S...
OH.
SORRY...?
FIDGET
FIDGET

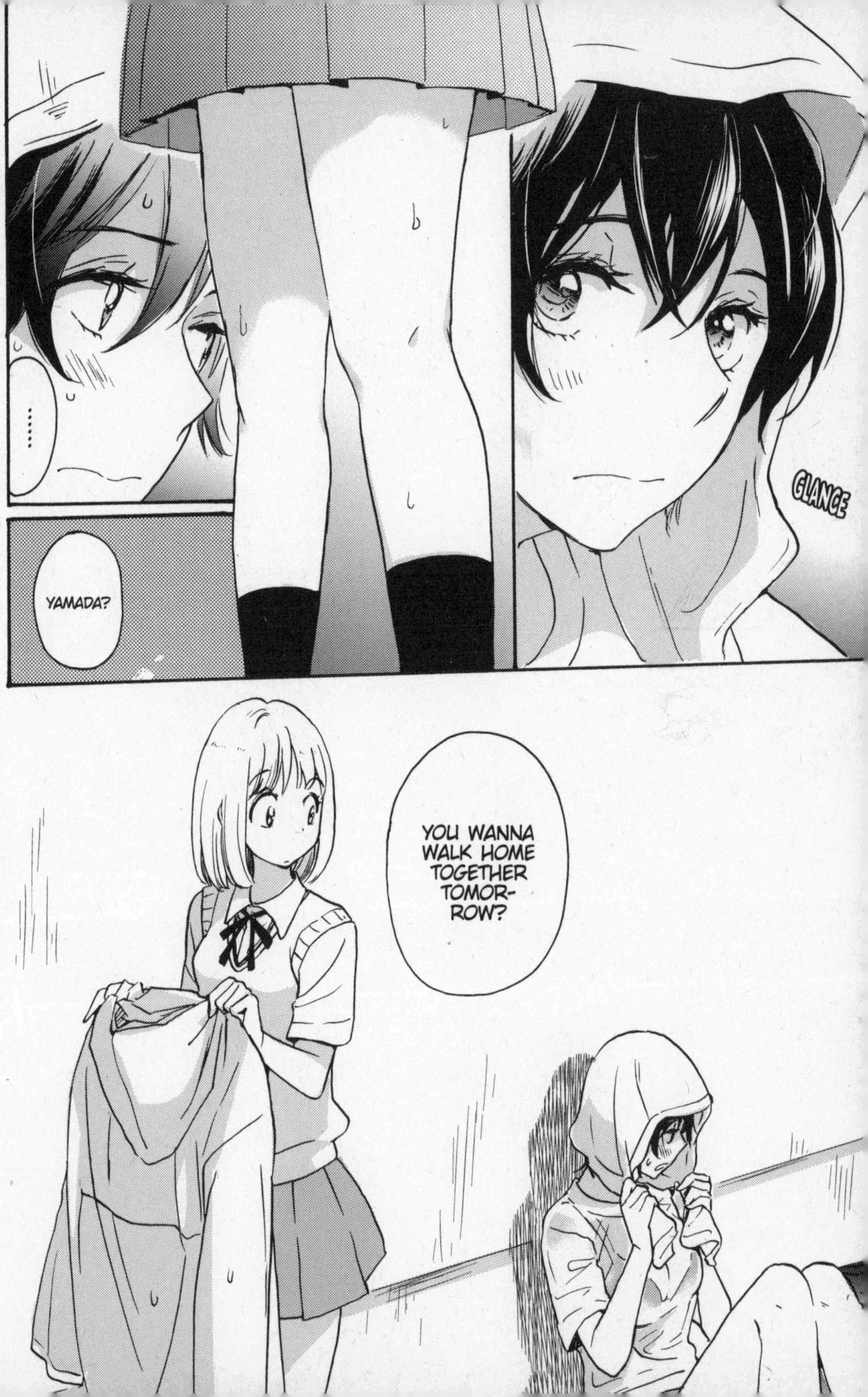
GLANCE
......
YAMADA?
YOU WANNA WALK HOME TOGETHER TOMOR-ROW?

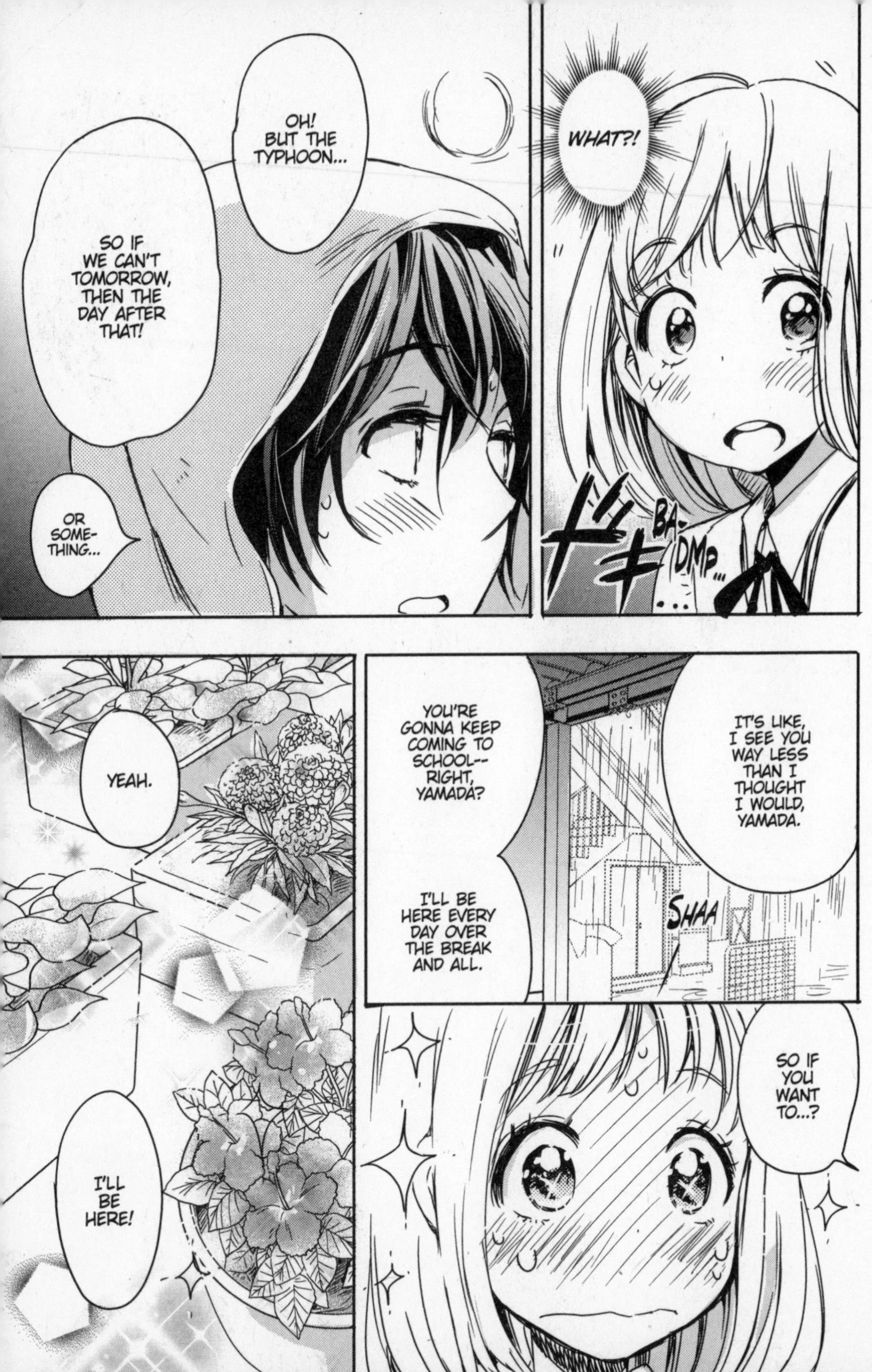
WHAT?!
BA-DMP...
...
OH! BUT THE TYPHOON...
SO IF WE CAN'T TOMORROW, THEN THE DAY AFTER THAT!
OR SOME-THING...
IT'S LIKE, I SEE YOU WAY LESS THAN I THOUGHT I WOULD, YAMADA.
YOU'RE GONNA KEEP COMING TO SCHOOL-- RIGHT, YAMADA?
I'LL BE HERE EVERY DAY OVER THE BREAK AND ALL.
SHAA
SO IF YOU WANT TO...?
YEAH.
I'LL BE HERE!

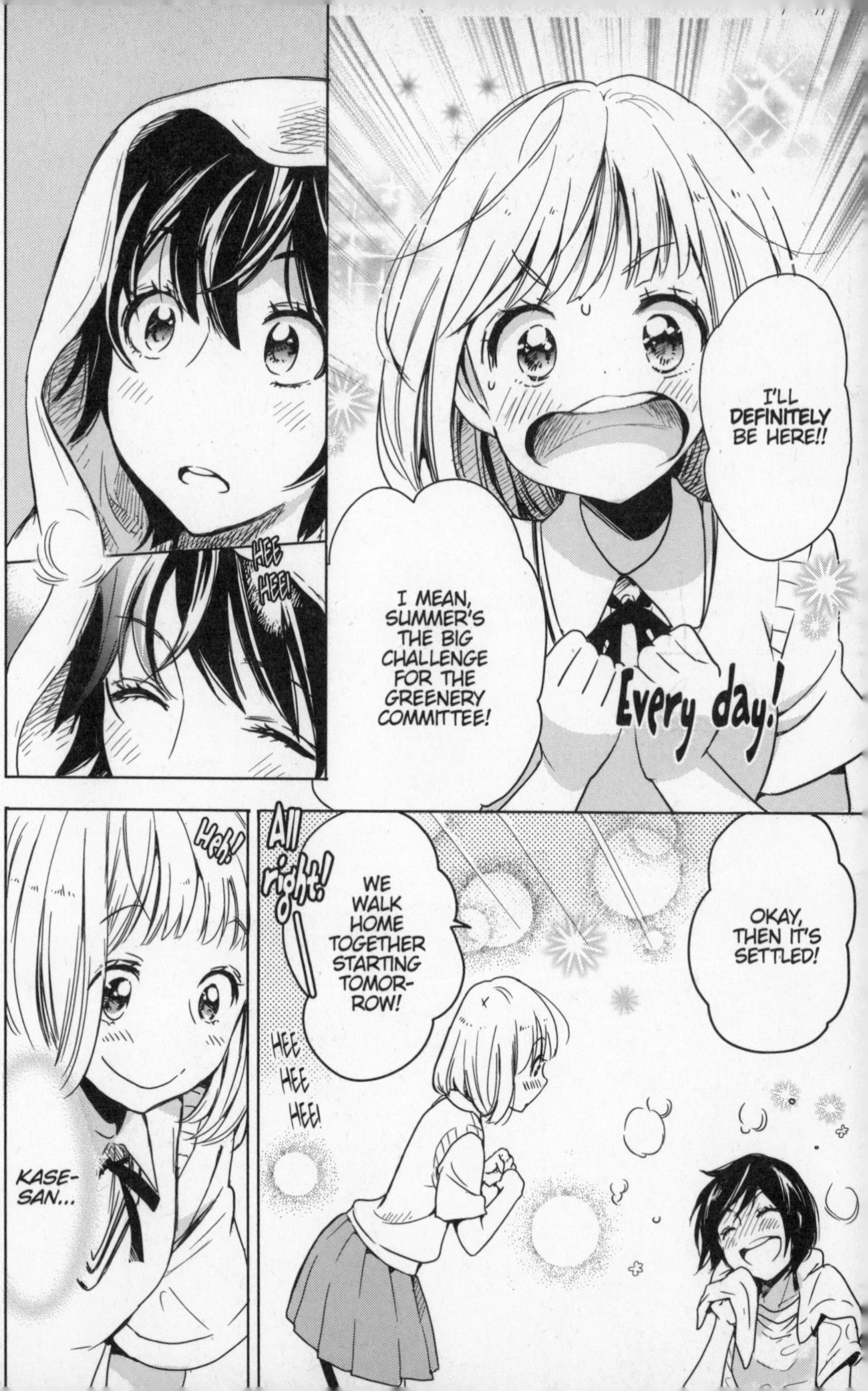
I'LL DEFINITELY BE HERE!!
Every day!
I MEAN, SUMMER'S THE BIG CHALLENGE FOR THE GREENERY COMMITTEE!
HEE HEE!
OKAY, THEN IT'S SETTLED!
WE WALK HOME TOGETHER STARTING TOMORROW!
All right!
HEE HEE HEE!
Heh!
KASE-SAN...

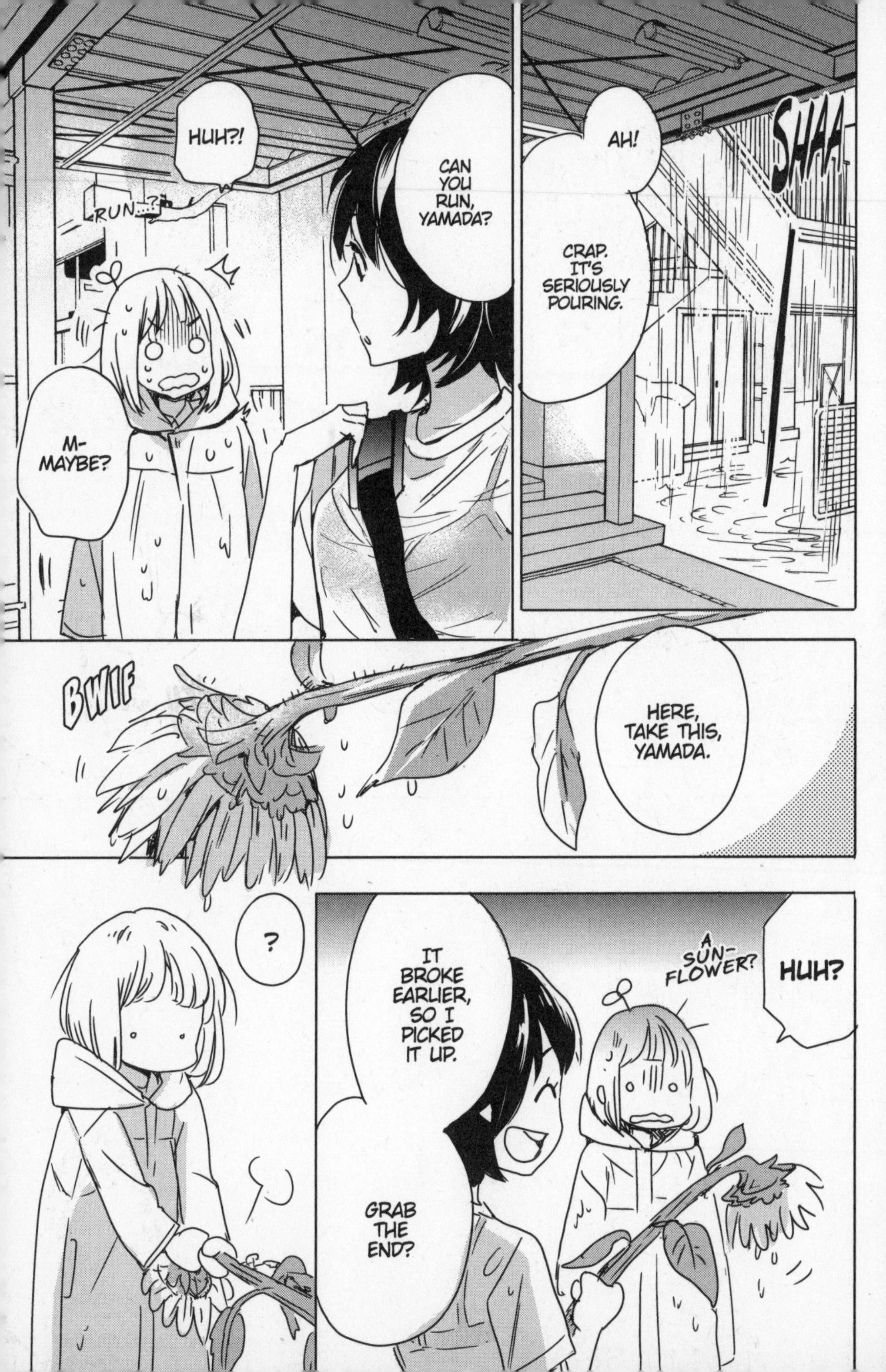
SHAA
AH!
CRAP. IT'S SERIOUSLY POURING.
CAN YOU RUN, YAMADA?
HUH?!
RUN...?
M-MAYBE?
HERE, TAKE THIS, YAMADA.
BWIF
HUH?
A SUN-FLOWER?
IT BROKE EARLIER, SO I PICKED IT UP.
GRAB THE END?
?

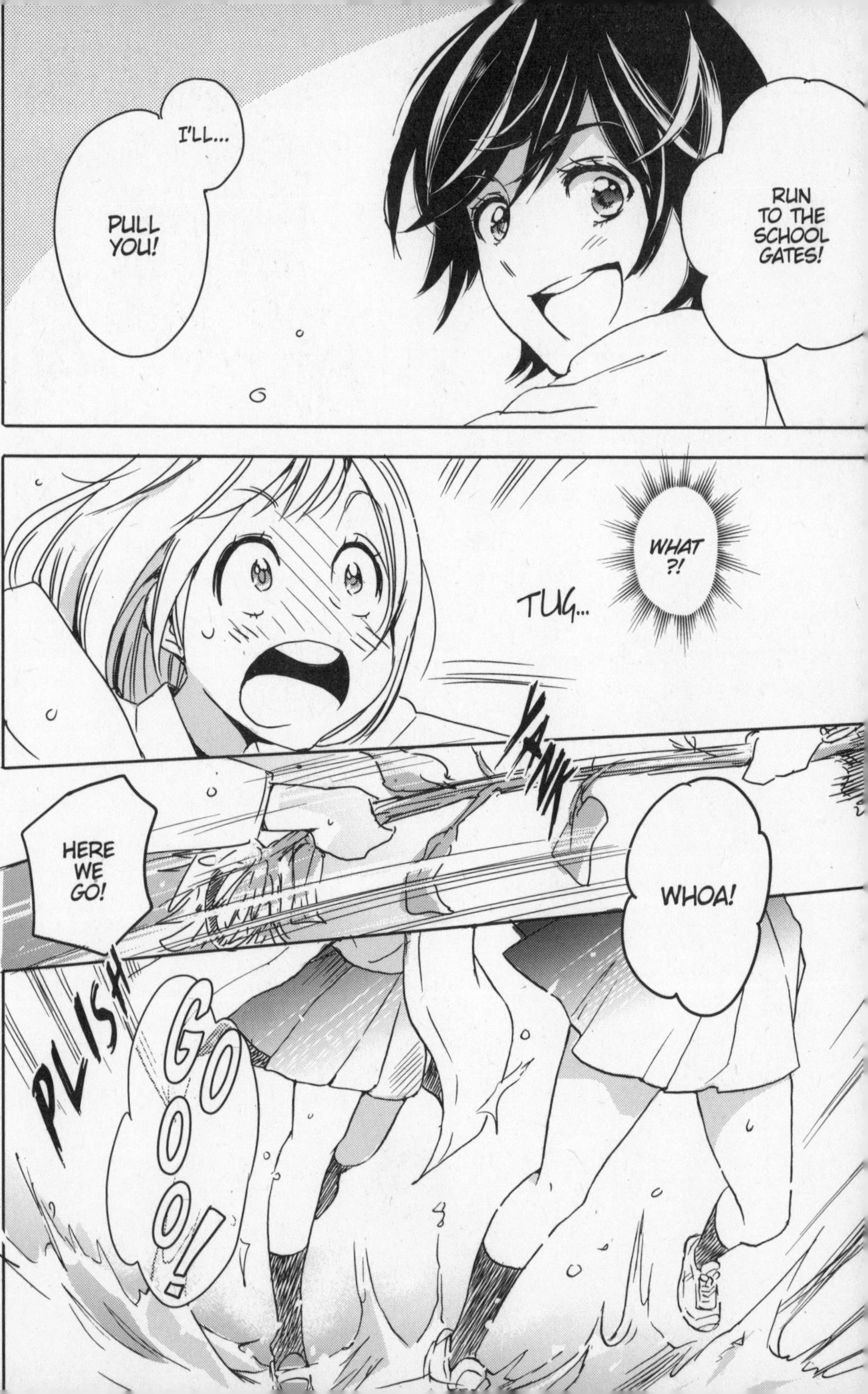
RUN TO THE SCHOOL GATES!
I'LL... PULL YOU!
WHAT?!
TUG...
YANK
WHOA!
HERE WE GO!
PLISH
GOOOO!

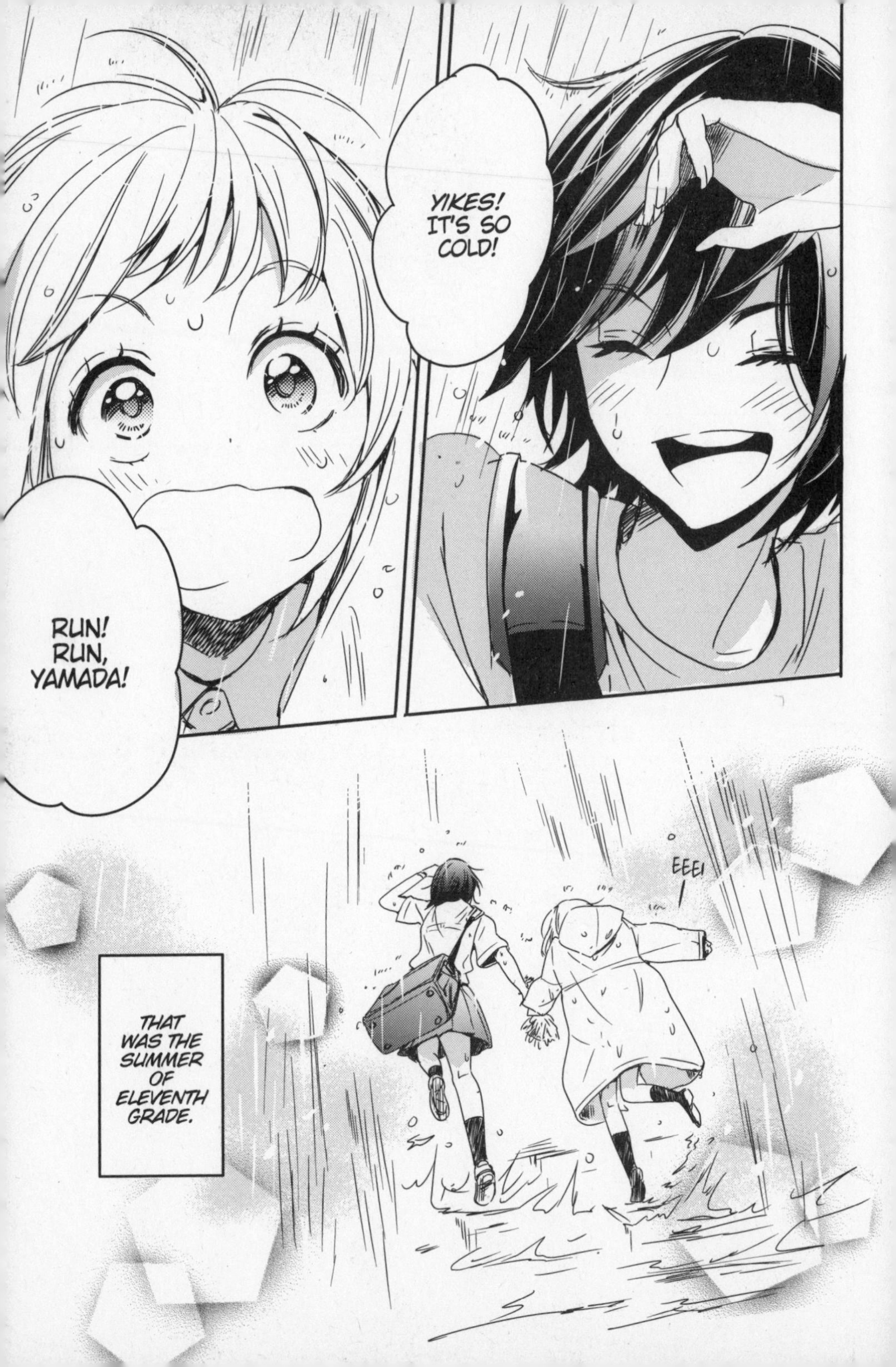
YIKES! IT'S SO COLD!
RUN! RUN, YAMADA!
EEEI
THAT WAS THE SUMMER OF ELEVENTH GRADE.

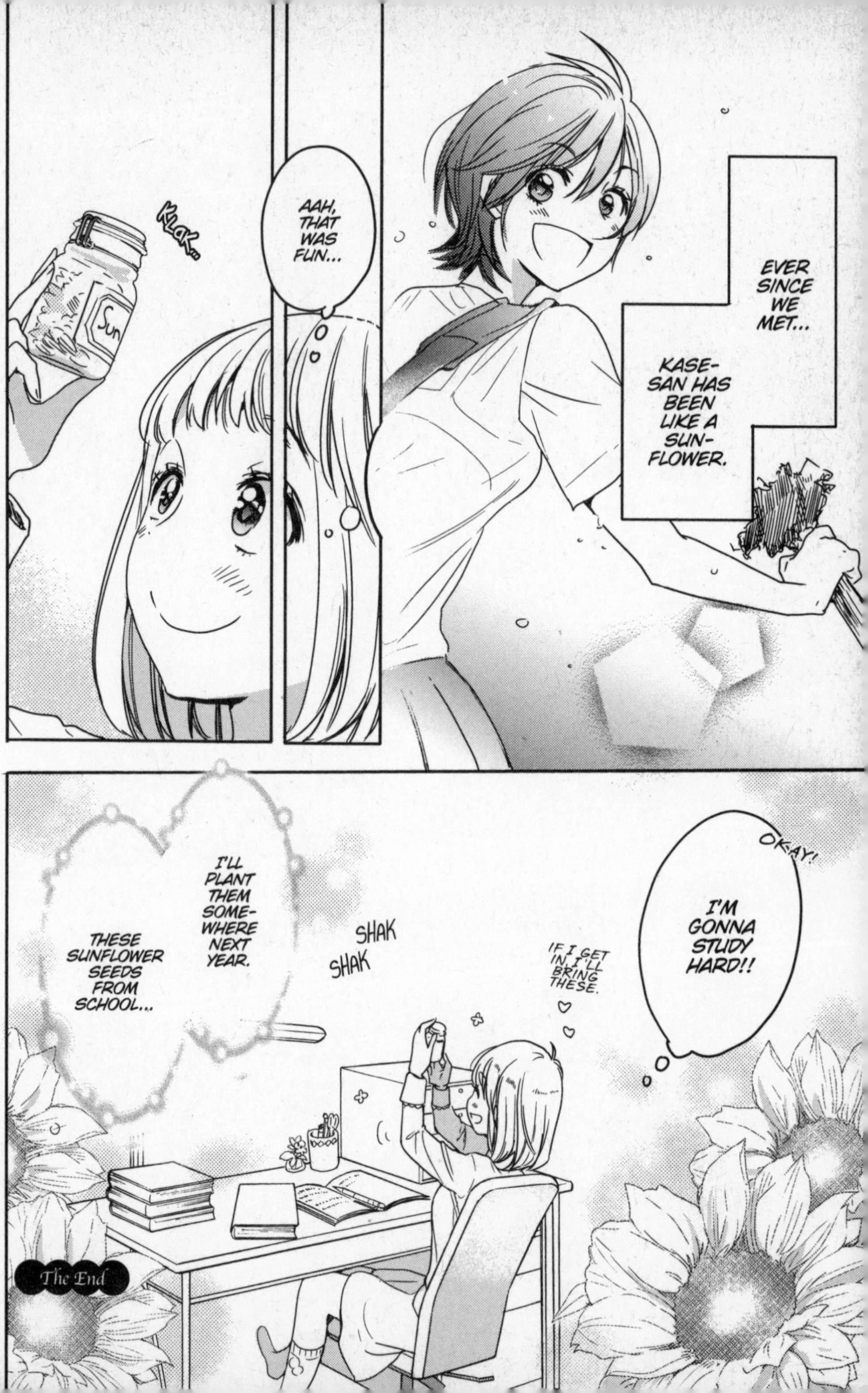
EVER SINCE WE MET...
KASE-SAN HAS BEEN LIKE A SUNFLOWER.
AAH, THAT WAS FUN...
KLAK...
OKAY!
I'M GONNA STUDY HARD!!
IF I GET IN, I'LL BRING THESE.
SHAK
SHAK
THESE SUNFLOWER SEEDS FROM SCHOOL...
I'LL PLANT THEM SOMEWHERE NEXT YEAR.
The End

Kase-san and Christmas

IT WAS CHRISTMAS EVE IN TWELFTH GRADE.

No. 1 University Acceptance Rate in the City

Shinsho Prep School

Ajito Dental

Makoba Law Firm

Ajito Dental Clinic

Shinsho Prep

隠家歯科クリ二ッ

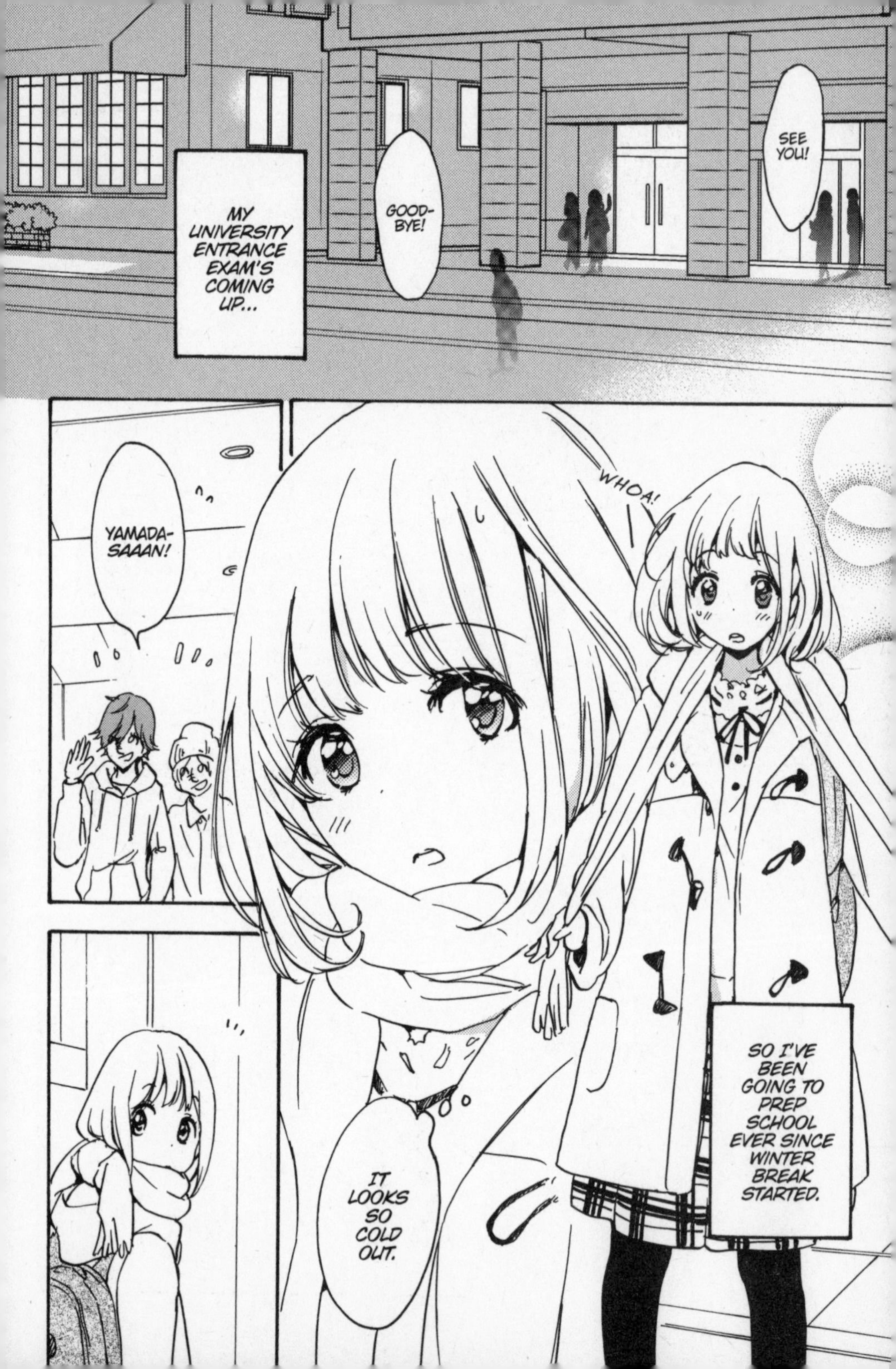
SEE YOU!
GOOD-BYE!
MY UNIVERSITY ENTRANCE EXAM'S COMING UP...
WHOA!
SO I'VE BEEN GOING TO PREP SCHOOL EVER SINCE WINTER BREAK STARTED.
IT LOOKS SO COLD OUT.
YAMADA-SAAAN!

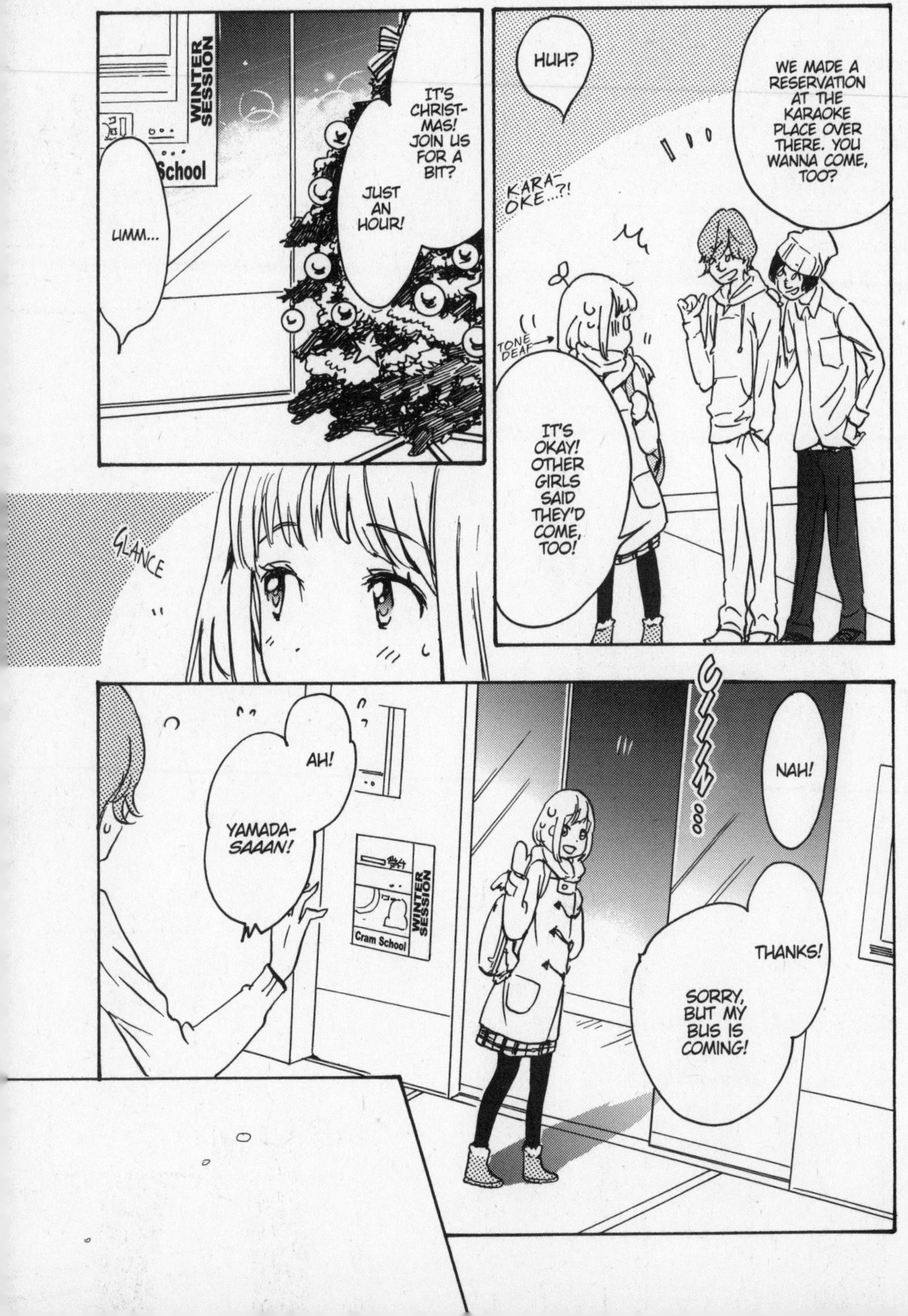
WE MADE A RESERVATION AT THE KARAOKE PLACE OVER THERE. YOU WANNA COME, TOO?
HUH?
KARA-OKE...?!
TONE DEAF
IT'S OKAY! OTHER GIRLS SAID THEY'D COME, TOO!
IT'S CHRISTMAS! JOIN US FOR A BIT?
JUST AN HOUR!
WINTER SESSION
School
UMM...
GLANCE
NAH!
THANKS!
SORRY, BUT MY BUS IS COMING!
AH!
YAMADA-SAAAN!
WINTER SESSION
Cram School

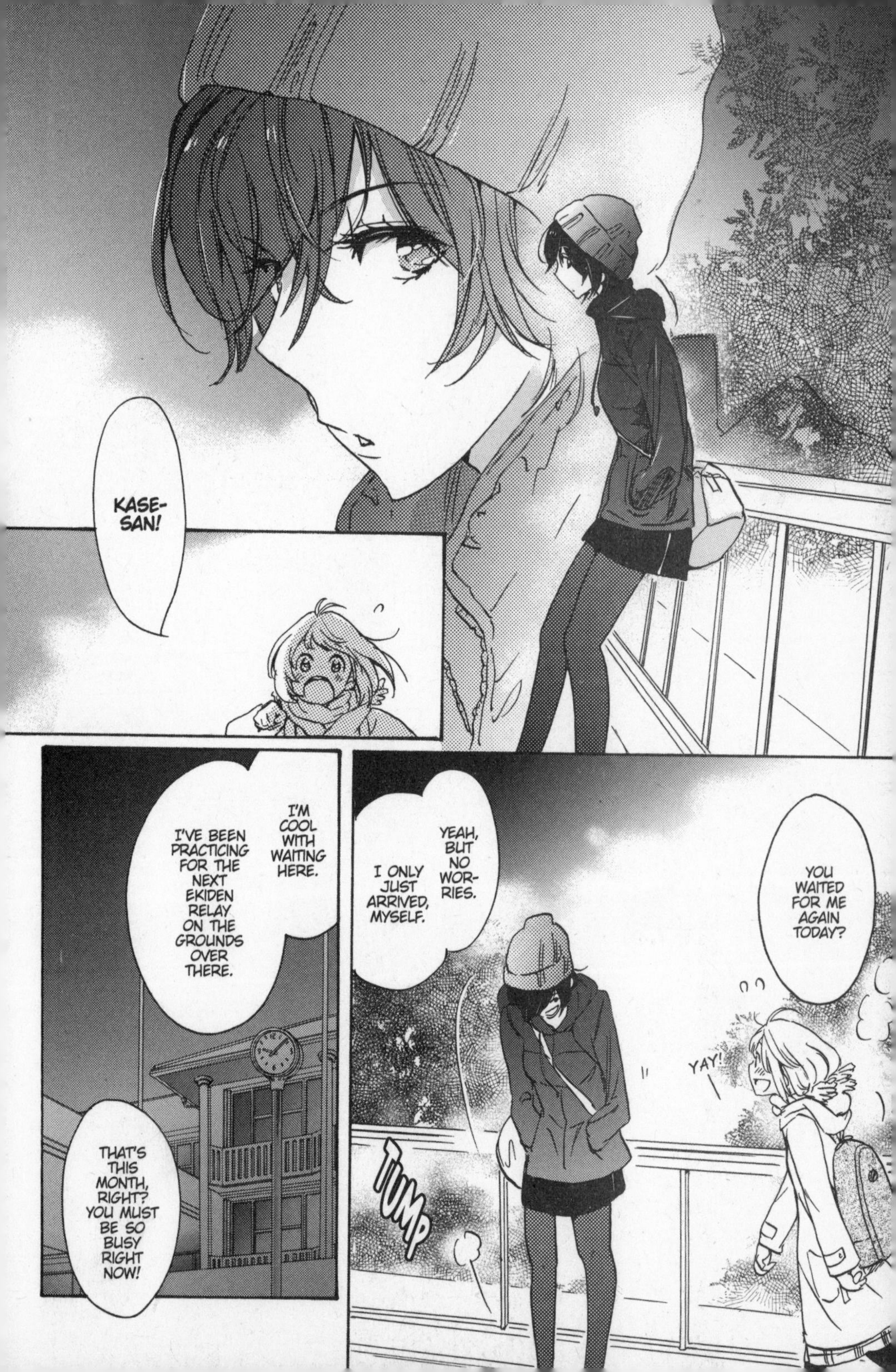
KASE-SAN!
YOU WAITED FOR ME AGAIN TODAY?
YAY!
YEAH, BUT NO WORRIES.
I ONLY JUST ARRIVED, MYSELF.
TUMP
I'M COOL WITH WAITING HERE.
I'VE BEEN PRACTICING FOR THE NEXT EKIDEN RELAY ON THE GROUNDS OVER THERE.
THAT'S THIS MONTH, RIGHT? YOU MUST BE SO BUSY RIGHT NOW!

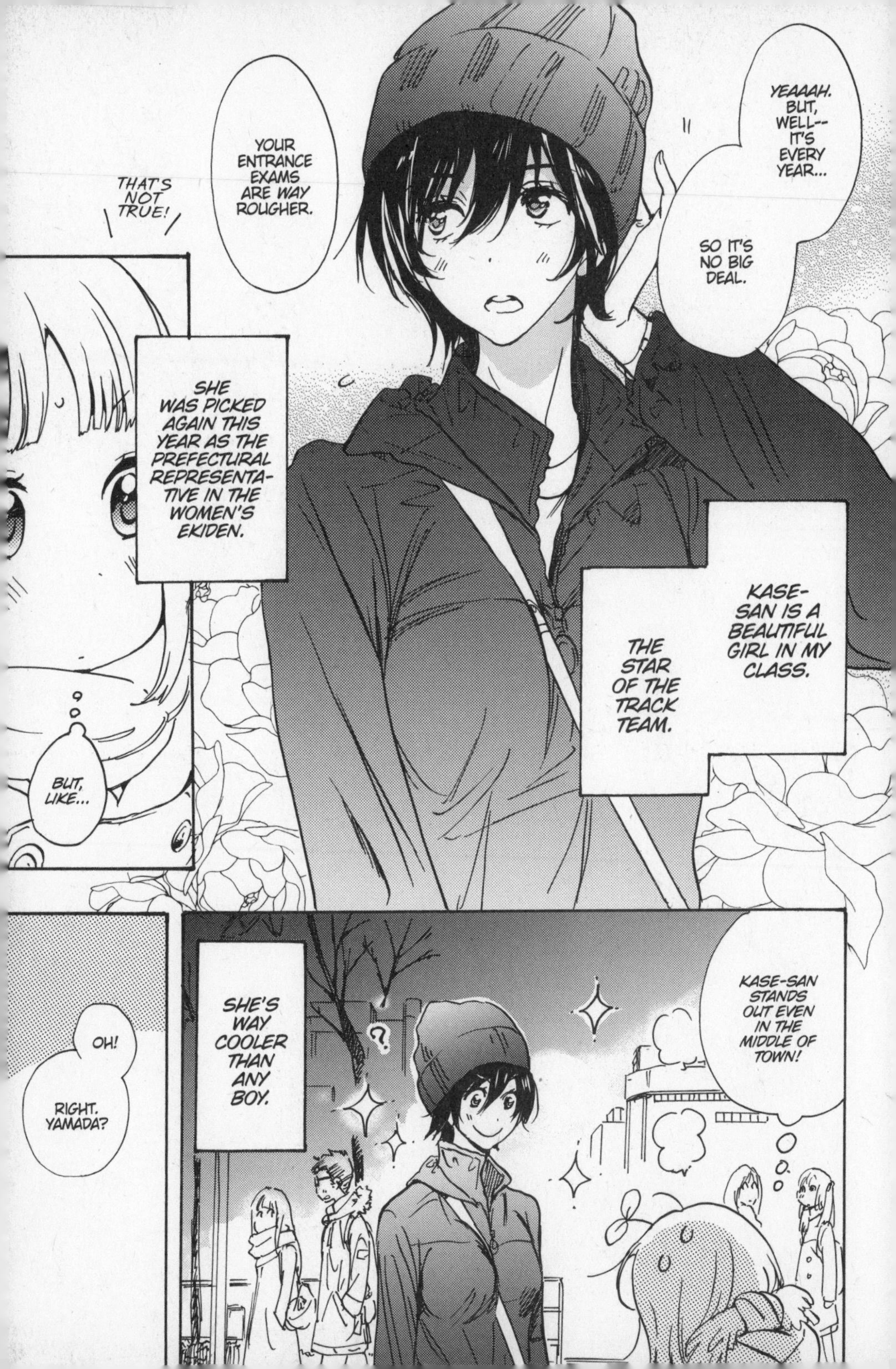
YEAAAH. BUT, WELL-- IT'S EVERY YEAR...
SO IT'S NO BIG DEAL.
YOUR ENTRANCE EXAMS ARE WAY ROUGHER.
THAT'S NOT TRUE!
KASE-SAN IS A BEAUTIFUL GIRL IN MY CLASS.
THE STAR OF THE TRACK TEAM.
SHE WAS PICKED AGAIN THIS YEAR AS THE PREFECTURAL REPRESENTA-TIVE IN THE WOMEN'S EKIDEN.
BUT, LIKE...
KASE-SAN STANDS OUT EVEN IN THE MIDDLE OF TOWN!
SHE'S WAY COOLER THAN ANY BOY.
OH!
RIGHT. YAMADA?

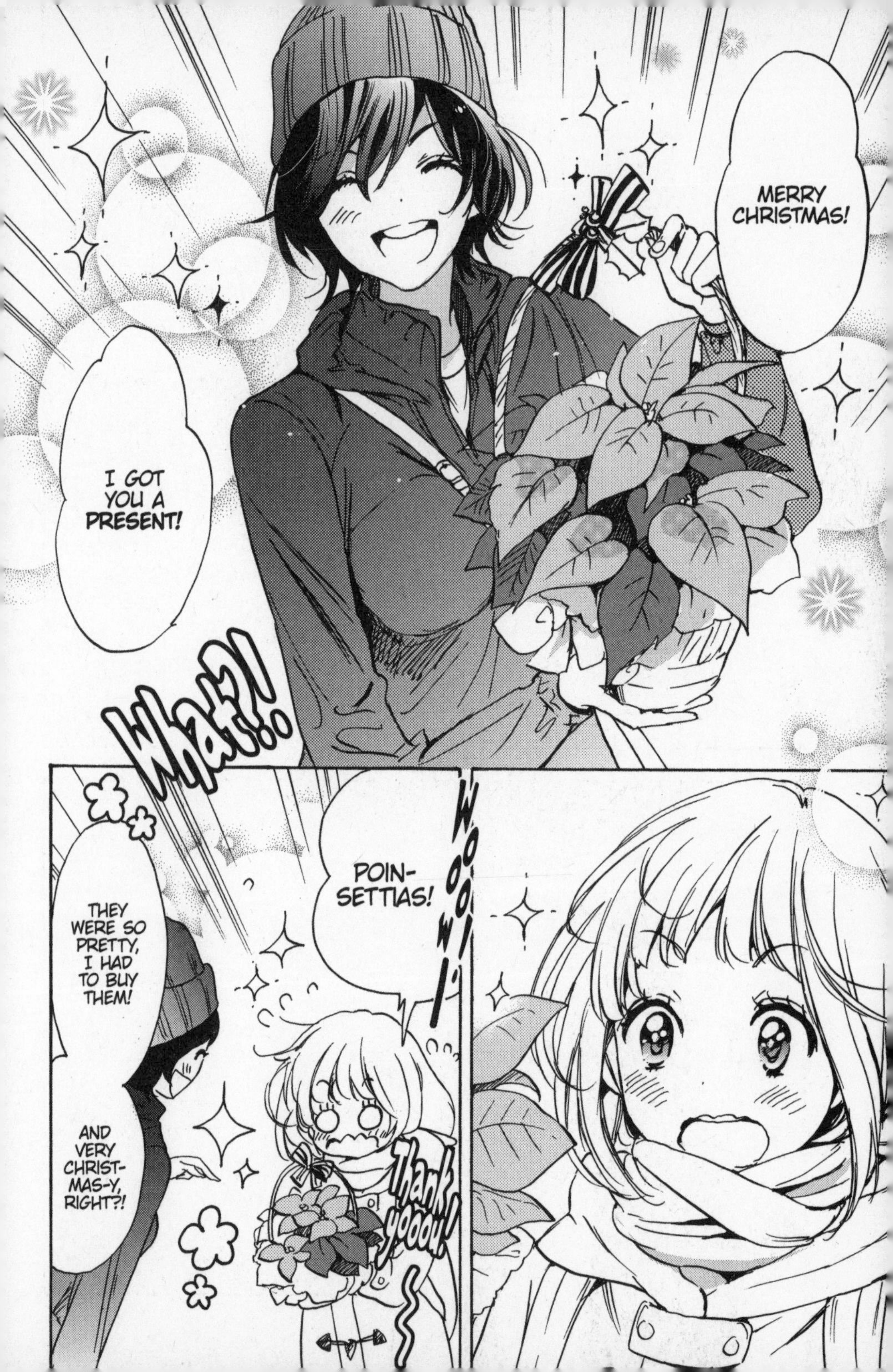
MERRY CHRISTMAS!
I GOT YOU A PRESENT!
What?!
WOOOW!
POIN-SETTIAS!
Thank yooou!
THEY WERE SO PRETTY, I HAD TO BUY THEM!
AND VERY CHRIST-MAS-Y, RIGHT?!

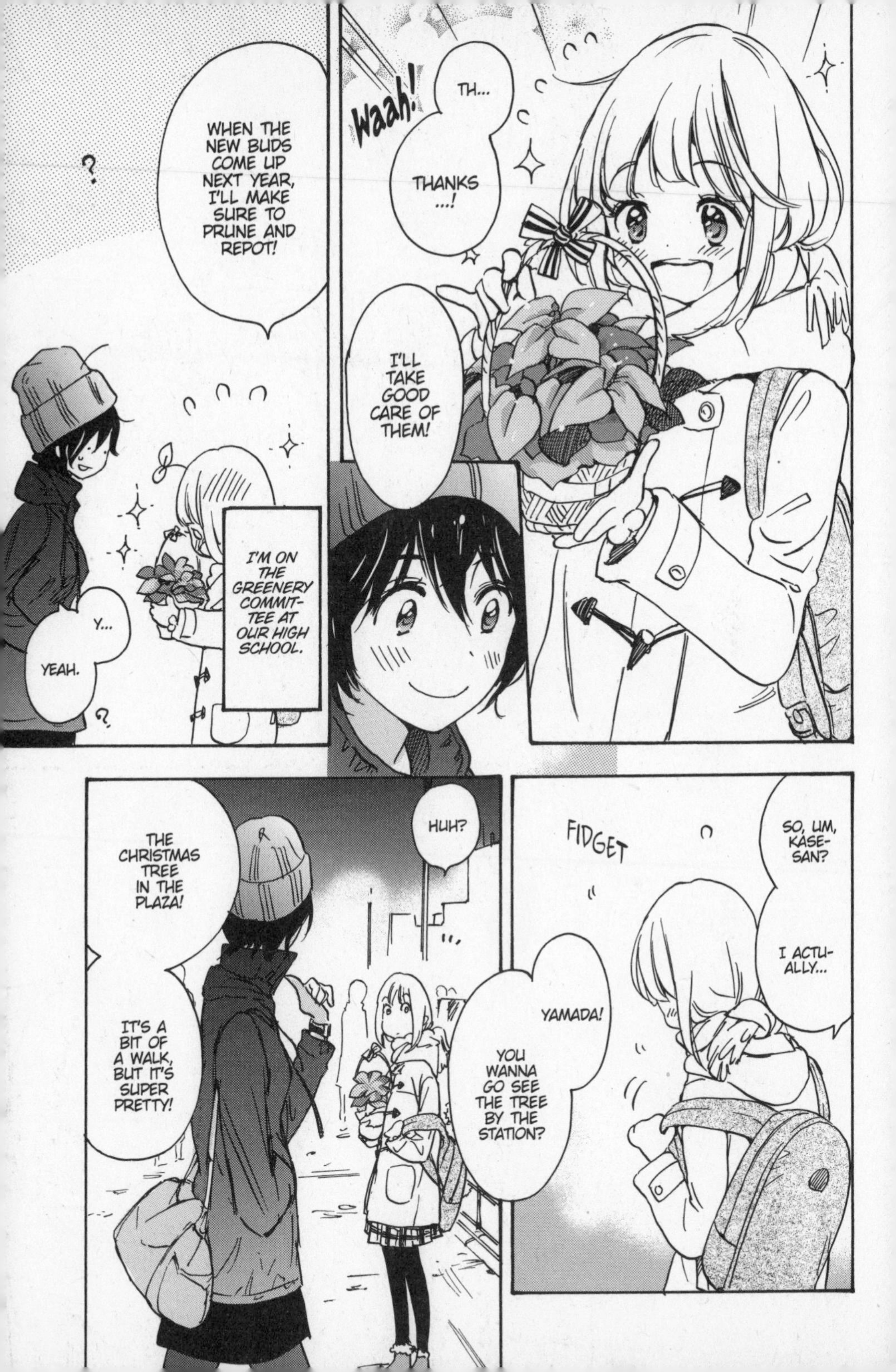

Waah!
TH... THANKS ...!
I'LL TAKE GOOD CARE OF THEM!
WHEN THE NEW BUDS COME UP NEXT YEAR, I'LL MAKE SURE TO PRUNE AND REPOT!
I'M ON THE GREENERY COMMITTEE AT OUR HIGH SCHOOL.
Y... YEAH.
FIDGET
SO, UM, KASE-SAN?
I ACTUALLY...
YAMADA!
YOU WANNA GO SEE THE TREE BY THE STATION?
HUH?
THE CHRISTMAS TREE IN THE PLAZA!
IT'S A BIT OF A WALK, BUT IT'S SUPER PRETTY!

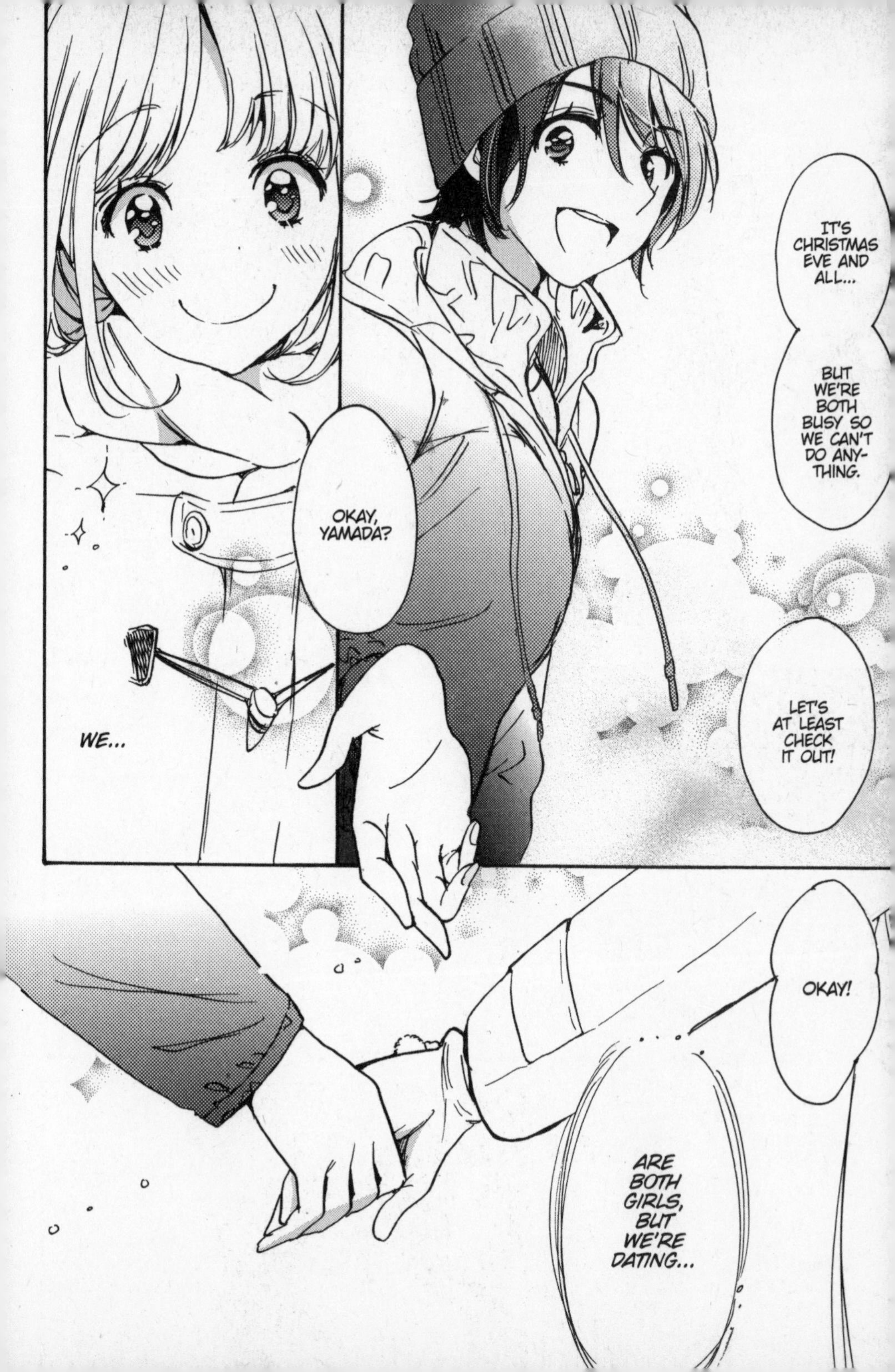
IT'S CHRISTMAS EVE AND ALL...
BUT WE'RE BOTH BUSY SO WE CAN'T DO ANY-THING.
LET'S AT LEAST CHECK IT OUT!
OKAY, YAMADA?
WE...
OKAY!
...
ARE BOTH GIRLS, BUT WE'RE DATING...

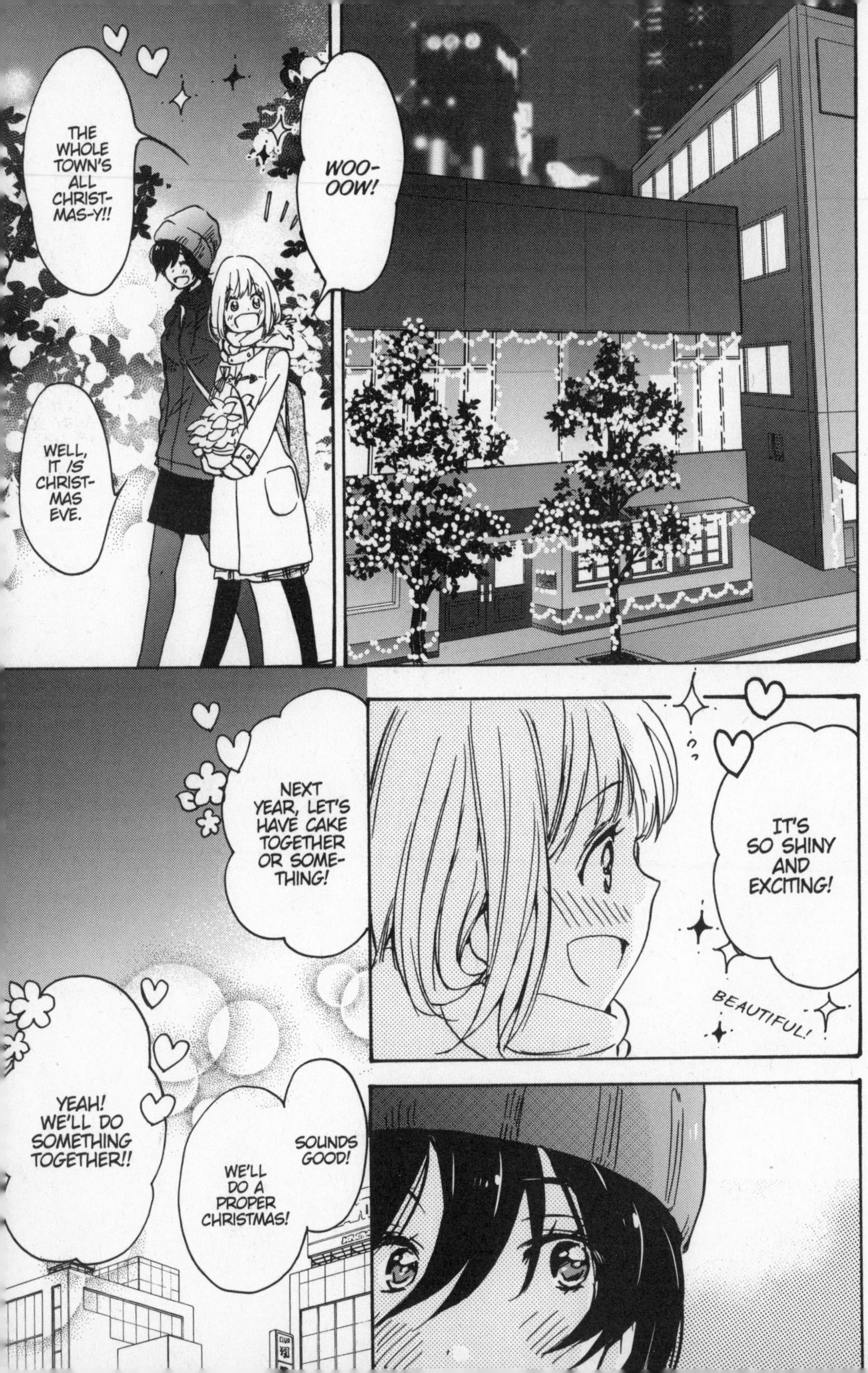
WOOO-OOW!
THE WHOLE TOWN'S ALL CHRIST-MAS-Y!!
WELL, IT IS CHRIST-MAS EVE.
IT'S SO SHINY AND EXCITING!
BEAUTIFUL!
NEXT YEAR, LET'S HAVE CAKE TOGETHER OR SOME-THING!
SOUNDS GOOD!
WE'LL DO A PROPER CHRISTMAS!
YEAH! WE'LL DO SOMETHING TOGETHER!!

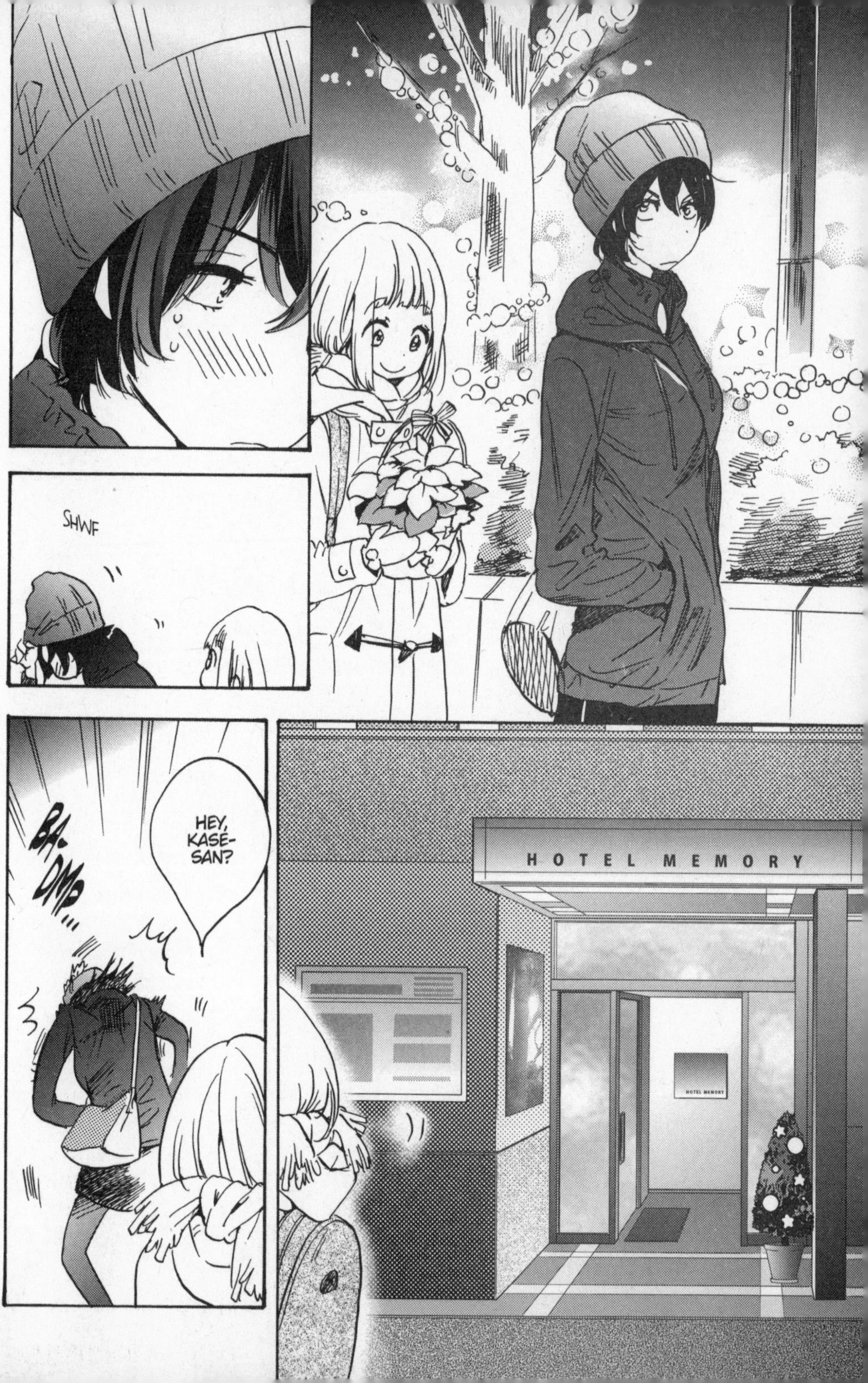
SHWF
HOTEL MEMORY
HEY, KASE-SAN?
BA-DMP...

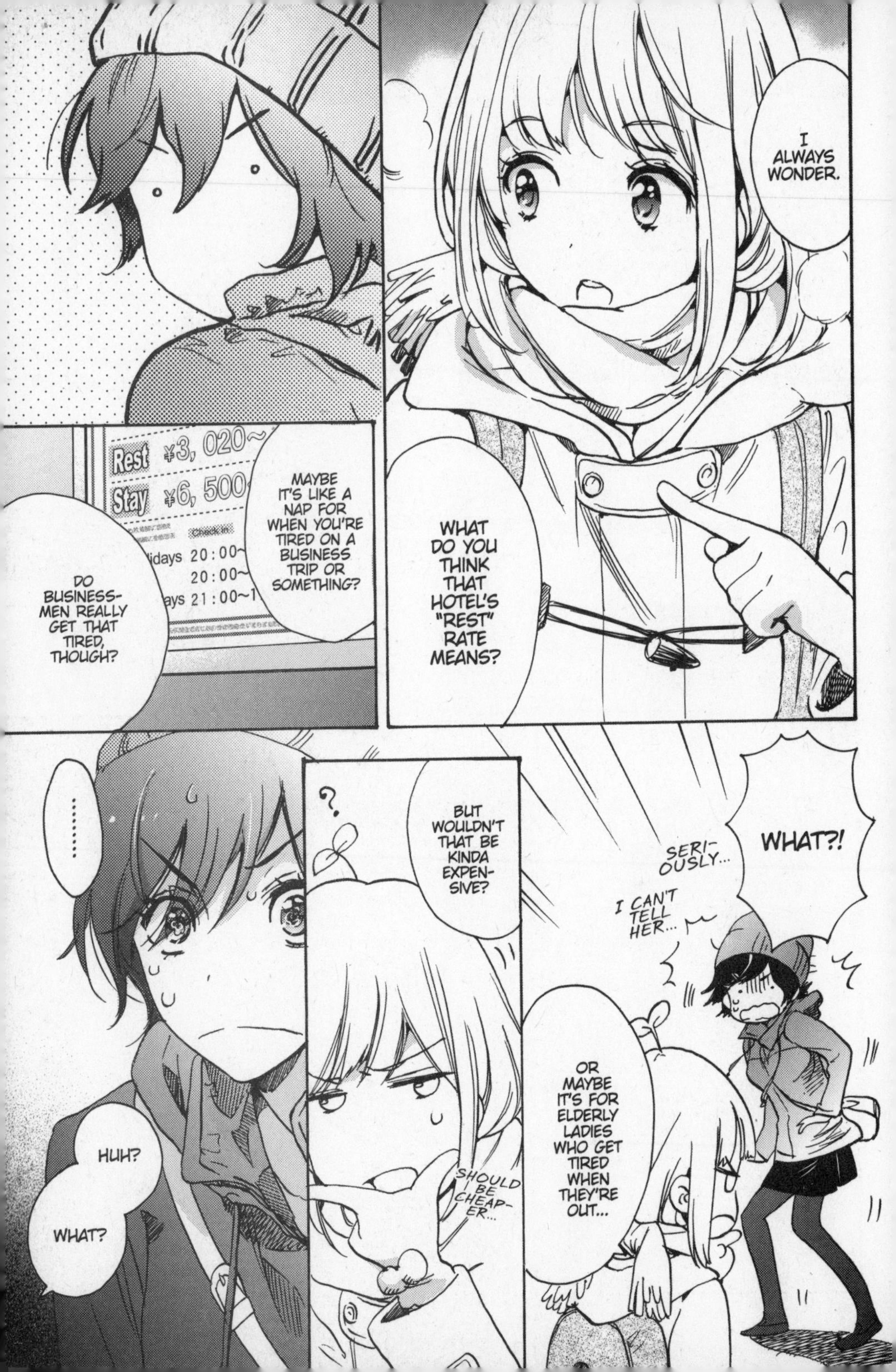
I ALWAYS WONDER.
WHAT DO YOU THINK THAT HOTEL'S "REST" RATE MEANS?
Rest ¥3, 020~
Stay ¥6, 500
Check in
MAYBE IT'S LIKE A NAP FOR WHEN YOU'RE TIRED ON A BUSINESS TRIP OR SOMETHING?
DO BUSINESSMEN REALLY GET THAT TIRED, THOUGH?
WHAT?!
SERIOUSLY...
I CAN'T TELL HER...
OR MAYBE IT'S FOR ELDERLY LADIES WHO GET TIRED WHEN THEY'RE OUT...
BUT WOULDN'T THAT BE KINDA EXPENSIVE?
SHOULD BE CHEAPER...
?
......
HUH?
WHAT?

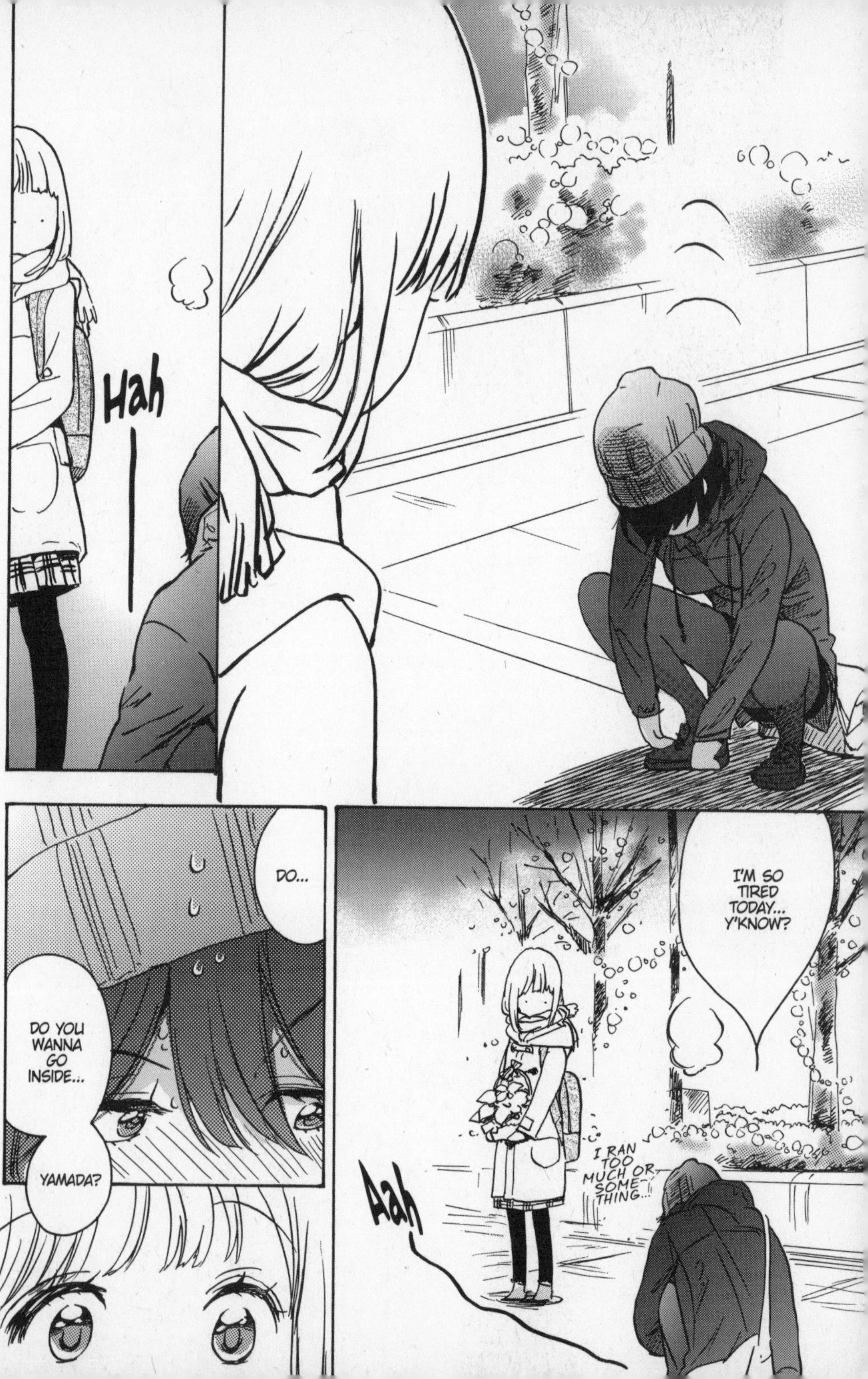
Hah
I'M SO TIRED TODAY... Y'KNOW?
I RAN TOO MUCH OR SOME-THING...
Aah
DO...
DO YOU WANNA GO INSIDE...
YAMADA?

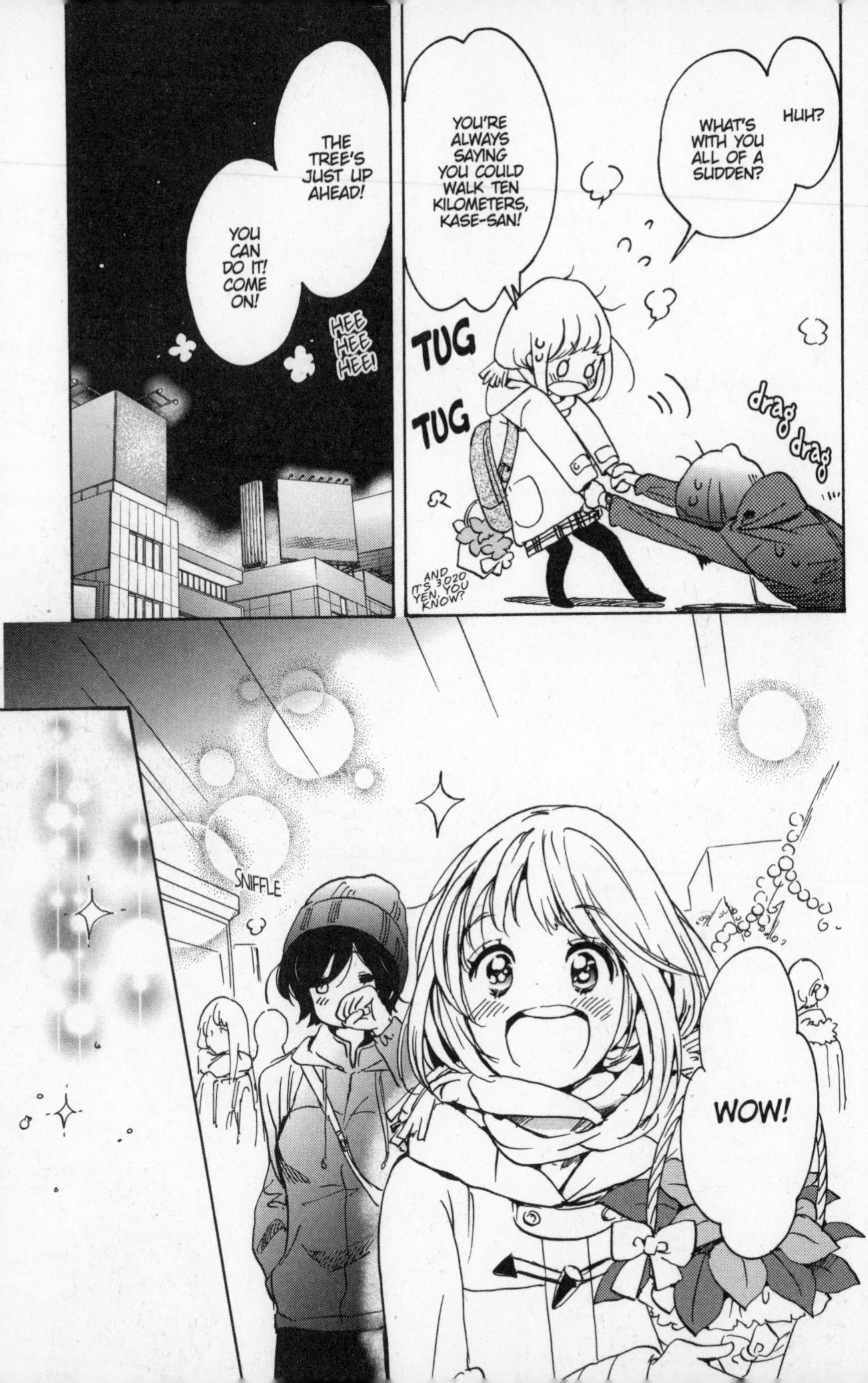
HUH?
WHAT'S WITH YOU ALL OF A SUDDEN?
YOU'RE ALWAYS SAYING YOU COULD WALK TEN KILOMETERS, KASE-SAN!
drag drag
TUG
TUG
AND IT'S 3,020 YEN, YOU KNOW?
THE TREE'S JUST UP AHEAD!
YOU CAN DO IT! COME ON!
HEE HEE HEE!
WOW!
SNIFFLE

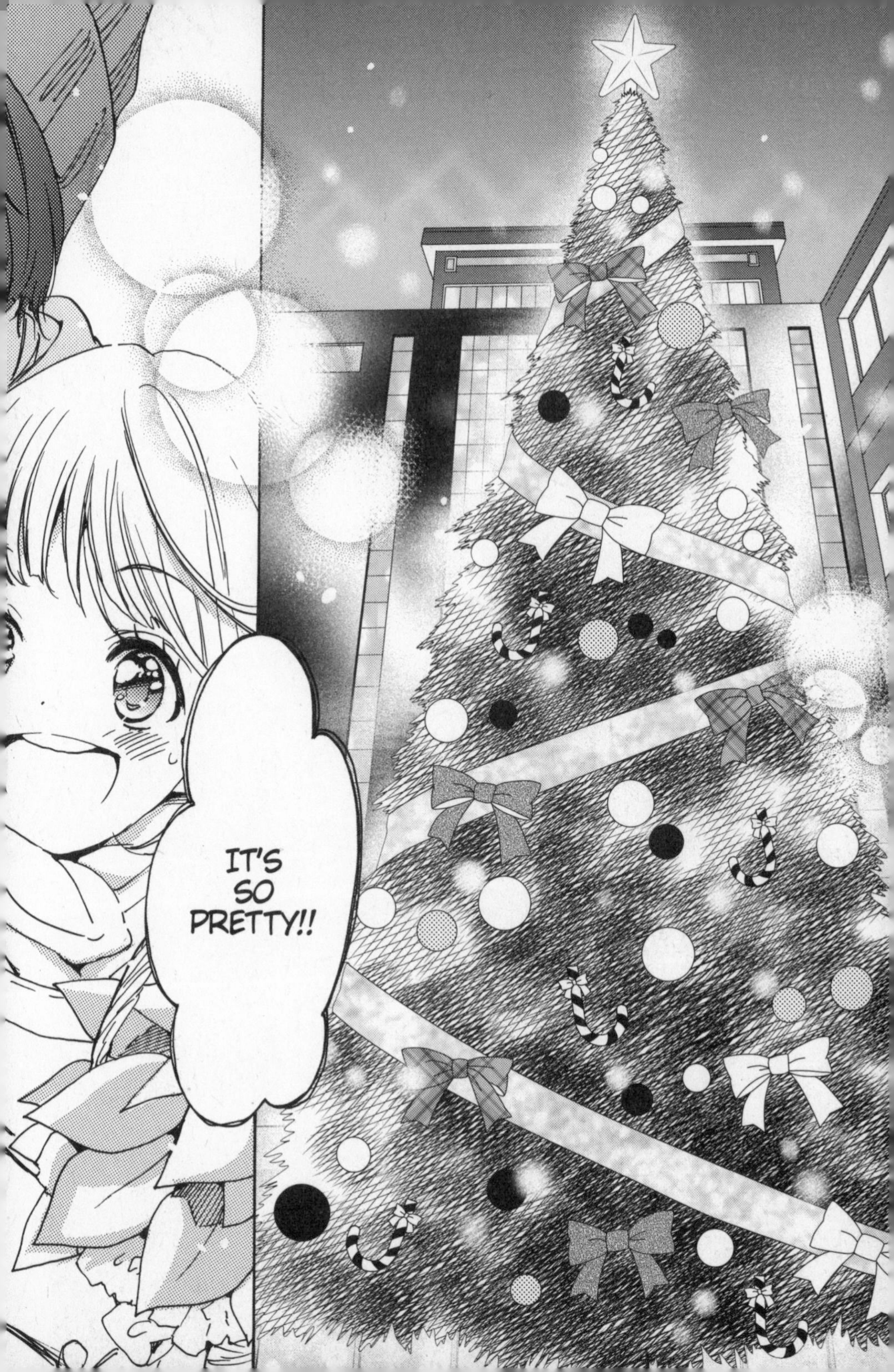
IT'S SO PRETTY!!

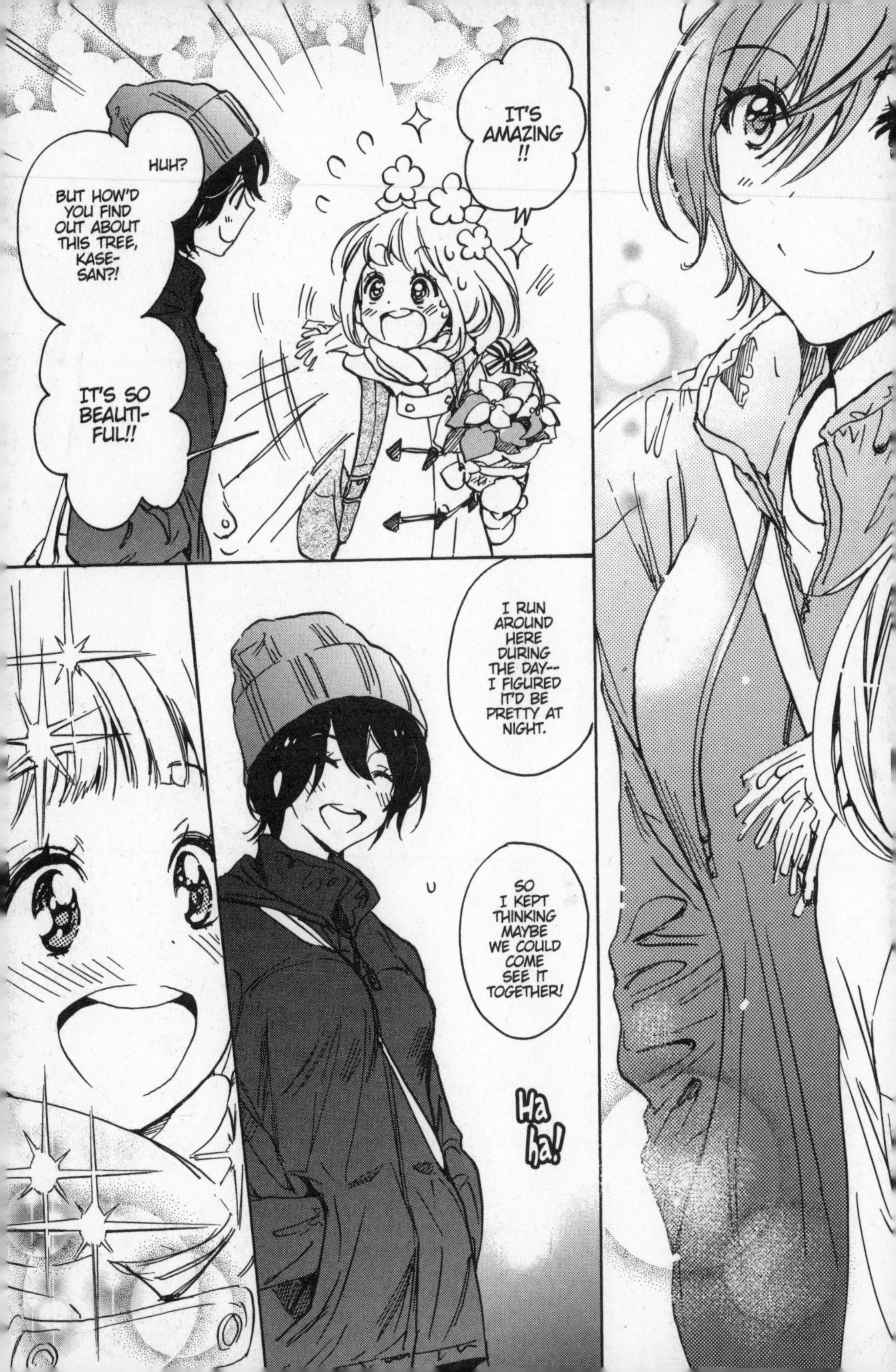
IT'S AMAZING!!
HUH? BUT HOW'D YOU FIND OUT ABOUT THIS TREE, KASE-SAN?!
IT'S SO BEAUTIFUL!!
I RUN AROUND HERE DURING THE DAY-- I FIGURED IT'D BE PRETTY AT NIGHT.
SO I KEPT THINKING MAYBE WE COULD COME SEE IT TOGETHER!
Ha ha!

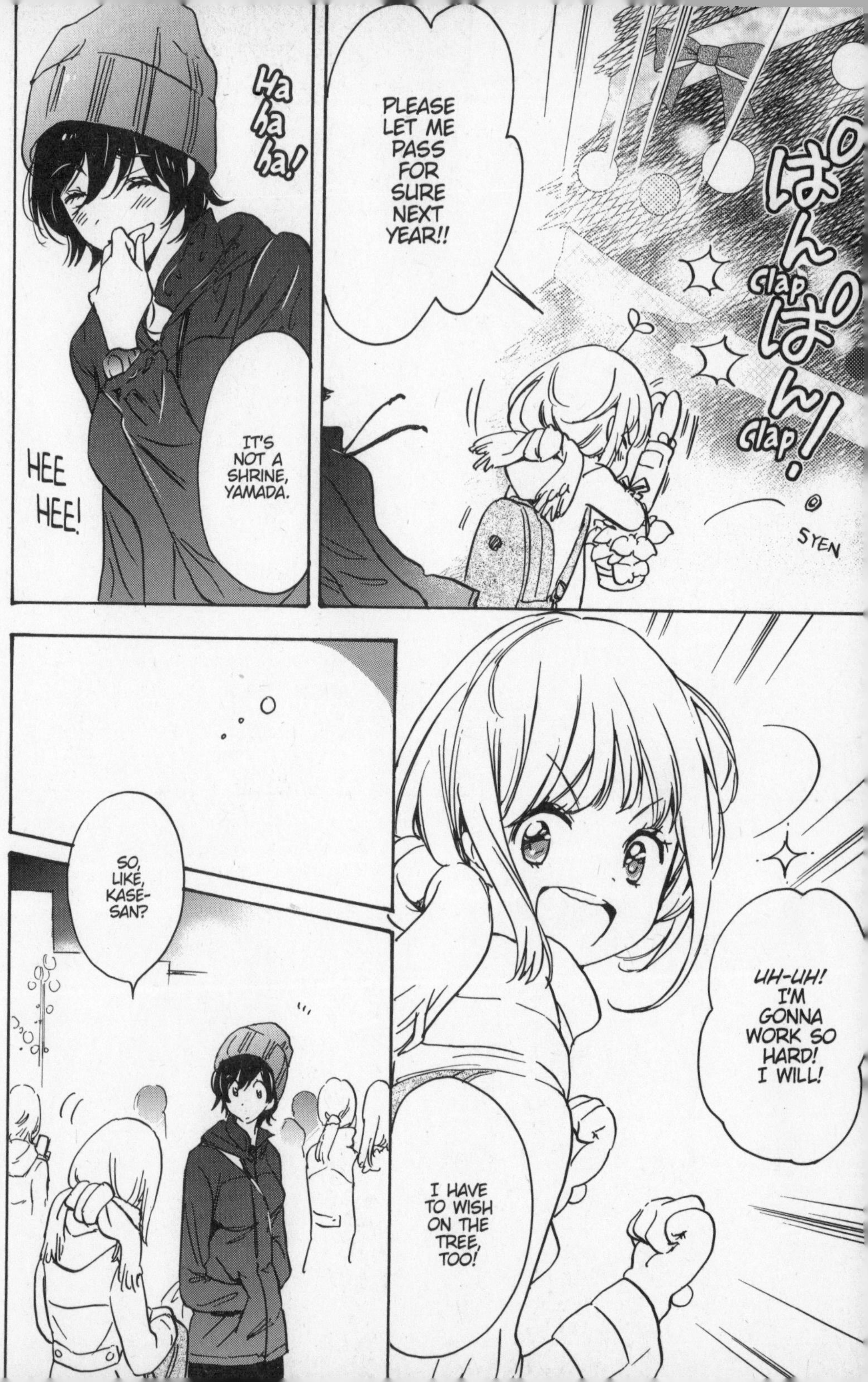
ぱんぱん!
clap
clap
SYEN
PLEASE LET ME PASS FOR SURE NEXT YEAR!!
IT'S NOT A SHRINE, YAMADA.
Ha ha ha!
HEE HEE!
UH-UH! I'M GONNA WORK SO HARD! I WILL!
I HAVE TO WISH ON THE TREE, TOO!
SO, LIKE, KASE-SAN?

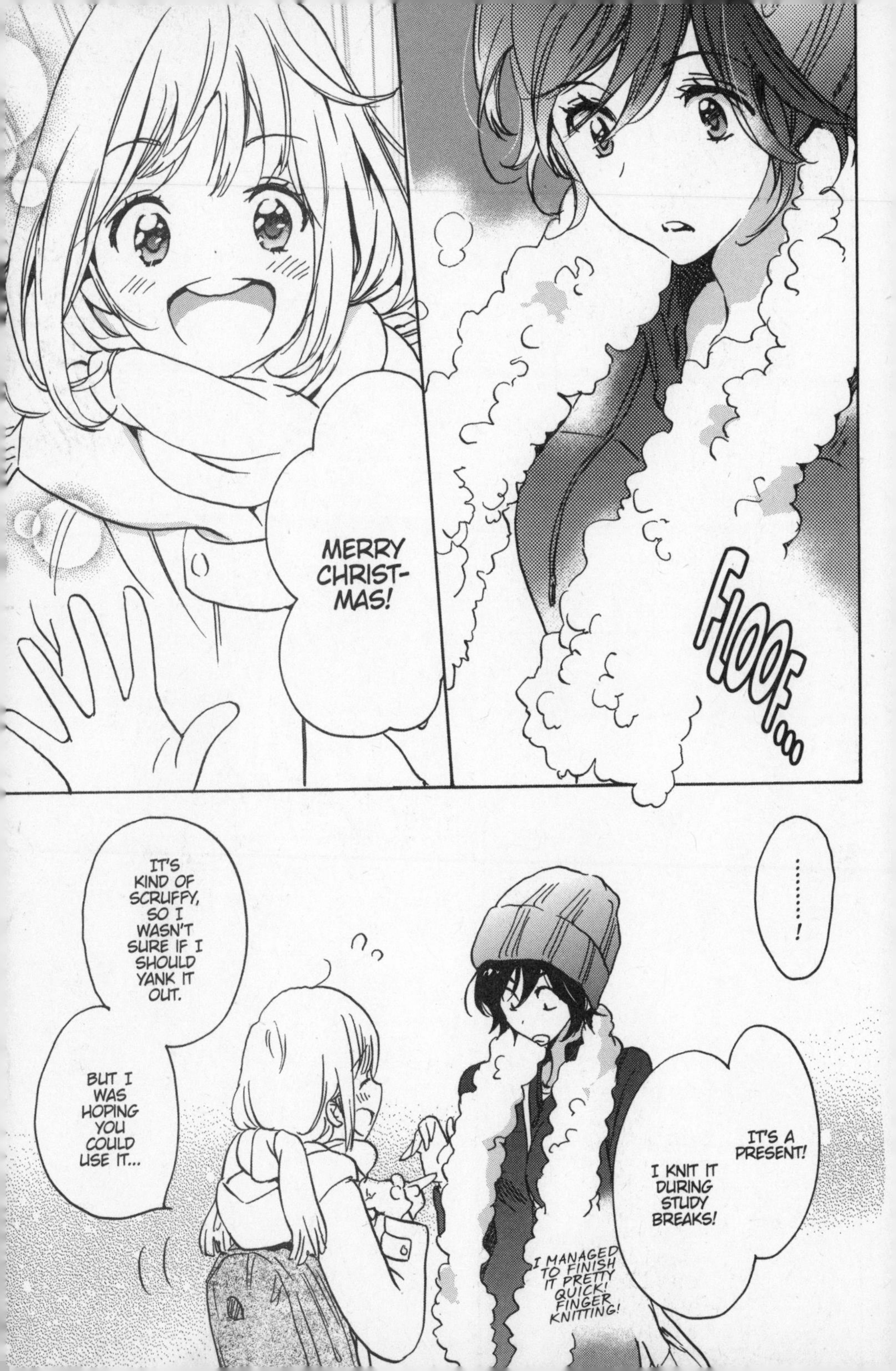
FLOOF...
MERRY CHRIST-MAS!
......!
IT'S A PRESENT!
I KNIT IT DURING STUDY BREAKS!
I MANAGED TO FINISH IT PRETTY QUICK! FINGER KNITTING!
IT'S KIND OF SCRUFFY, SO I WASN'T SURE IF I SHOULD YANK IT OUT.
BUT I WAS HOPING YOU COULD USE IT...

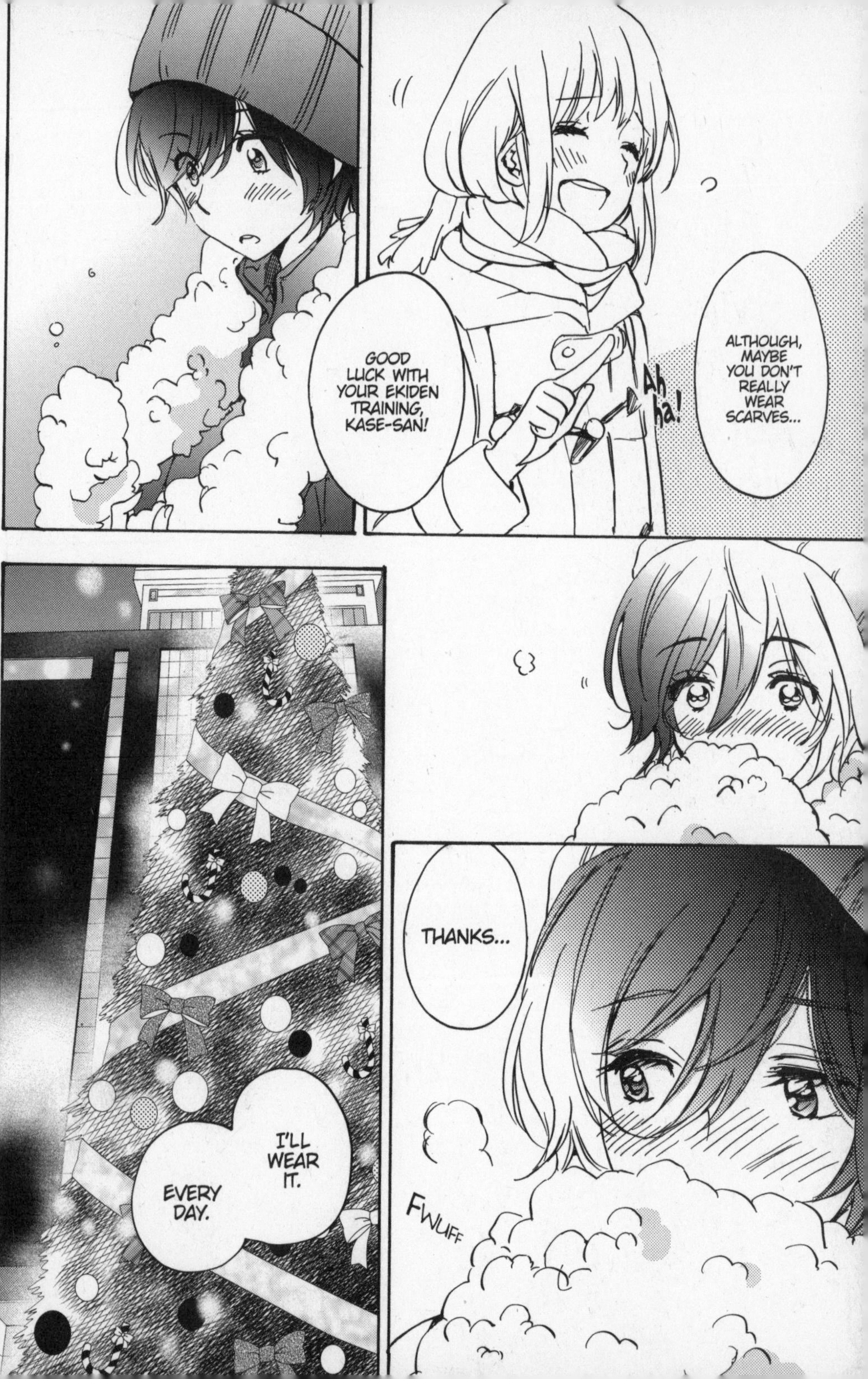
ALTHOUGH, MAYBE YOU DON'T REALLY WEAR SCARVES...
Ah ha!
GOOD LUCK WITH YOUR EKIDEN TRAINING, KASE-SAN!
THANKS...
FWUFF
I'LL WEAR IT.
EVERY DAY.

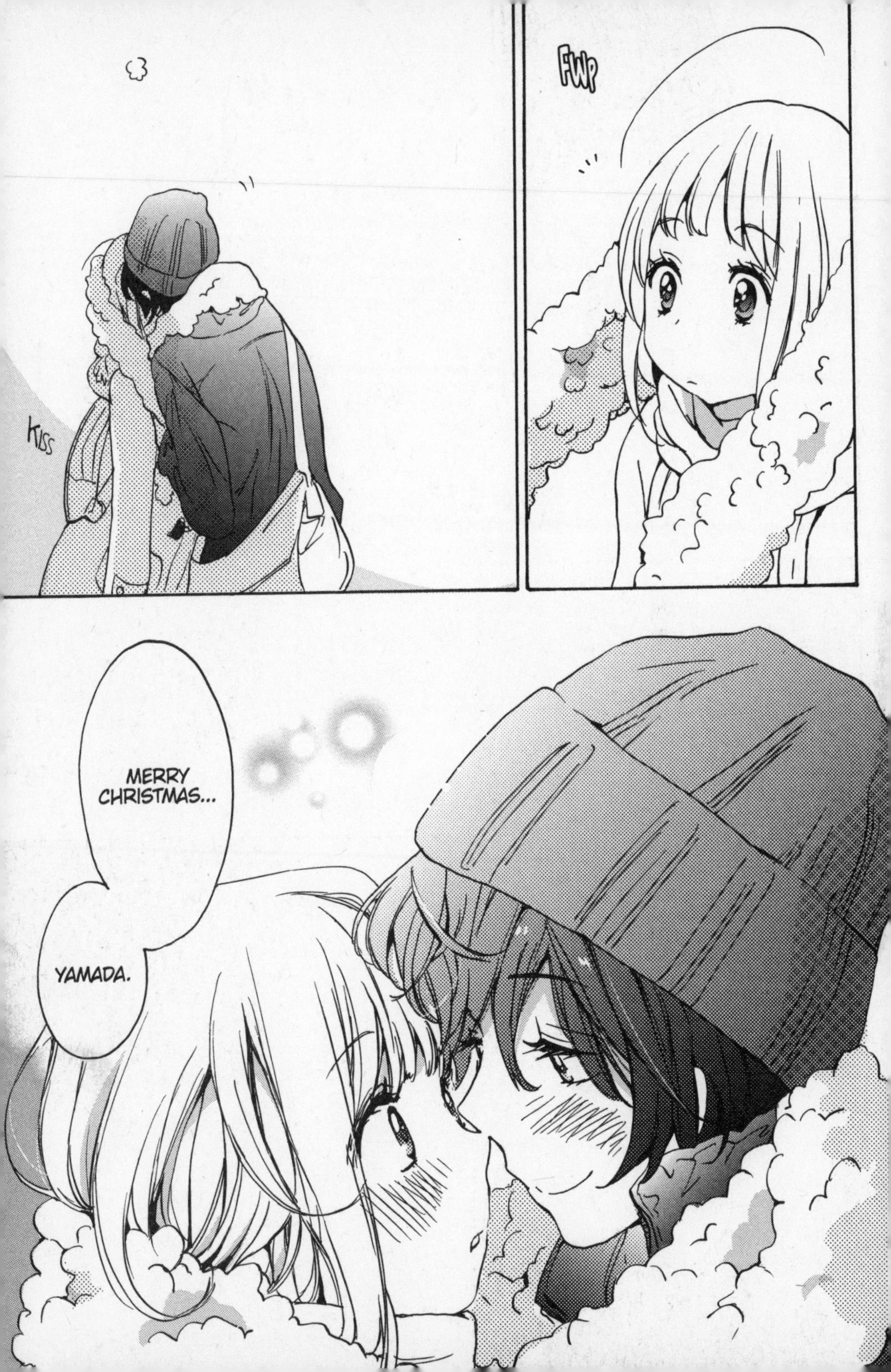
FWP
KISS
MERRY CHRISTMAS...
YAMADA.

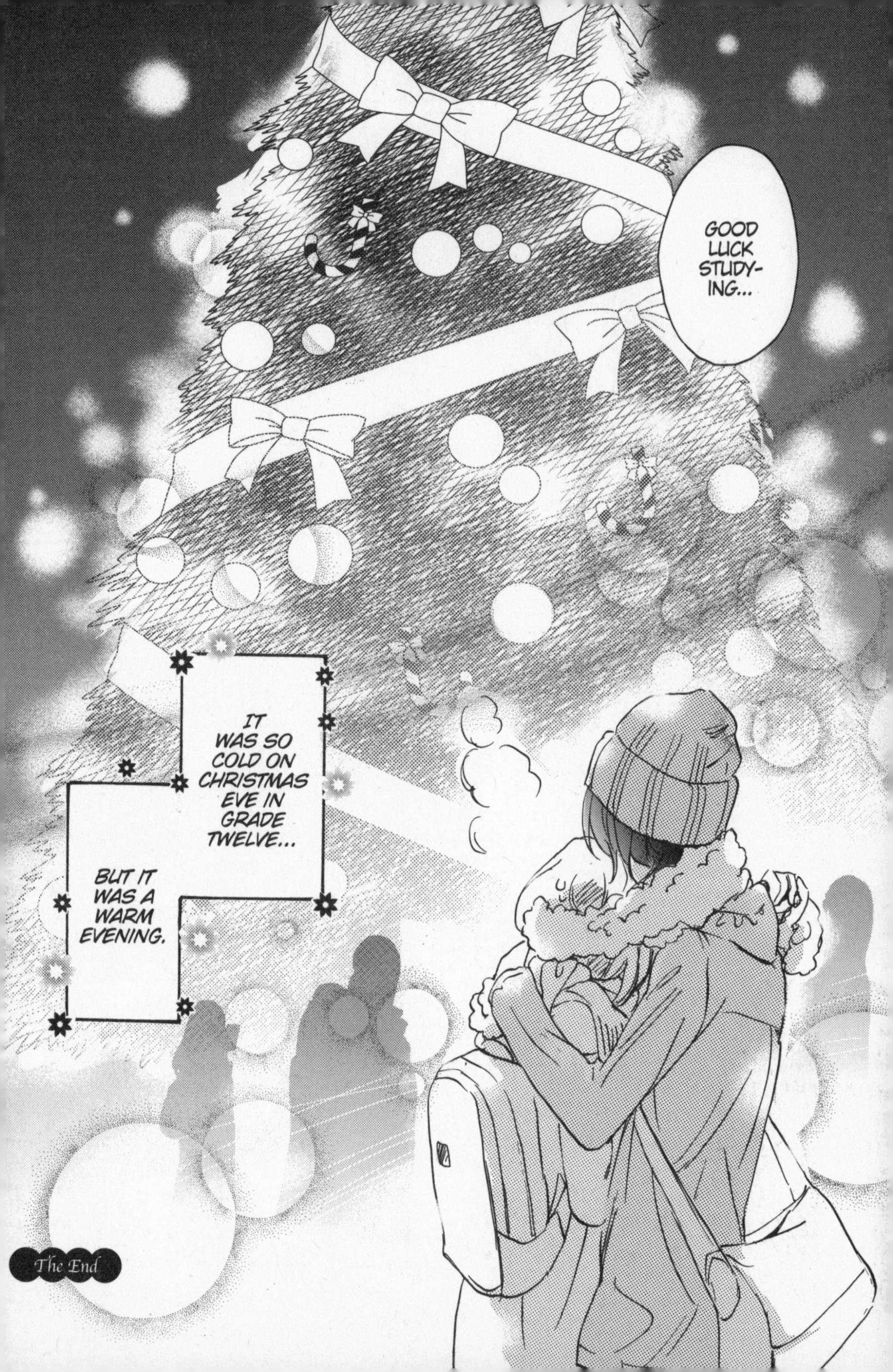
GOOD LUCK STUDY-ING...
IT WAS SO COLD ON CHRISTMAS EVE IN GRADE TWELVE...
BUT IT WAS A WARM EVENING.
The End

Kase-san and Powder Snow

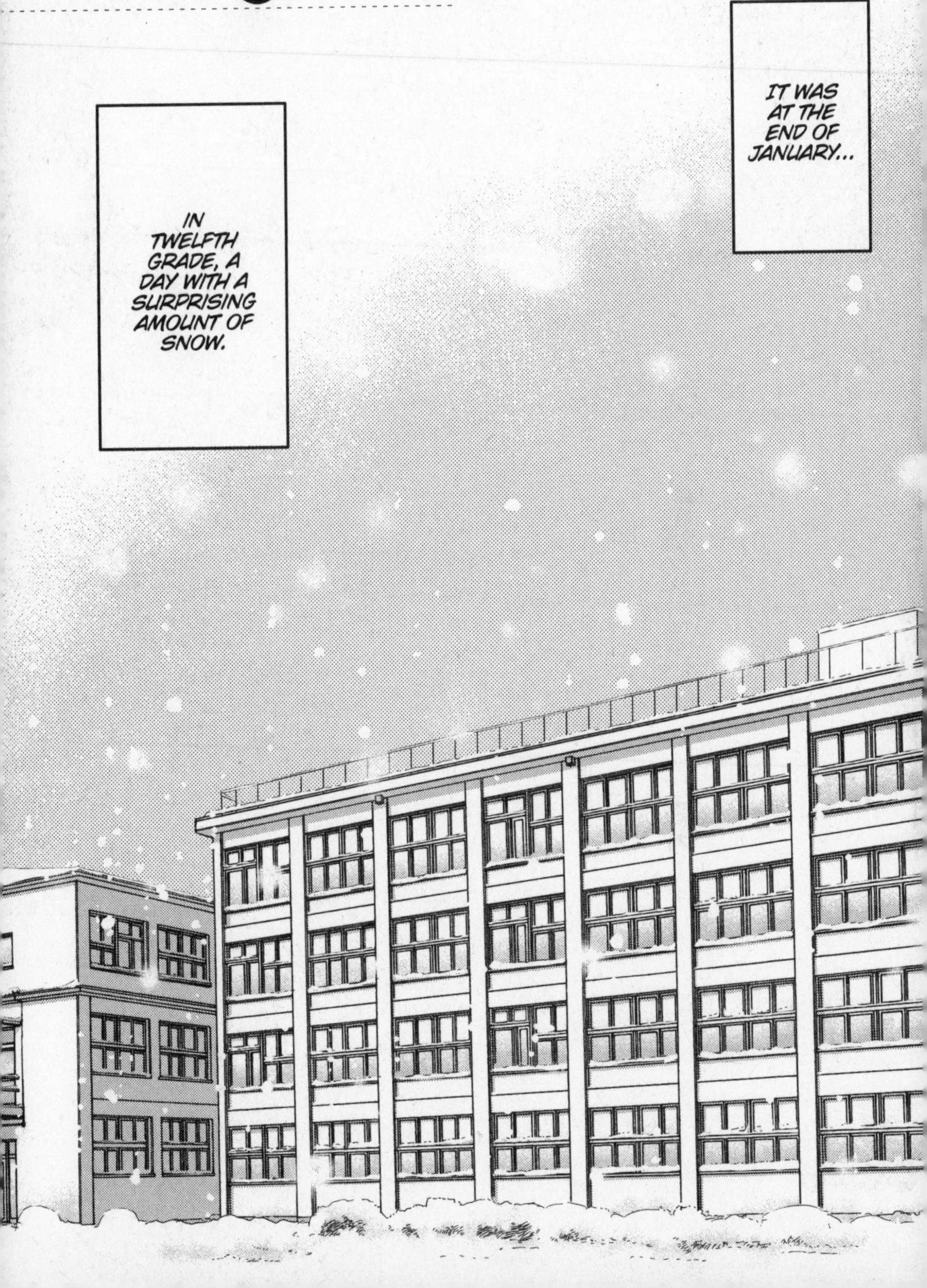
IT WAS AT THE END OF JANUARY...
IN TWELFTH GRADE, A DAY WITH A SURPRISING AMOUNT OF SNOW.

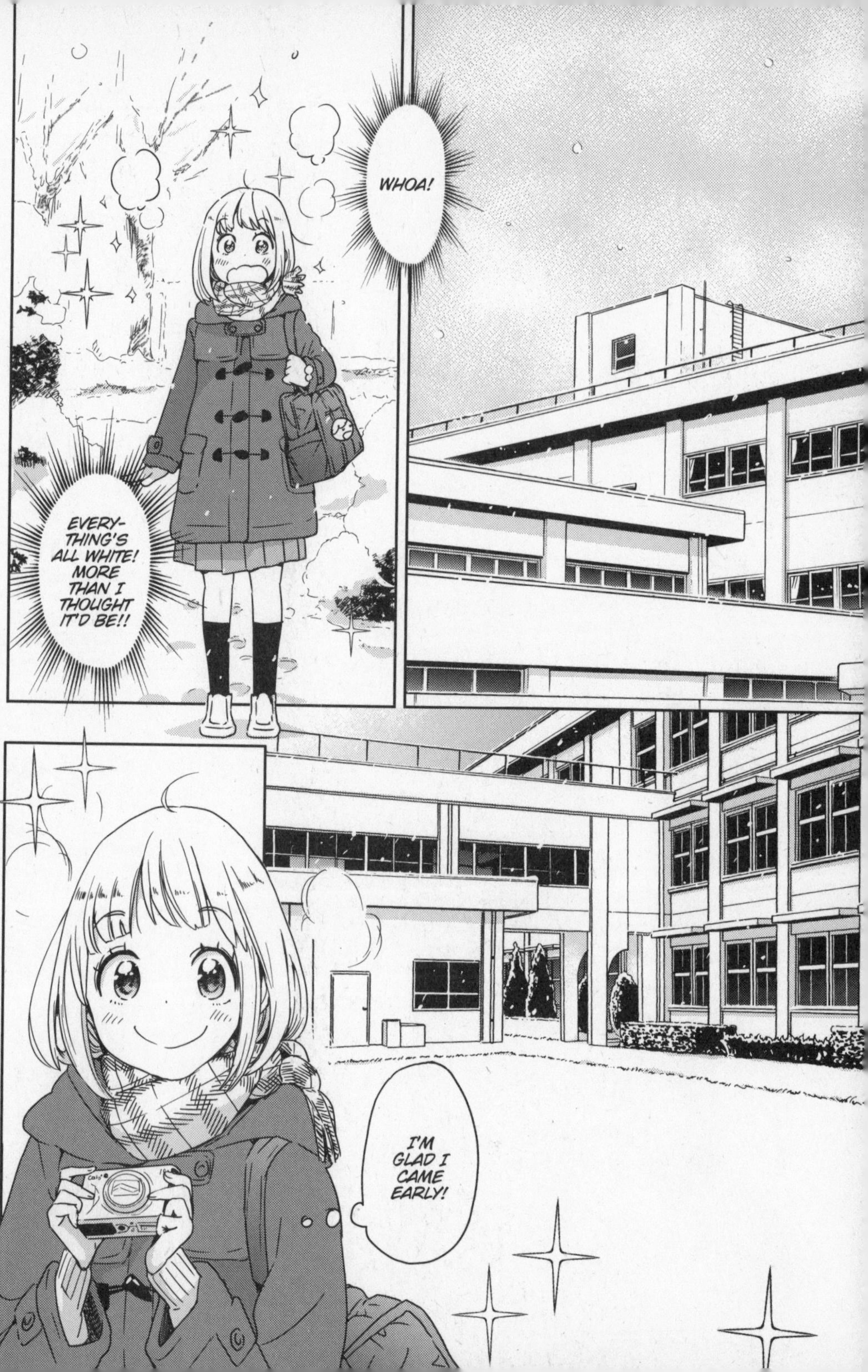
WHOA!
EVERYTHING'S ALL WHITE! MORE THAN I THOUGHT IT'D BE!!
I'M GLAD I CAME EARLY!

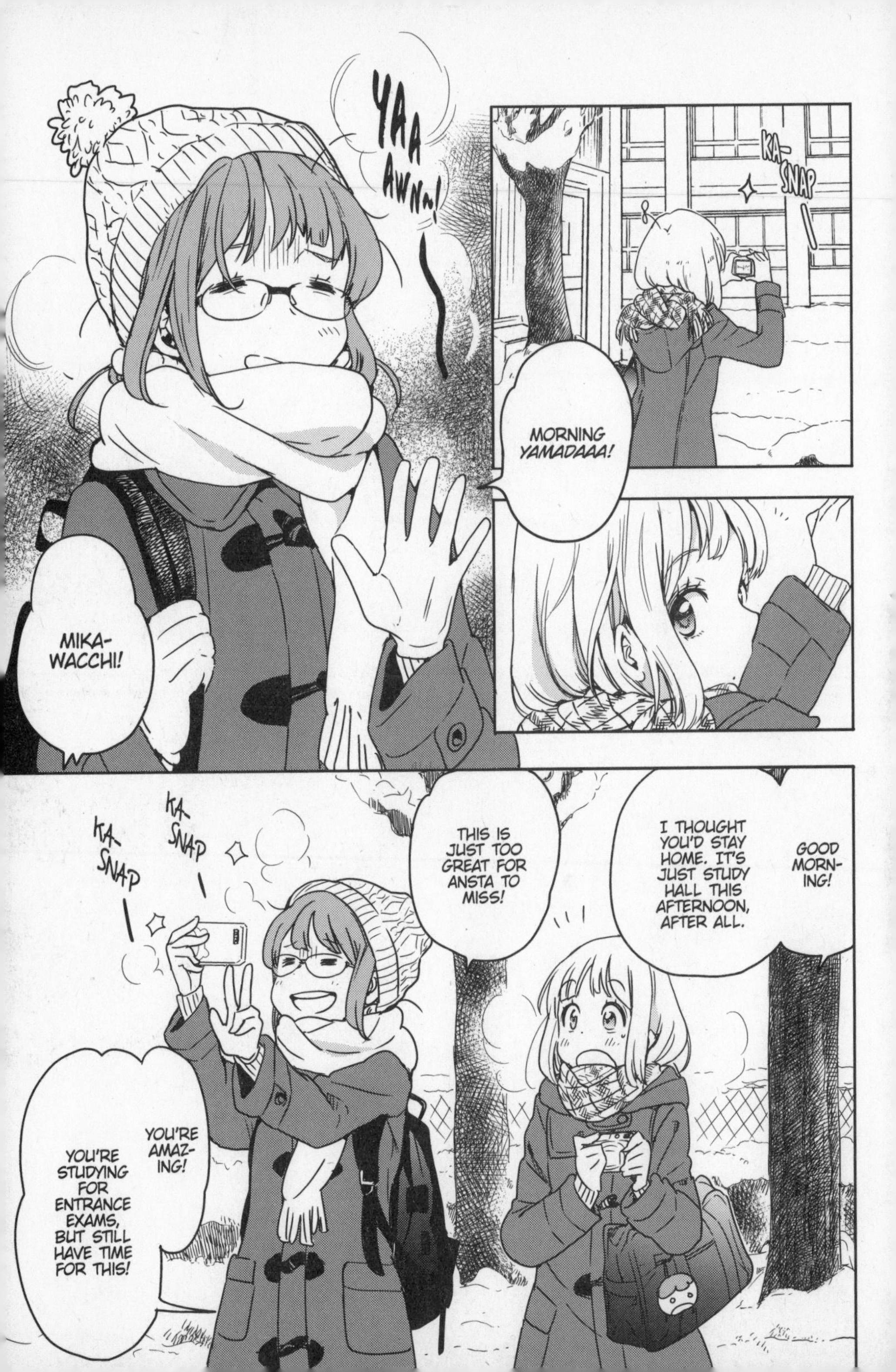
KA-SNAP
MORNING YAMADAAA!
YAAAWN~!
MIKA-WACCHI!
GOOD MORN-ING!
I THOUGHT YOU'D STAY HOME. IT'S JUST STUDY HALL THIS AFTERNOON, AFTER ALL.
THIS IS JUST TOO GREAT FOR ANSTA TO MISS!
KA-SNAP
KA-SNAP
YOU'RE AMAZ-ING!
YOU'RE STUDYING FOR ENTRANCE EXAMS, BUT STILL HAVE TIME FOR THIS!

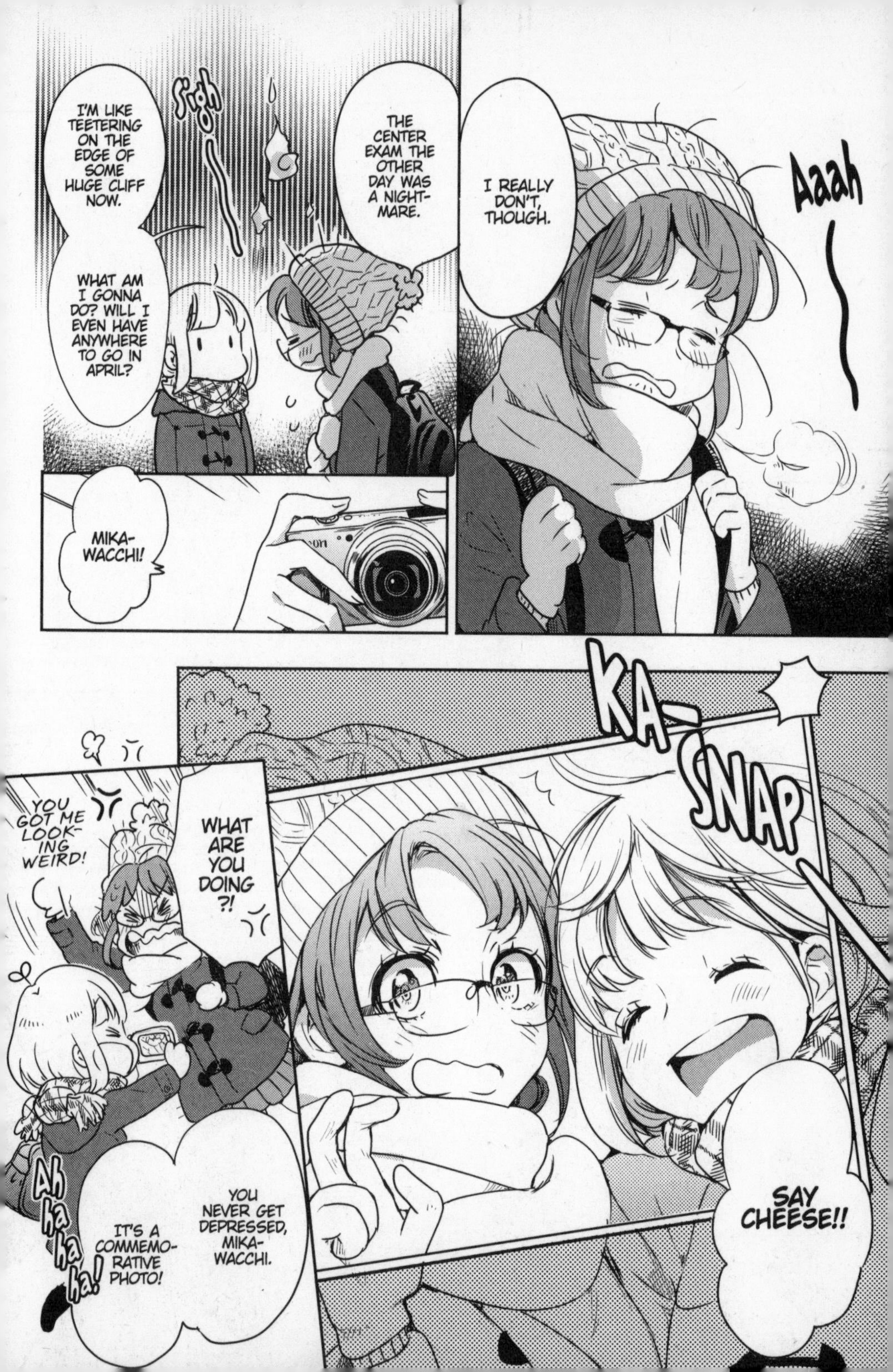
Aaah
I REALLY DON'T, THOUGH.
THE CENTER EXAM THE OTHER DAY WAS A NIGHT-MARE.
sigh
I'M LIKE TEETERING ON THE EDGE OF SOME HUGE CLIFF NOW.
WHAT AM I GONNA DO? WILL I EVEN HAVE ANYWHERE TO GO IN APRIL?
MIKA-WACCHI!
KA-SNAP
SAY CHEESE!!
WHAT ARE YOU DOING ?!
YOU GOT ME LOOK-ING WEIRD!
YOU NEVER GET DEPRESSED, MIKA-WACCHI.
IT'S A COMMEMO-RATIVE PHOTO!
Ah ha ha ha!

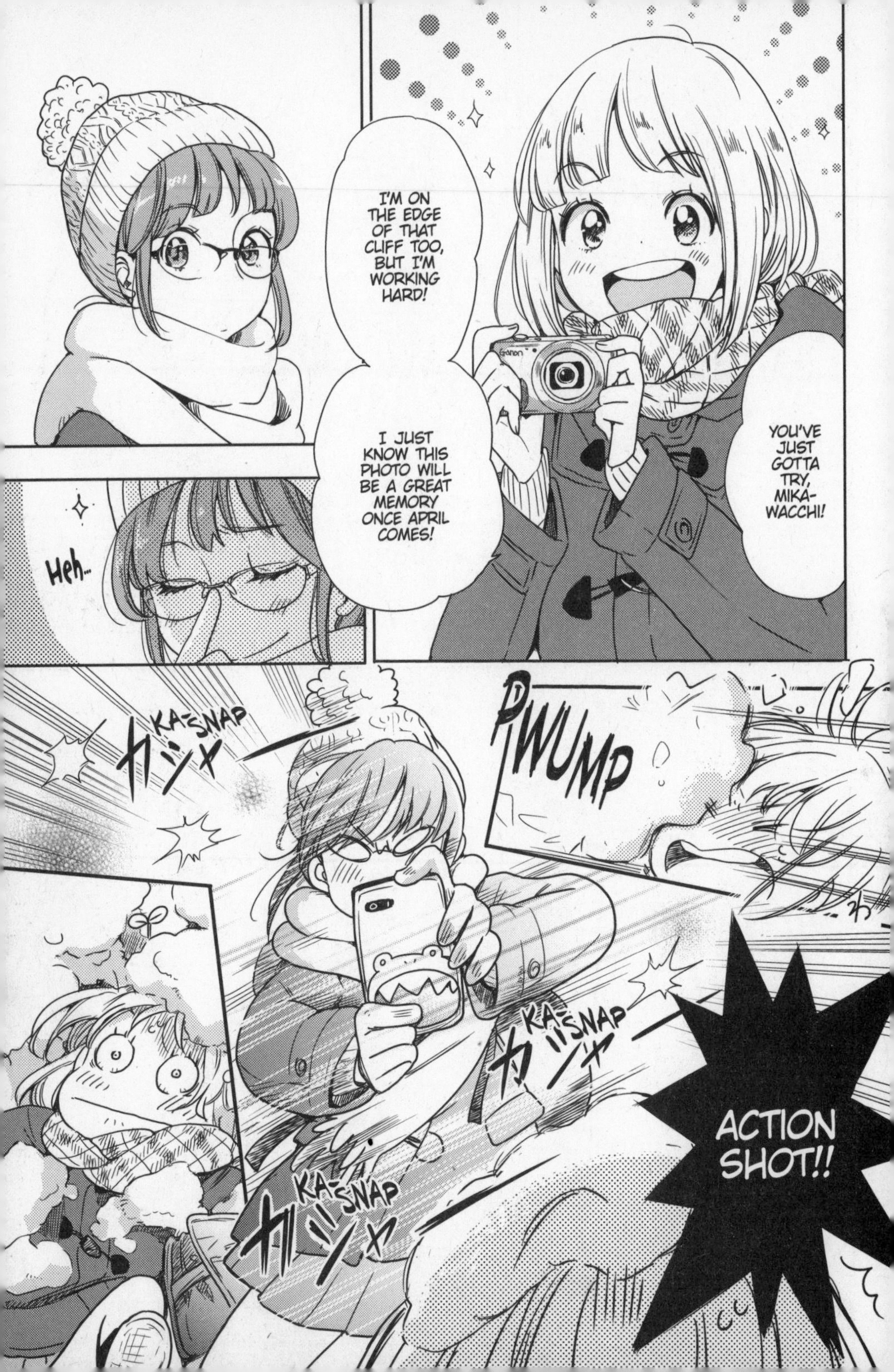
YOU'VE JUST GOTTA TRY, MIKA-WACCHI!
I'M ON THE EDGE OF THAT CLIFF TOO, BUT I'M WORKING HARD!
I JUST KNOW THIS PHOTO WILL BE A GREAT MEMORY ONCE APRIL COMES!
Heh...
PWUMP
KA-SNAP
KA-SNAP
ACTION SHOT!!
KA-SNAP

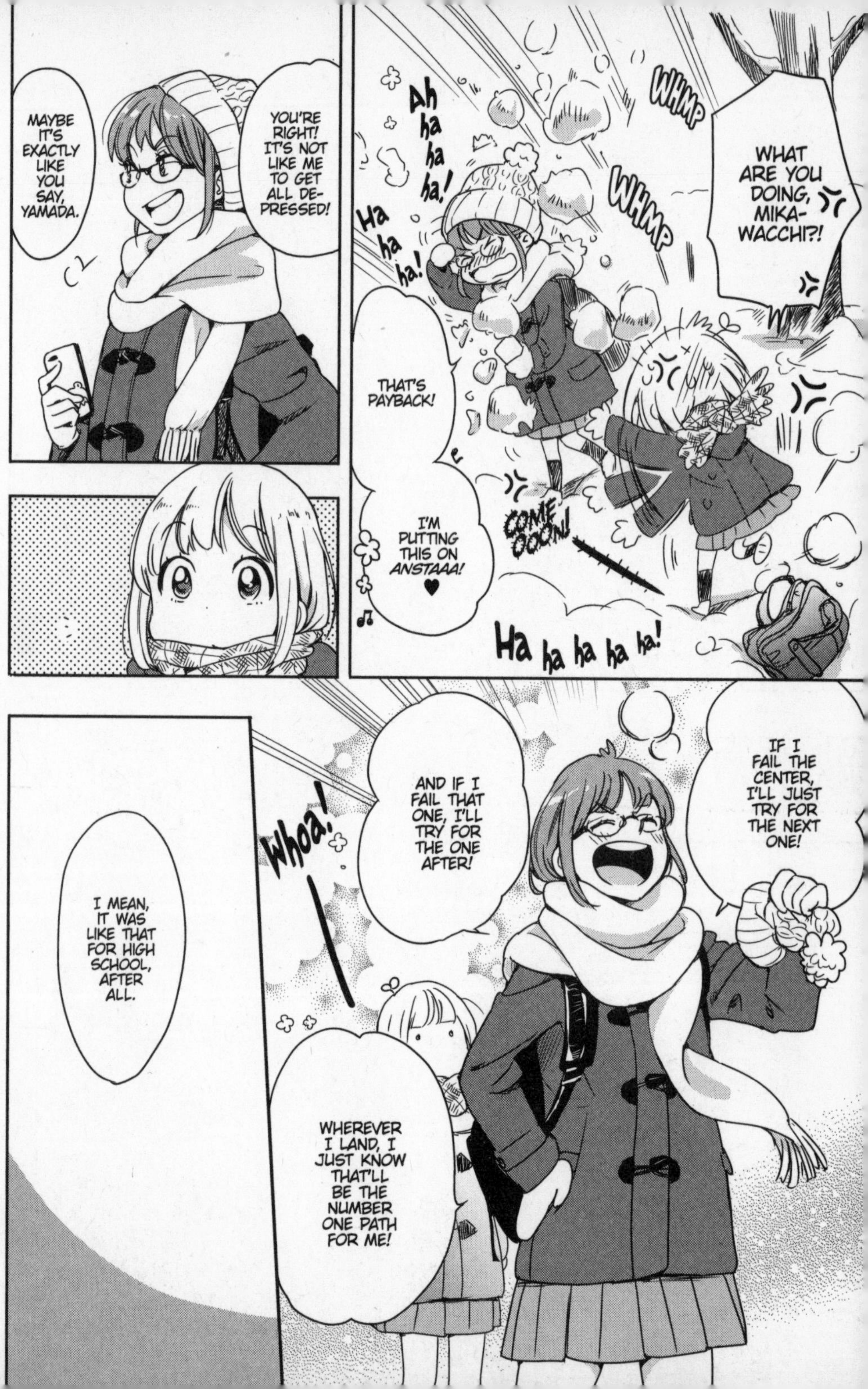
WHAT ARE YOU DOING, MIKA-WACCHI?!
WHMP
WHMP
Ah ha ha ha!
Ha ha ha!
THAT'S PAYBACK!
I'M PUTTING THIS ON ANSTAAA! ♥
COME OOON!
Ha ha ha ha ha!
YOU'RE RIGHT! IT'S NOT LIKE ME TO GET ALL DE-PRESSED!
MAYBE IT'S EXACTLY LIKE YOU SAY, YAMADA.
IF I FAIL THE CENTER, I'LL JUST TRY FOR THE NEXT ONE!
AND IF I FAIL THAT ONE, I'LL TRY FOR THE ONE AFTER!
Whoa!
WHEREVER I LAND, I JUST KNOW THAT'LL BE THE NUMBER ONE PATH FOR ME!
I MEAN, IT WAS LIKE THAT FOR HIGH SCHOOL, AFTER ALL.

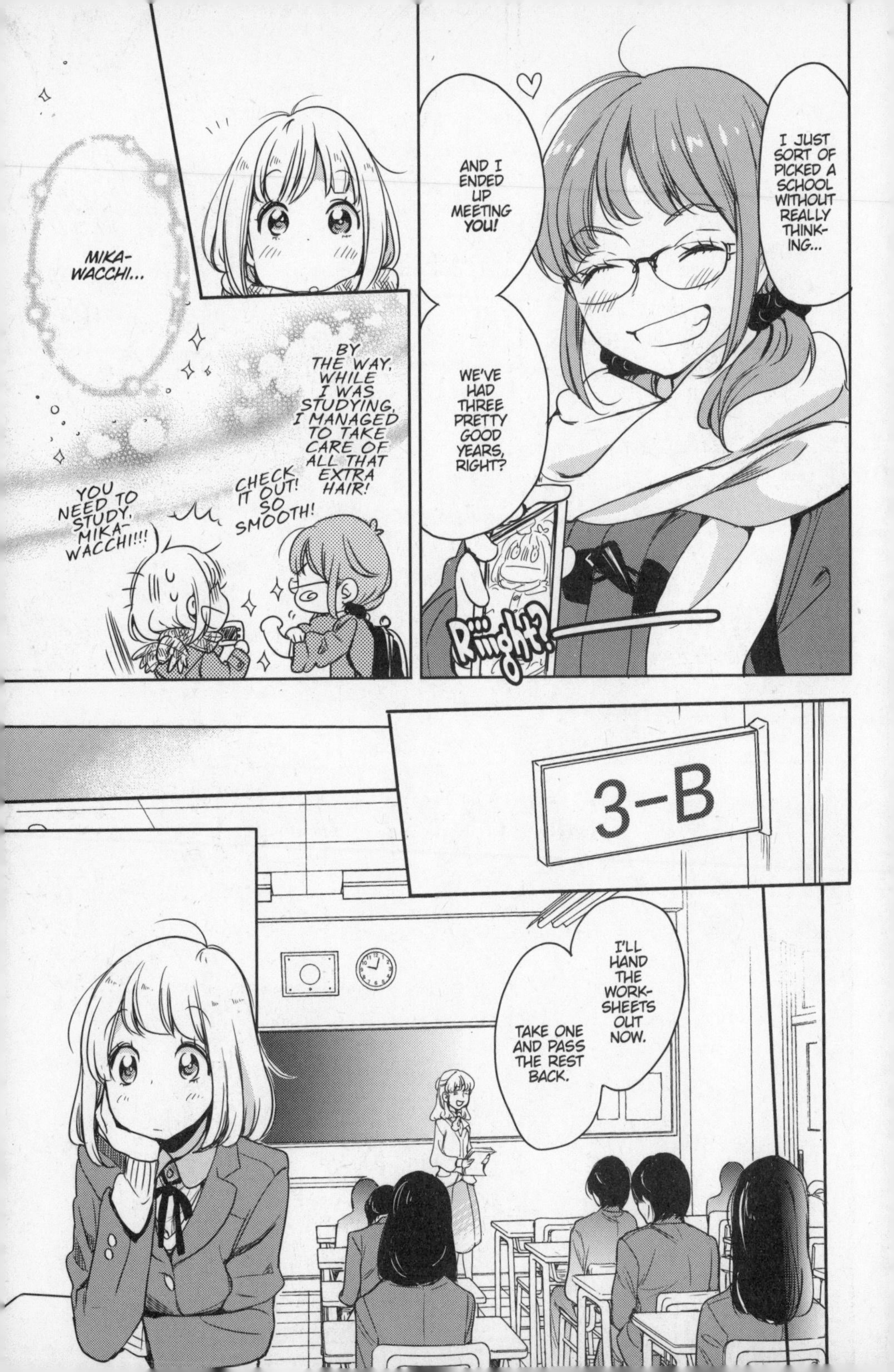
I JUST SORT OF PICKED A SCHOOL WITHOUT REALLY THINKING...
AND I ENDED UP MEETING YOU!
WE'VE HAD THREE PRETTY GOOD YEARS, RIGHT?
R...ight?
MIKA-WACCHI...
BY THE WAY, WHILE I WAS STUDYING, I MANAGED TO TAKE CARE OF ALL THAT EXTRA HAIR!
CHECK IT OUT! SO SMOOTH!
YOU NEED TO STUDY, MIKA-WACCHI!!!
3-B
I'LL HAND THE WORKSHEETS OUT NOW.
TAKE ONE AND PASS THE REST BACK.

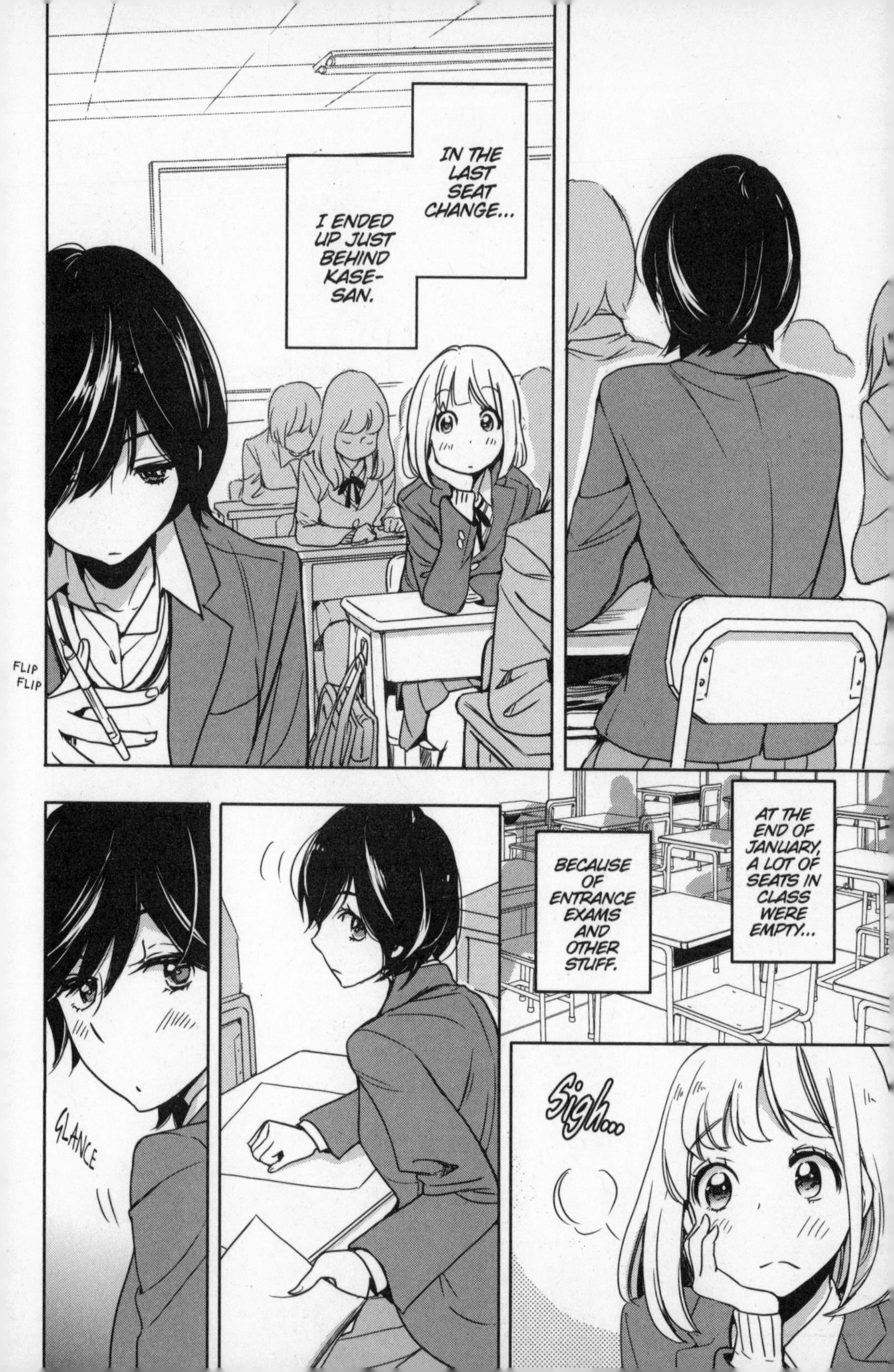
IN THE LAST SEAT CHANGE...
I ENDED UP JUST BEHIND KASE-SAN.
FLIP FLIP
AT THE END OF JANUARY, A LOT OF SEATS IN CLASS WERE EMPTY...
BECAUSE OF ENTRANCE EXAMS AND OTHER STUFF.
Sigh...
GLANCE

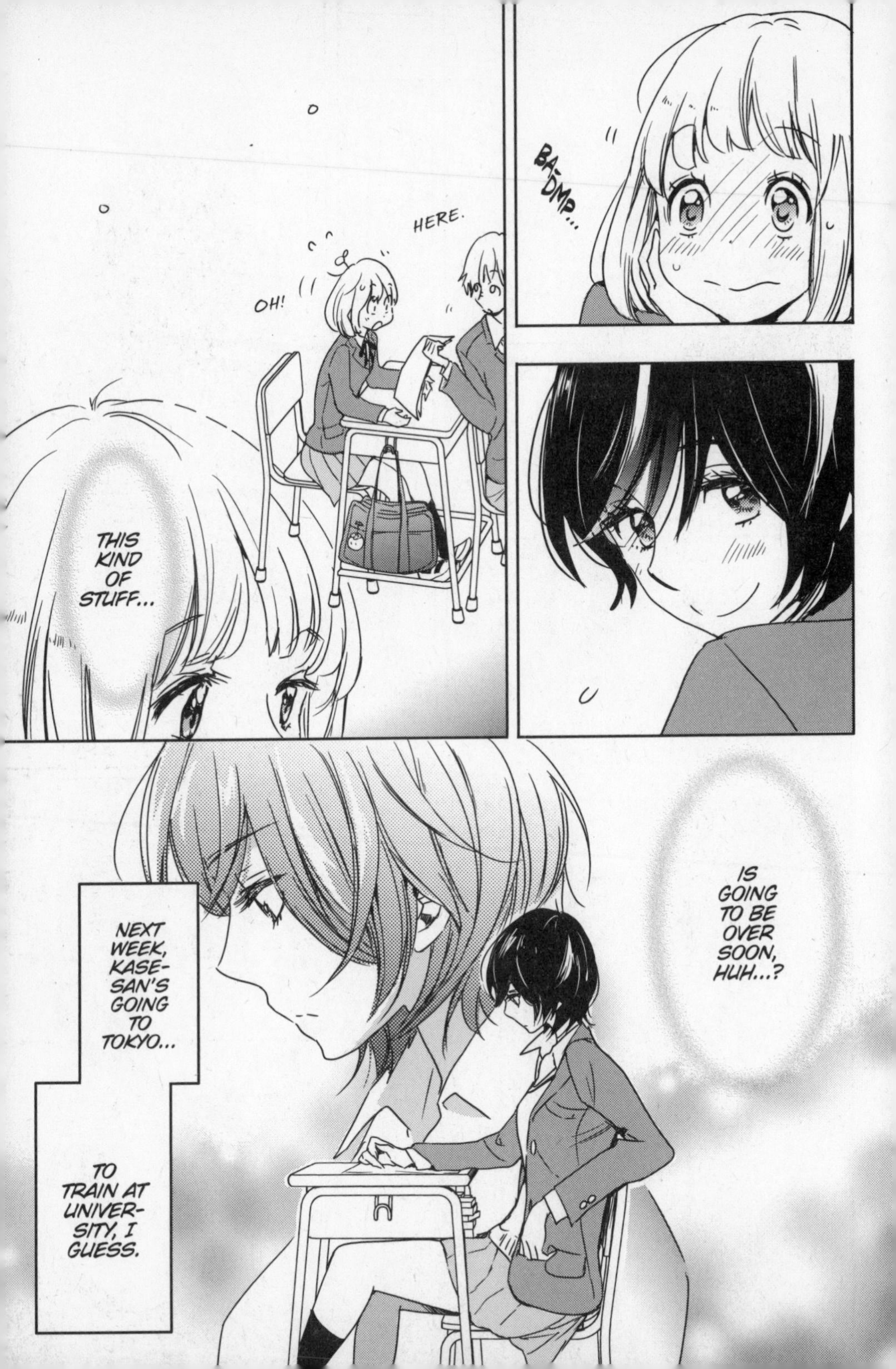
BA-DMP...
HERE.
OH!
THIS KIND OF STUFF...
IS GOING TO BE OVER SOON, HUH...?
NEXT WEEK, KASE-SAN'S GOING TO TOKYO...
TO TRAIN AT UNIVERSITY, I GUESS.

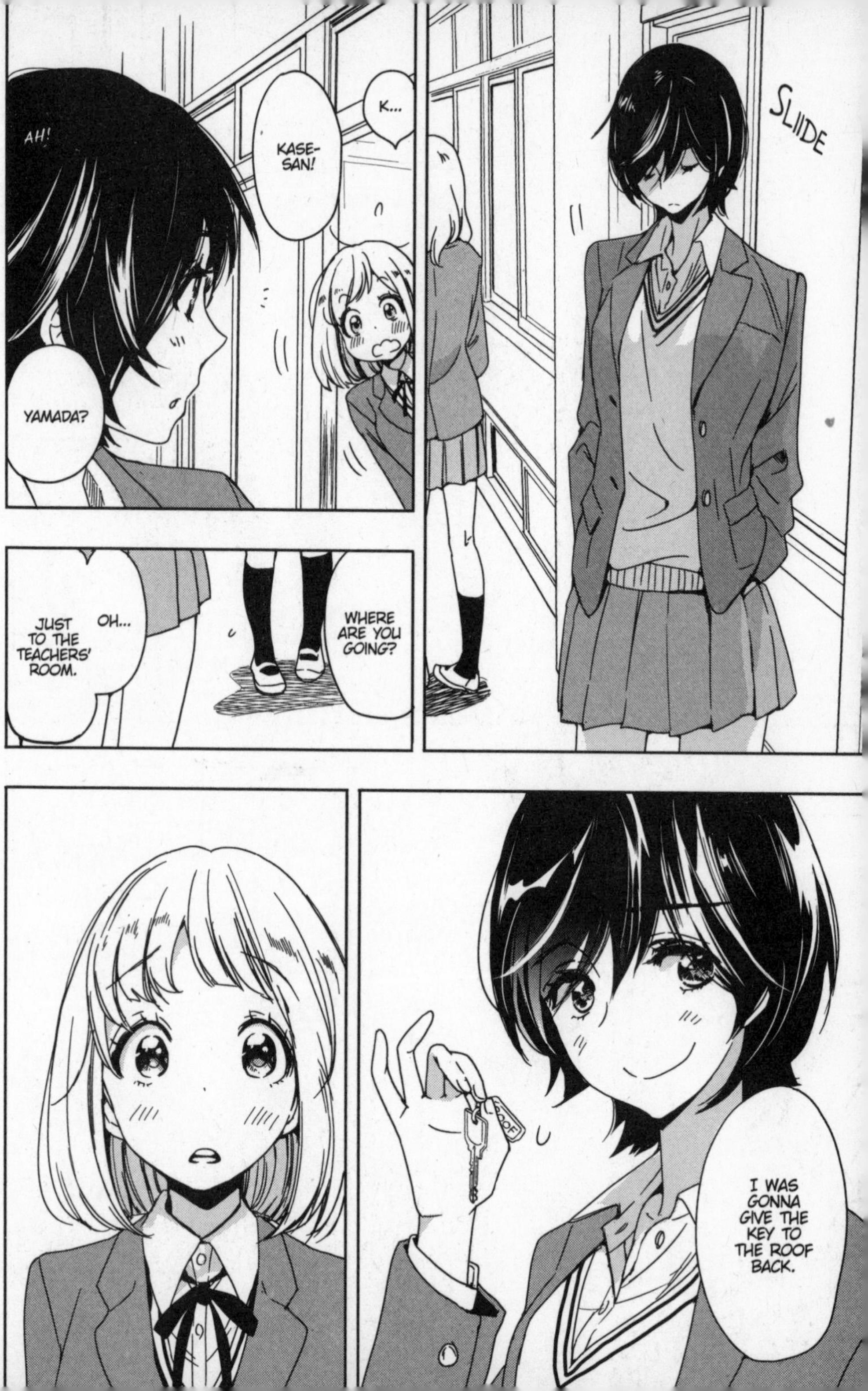
SLIIDE
K...
KASE-SAN!
AH!
YAMADA?
WHERE ARE YOU GOING?
OH...
JUST TO THE TEACHERS' ROOM.
I WAS GONNA GIVE THE KEY TO THE ROOF BACK.

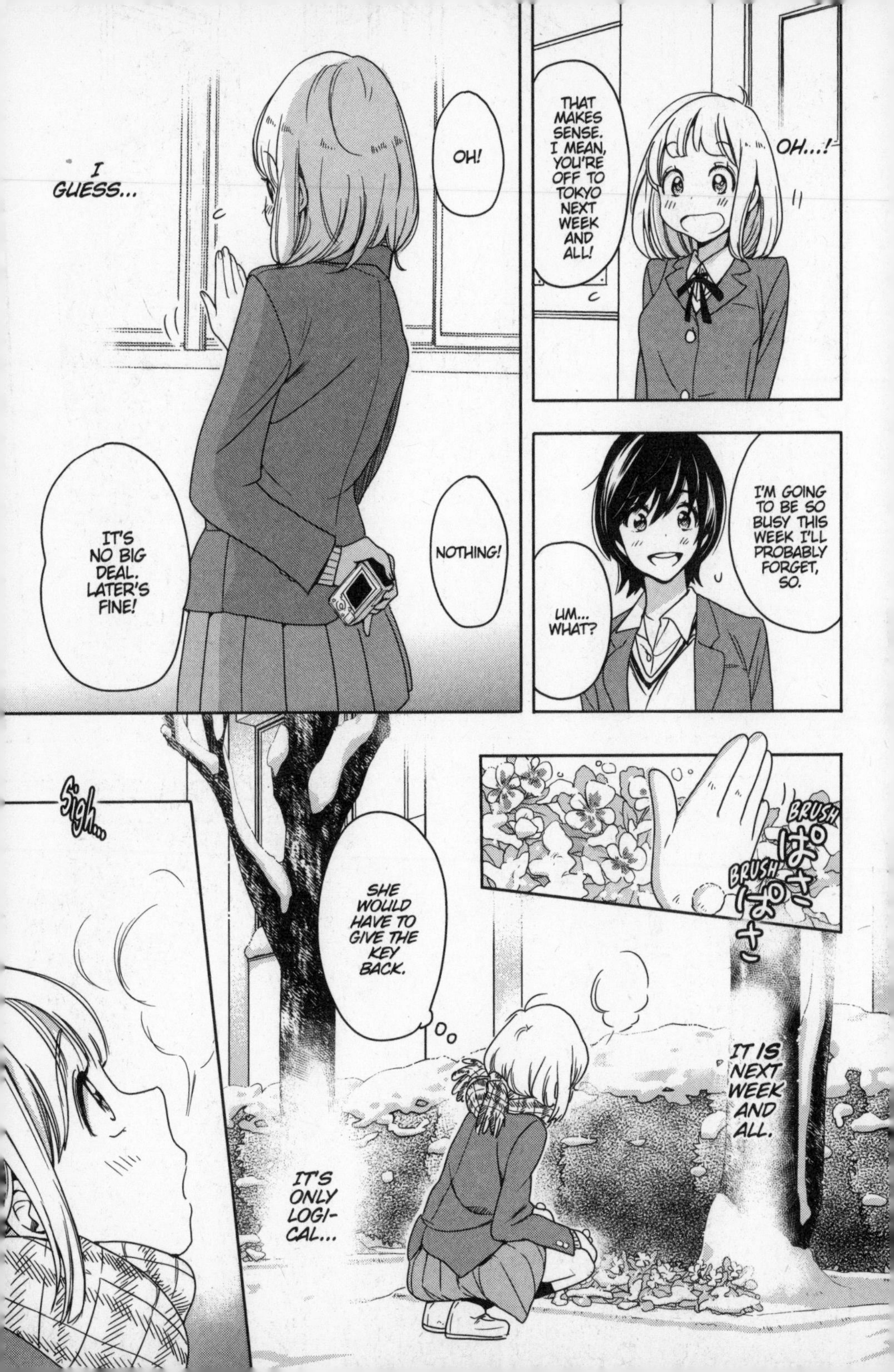
OH...!
THAT MAKES SENSE. I MEAN, YOU'RE OFF TO TOKYO NEXT WEEK AND ALL!
I'M GOING TO BE SO BUSY THIS WEEK I'LL PROBABLY FORGET, SO.
UM... WHAT?
OH!
I GUESS...
NOTHING!
IT'S NO BIG DEAL. LATER'S FINE!
BRUSH
ぱさー
BRUSH
ぱさ
IT IS NEXT WEEK AND ALL.
SHE WOULD HAVE TO GIVE THE KEY BACK.
IT'S ONLY LOGICAL...
Sigh...

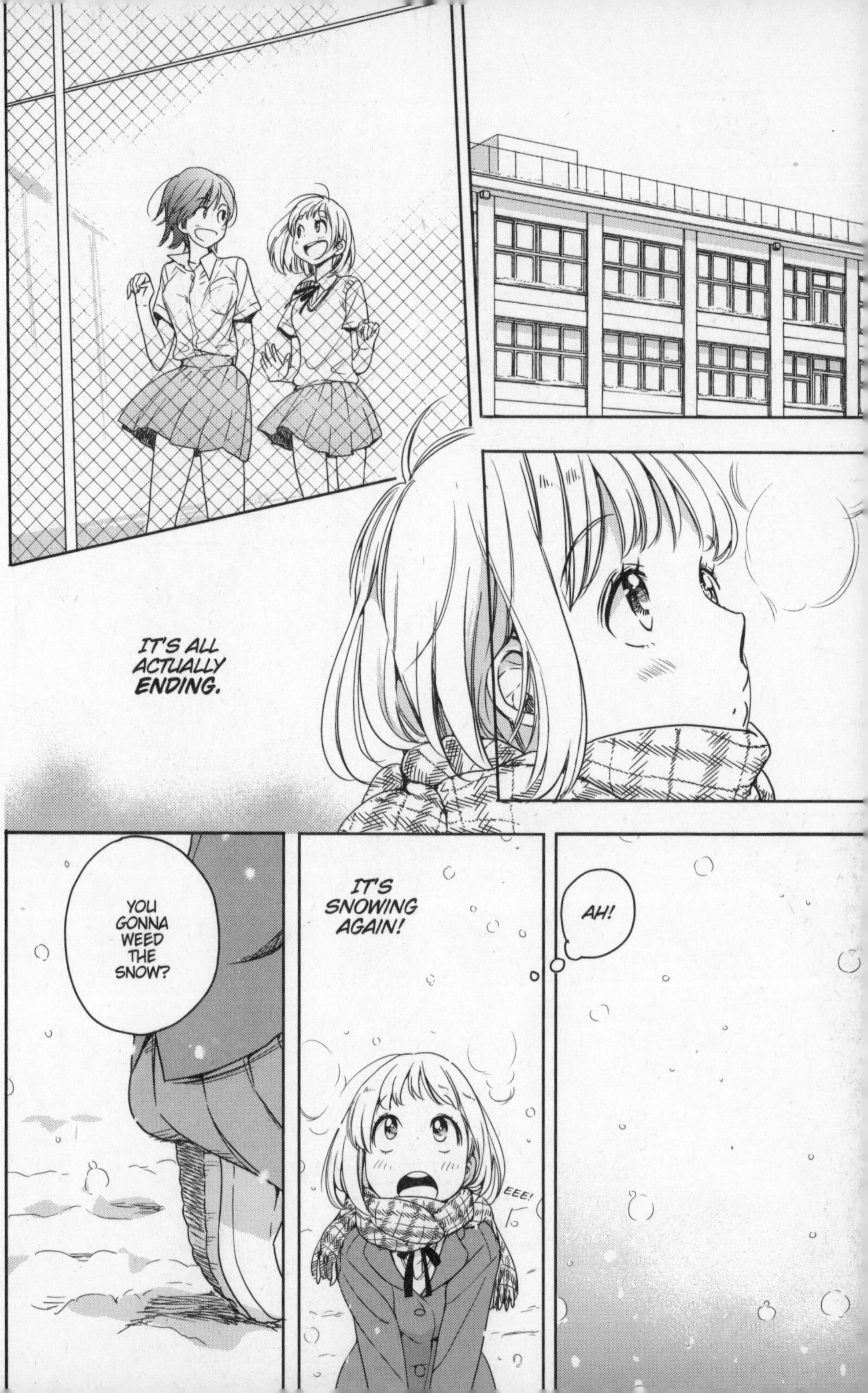
IT'S ALL ACTUALLY ENDING.
AH!
IT'S SNOWING AGAIN!
EEE!
YOU GONNA WEED THE SNOW?

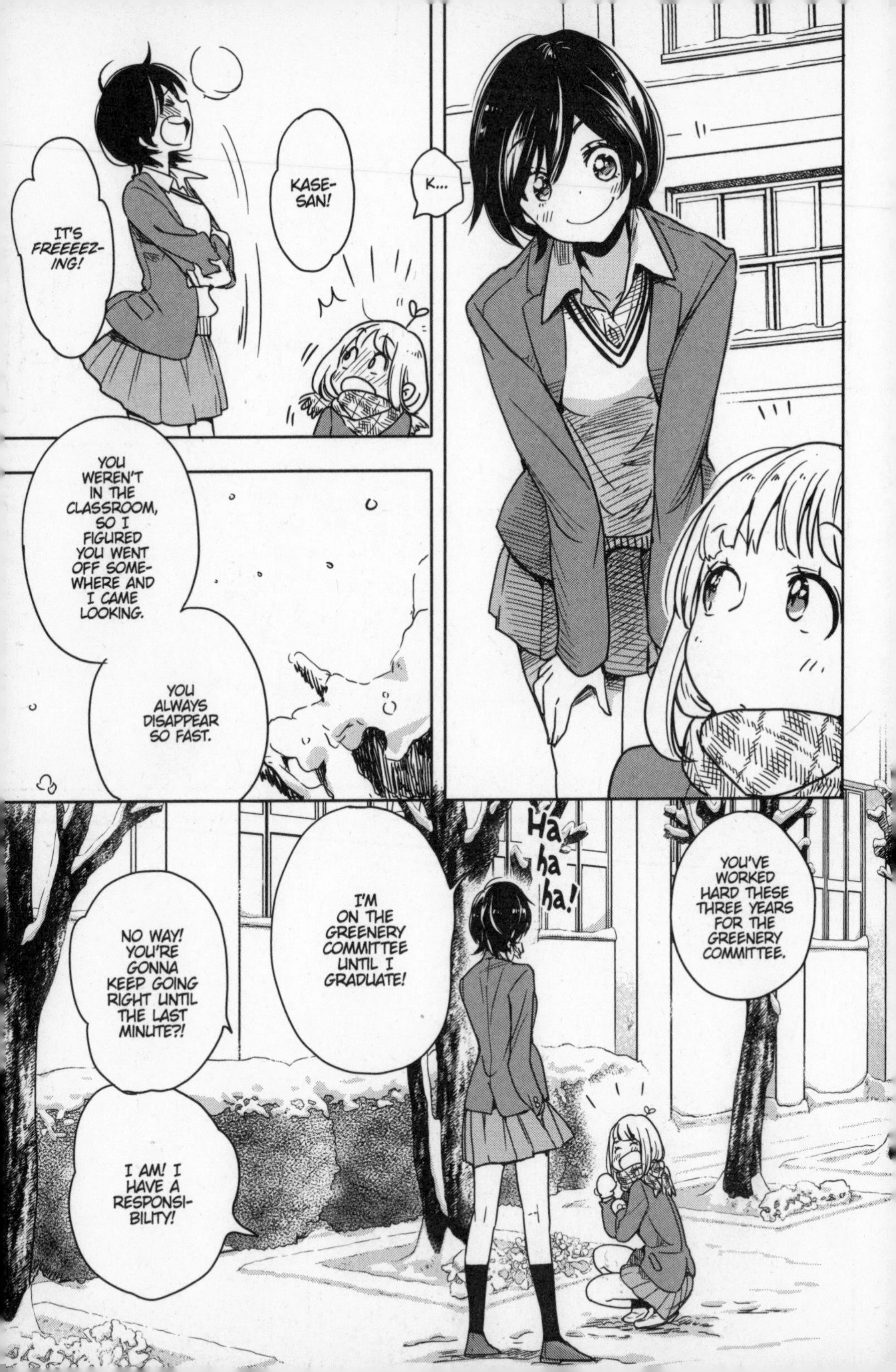
K...
KASE-SAN!
IT'S FREEEEZ-ING!
YOU WEREN'T IN THE CLASSROOM, SO I FIGURED YOU WENT OFF SOME-WHERE AND I CAME LOOKING.
YOU ALWAYS DISAPPEAR SO FAST.
YOU'VE WORKED HARD THESE THREE YEARS FOR THE GREENERY COMMITTEE.
Ha ha ha!
I'M ON THE GREENERY COMMITTEE UNTIL I GRADUATE!
NO WAY! YOU'RE GONNA KEEP GOING RIGHT UNTIL THE LAST MINUTE?!
I AM! I HAVE A RESPONSI-BILITY!

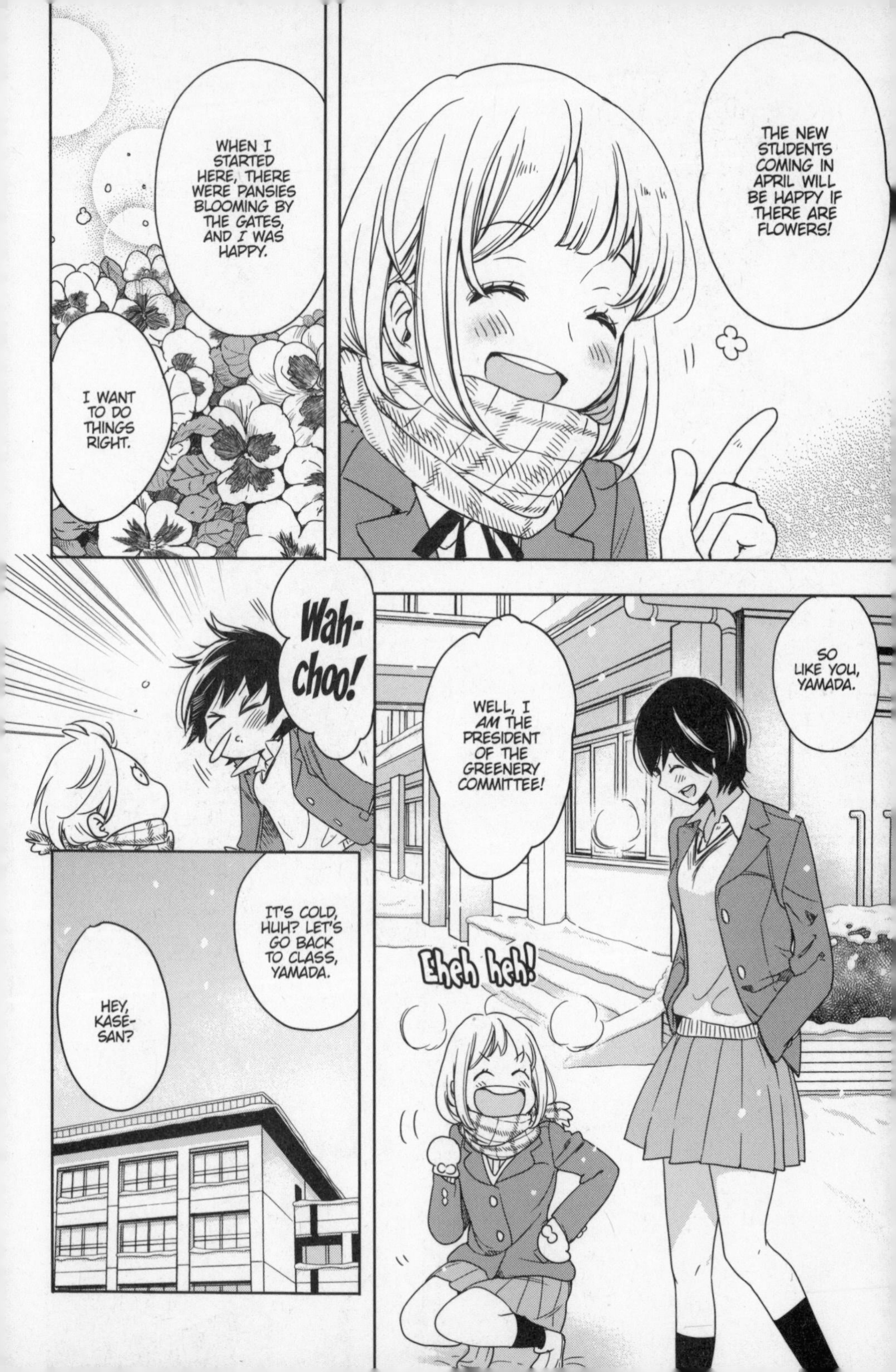
THE NEW STUDENTS COMING IN APRIL WILL BE HAPPY IF THERE ARE FLOWERS!
WHEN I STARTED HERE, THERE WERE PANSIES BLOOMING BY THE GATES, AND *I* WAS HAPPY.
I WANT TO DO THINGS RIGHT.
SO LIKE YOU, YAMADA.
WELL, I *AM* THE PRESIDENT OF THE GREENERY COMMITTEE!
Eheh heh!
Wah-choo!
IT'S COLD, HUH? LET'S GO BACK TO CLASS, YAMADA.
HEY, KASE-SAN?

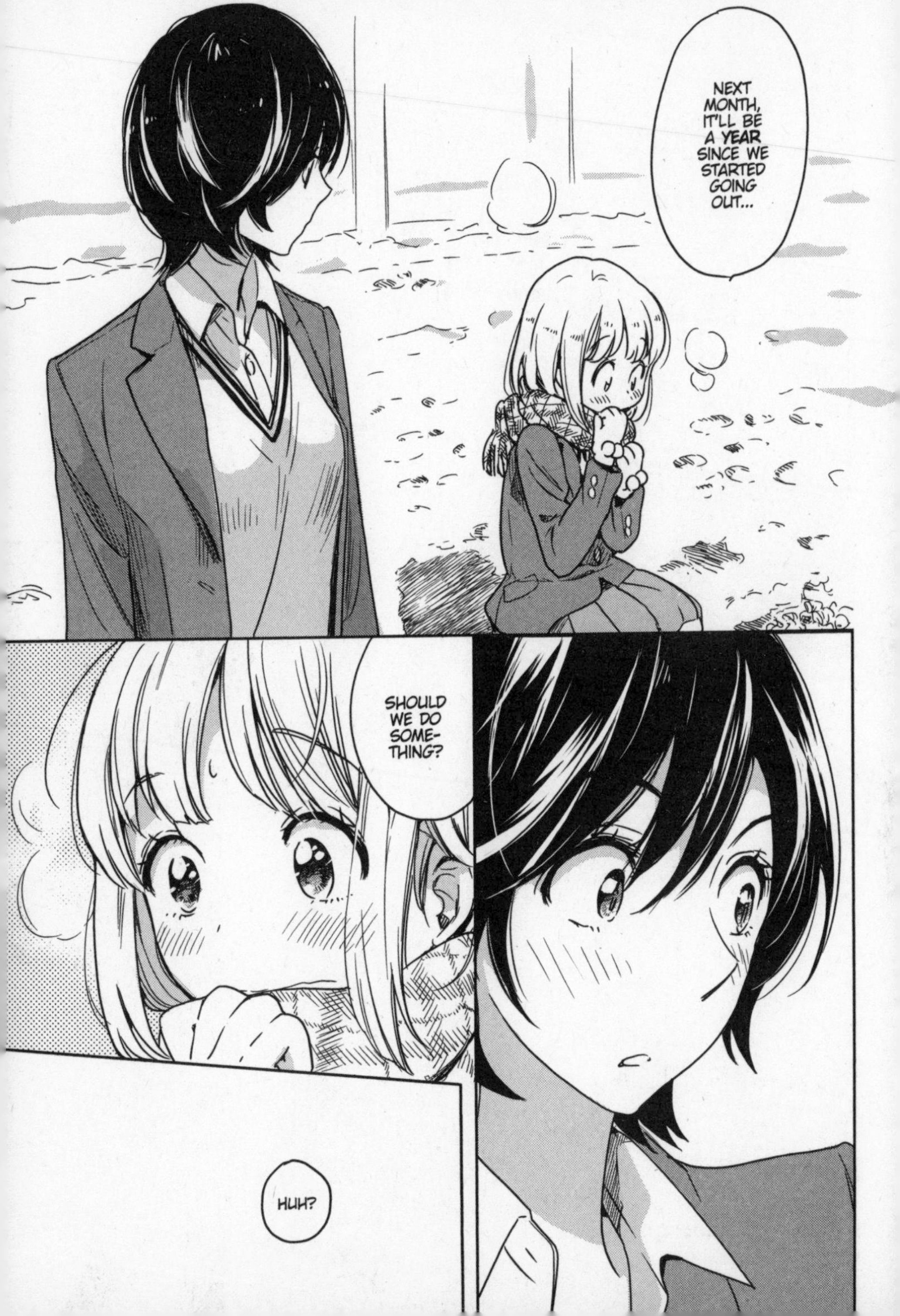
NEXT MONTH, IT'LL BE A YEAR SINCE WE STARTED GOING OUT...
SHOULD WE DO SOME-THING?
HUH?

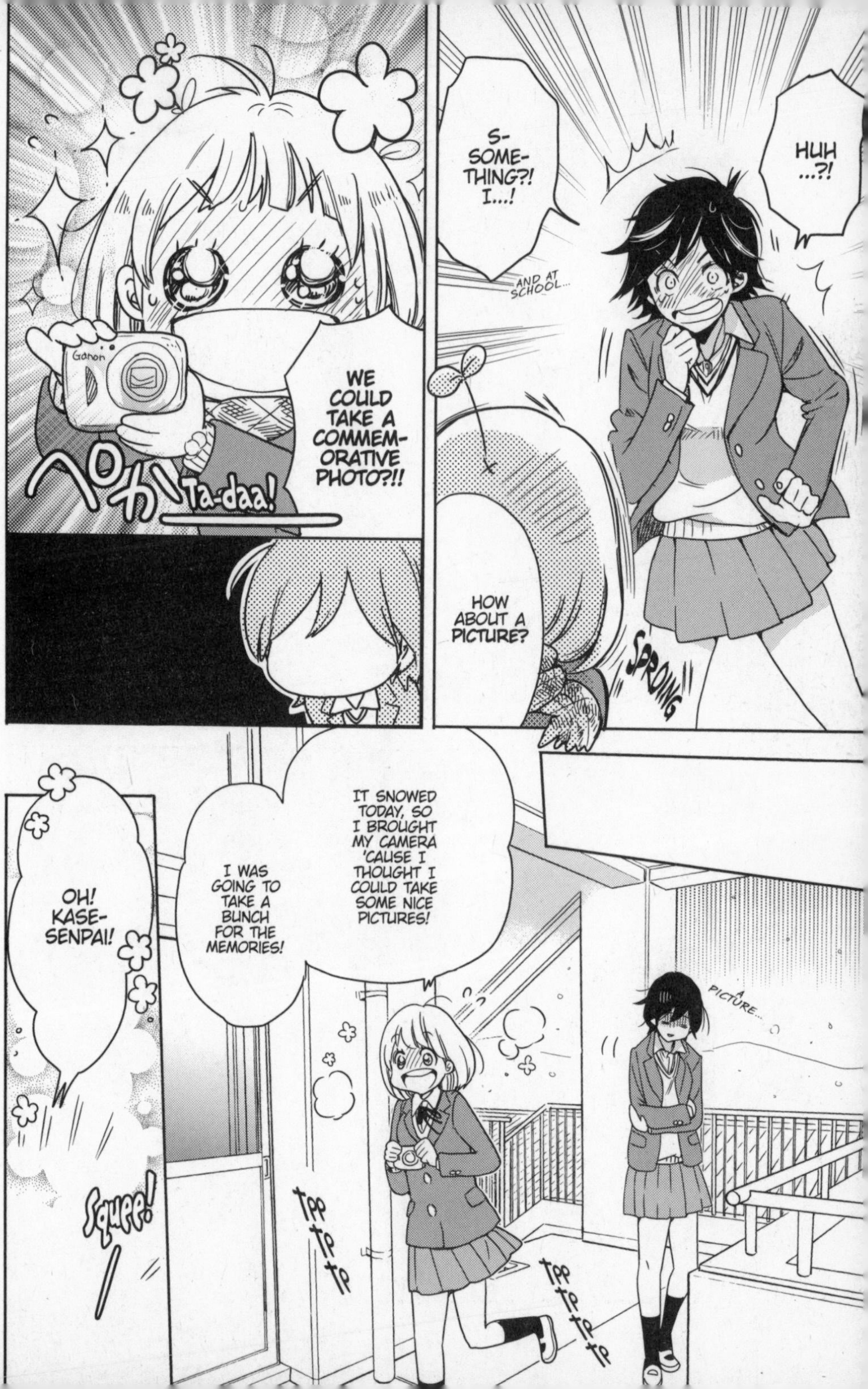
HUH ...?!
S-SOMETHING?! I...!
AND AT SCHOOL...
HOW ABOUT A PICTURE?
SPROING
WE COULD TAKE A COMMEMORATIVE PHOTO?!!
Ganon
Ta-daa!
A PICTURE...
IT SNOWED TODAY, SO I BROUGHT MY CAMERA 'CAUSE I THOUGHT I COULD TAKE SOME NICE PICTURES!
I WAS GOING TO TAKE A BUNCH FOR THE MEMORIES!
OH! KASE-SENPAI!
TPP TP TP TP
TPP TP TP TP
Squee!

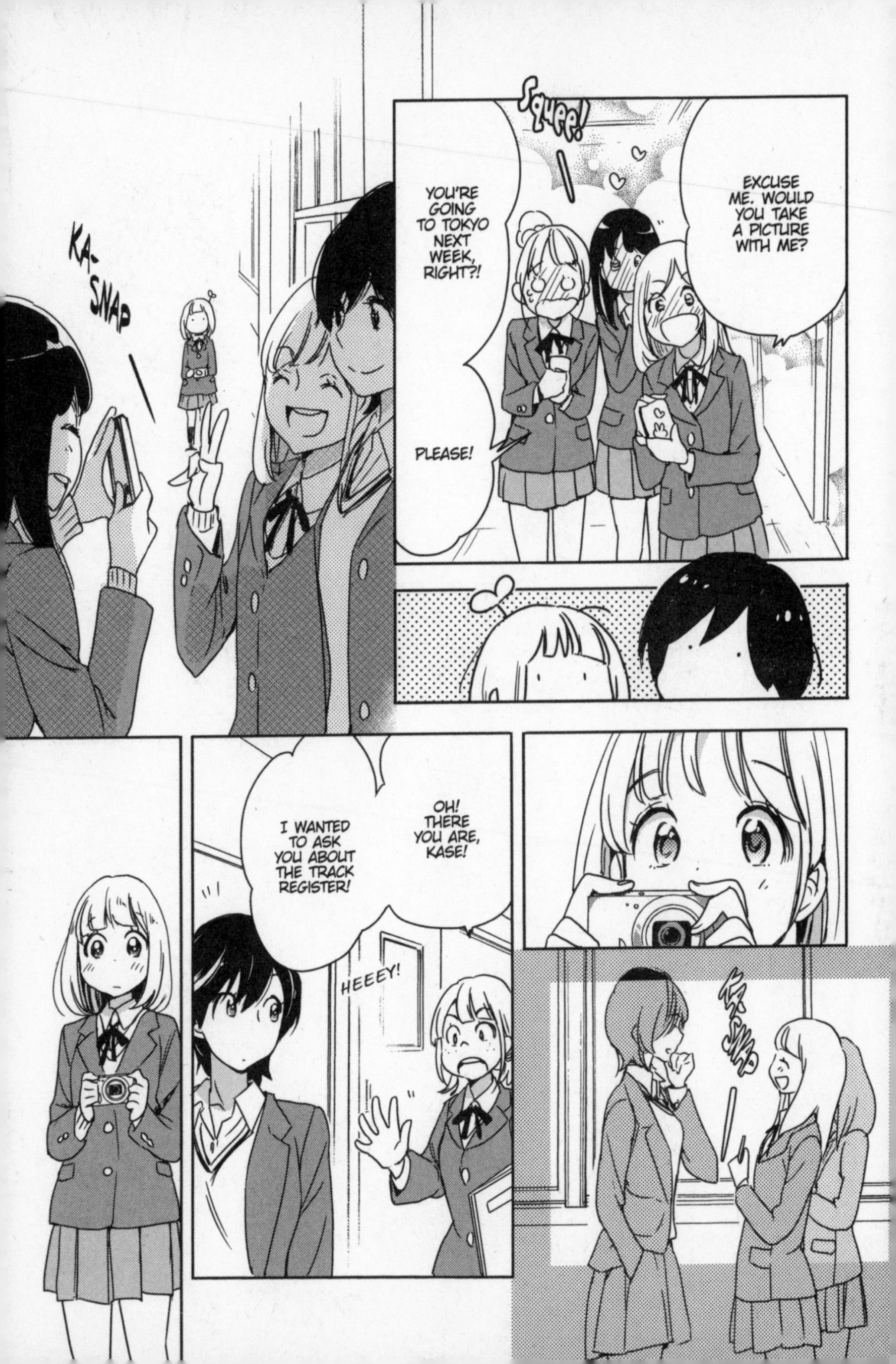
EXCUSE ME. WOULD YOU TAKE A PICTURE WITH ME?
Squee!
YOU'RE GOING TO TOKYO NEXT WEEK, RIGHT?!
PLEASE!
KA-SNAP
KA-SNAP
OH! THERE YOU ARE, KASE!
I WANTED TO ASK YOU ABOUT THE TRACK REGISTER!
HEEEY!

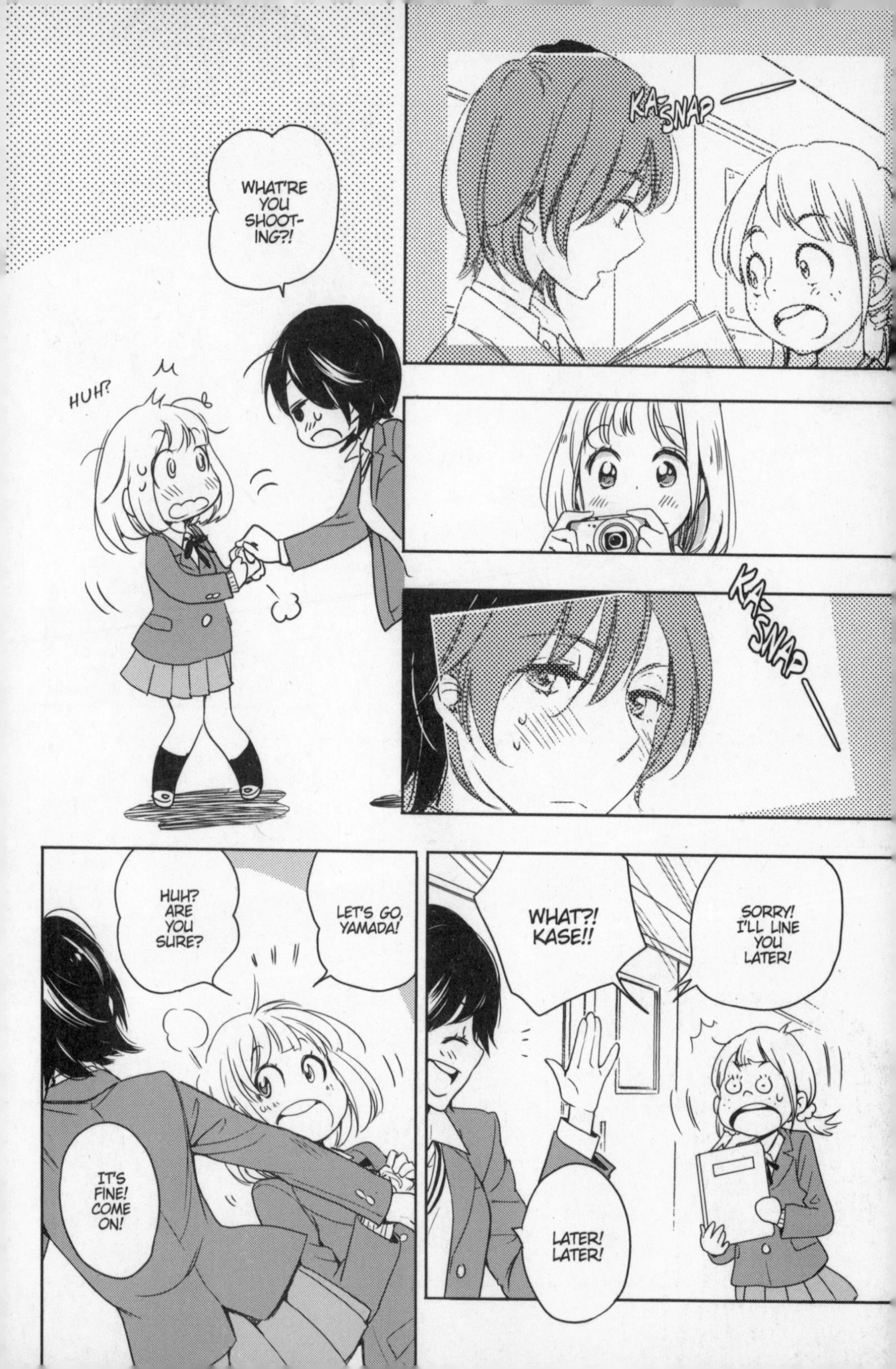
KA-SNAP
KA-SNAP
WHAT'RE YOU SHOOTING?!
HUH?
SORRY! I'LL LINE YOU LATER!
WHAT?! KASE!!
LATER! LATER!
LET'S GO, YAMADA!
HUH? ARE YOU SURE?
IT'S FINE! COME ON!

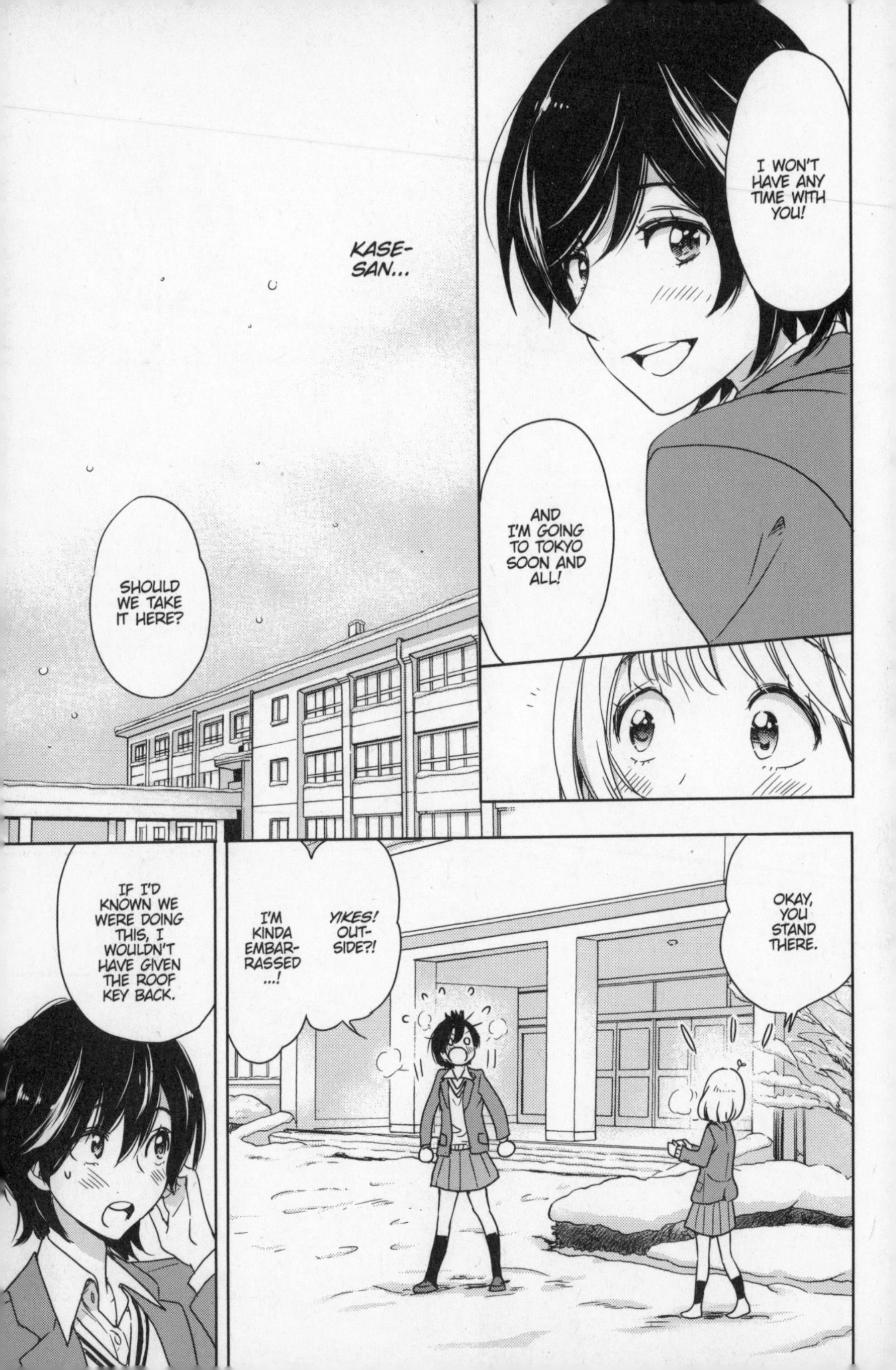

I WON'T HAVE ANY TIME WITH YOU!
AND I'M GOING TO TOKYO SOON AND ALL!
KASE-SAN...
SHOULD WE TAKE IT HERE?
OKAY, YOU STAND THERE.
YIKES! OUT-SIDE?!
I'M KINDA EMBAR-RASSED ...!
IF I'D KNOWN WE WERE DOING THIS, I WOULDN'T HAVE GIVEN THE ROOF KEY BACK.

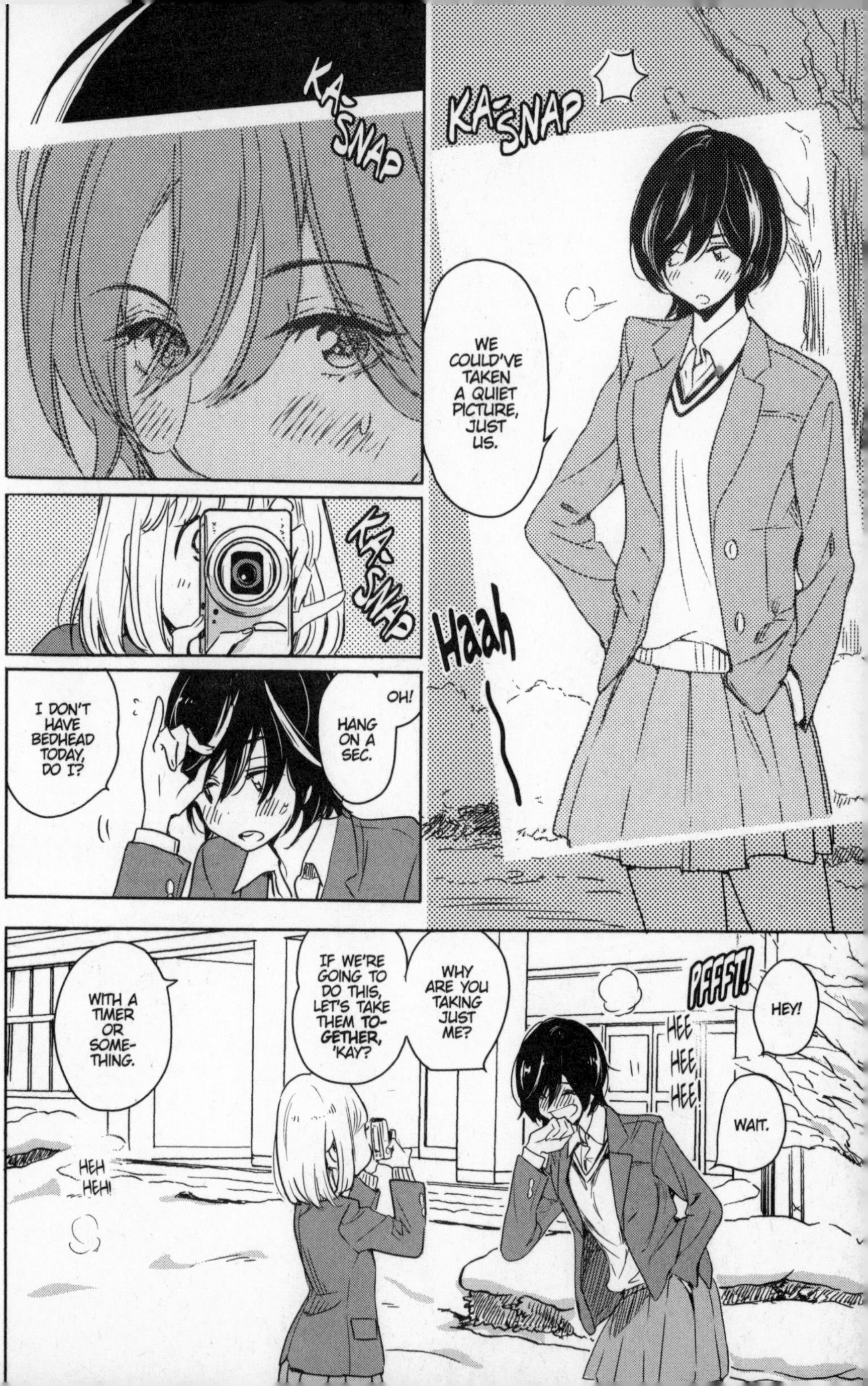
KA-SNAP
WE COULD'VE TAKEN A QUIET PICTURE, JUST US.
Haah
KA-SNAP
KA-SNAP
OH!
HANG ON A SEC.
I DON'T HAVE BEDHEAD TODAY, DO I?
HEY!
WAIT.
PFFFT!
HEE HEE, HEE!
WHY ARE YOU TAKING JUST ME?
IF WE'RE GOING TO DO THIS, LET'S TAKE THEM TO-GETHER, 'KAY?
WITH A TIMER OR SOMETHING.
HEH HEH!

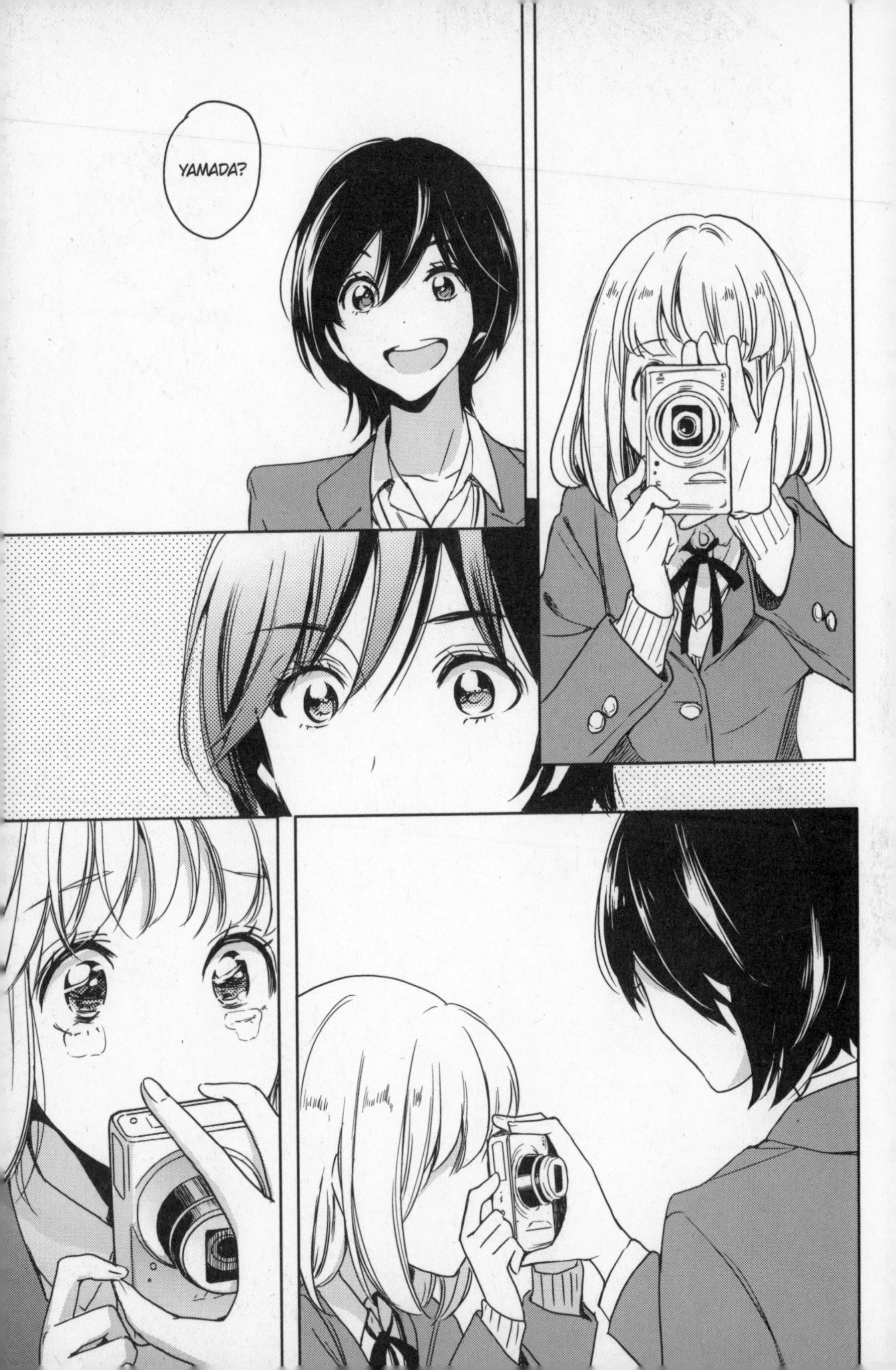
YAMADA?

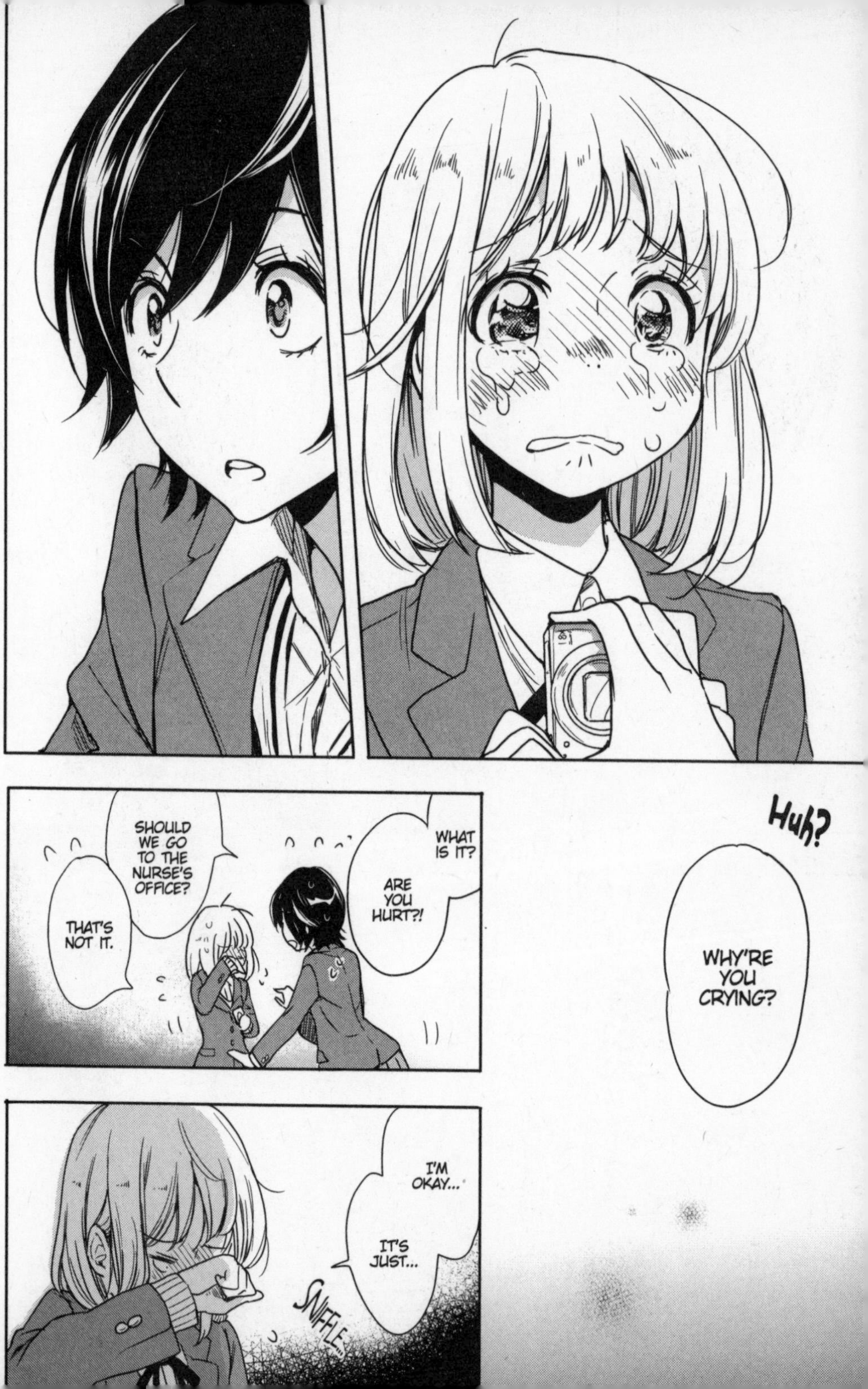
Huh?
WHY'RE YOU CRYING?
WHAT IS IT?
ARE YOU HURT?!
SHOULD WE GO TO THE NURSE'S OFFICE?
THAT'S NOT IT.
I'M OKAY...
IT'S JUST...
SNIFFLE...

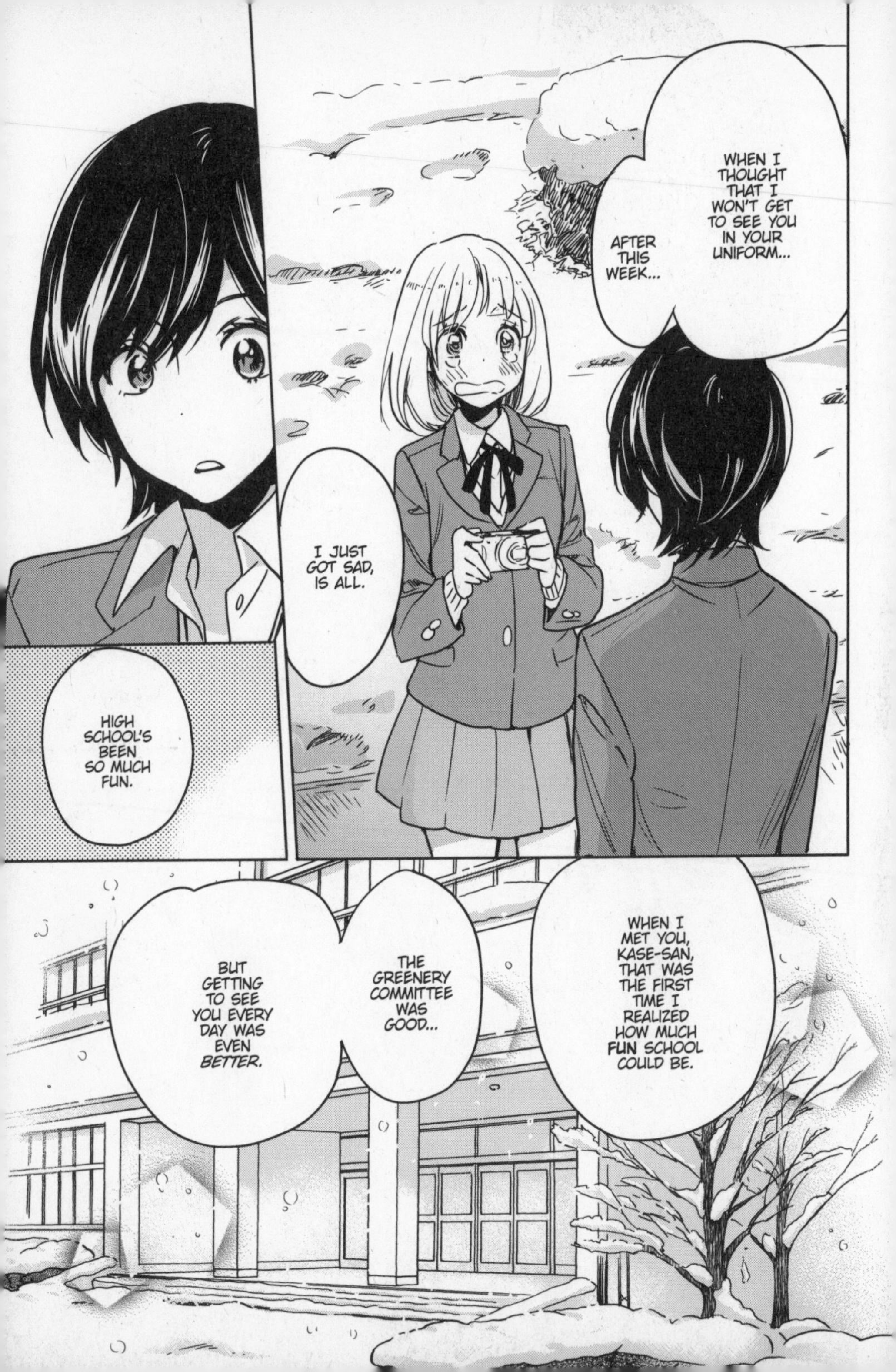
WHEN I THOUGHT THAT I WON'T GET TO SEE YOU IN YOUR UNIFORM...
AFTER THIS WEEK...
I JUST GOT SAD, IS ALL.
HIGH SCHOOL'S BEEN SO MUCH FUN.
WHEN I MET YOU, KASE-SAN, THAT WAS THE FIRST TIME I REALIZED HOW MUCH **FUN** SCHOOL COULD BE.
THE GREENERY COMMITTEE WAS GOOD...
BUT GETTING TO SEE YOU EVERY DAY WAS EVEN *BETTER*.

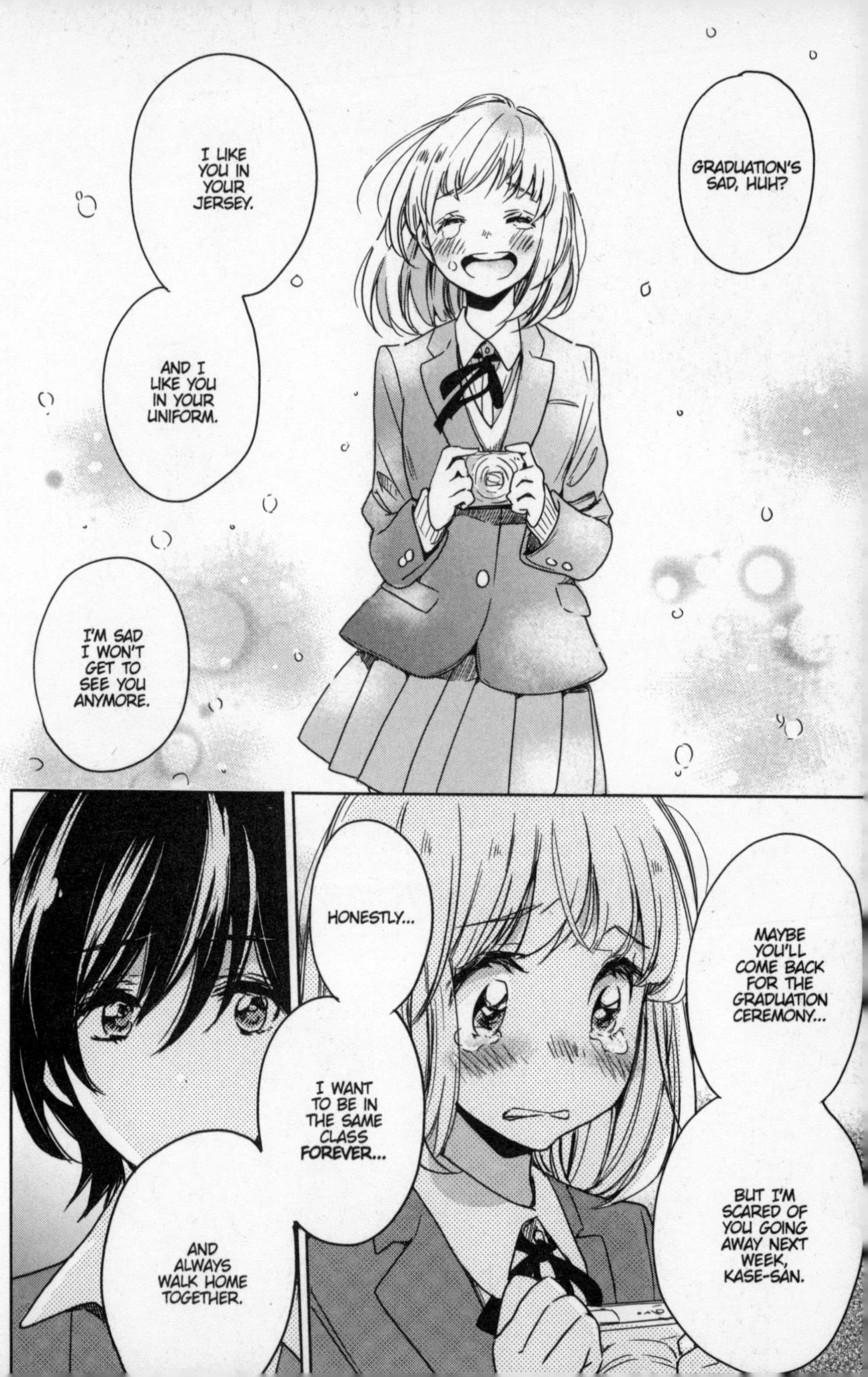
GRADUATION'S SAD, HUH?
I LIKE YOU IN YOUR JERSEY.
AND I LIKE YOU IN YOUR UNIFORM.
I'M SAD I WON'T GET TO SEE YOU ANYMORE.
MAYBE YOU'LL COME BACK FOR THE GRADUATION CEREMONY...
BUT I'M SCARED OF YOU GOING AWAY NEXT WEEK, KASE-SAN.
HONESTLY...
I WANT TO BE IN THE SAME CLASS FOREVER...
AND ALWAYS WALK HOME TOGETHER.

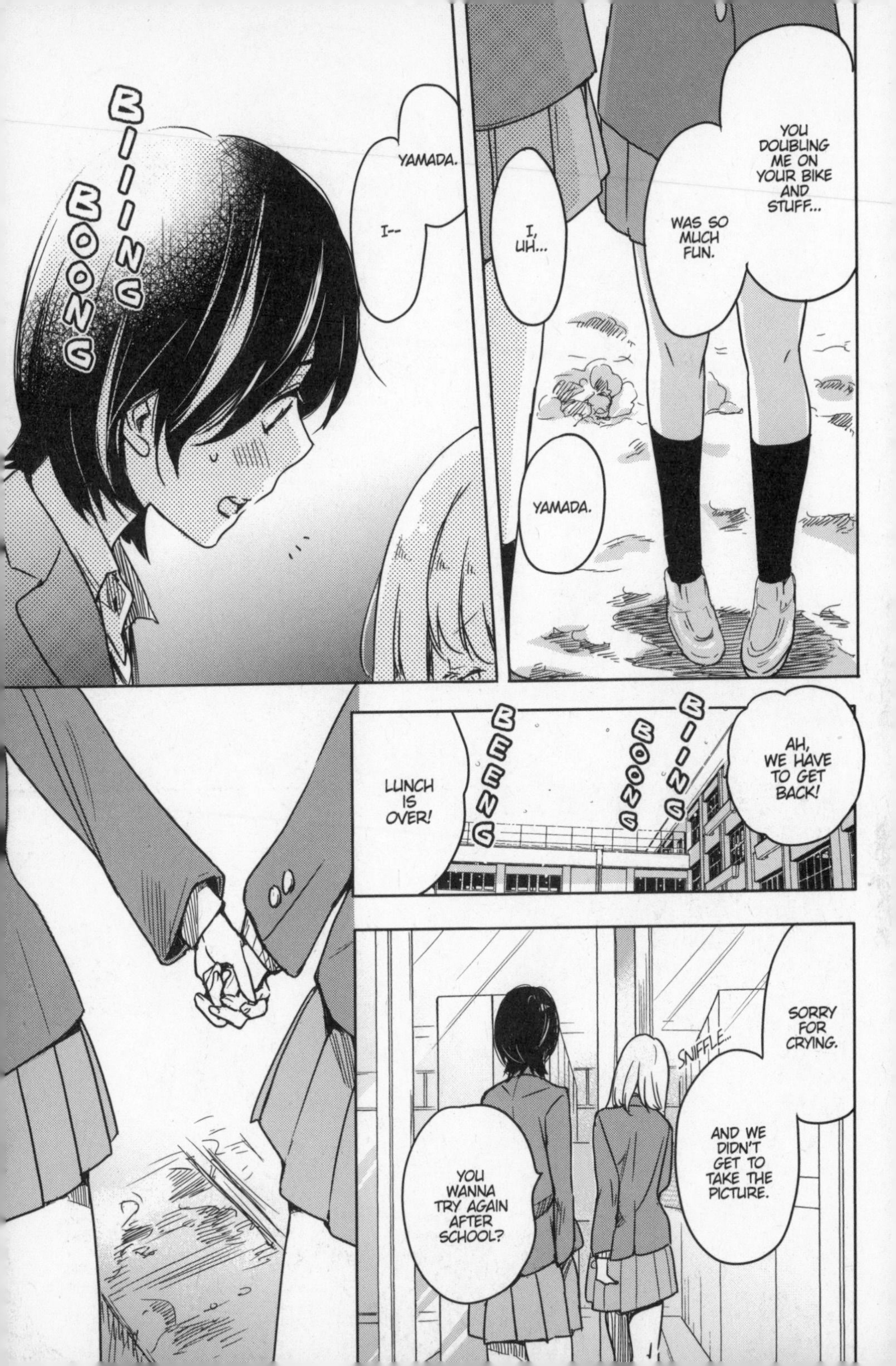
YOU DOUBLING ME ON YOUR BIKE AND STUFF...
WAS SO MUCH FUN.
YAMADA.
I, UH...
YAMADA.
I--
BIIING
BOONG
AH, WE HAVE TO GET BACK!
BIING
BOONG
BEENG
LUNCH IS OVER!
SORRY FOR CRYING.
SNIFFLE...
AND WE DIDN'T GET TO TAKE THE PICTURE.
YOU WANNA TRY AGAIN AFTER SCHOOL?

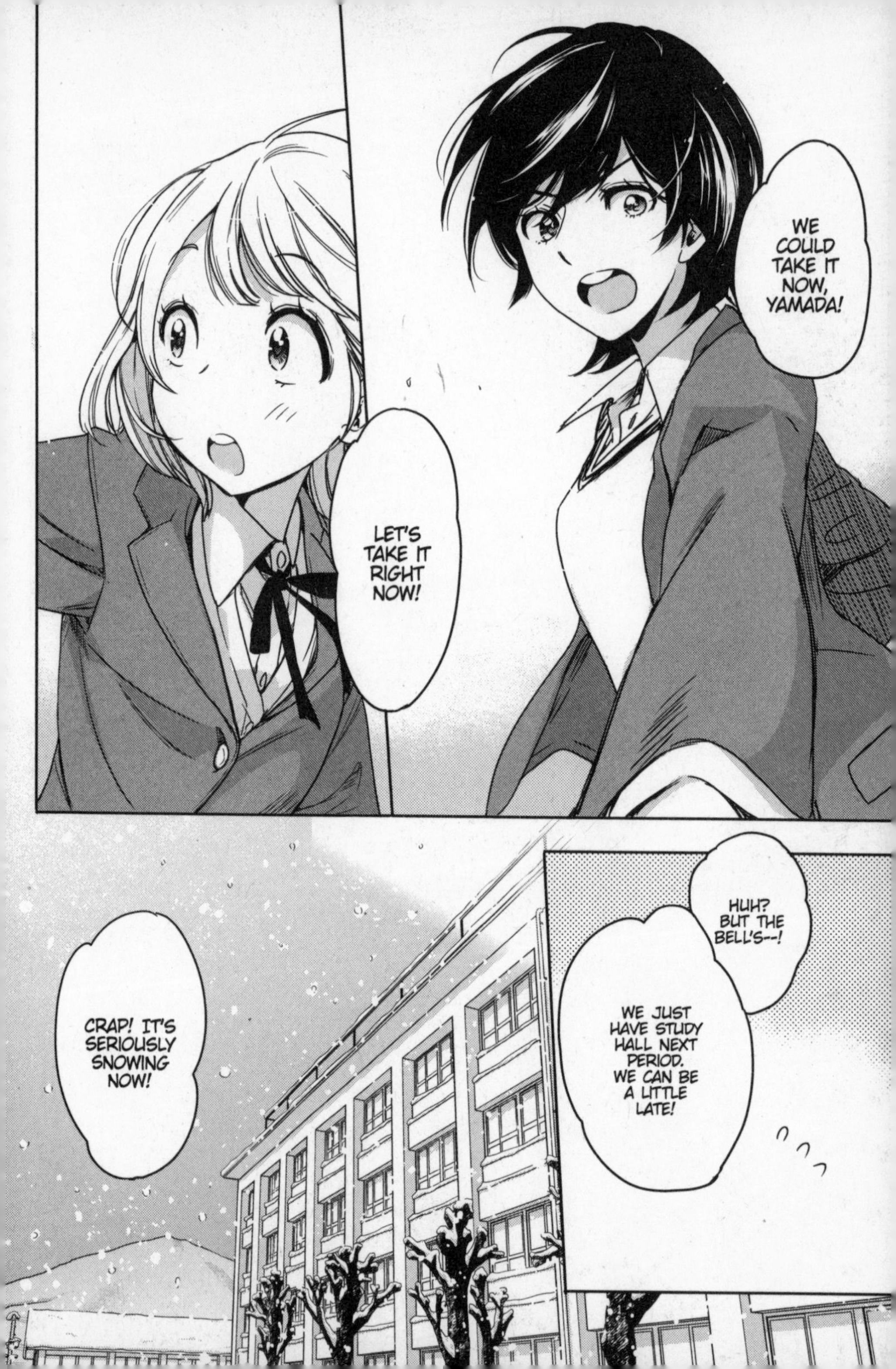
WE COULD TAKE IT NOW, YAMADA!
LET'S TAKE IT RIGHT NOW!
HUH? BUT THE BELL'S--!
WE JUST HAVE STUDY HALL NEXT PERIOD. WE CAN BE A LITTLE LATE!
CRAP! IT'S SERIOUSLY SNOWING NOW!

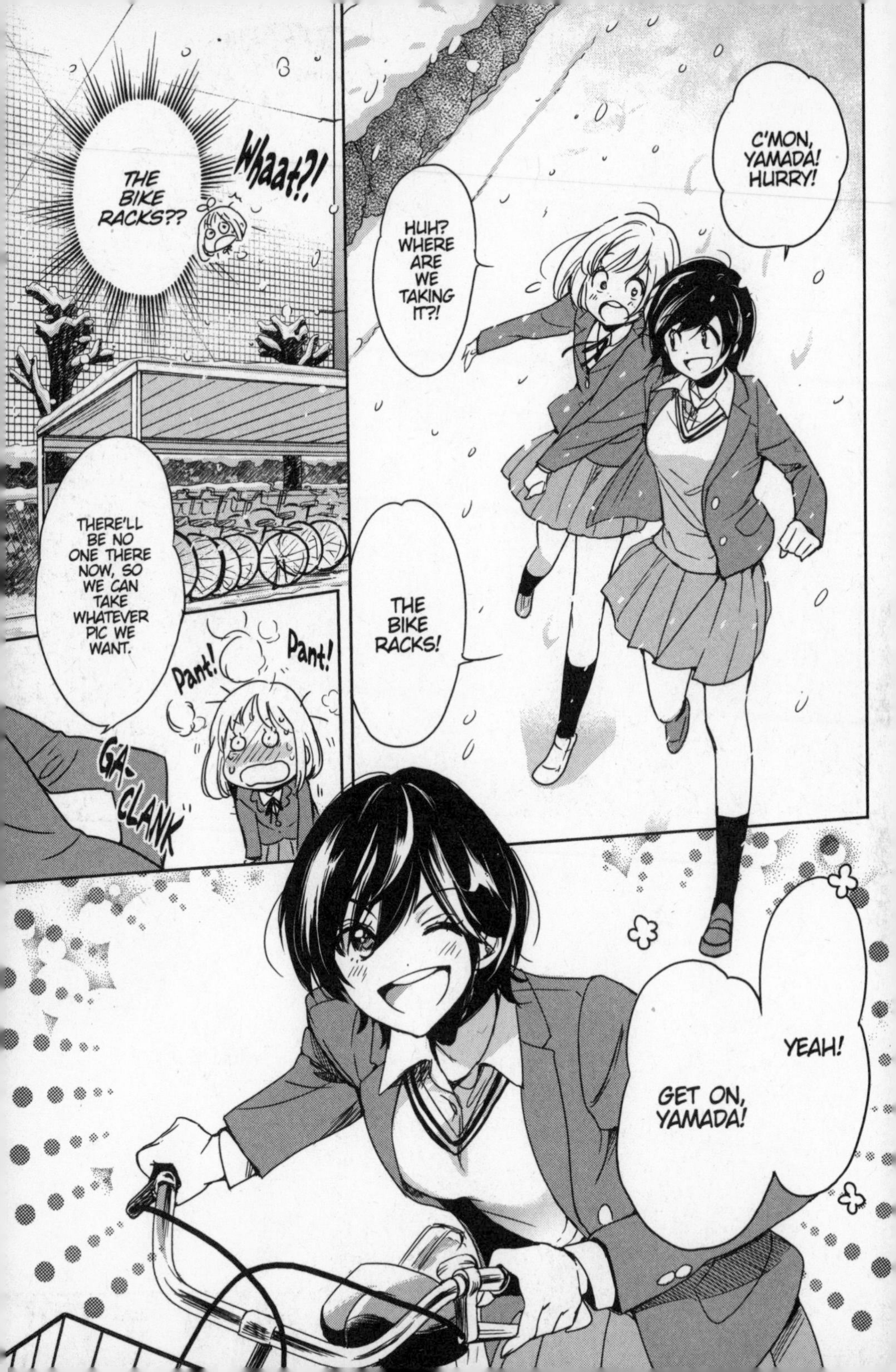
C'MON, YAMADA! HURRY!
HUH? WHERE ARE WE TAKING IT?!
THE BIKE RACKS!
THE BIKE RACKS??
Whaaat?!
THERE'LL BE NO ONE THERE NOW, SO WE CAN TAKE WHATEVER PIC WE WANT.
Pant!
Pant!
GA-CLANK
YEAH!
GET ON, YAMADA!

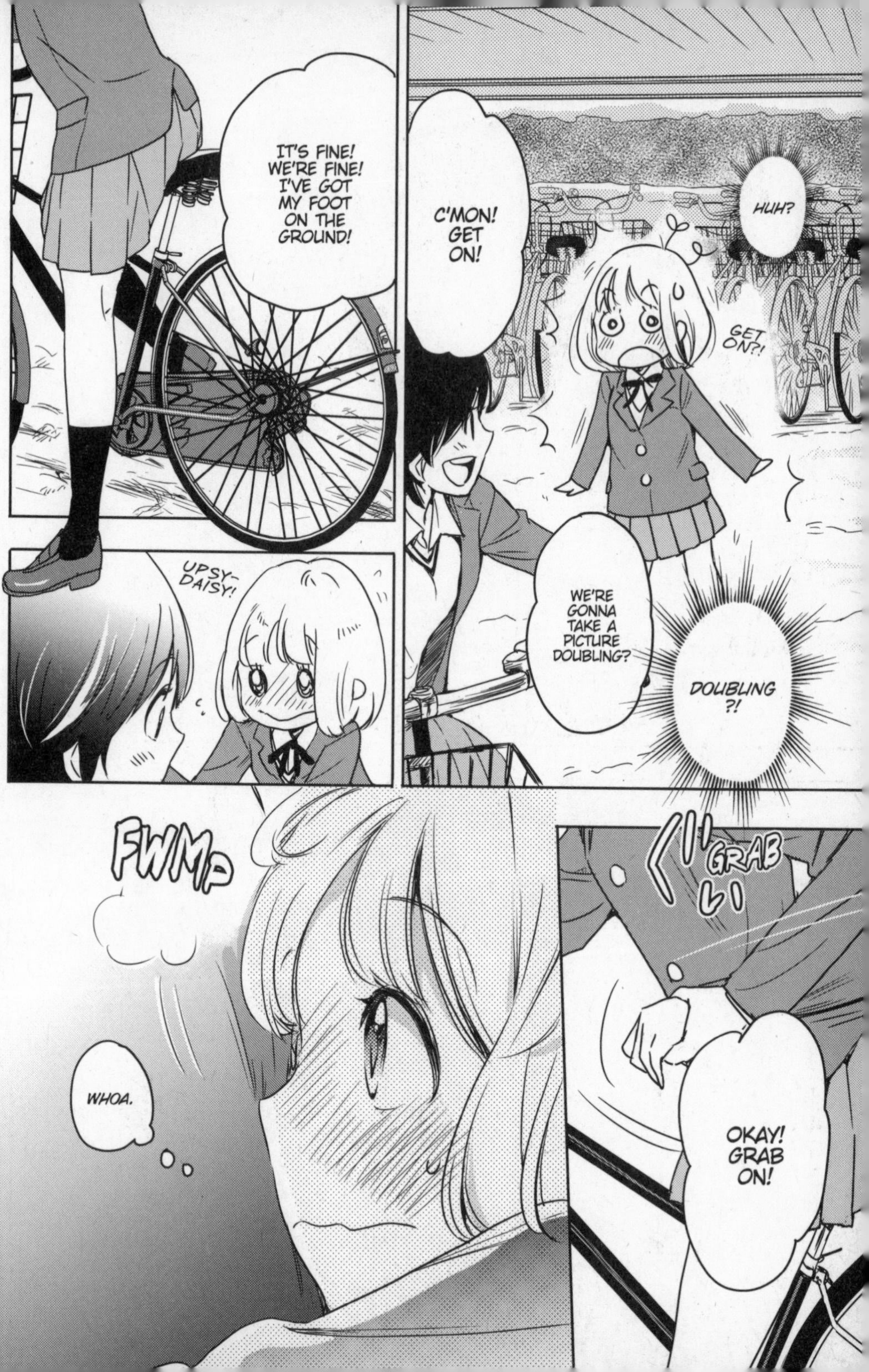
HUH?
C'MON! GET ON!
GET ON?!
WE'RE GONNA TAKE A PICTURE DOUBLING?
DOUBLING?!
IT'S FINE! WE'RE FINE! I'VE GOT MY FOOT ON THE GROUND!
UPSY-DAISY!
GRAB
OKAY! GRAB ON!
FWMP
WHOA.

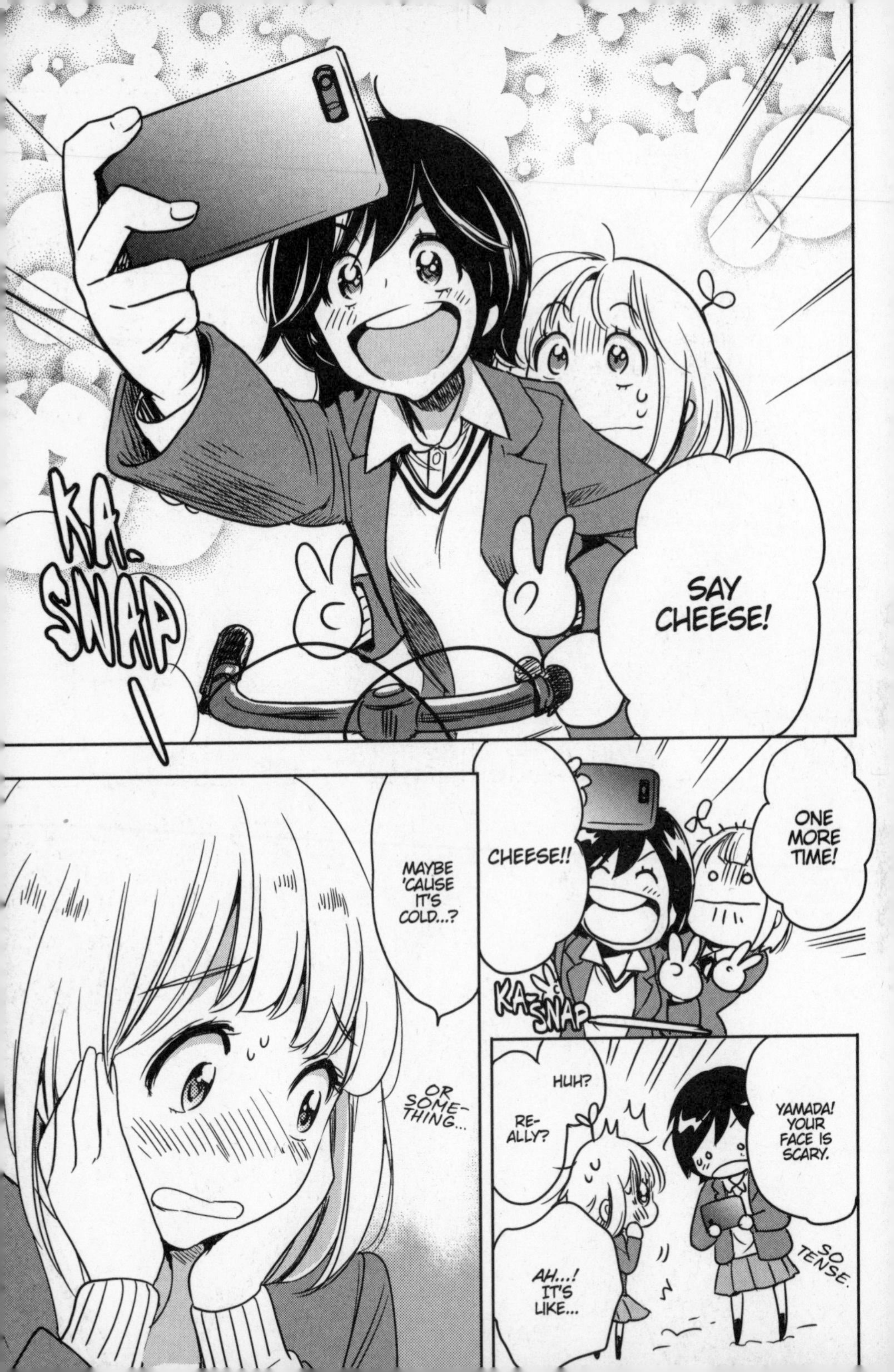
SAY CHEESE!
KA-SNAP
ONE MORE TIME!
CHEESE!!
KA-SNAP
YAMADA! YOUR FACE IS SCARY.
SO TENSE.
HUH?
RE-ALLY?
AH...! IT'S LIKE...
MAYBE 'CAUSE IT'S COLD...?
OR SOME-THING...

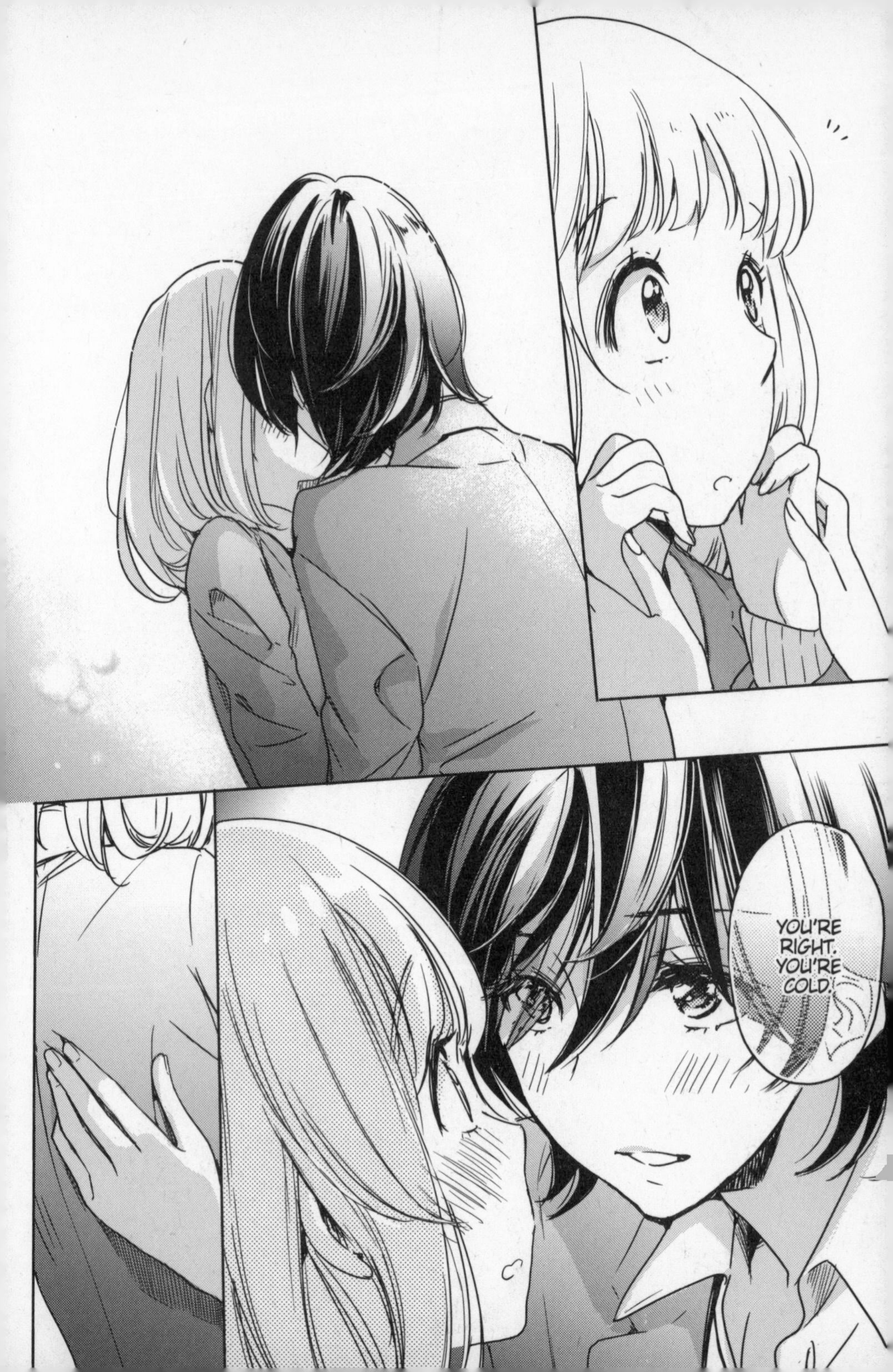
YOU'RE RIGHT. YOU'RE COLD.

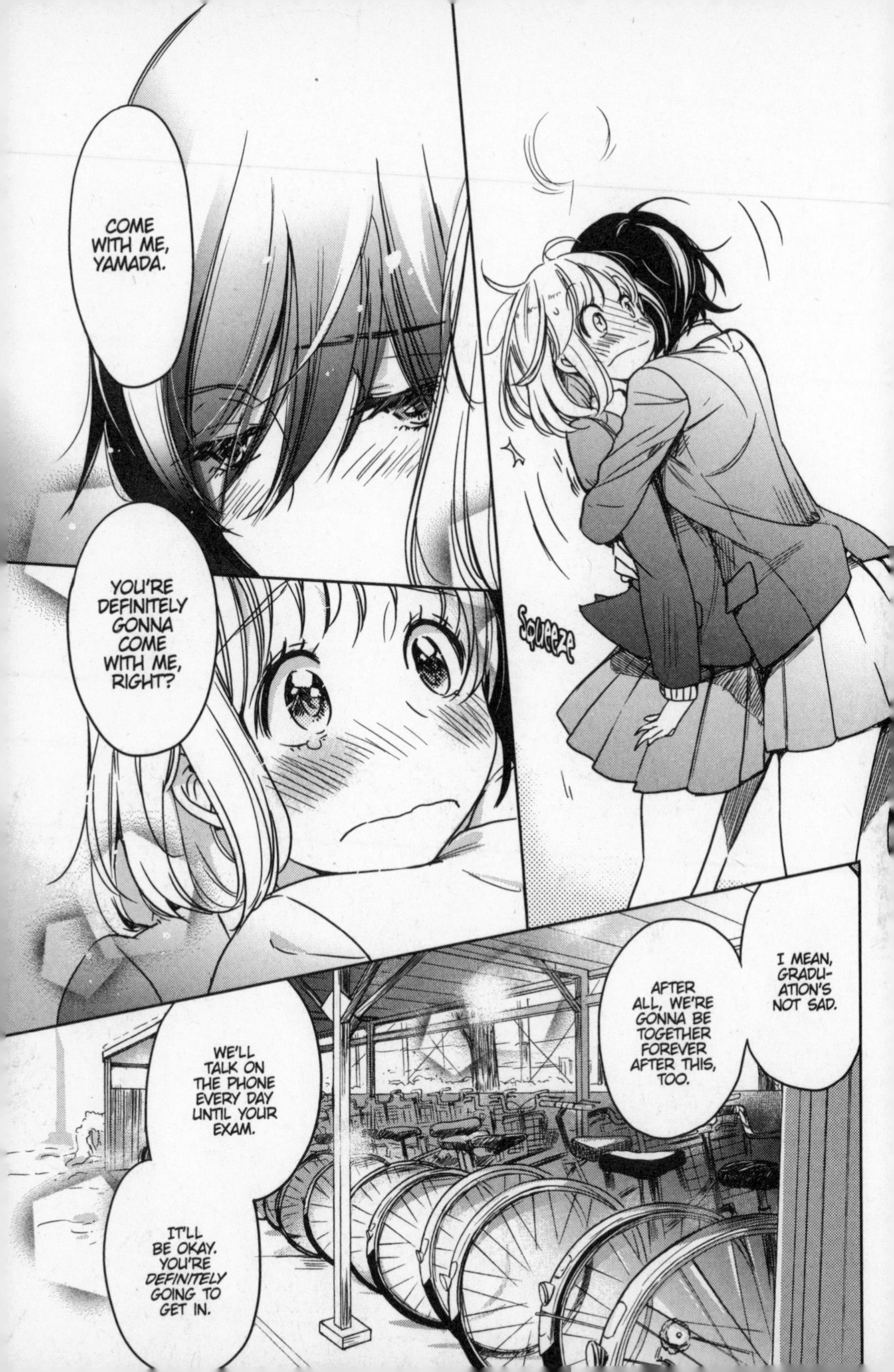
SQUEEZE
COME WITH ME, YAMADA.
YOU'RE DEFINITELY GONNA COME WITH ME, RIGHT?
I MEAN, GRADU-ATION'S NOT SAD.
AFTER ALL, WE'RE GONNA BE TOGETHER FOREVER AFTER THIS, TOO.
WE'LL TALK ON THE PHONE EVERY DAY UNTIL YOUR EXAM.
IT'LL BE OKAY. YOU'RE *DEFINITELY* GOING TO GET IN.

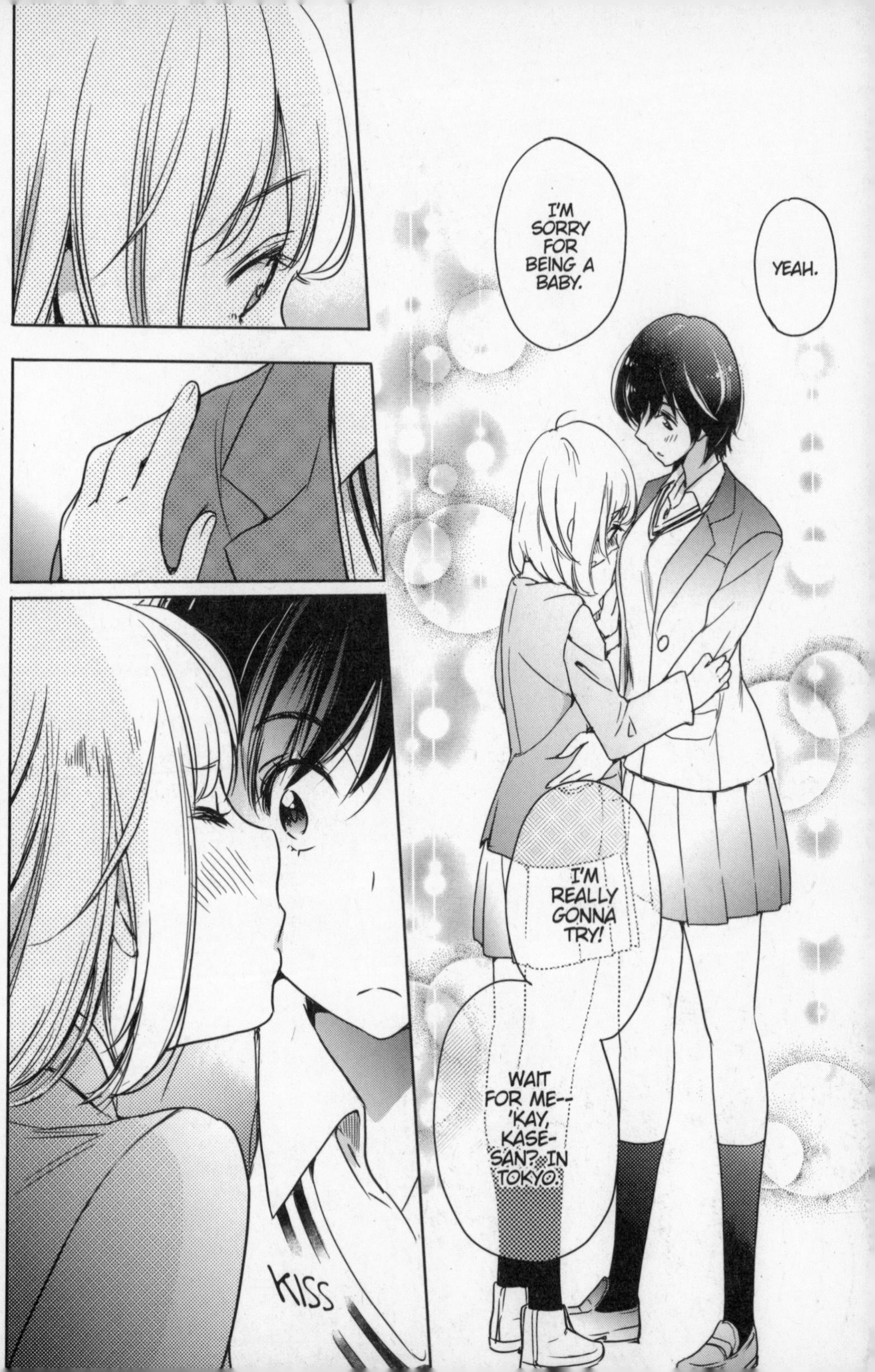
YEAH.
I'M SORRY FOR BEING A BABY.
I'M REALLY GONNA TRY!
WAIT FOR ME-- 'KAY, KASE-SAN? IN TOKYO.
KISS

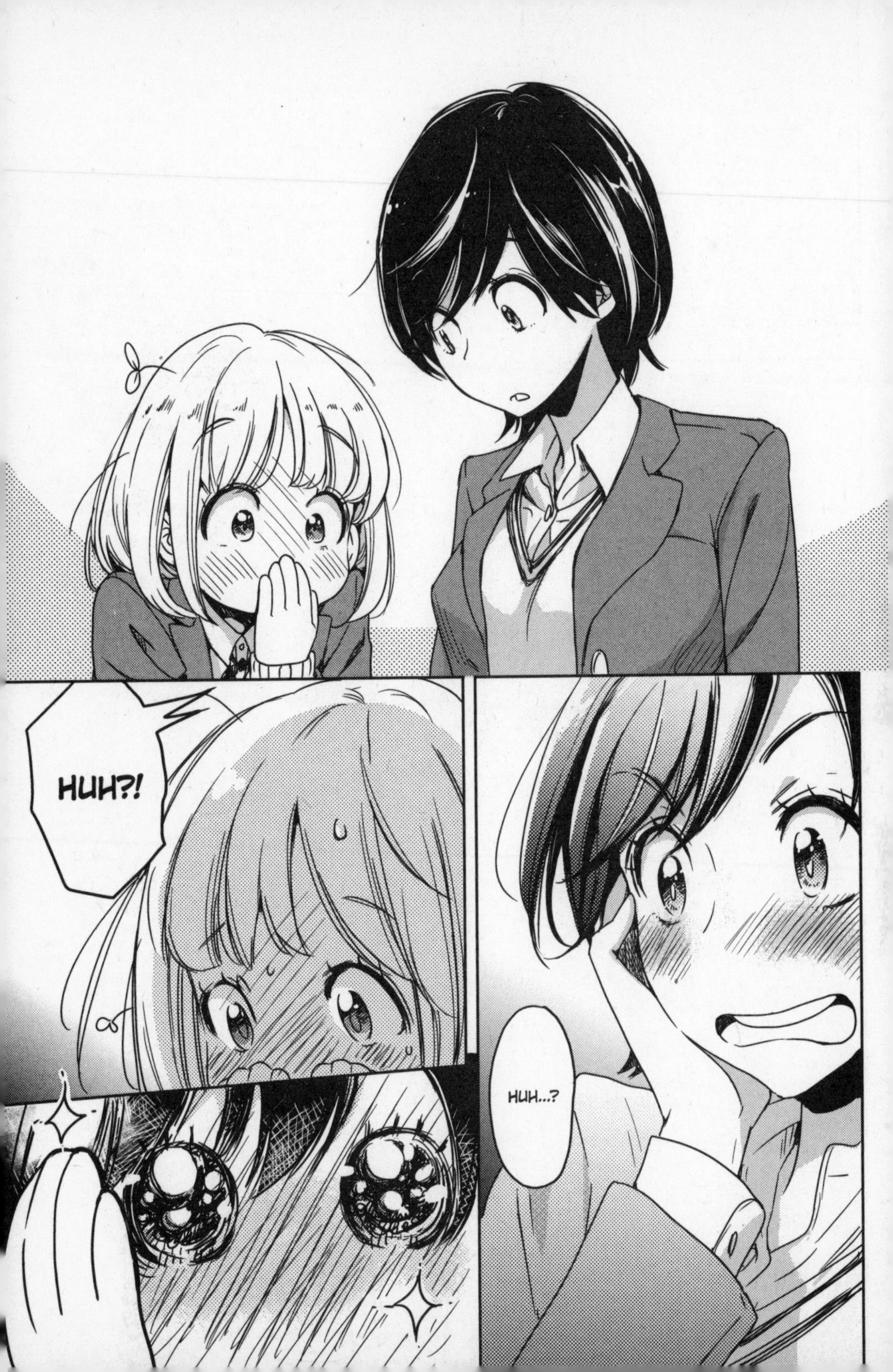
HUH...?
HUH?!

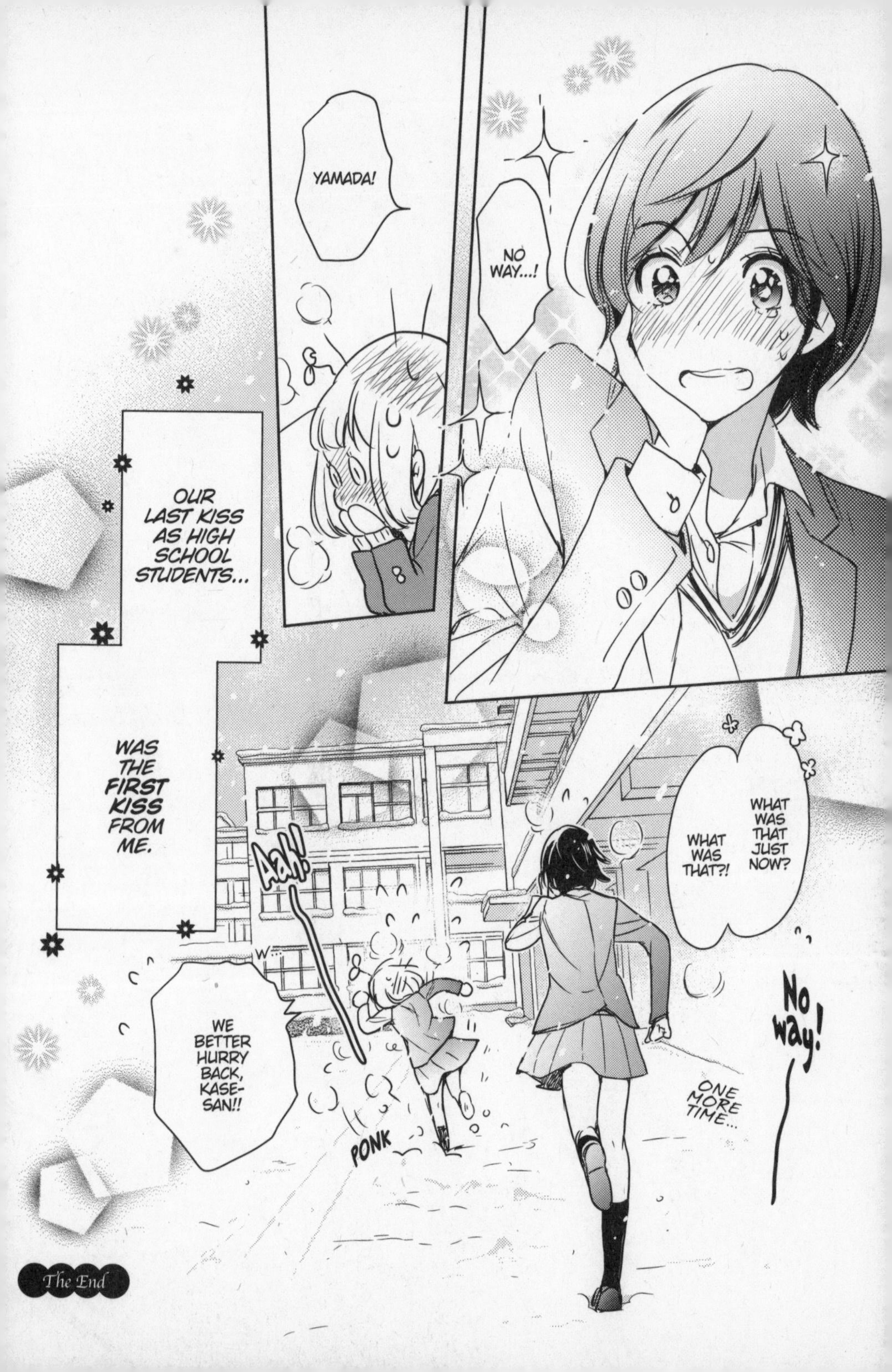
NO WAY...!
YAMADA!
OUR LAST KISS AS HIGH SCHOOL STUDENTS...
WAS THE FIRST KISS FROM ME.
No way!
WHAT WAS THAT JUST NOW?
WHAT WAS THAT?!
ONE MORE TIME...
Aah!
W...
WE BETTER HURRY BACK, KASE-SAN!!
PONK

The End

Kase-san and the Glove

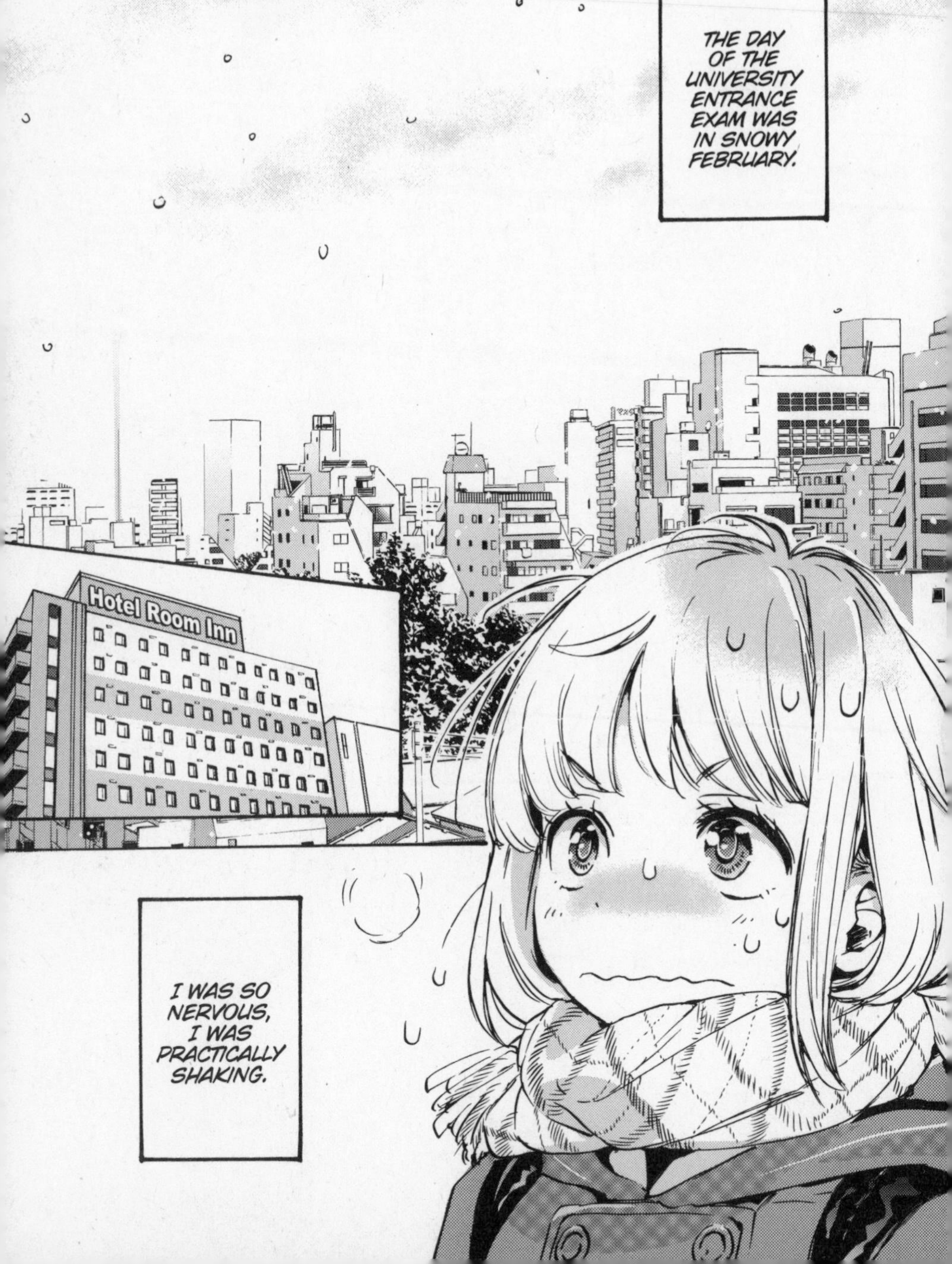
THE DAY OF THE UNIVERSITY ENTRANCE EXAM WAS IN SNOWY FEBRUARY.
Hotel Room Inn
I WAS SO NERVOUS, I WAS PRACTICALLY SHAKING.

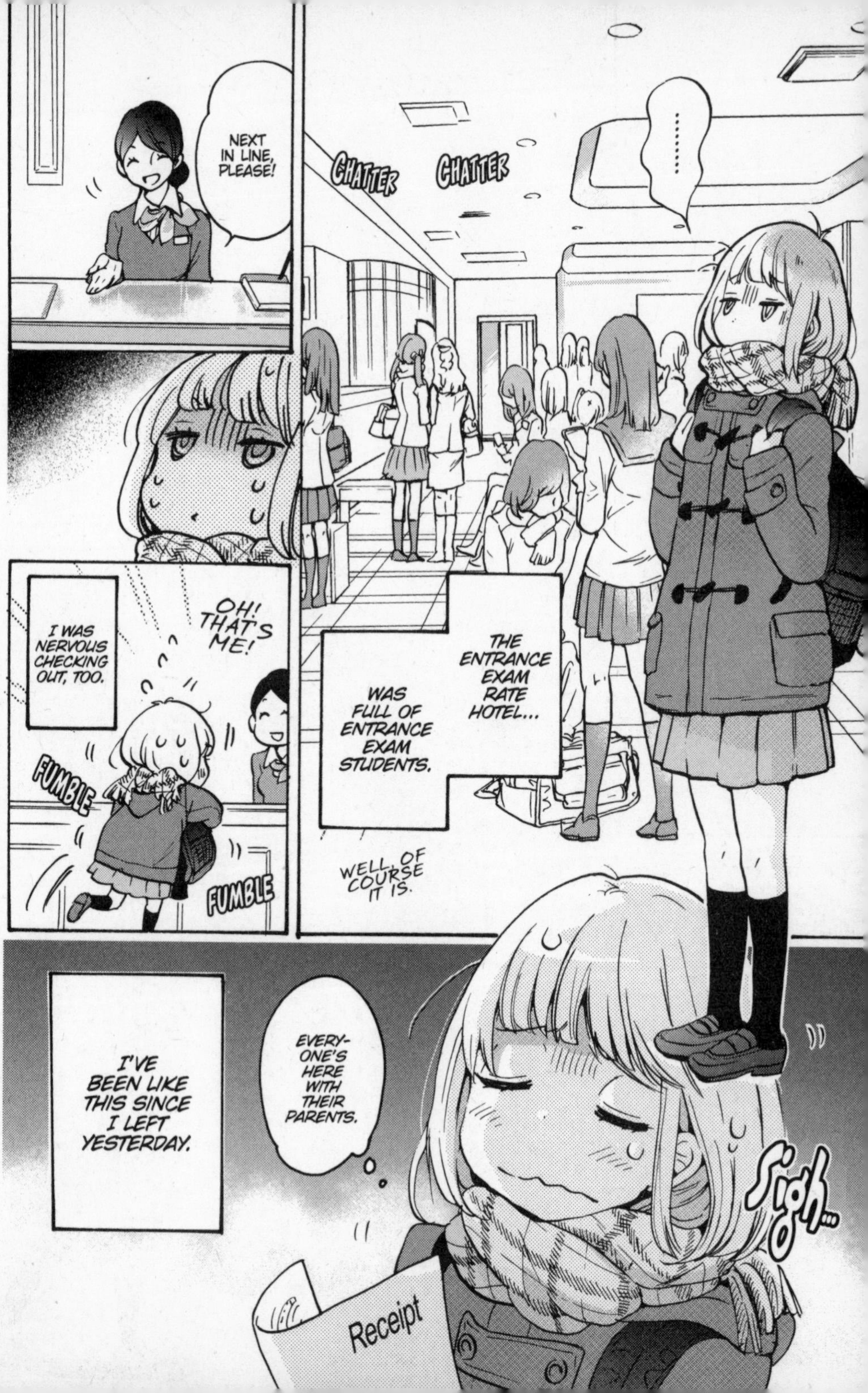

......
CHATTER
CHATTER
THE ENTRANCE EXAM RATE HOTEL...
WAS FULL OF ENTRANCE EXAM STUDENTS.
WELL, OF COURSE IT IS.
NEXT IN LINE, PLEASE!
OH! THAT'S ME!
I WAS NERVOUS CHECKING OUT, TOO.
FUMBLE
FUMBLE
Sigh...
EVERY-ONE'S HERE WITH THEIR PARENTS.
I'VE BEEN LIKE THIS SINCE I LEFT YESTERDAY.
Receipt

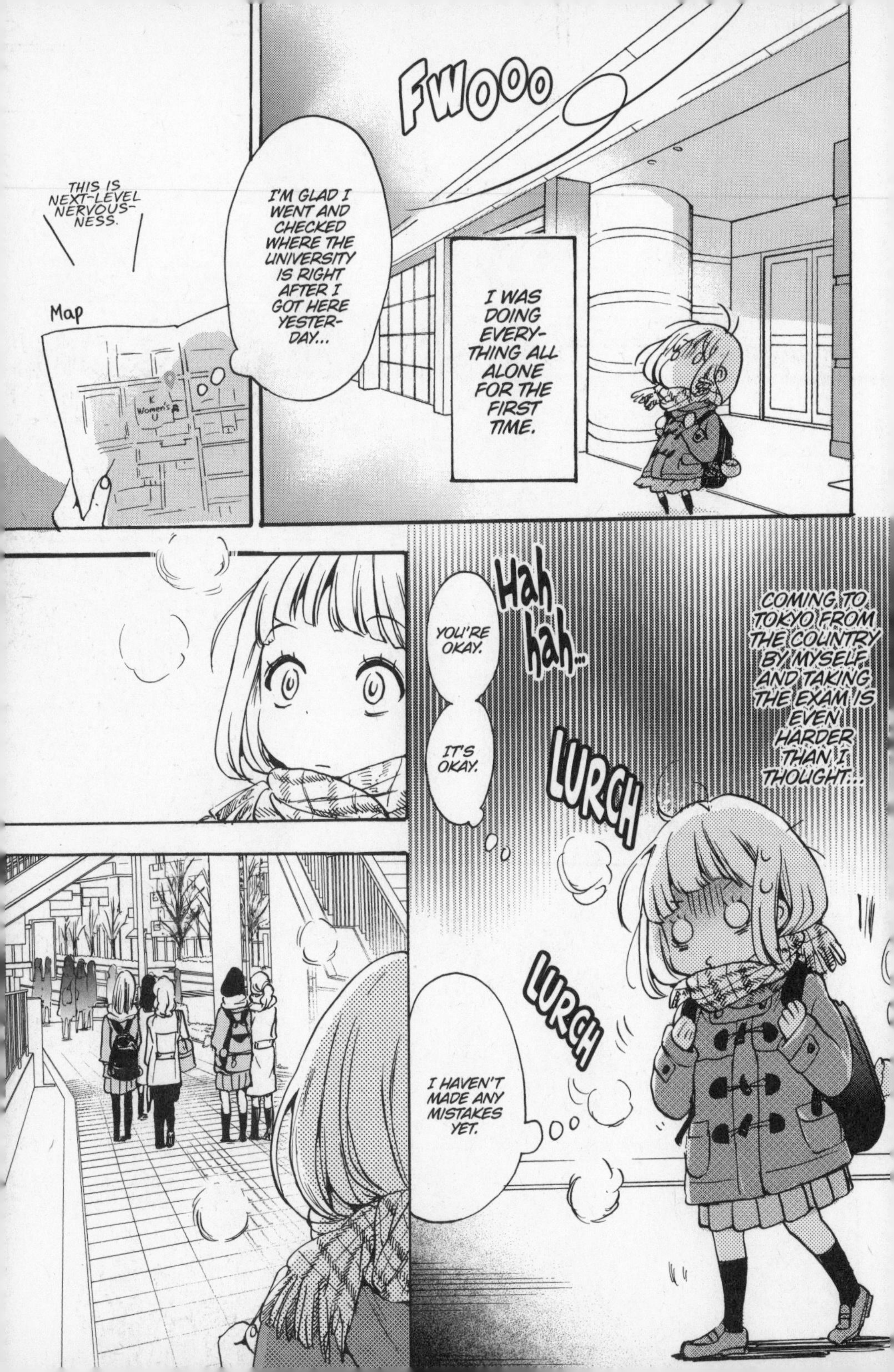
FWOOO
I WAS DOING EVERY-THING ALL ALONE FOR THE FIRST TIME.
I'M GLAD I WENT AND CHECKED WHERE THE UNIVERSITY IS RIGHT AFTER I GOT HERE YESTER-DAY...
THIS IS NEXT-LEVEL NERVOUS-NESS.
Map
K Women's U
COMING TO TOKYO FROM THE COUNTRY BY MYSELF AND TAKING THE EXAM IS EVEN HARDER THAN I THOUGHT...
Hah hah...
YOU'RE OKAY.
IT'S OKAY.
LURCH
LURCH
I HAVEN'T MADE ANY MISTAKES YET.

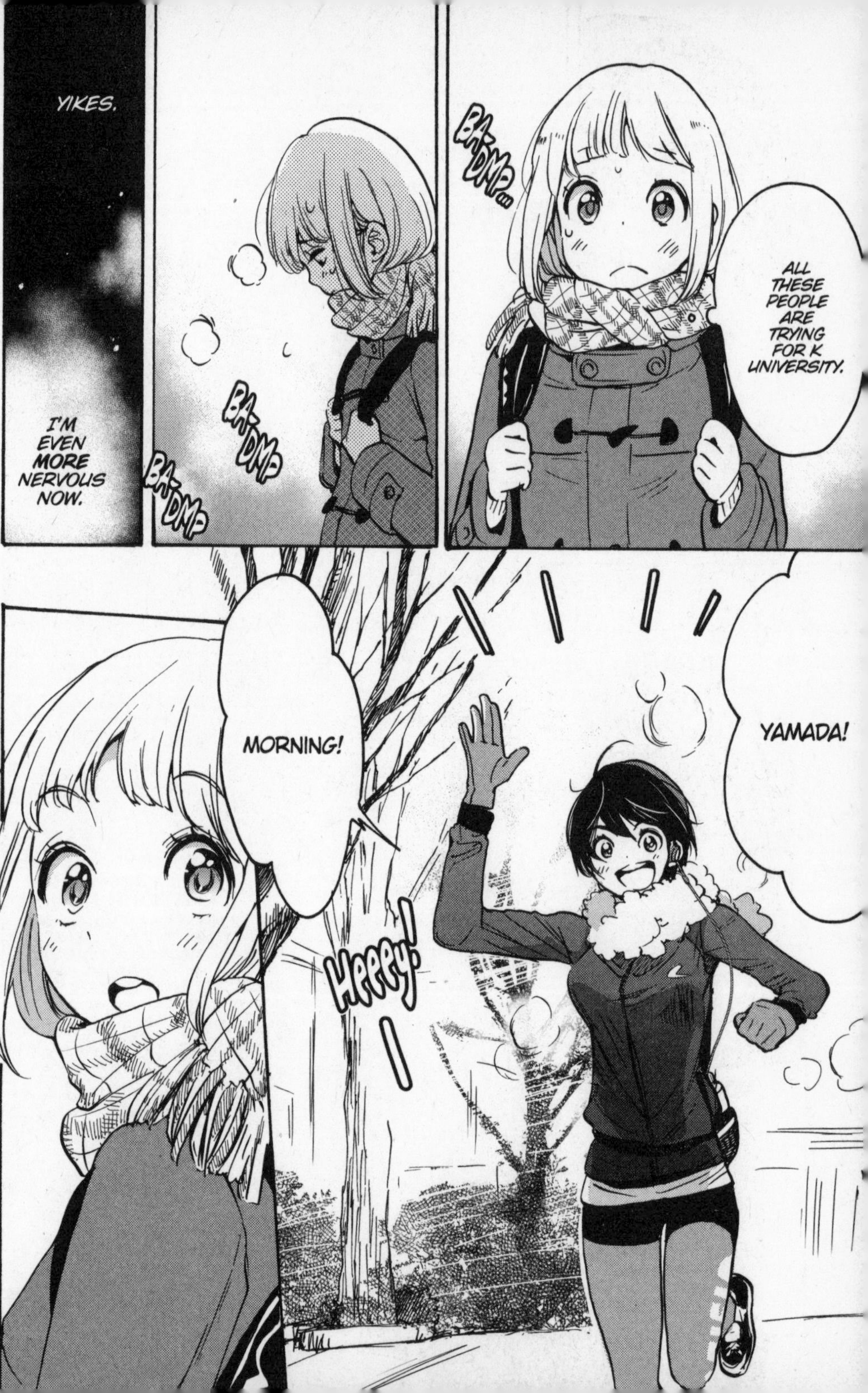

ALL THESE PEOPLE ARE TRYING FOR K UNIVERSITY.
BA-DMP...
BA-DMP
BA-DMP
YIKES.
I'M EVEN MORE NERVOUS NOW.
YAMADA!
MORNING!
Heeey!

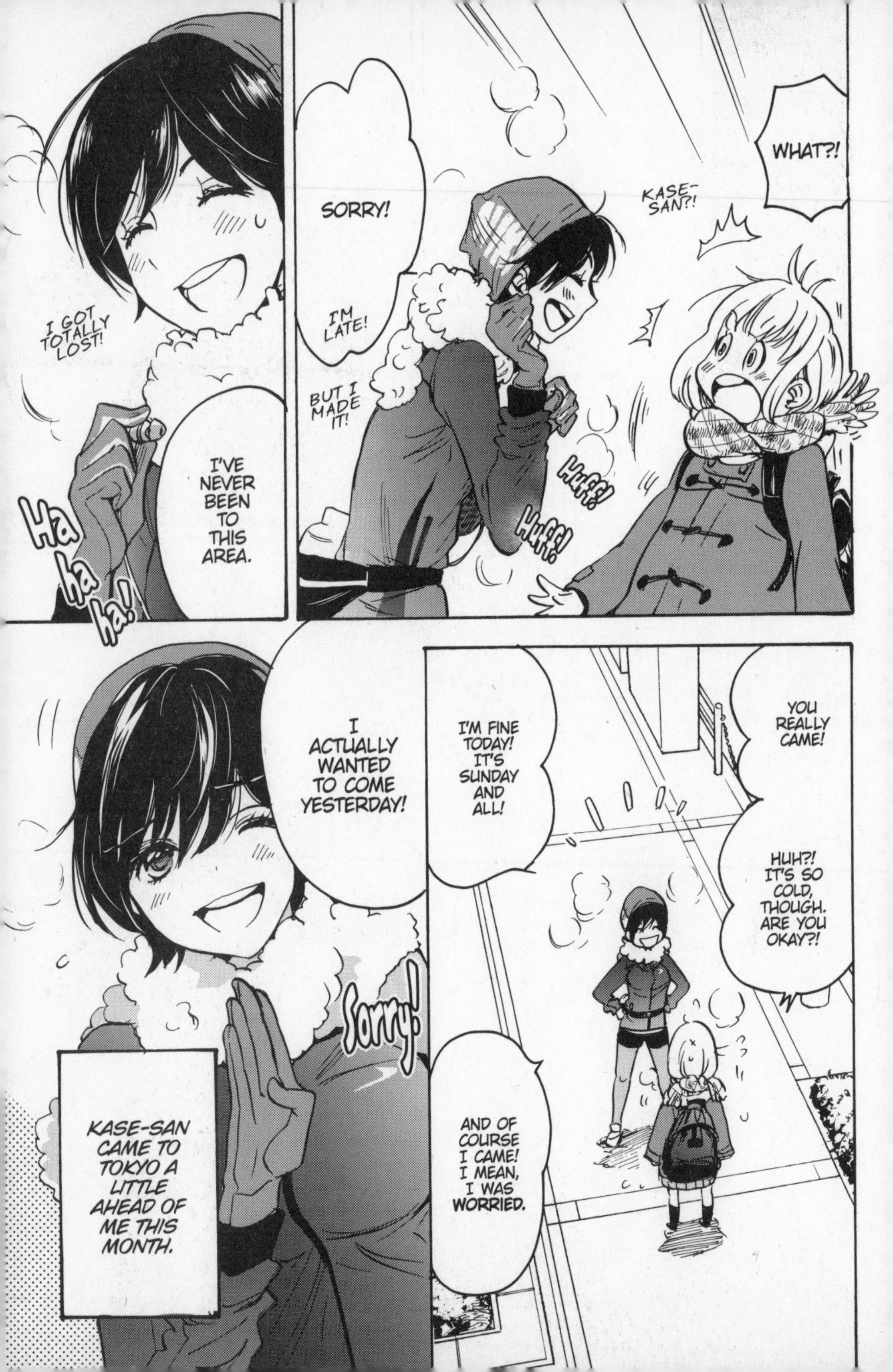
WHAT?!
KASE-SAN?!
SORRY!
I'M LATE!
BUT I MADE IT!
Huff!
Huff!
I GOT TOTALLY LOST!
I'VE NEVER BEEN TO THIS AREA.
Ha ha ha!
YOU REALLY CAME!
HUH?! IT'S SO COLD, THOUGH. ARE YOU OKAY?!
I'M FINE TODAY! IT'S SUNDAY AND ALL!
AND OF COURSE I CAME! I MEAN, I WAS WORRIED.
I ACTUALLY WANTED TO COME YESTERDAY!
Sorry!
KASE-SAN CAME TO TOKYO A LITTLE AHEAD OF ME THIS MONTH.

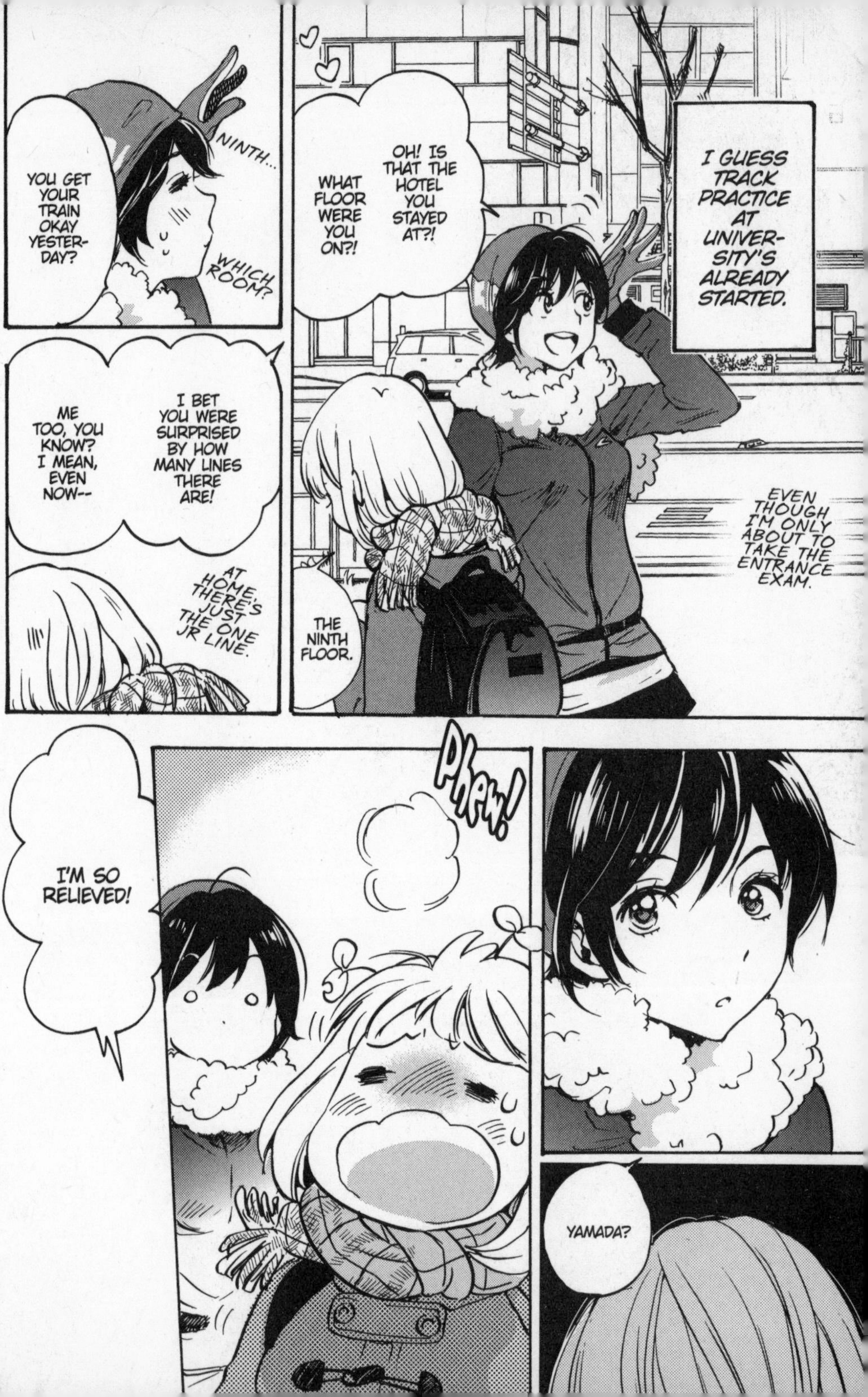
I GUESS TRACK PRACTICE AT UNIVERSITY'S ALREADY STARTED.
OH! IS THAT THE HOTEL YOU STAYED AT?!
WHAT FLOOR WERE YOU ON?!
EVEN THOUGH I'M ONLY ABOUT TO TAKE THE ENTRANCE EXAM.
THE NINTH FLOOR.
NINTH...
WHICH ROOM?
YOU GET YOUR TRAIN OKAY YESTER-DAY?
I BET YOU WERE SURPRISED BY HOW MANY LINES THERE ARE!
ME TOO, YOU KNOW? I MEAN, EVEN NOW--
AT HOME, THERE'S JUST THE ONE JR LINE.
YAMADA?
Phew!
I'M SO RELIEVED!

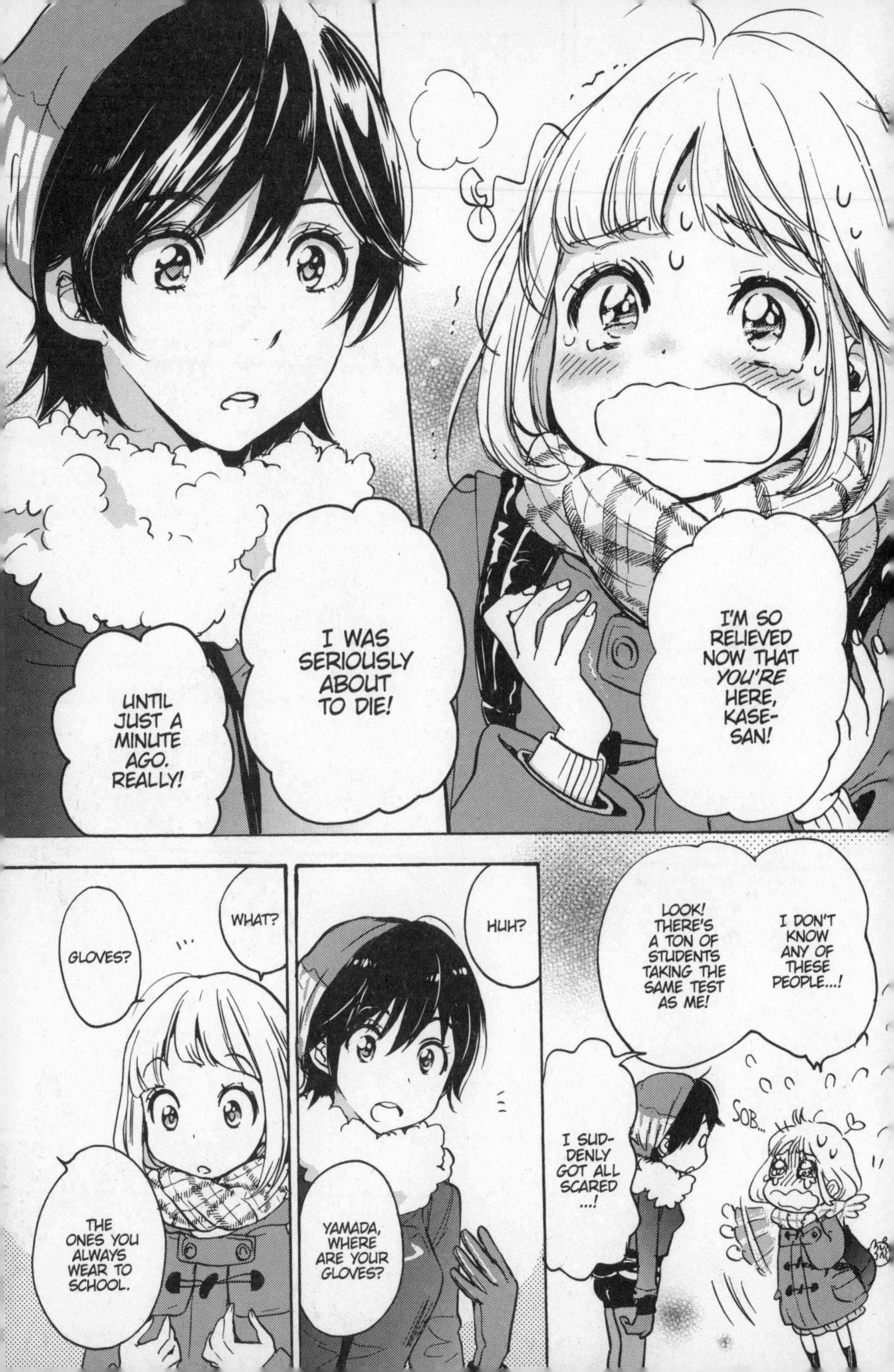
I'M SO RELIEVED NOW THAT *YOU'RE* HERE, KASE-SAN!
I WAS SERIOUSLY ABOUT TO DIE!
UNTIL JUST A MINUTE AGO. REALLY!
I DON'T KNOW ANY OF THESE PEOPLE...!
LOOK! THERE'S A TON OF STUDENTS TAKING THE SAME TEST AS ME!
I SUDDENLY GOT ALL SCARED ...!
SOB...
HUH?
YAMADA, WHERE ARE YOUR GLOVES?
WHAT?
GLOVES?
THE ONES YOU ALWAYS WEAR TO SCHOOL.

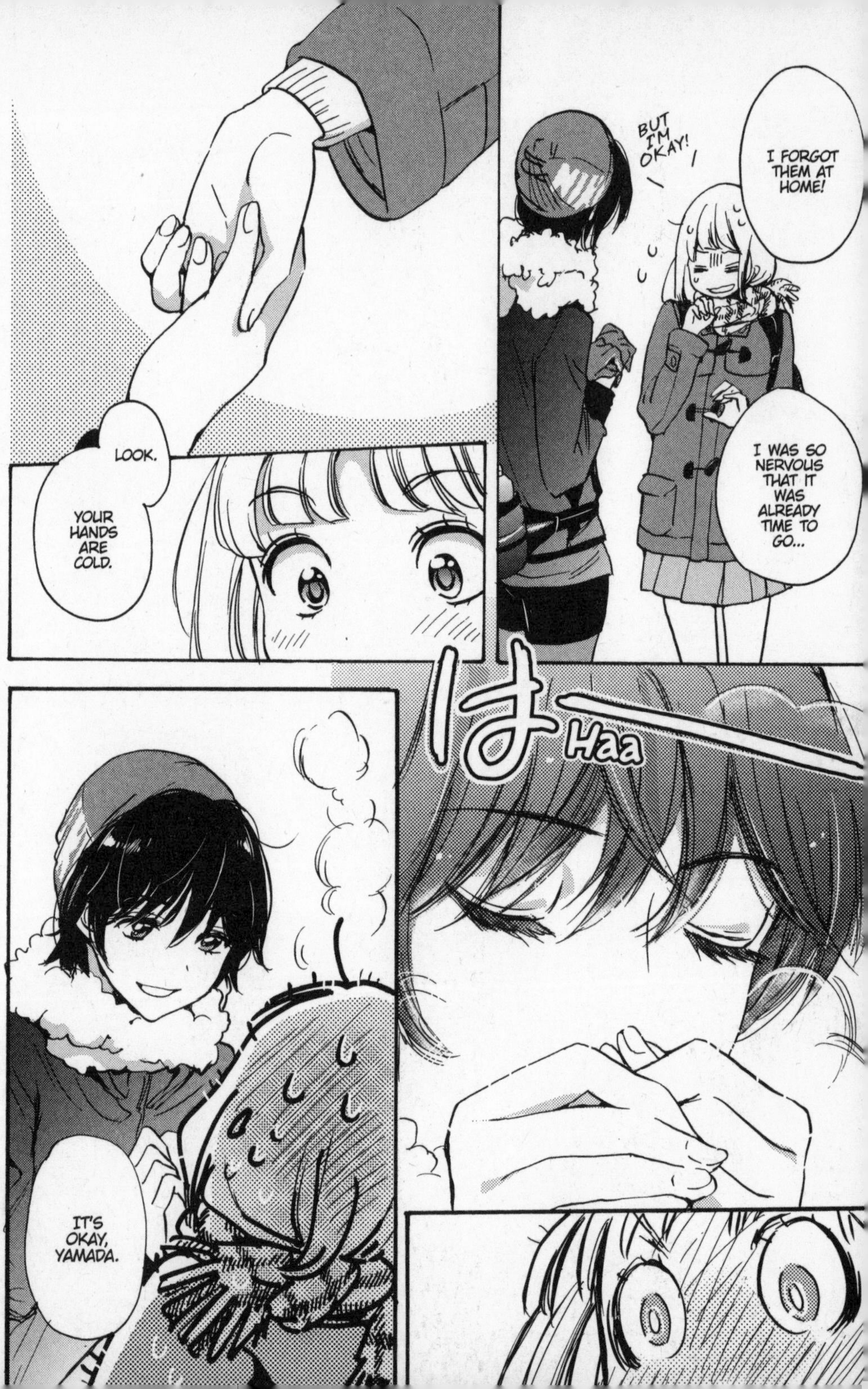

I FORGOT THEM AT HOME!
BUT I'M OKAY!
I WAS SO NERVOUS THAT IT WAS ALREADY TIME TO GO...
LOOK.
YOUR HANDS ARE COLD.
は Haa
IT'S OKAY, YAMADA.

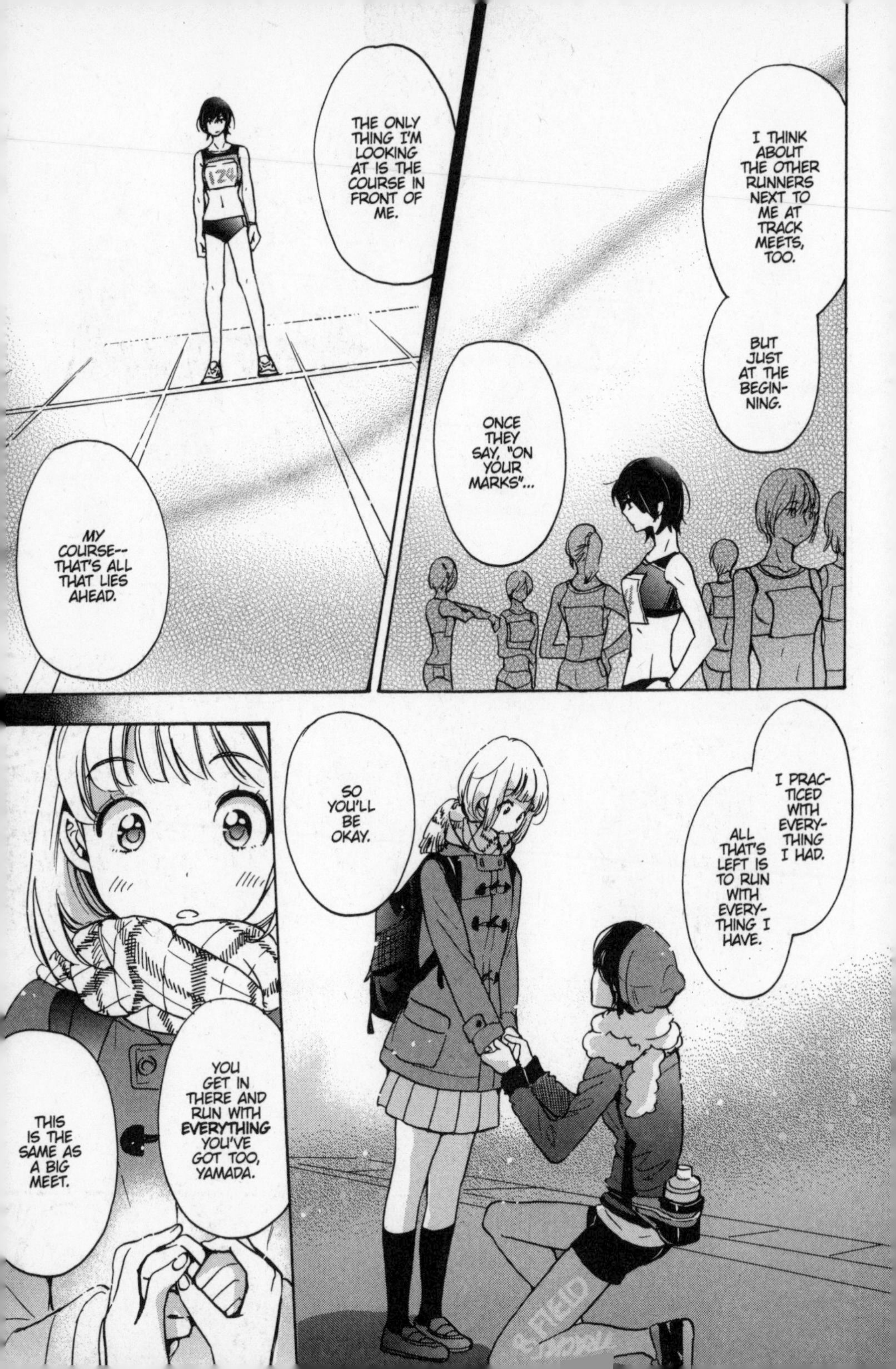
I THINK ABOUT THE OTHER RUNNERS NEXT TO ME AT TRACK MEETS, TOO.
BUT JUST AT THE BEGINNING.
ONCE THEY SAY, "ON YOUR MARKS"...
THE ONLY THING I'M LOOKING AT IS THE COURSE IN FRONT OF ME.
MY COURSE--THAT'S ALL THAT LIES AHEAD.
I PRACTICED WITH EVERYTHING I HAD.
ALL THAT'S LEFT IS TO RUN WITH EVERYTHING I HAVE.
SO YOU'LL BE OKAY.
YOU GET IN THERE AND RUN WITH **EVERYTHING** YOU'VE GOT TOO, YAMADA.
THIS IS THE SAME AS A BIG MEET.

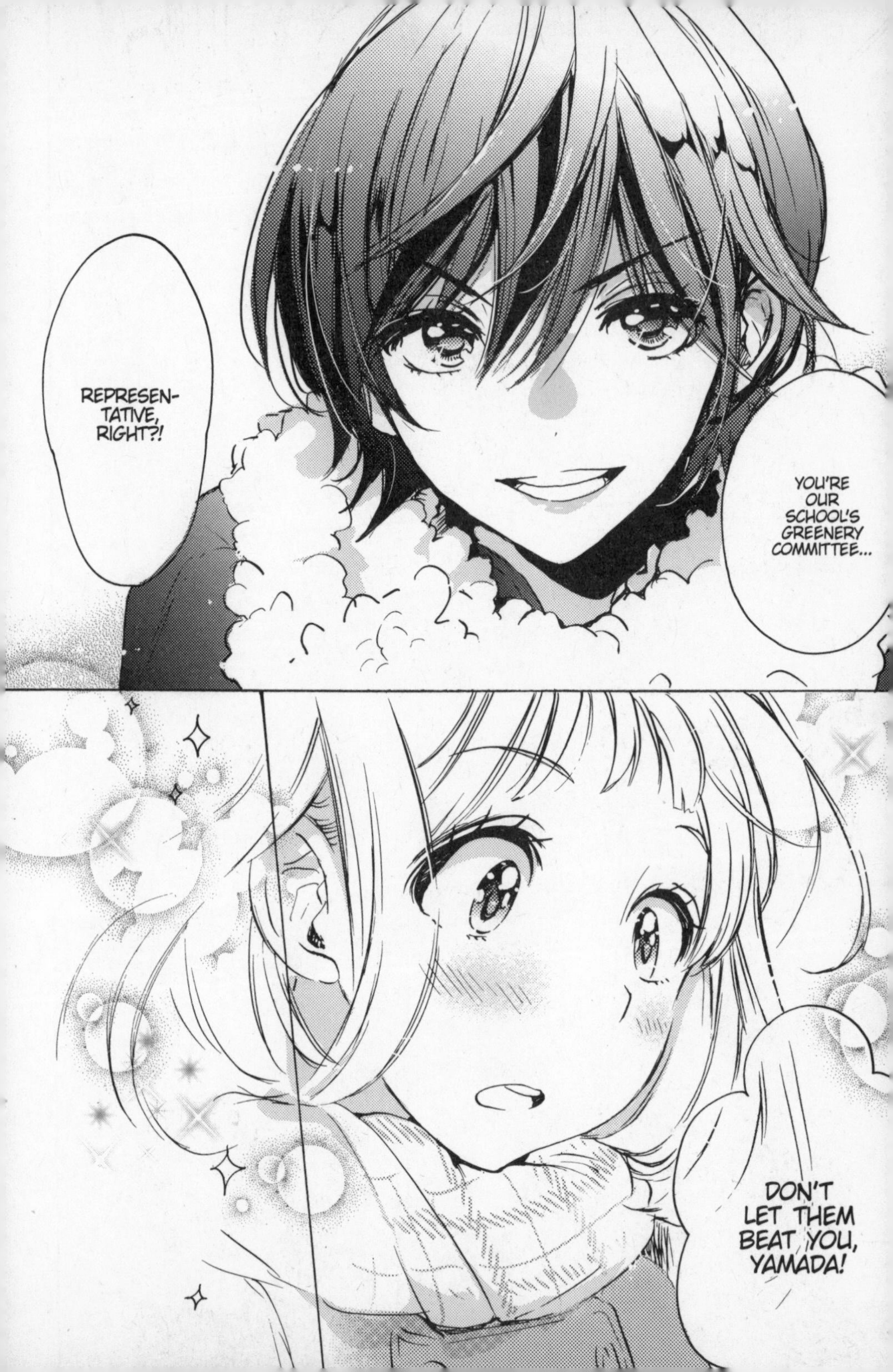
YOU'RE OUR SCHOOL'S GREENERY COMMITTEE...
REPRESEN-TATIVE, RIGHT?!
DON'T LET THEM BEAT YOU, YAMADA!

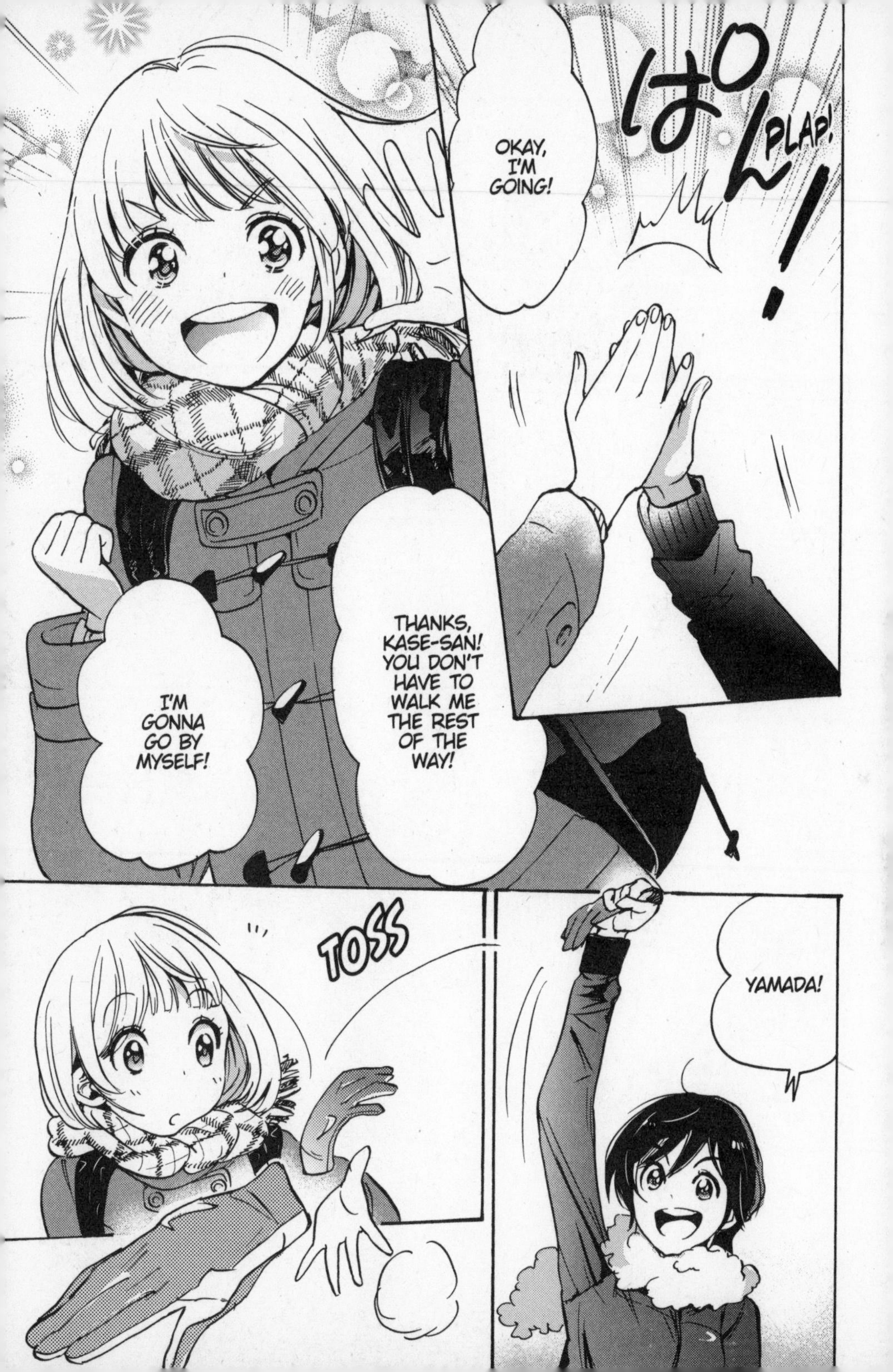
OKAY, I'M GOING!
ぱん!!
PLAP!
THANKS, KASE-SAN! YOU DON'T HAVE TO WALK ME THE REST OF THE WAY!
I'M GONNA GO BY MYSELF!
YAMADA!
TOSS

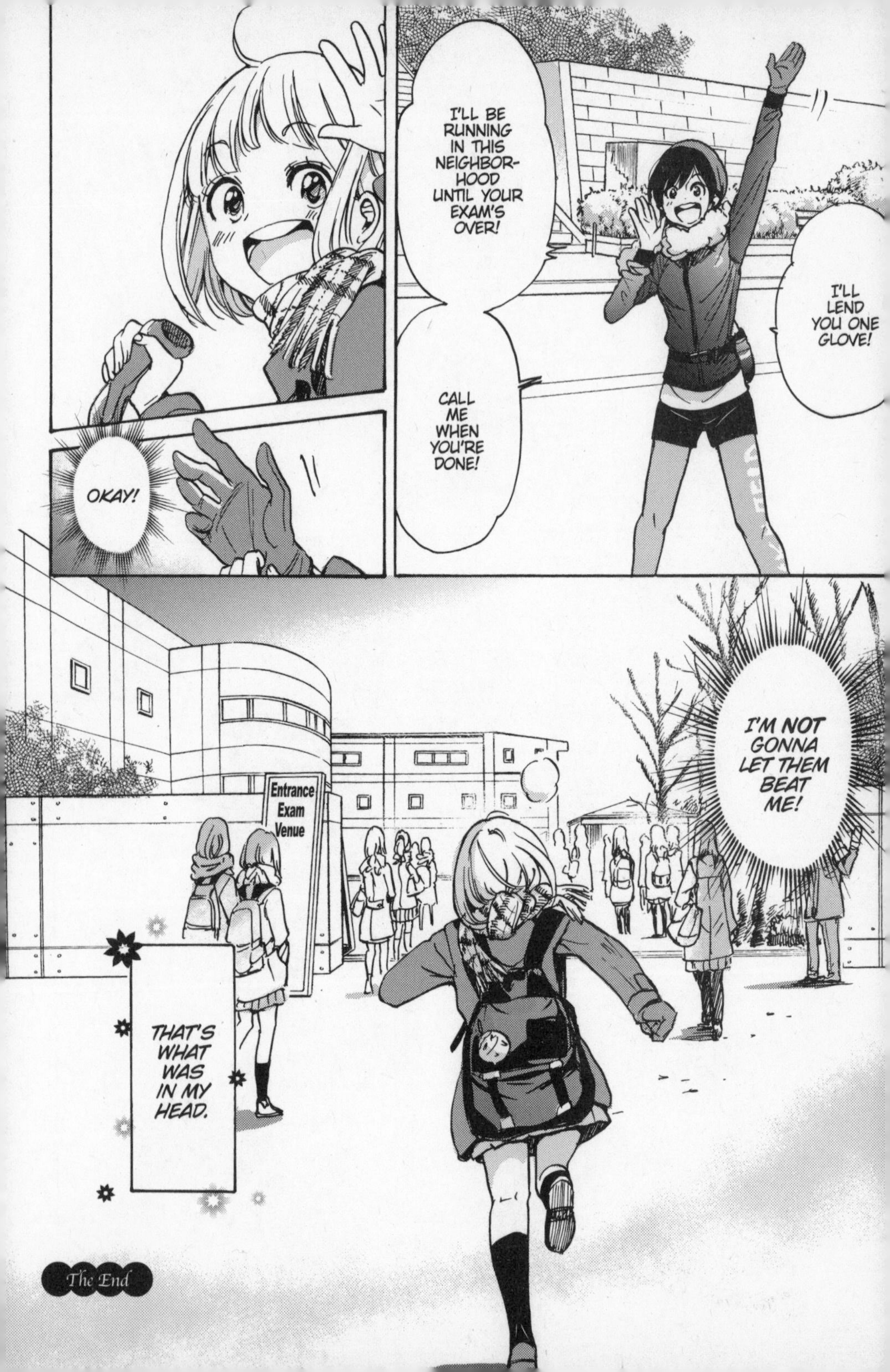
I'LL LEND YOU ONE GLOVE!
I'LL BE RUNNING IN THIS NEIGHBOR-HOOD UNTIL YOUR EXAM'S OVER!
CALL ME WHEN YOU'RE DONE!
OKAY!
I'M NOT GONNA LET THEM BEAT ME!
Entrance Exam Venue
THAT'S WHAT WAS IN MY HEAD.
The End

Kase-san _and_
Cherry Blossoms ✽

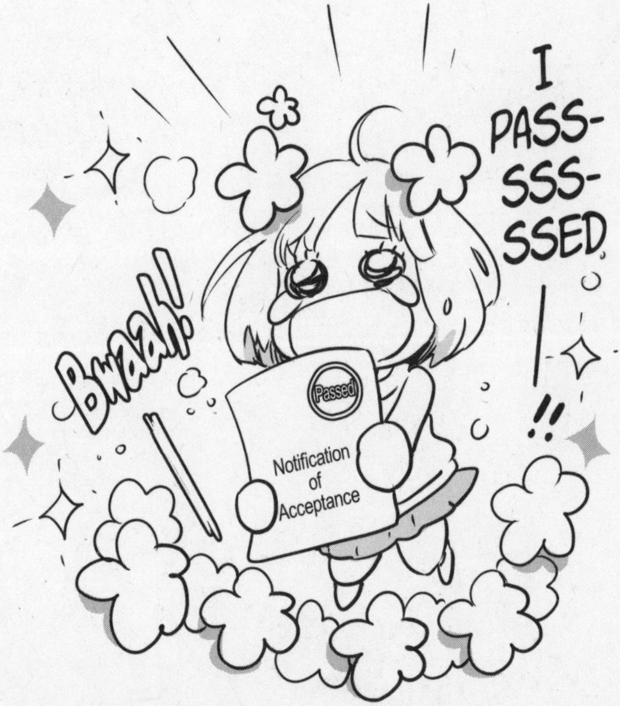
I PASS-SSS-SSED!!
Passed
Notification of Acceptance
Bwaah!

Kase-san and Cherry Blossoms

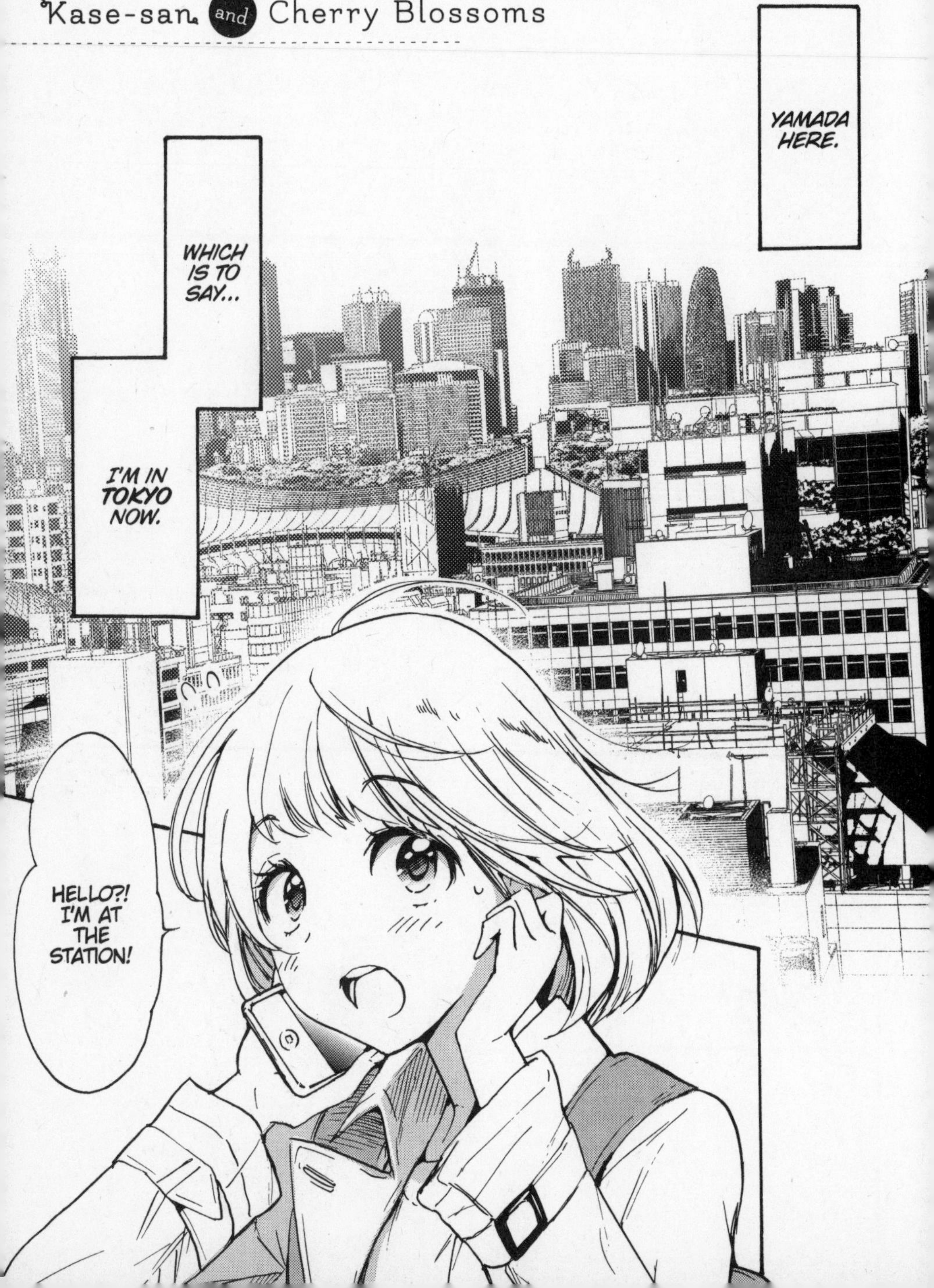
YAMADA HERE.
WHICH IS TO SAY...
I'M IN TOKYO NOW.
HELLO?! I'M AT THE STATION!

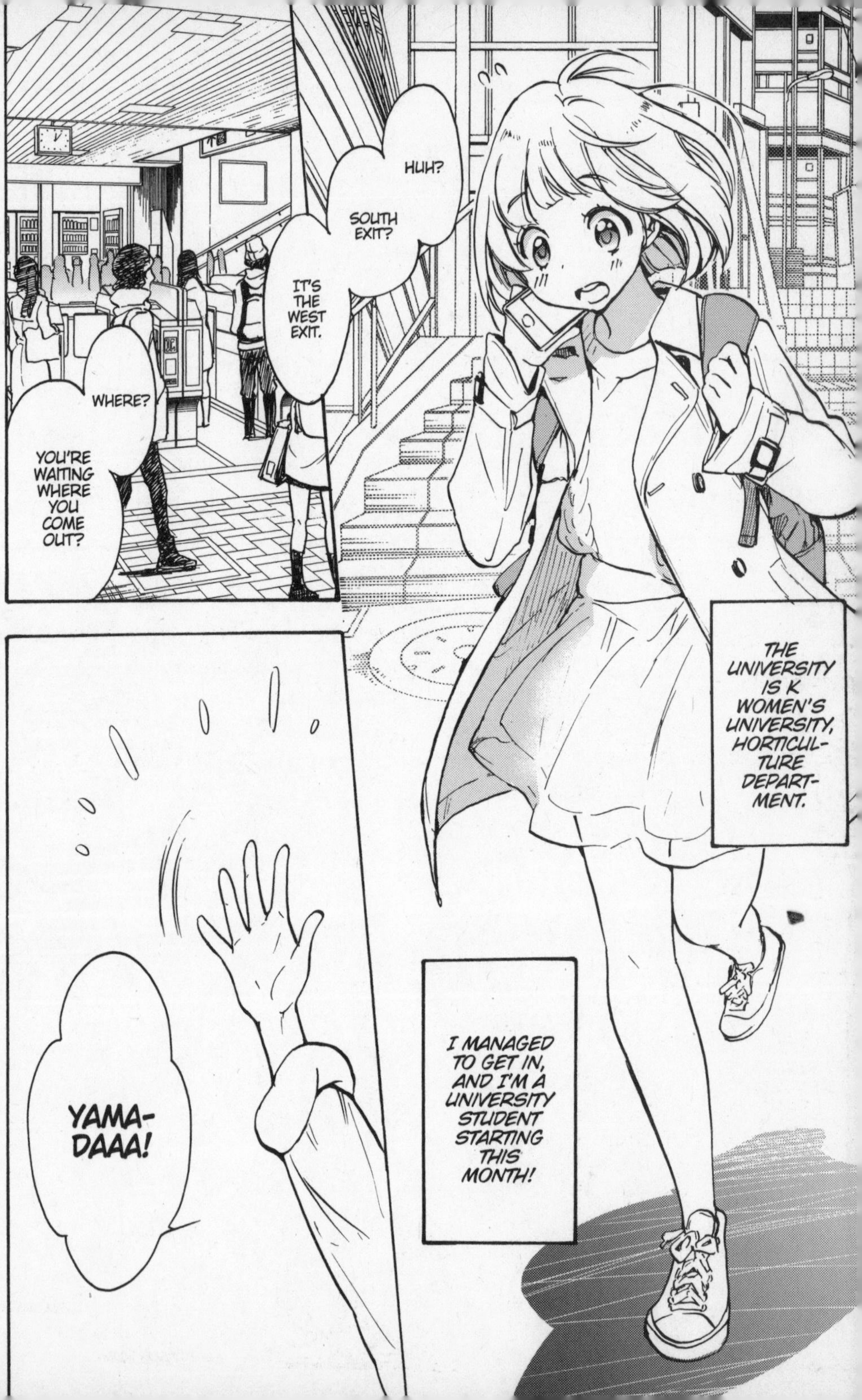
HUH?
SOUTH EXIT?
IT'S THE WEST EXIT.
WHERE?
YOU'RE WAITING WHERE YOU COME OUT?
THE UNIVERSITY IS K WOMEN'S UNIVERSITY, HORTICUL-TURE DEPART-MENT.
I MANAGED TO GET IN, AND I'M A UNIVERSITY STUDENT STARTING THIS MONTH!
YAMA-DAAA!

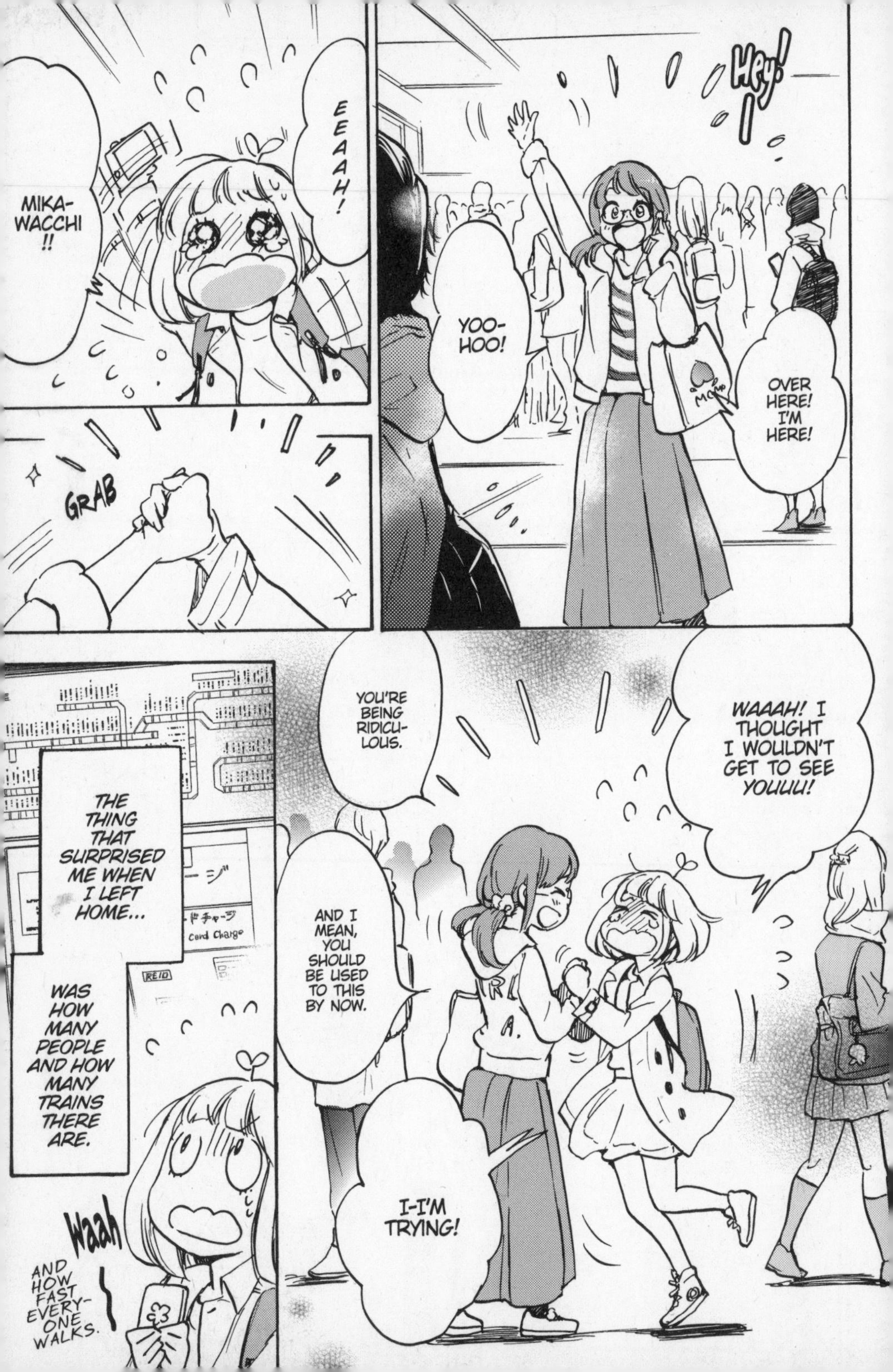
Hey!
YOO-HOO!
OVER HERE! I'M HERE!
EEAAAH!
MIKA-WACCHI!!
GRAB
WAAAH! I THOUGHT I WOULDN'T GET TO SEE YOUUU!
YOU'RE BEING RIDICULOUS.
AND I MEAN, YOU SHOULD BE USED TO THIS BY NOW.
I-I'M TRYING!
THE THING THAT SURPRISED ME WHEN I LEFT HOME...
Card Charge
WAS HOW MANY PEOPLE AND HOW MANY TRAINS THERE ARE.
Waah
AND HOW FAST EVERYONE WALKS.

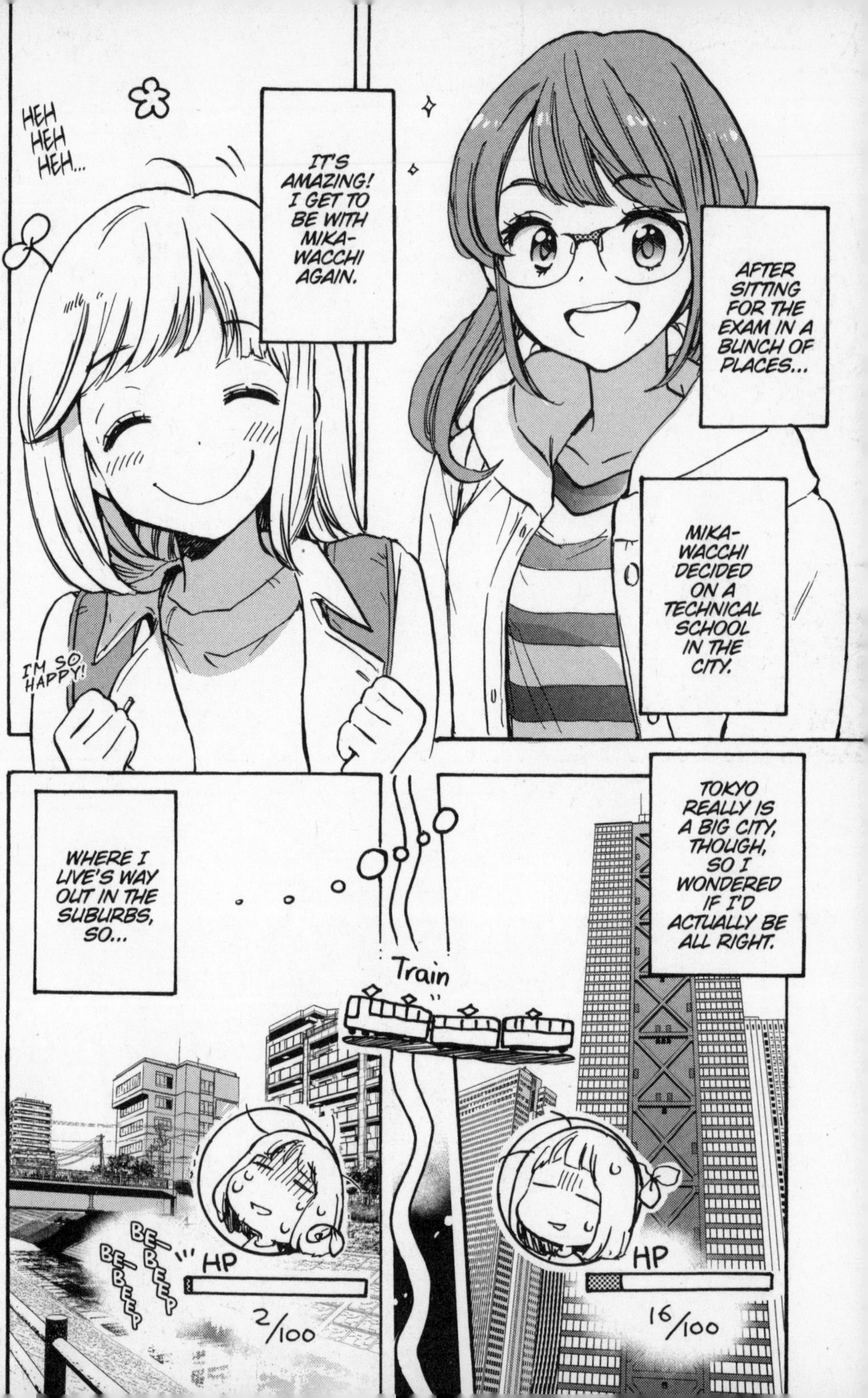
AFTER SITTING FOR THE EXAM IN A BUNCH OF PLACES...
MIKA-WACCHI DECIDED ON A TECHNICAL SCHOOL IN THE CITY.
IT'S AMAZING! I GET TO BE WITH MIKA-WACCHI AGAIN.
HEH HEH HEH...
I'M SO HAPPY!
TOKYO REALLY IS A BIG CITY, THOUGH, SO I WONDERED IF I'D ACTUALLY BE ALL RIGHT.
HP
16/100
WHERE I LIVE'S WAY OUT IN THE SUBURBS, SO...
Train
BE-BEEP
BE-BEEP
HP
2/100

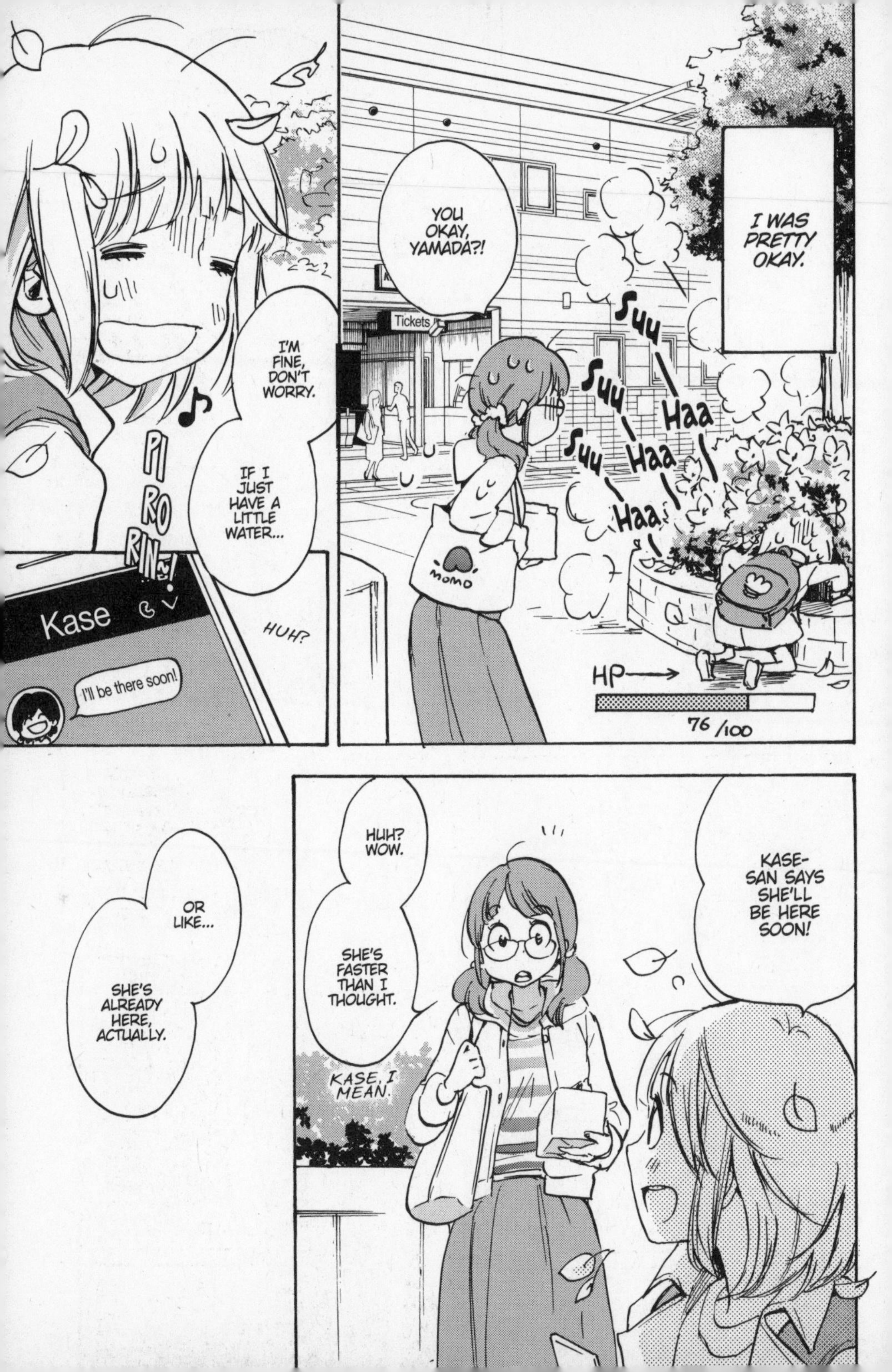
I WAS PRETTY OKAY.
YOU OKAY, YAMADA?!
Tickets
Suu Haa Suu Haa Suu Haa
MOMO
HP
76/100
I'M FINE, DON'T WORRY.
IF I JUST HAVE A LITTLE WATER...
PI RO RIN!
Kase
I'll be there soon!
HUH?
KASE-SAN SAYS SHE'LL BE HERE SOON!
HUH? WOW.
SHE'S FASTER THAN I THOUGHT.
KASE, I MEAN.
OR LIKE...
SHE'S ALREADY HERE, ACTUALLY.

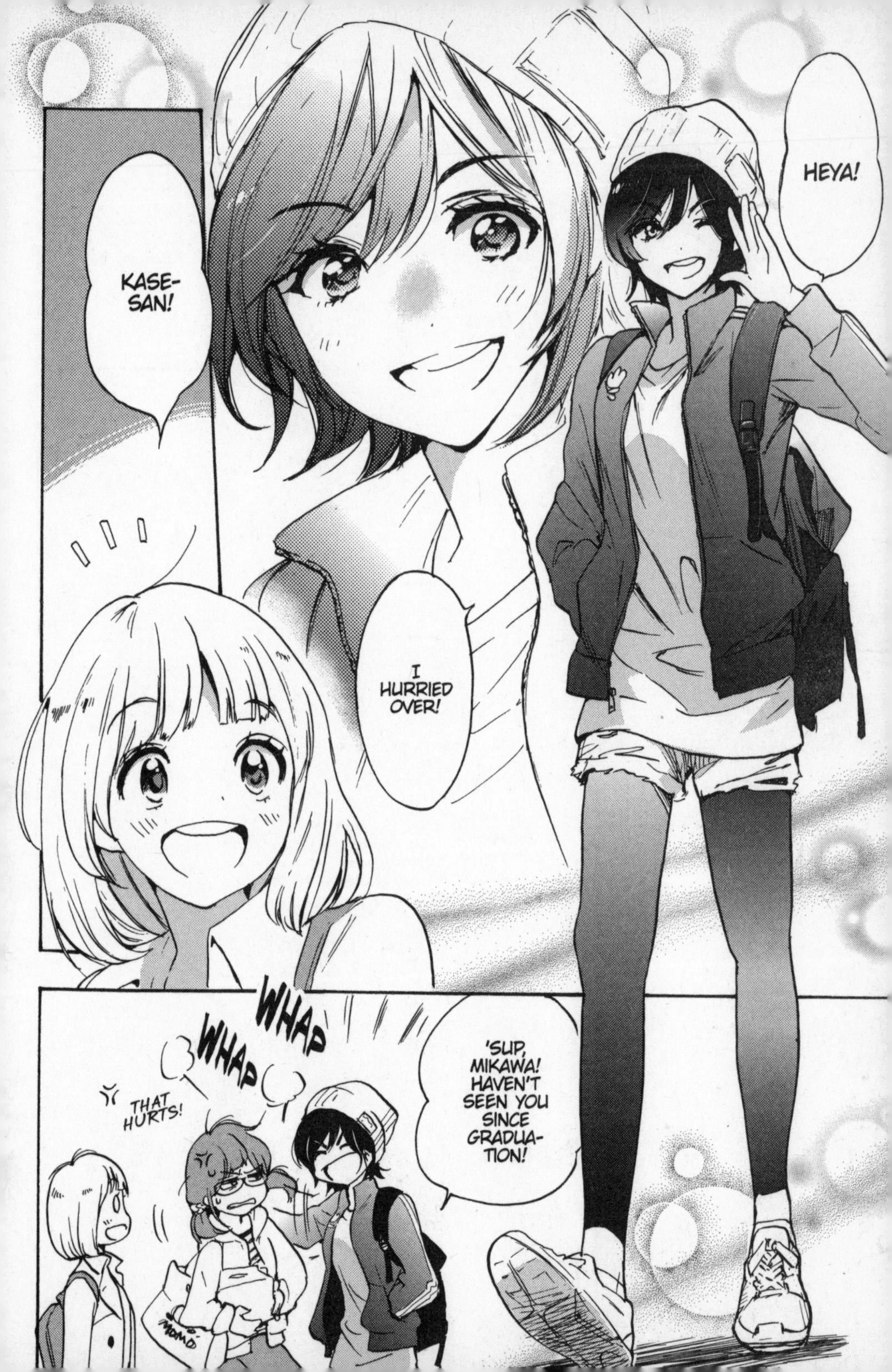
HEYA!
I HURRIED OVER!
KASE-SAN!
'SUP, MIKAWA! HAVEN'T SEEN YOU SINCE GRADUA-TION!
WHAP
WHAP
THAT HURTS!

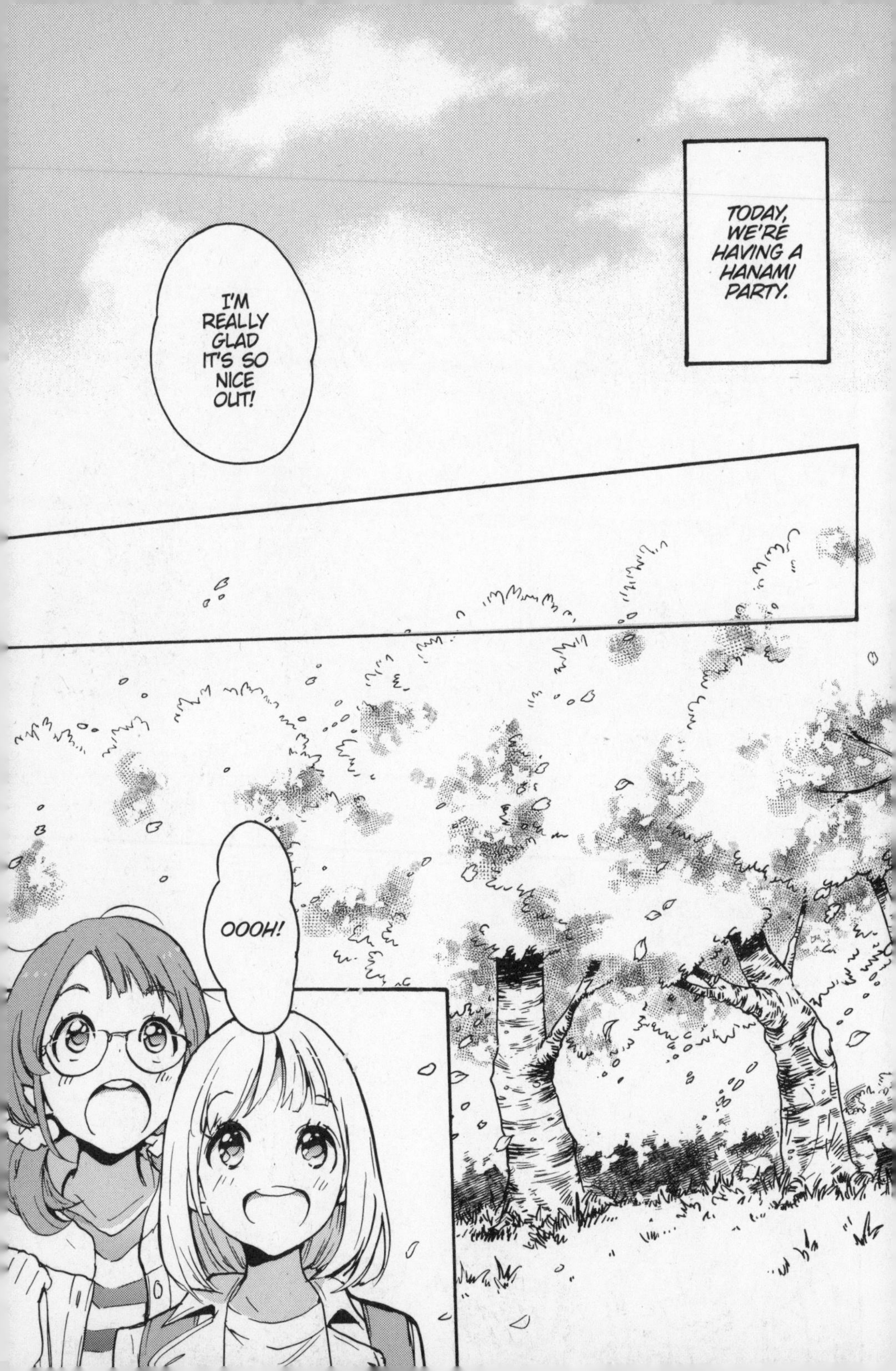
TODAY, WE'RE HAVING A HANAMI PARTY.
I'M REALLY GLAD IT'S SO NICE OUT!
OOOH!

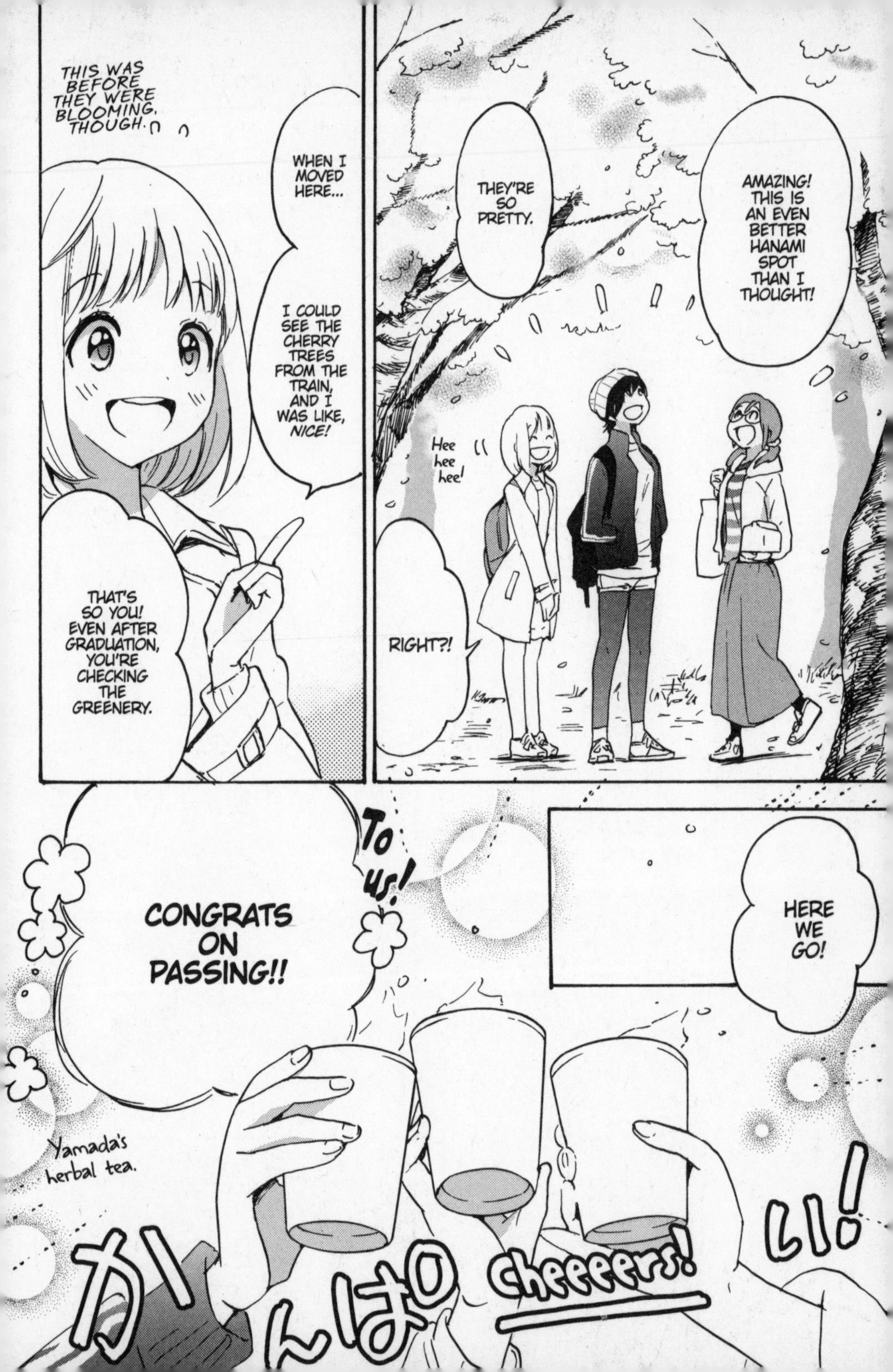

AMAZING! THIS IS AN EVEN BETTER HANAMI SPOT THAN I THOUGHT!
THEY'RE SO PRETTY.
Hee hee hee!
RIGHT?!
WHEN I MOVED HERE...
I COULD SEE THE CHERRY TREES FROM THE TRAIN, AND I WAS LIKE, *NICE!*
THIS WAS BEFORE THEY WERE BLOOMING, THOUGH.
THAT'S SO YOU! EVEN AFTER GRADUATION, YOU'RE CHECKING THE GREENERY.
HERE WE GO!
To us!
CONGRATS ON PASSING!!
Yamada's herbal tea.
かんぱい!
cheeeers!

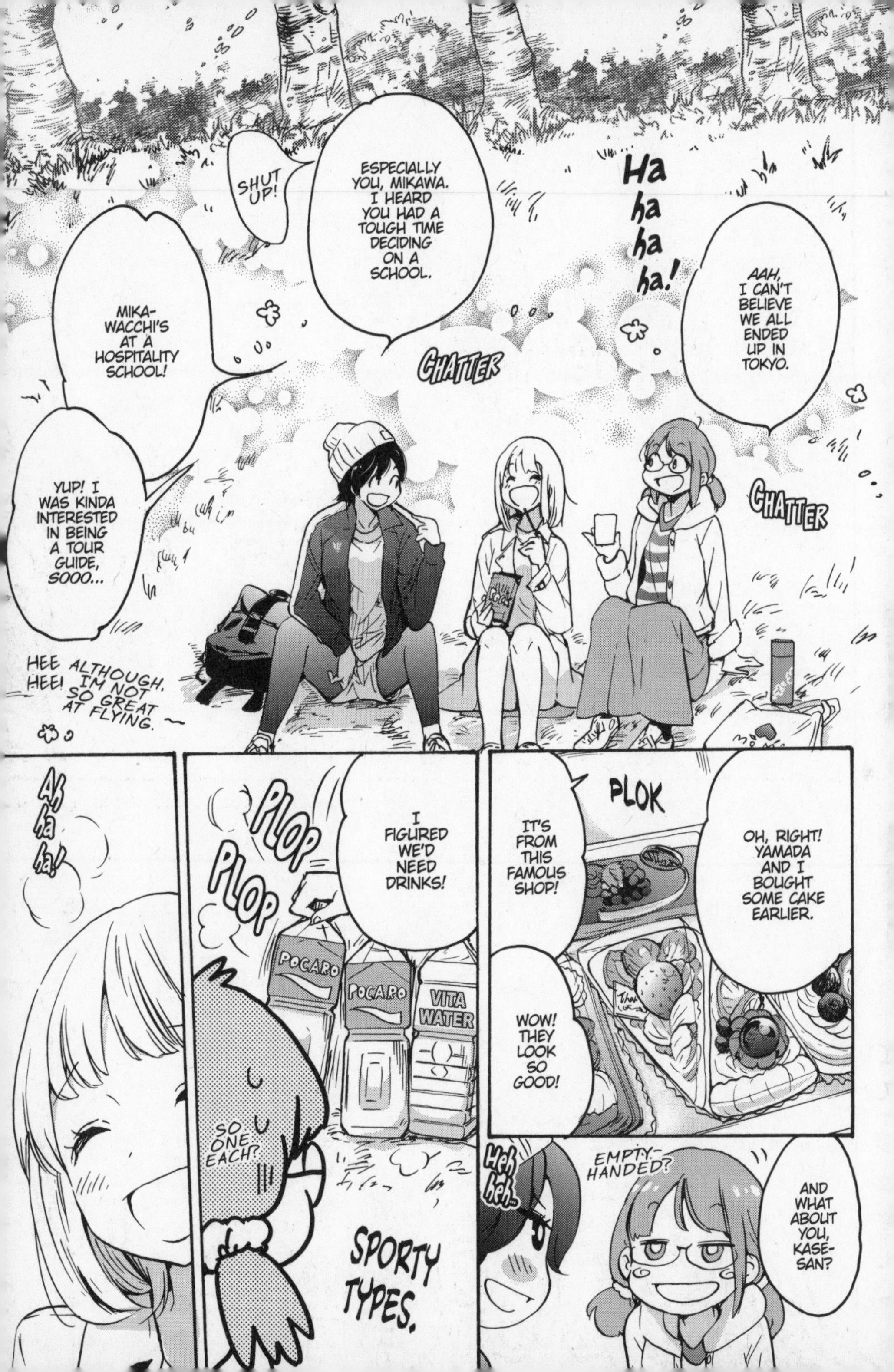
AAH, I CAN'T BELIEVE WE ALL ENDED UP IN TOKYO.
Ha ha ha ha!
CHATTER
ESPECIALLY YOU, MIKAWA. I HEARD YOU HAD A TOUGH TIME DECIDING ON A SCHOOL.
SHUT UP!
CHATTER
MIKA-WACCHI'S AT A HOSPITALITY SCHOOL!
YUP! I WAS KINDA INTERESTED IN BEING A TOUR GUIDE, SOOO...
ALTHOUGH, I'M NOT SO GREAT AT FLYING.
HEE HEE!
PLOK
OH, RIGHT! YAMADA AND I BOUGHT SOME CAKE EARLIER.
IT'S FROM THIS FAMOUS SHOP!
WOW! THEY LOOK SO GOOD!
AND WHAT ABOUT YOU, KASE-SAN?
EMPTY-HANDED?
Heh heh...
PLOP
PLOP
I FIGURED WE'D NEED DRINKS!
POCARO
POCARO
VITA WATER
SO ONE EACH?
SPORTY TYPES.
Ah ha ha!

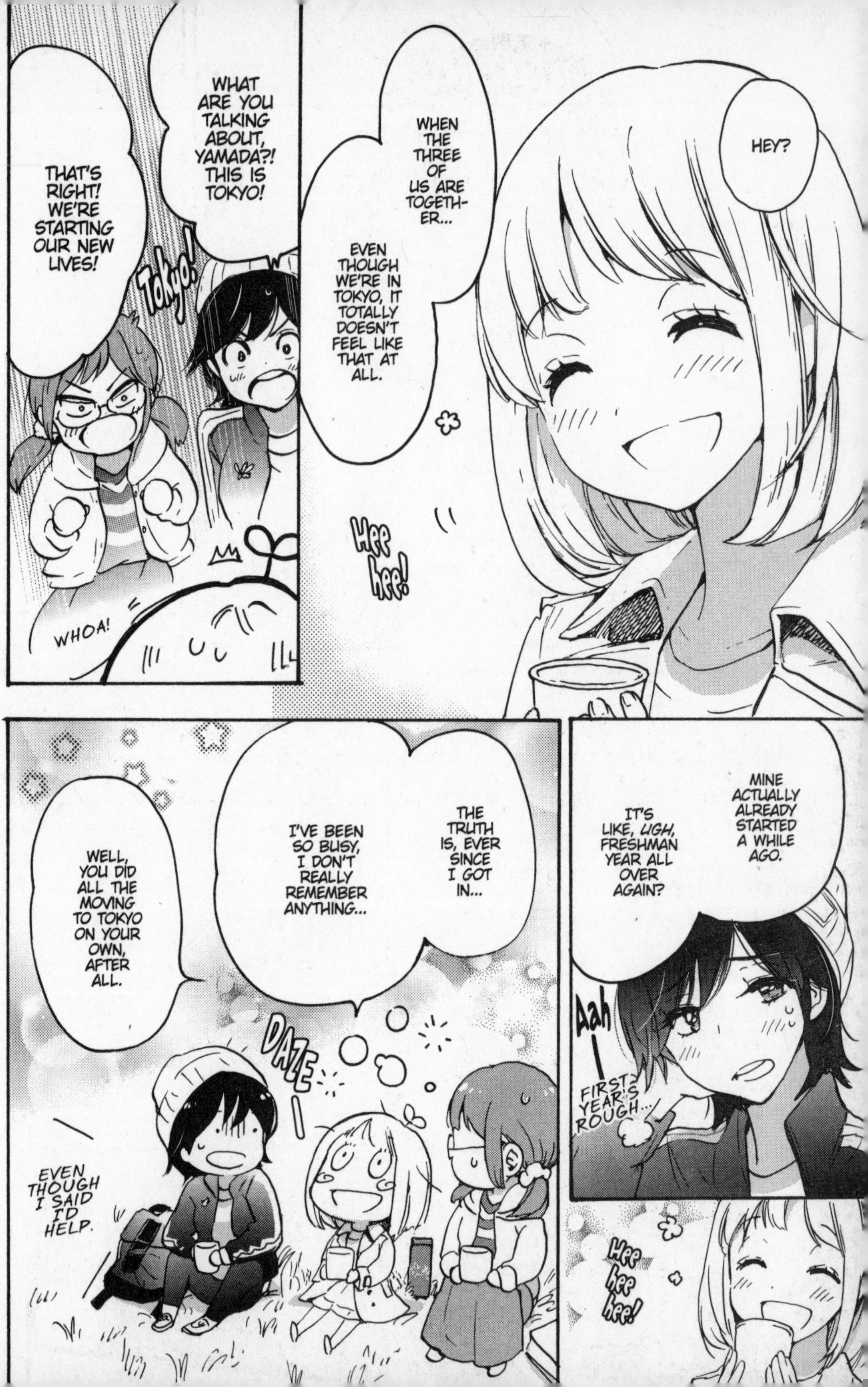
HEY?
WHEN THE THREE OF US ARE TOGETHER...
EVEN THOUGH WE'RE IN TOKYO, IT TOTALLY DOESN'T FEEL LIKE THAT AT ALL.
Hee hee!
WHAT ARE YOU TALKING ABOUT, YAMADA?! THIS IS TOKYO!
Tokyo!
THAT'S RIGHT! WE'RE STARTING OUR NEW LIVES!
WHOA!
MINE ACTUALLY ALREADY STARTED A WHILE AGO.
IT'S LIKE, *UGH*, FRESHMAN YEAR ALL OVER AGAIN?
Aah
FIRST YEAR'S ROUGH...
Hee hee hee!
THE TRUTH IS, EVER SINCE I GOT IN...
I'VE BEEN SO BUSY, I DON'T REALLY REMEMBER ANYTHING...
DAZE
WELL, YOU DID ALL THE MOVING TO TOKYO ON YOUR OWN, AFTER ALL.
EVEN THOUGH I SAID I'D HELP.

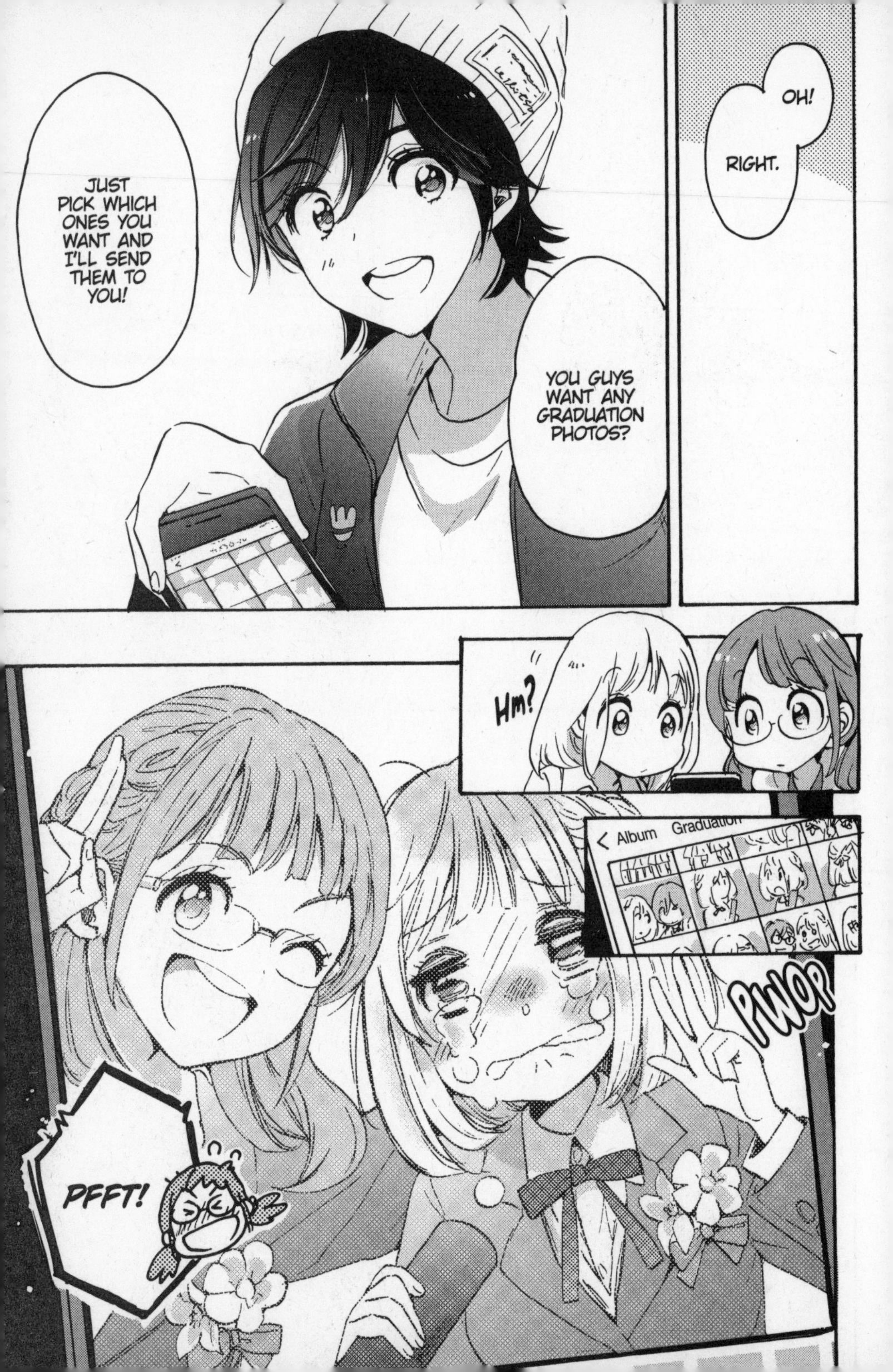
OH!
RIGHT.
YOU GUYS WANT ANY GRADUATION PHOTOS?
JUST PICK WHICH ONES YOU WANT AND I'LL SEND THEM TO YOU!
Hm?
Album Graduation
PWOP
PFFT!

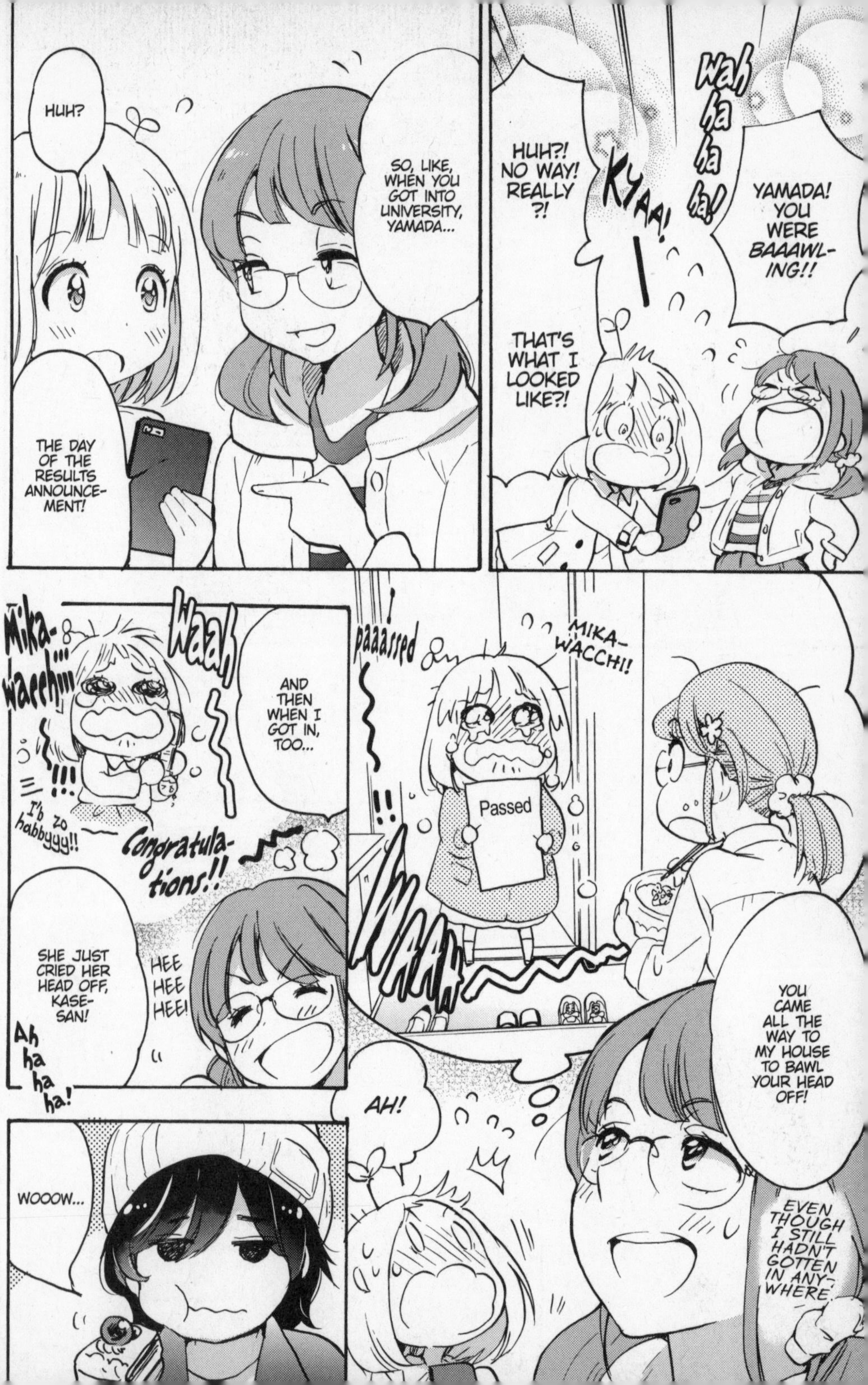
Wah ha ha ha!
YAMADA! YOU WERE BAAAWLING!!
KYAA!
HUH?! NO WAY! REALLY?!
THAT'S WHAT I LOOKED LIKE?!
SO, LIKE, WHEN YOU GOT INTO UNIVERSITY, YAMADA...
HUH?
THE DAY OF THE RESULTS ANNOUNCEMENT!
MIKA-WACCHI!!
paaassed
Passed
AND THEN WHEN I GOT IN, TOO...
Waaah
Mika-waech!!!
I'b zo habbyyy!!
Congratulations!!
SHE JUST CRIED HER HEAD OFF, KASE-SAN!
HEE HEE HEE!
Ah ha ha ha!
YOU CAME ALL THE WAY TO MY HOUSE TO BAWL YOUR HEAD OFF!
EVEN THOUGH I STILL HADN'T GOTTEN IN ANYWHERE.
AH!
WOOOW...

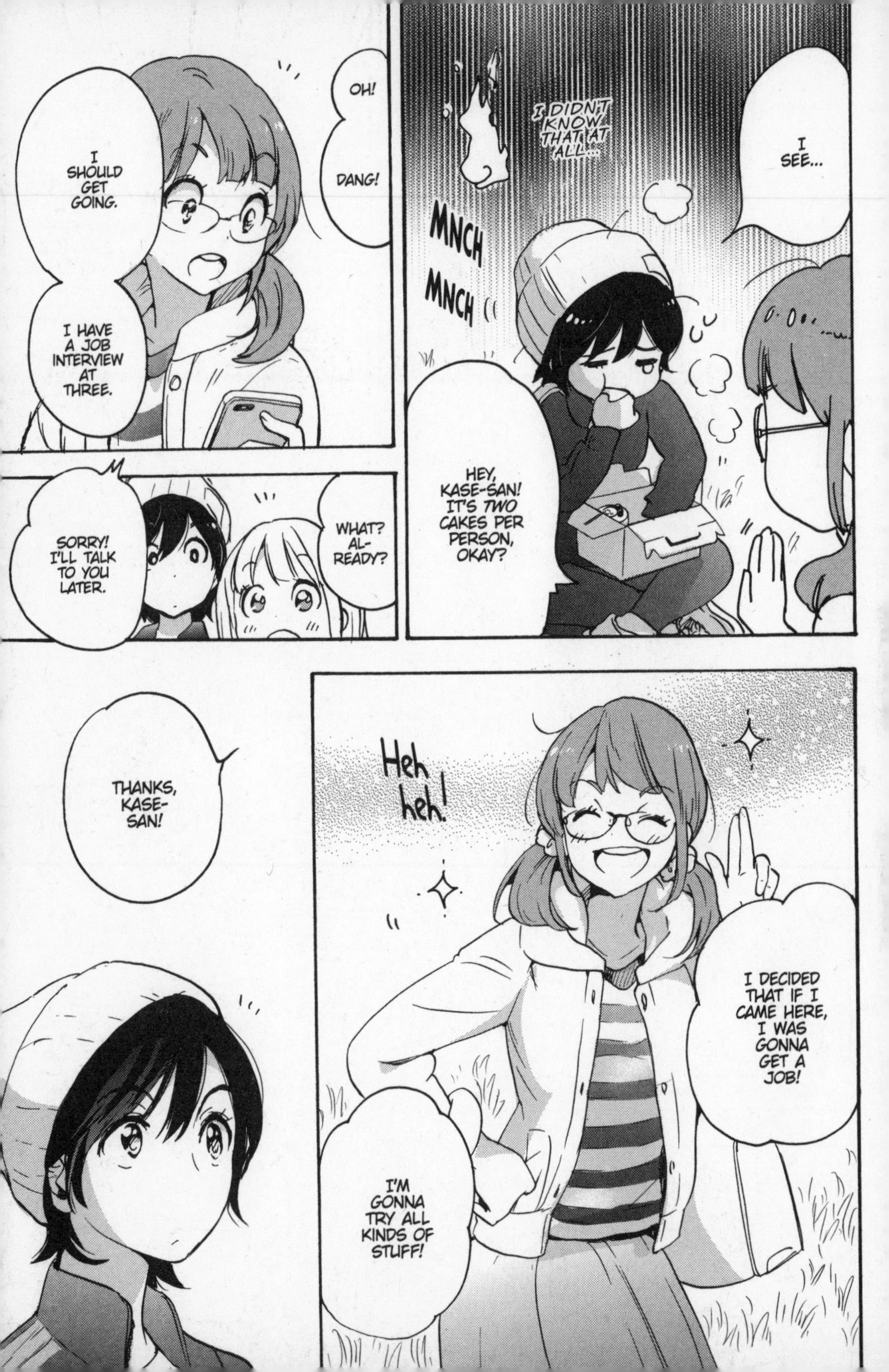
I SEE...
I DIDN'T KNOW THAT AT ALL...
MNCH MNCH
HEY, KASE-SAN! IT'S *TWO* CAKES PER PERSON, OKAY?
OH! DANG!
I SHOULD GET GOING.
I HAVE A JOB INTERVIEW AT THREE.
WHAT? AL-READY?
SORRY! I'LL TALK TO YOU LATER.
Heh heh!
I DECIDED THAT IF I CAME HERE, I WAS GONNA GET A JOB!
I'M GONNA TRY ALL KINDS OF STUFF!
THANKS, KASE-SAN!

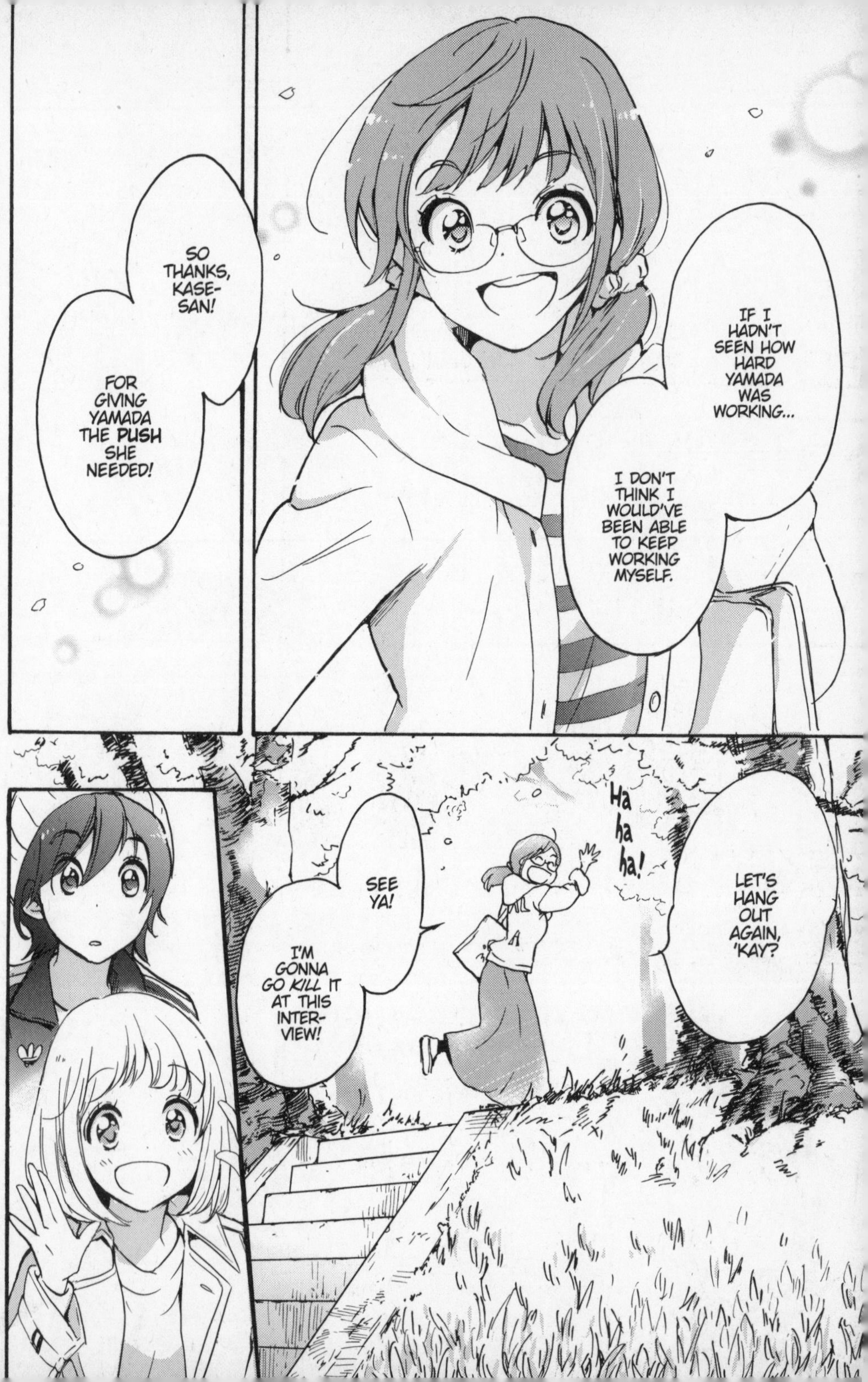
IF I HADN'T SEEN HOW HARD YAMADA WAS WORKING...
I DON'T THINK I WOULD'VE BEEN ABLE TO KEEP WORKING MYSELF.
SO THANKS, KASE-SAN!
FOR GIVING YAMADA THE PUSH SHE NEEDED!
LET'S HANG OUT AGAIN, 'KAY?
Ha ha ha!
SEE YA!
I'M GONNA GO KILL IT AT THIS INTERVIEW!

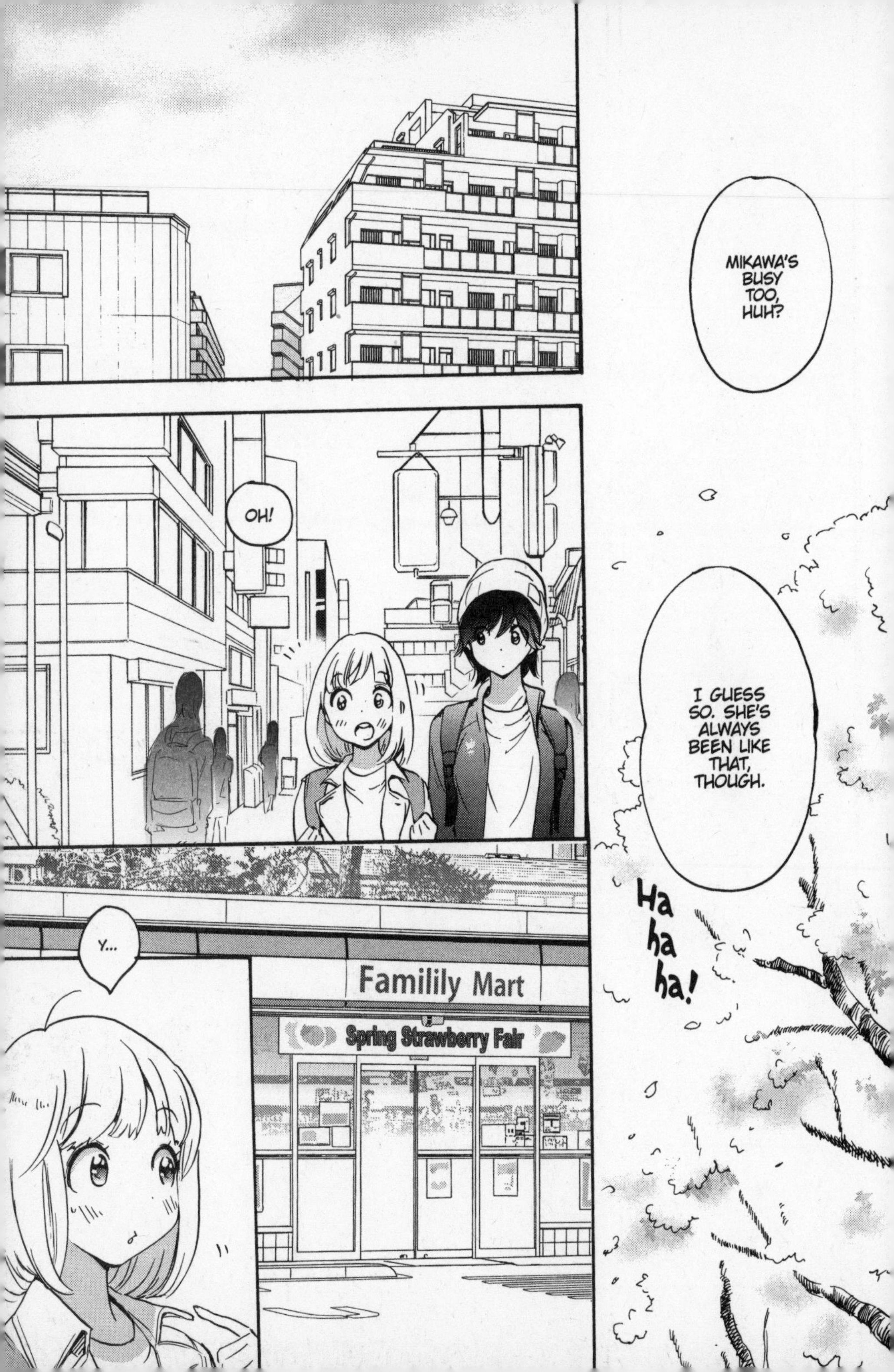
MIKAWA'S BUSY TOO, HUH?
I GUESS SO. SHE'S ALWAYS BEEN LIKE THAT, THOUGH.
Ha ha ha!
OH!
Familily Mart
Spring Strawberry Fair
Y...

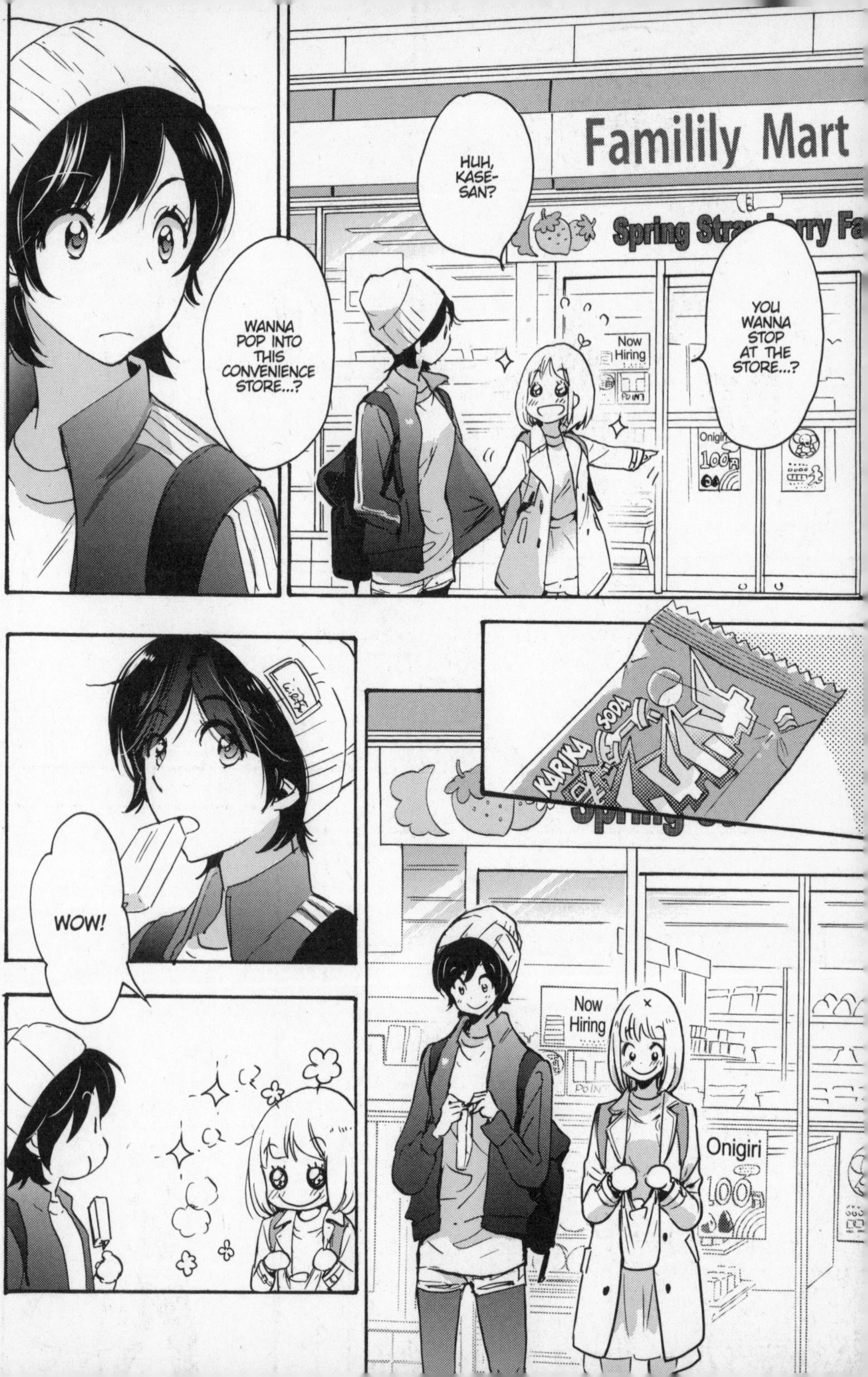
Familily Mart
Spring Straw
erry Fa
HUH, KASE-SAN?
YOU WANNA STOP AT THE STORE...?
Now Hiring
Onigiri
WANNA POP INTO THIS CONVENIENCE STORE...?
KARIKA SODA
Now Hiring
Onigiri
WOW!

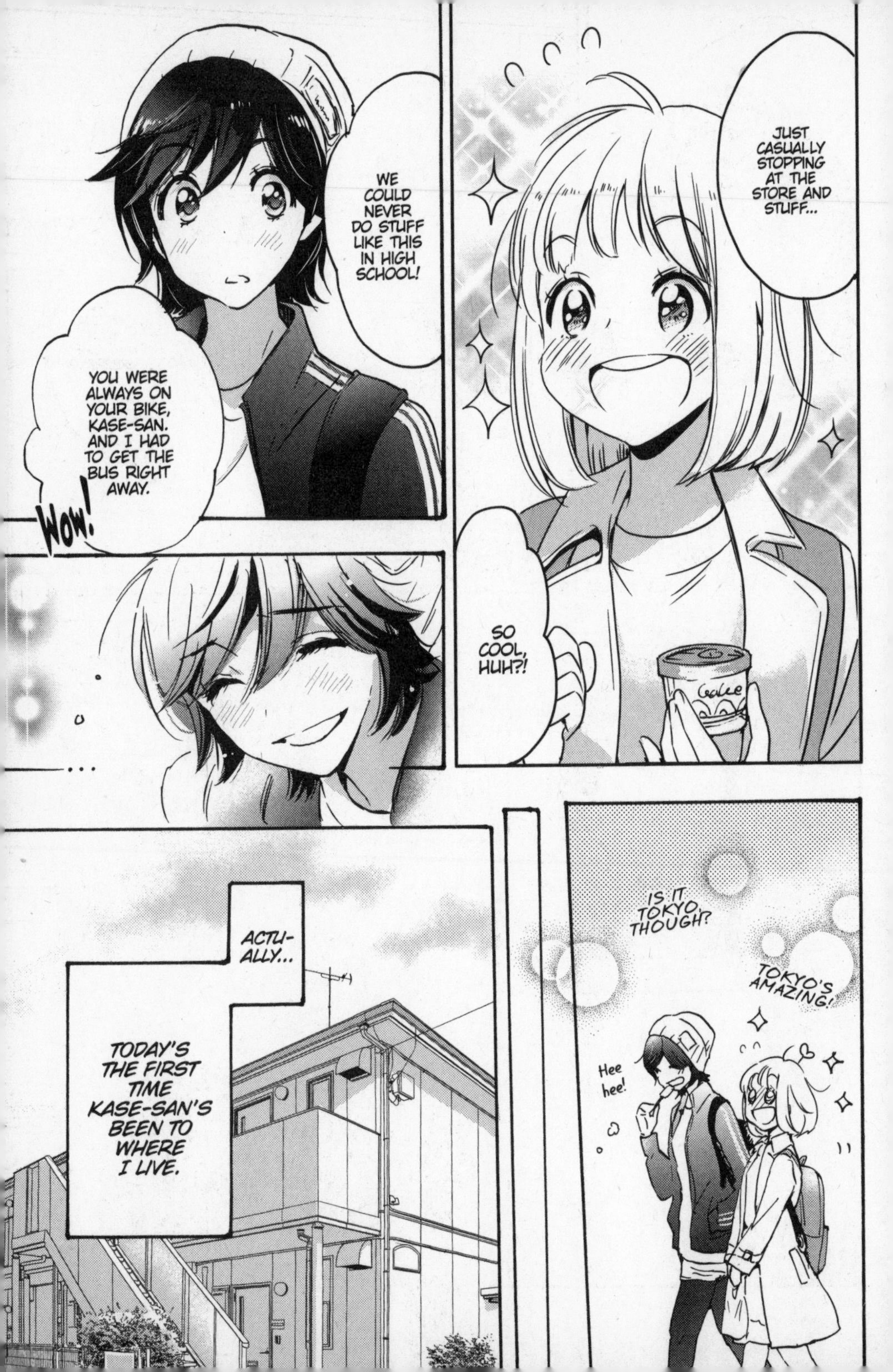
JUST CASUALLY STOPPING AT THE STORE AND STUFF...
SO COOL, HUH?!
WE COULD NEVER DO STUFF LIKE THIS IN HIGH SCHOOL!
YOU WERE ALWAYS ON YOUR BIKE, KASE-SAN. AND I HAD TO GET THE BUS RIGHT AWAY.
WOW!
—...
TOKYO'S AMAZING!
IS IT TOKYO, THOUGH?
Hee hee!
ACTU-ALLY...
TODAY'S THE FIRST TIME KASE-SAN'S BEEN TO WHERE I LIVE.

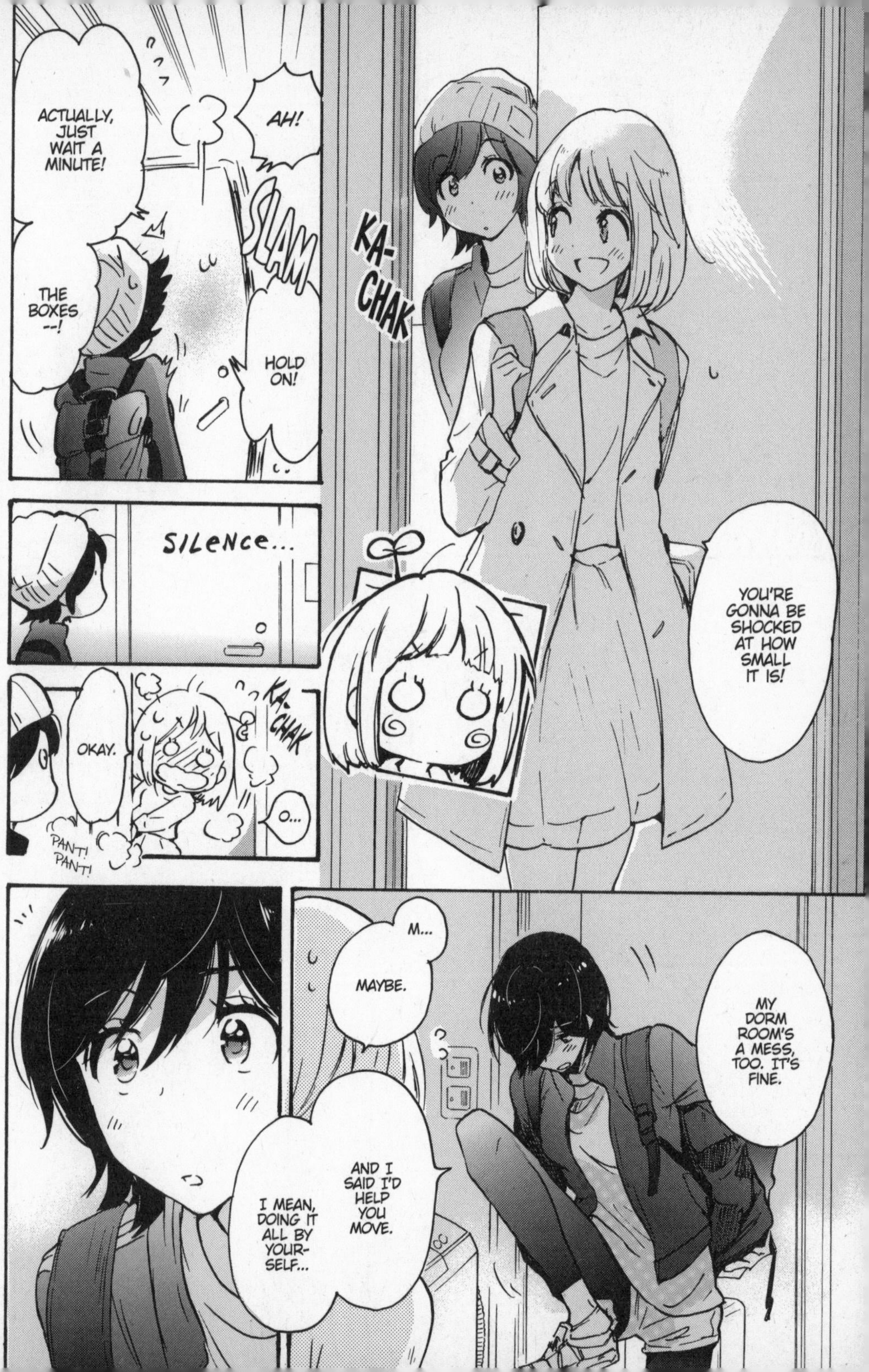
KA-CHAK
YOU'RE GONNA BE SHOCKED AT HOW SMALL IT IS!
AH!
SLAM
HOLD ON!
ACTUALLY, JUST WAIT A MINUTE!
THE BOXES --!
SILENCE...
KA-CHAK
O...
OKAY.
PANT! PANT!
MY DORM ROOM'S A MESS, TOO. IT'S FINE.
M...
MAYBE.
AND I SAID I'D HELP YOU MOVE.
I MEAN, DOING IT ALL BY YOURSELF...

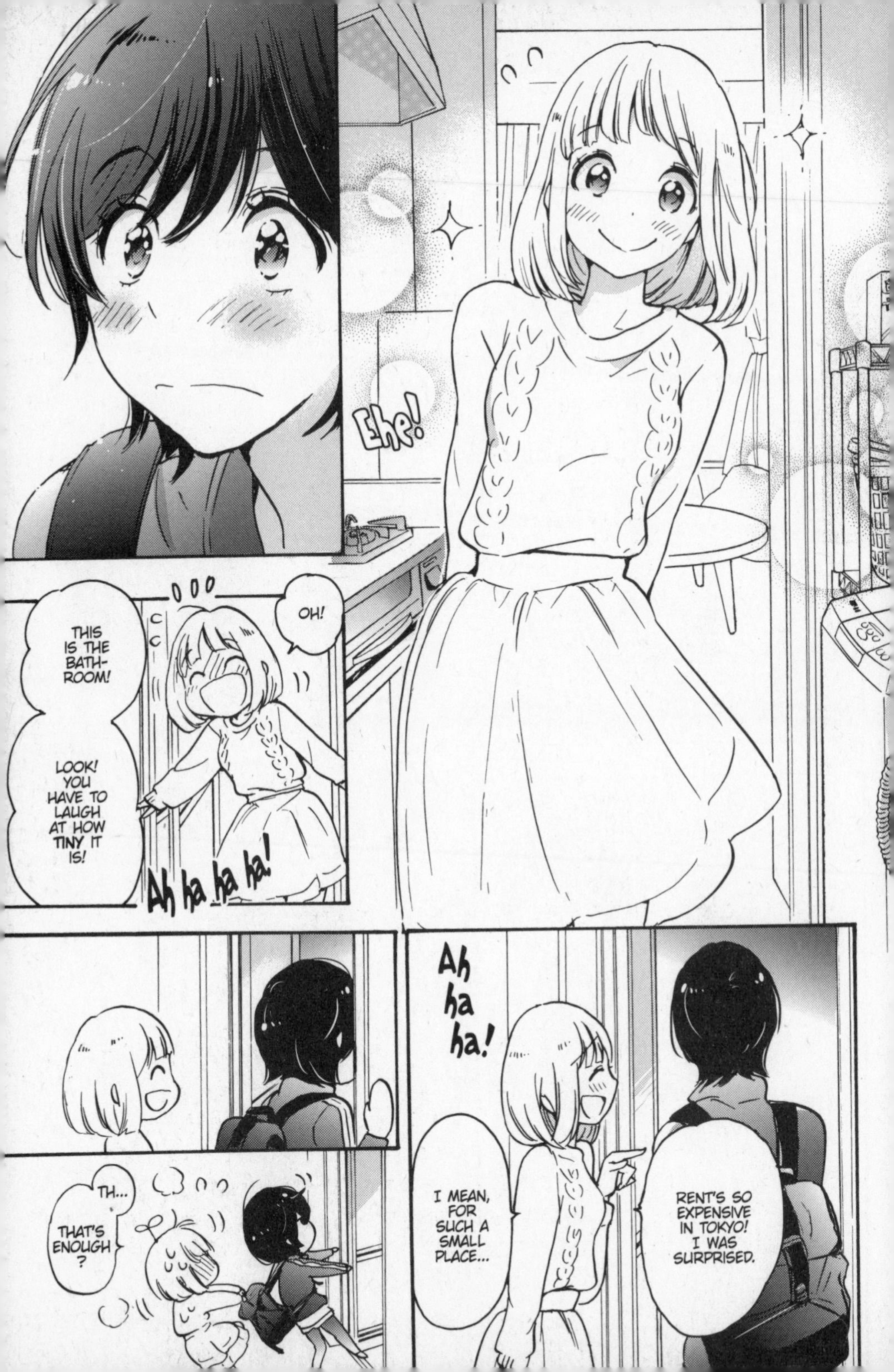
Ehe!
OH!
THIS IS THE BATHROOM!
LOOK! YOU HAVE TO LAUGH AT HOW TINY IT IS!
Ah ha ha ha!
Ah ha ha!
RENT'S SO EXPENSIVE IN TOKYO! I WAS SURPRISED.
I MEAN, FOR SUCH A SMALL PLACE...
TH... THAT'S ENOUGH?

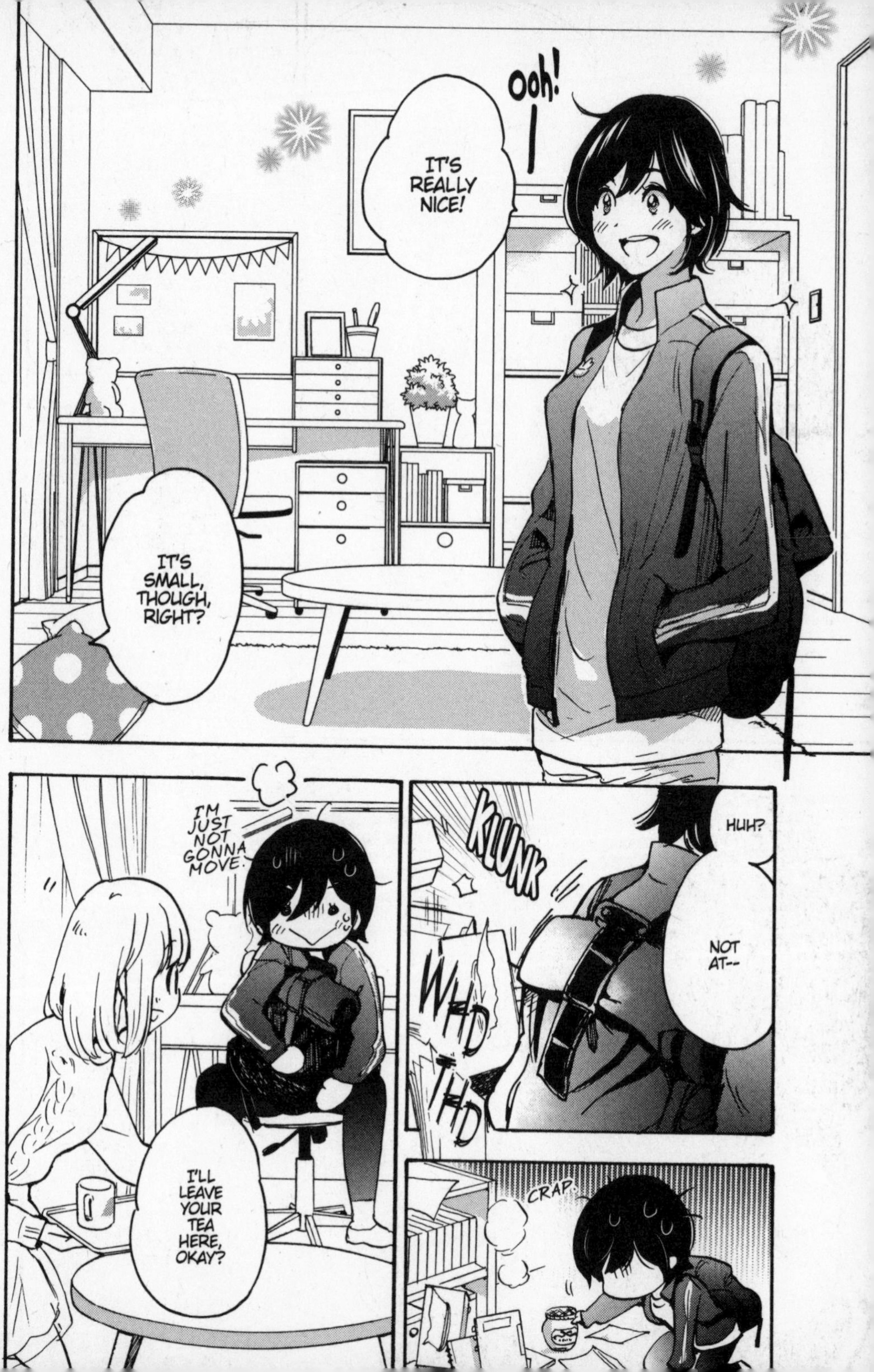
Ooh!
IT'S REALLY NICE!
IT'S SMALL, THOUGH, RIGHT?
HUH?
NOT AT--
KLUNK
WHD THD
CRAP.
I'M JUST NOT GONNA MOVE.
I'LL LEAVE YOUR TEA HERE, OKAY?

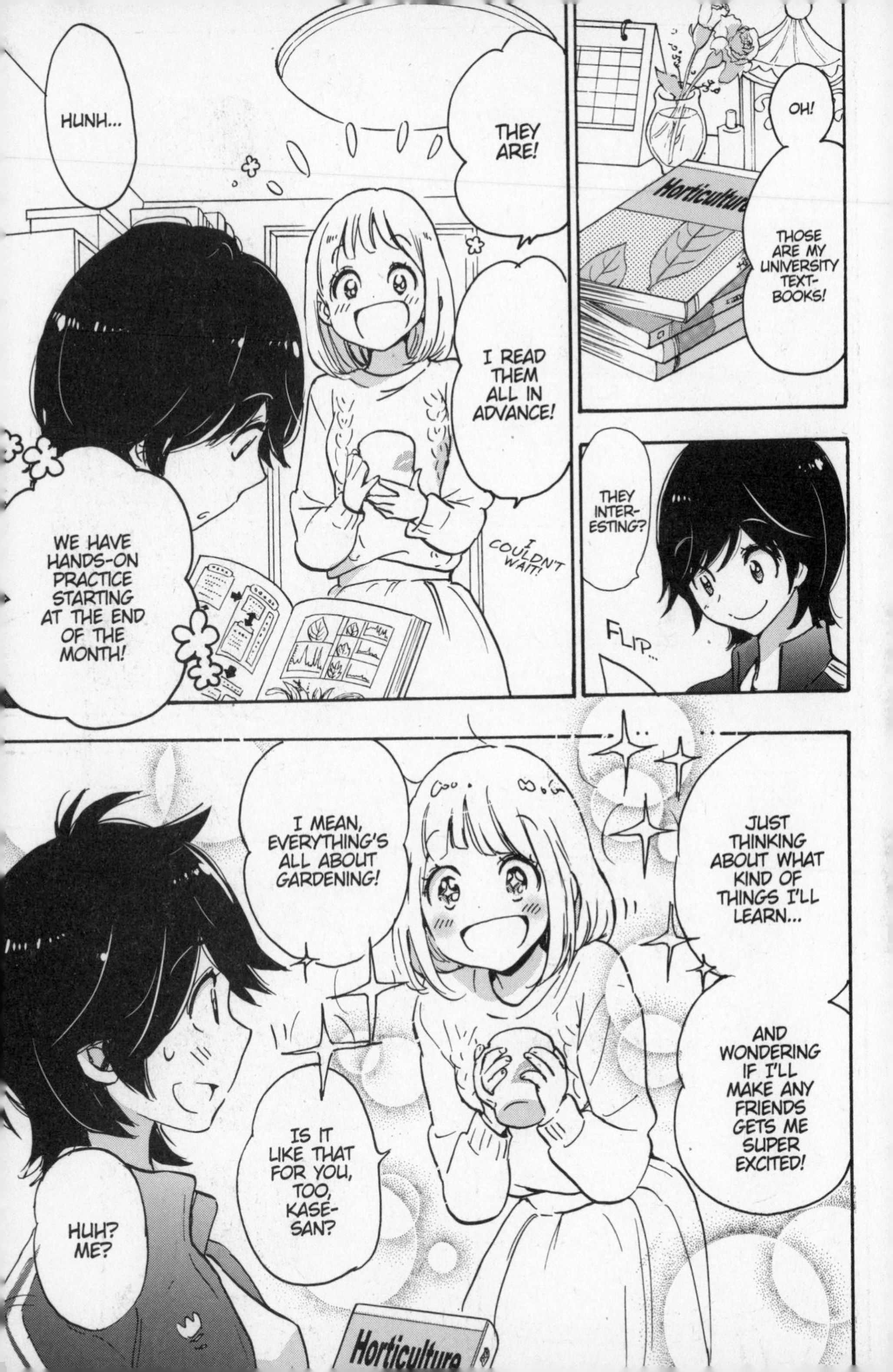
OH!
THOSE ARE MY UNIVERSITY TEXT-BOOKS!
Horticulture
THEY INTERESTING?
FLIP...
THEY ARE!
I READ THEM ALL IN ADVANCE!
I COULDN'T WAIT!
HUNH...
WE HAVE HANDS-ON PRACTICE STARTING AT THE END OF THE MONTH!
JUST THINKING ABOUT WHAT KIND OF THINGS I'LL LEARN...
AND WONDERING IF I'LL MAKE ANY FRIENDS GETS ME SUPER EXCITED!
I MEAN, EVERYTHING'S ALL ABOUT GARDENING!
IS IT LIKE THAT FOR YOU, TOO, KASE-SAN?
HUH? ME?
Horticulture

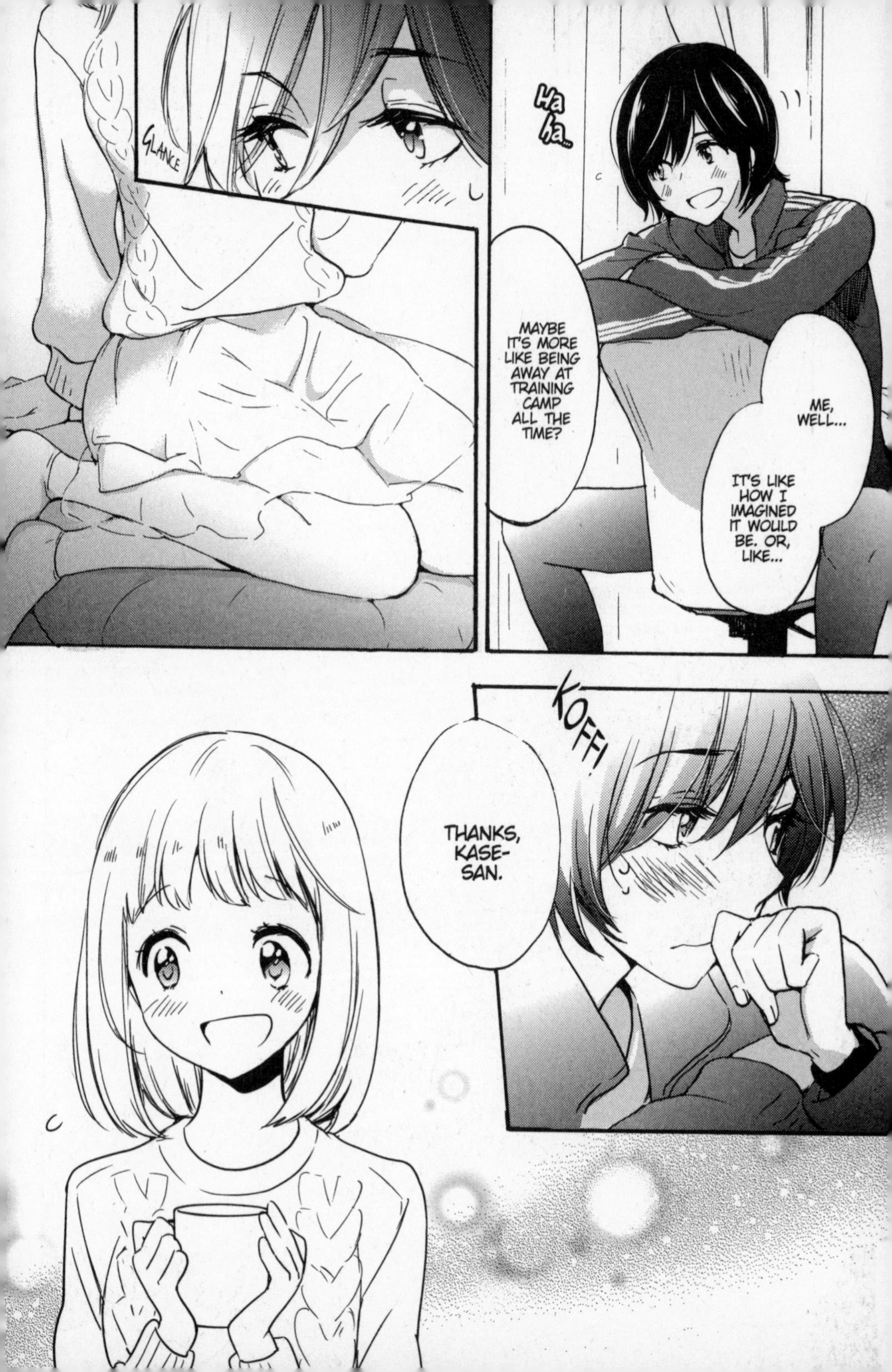
Ha ha...
ME, WELL...
IT'S LIKE HOW I IMAGINED IT WOULD BE. OR, LIKE...
MAYBE IT'S MORE LIKE BEING AWAY AT TRAINING CAMP ALL THE TIME?
GLANCE
KOFF!
THANKS, KASE-SAN.

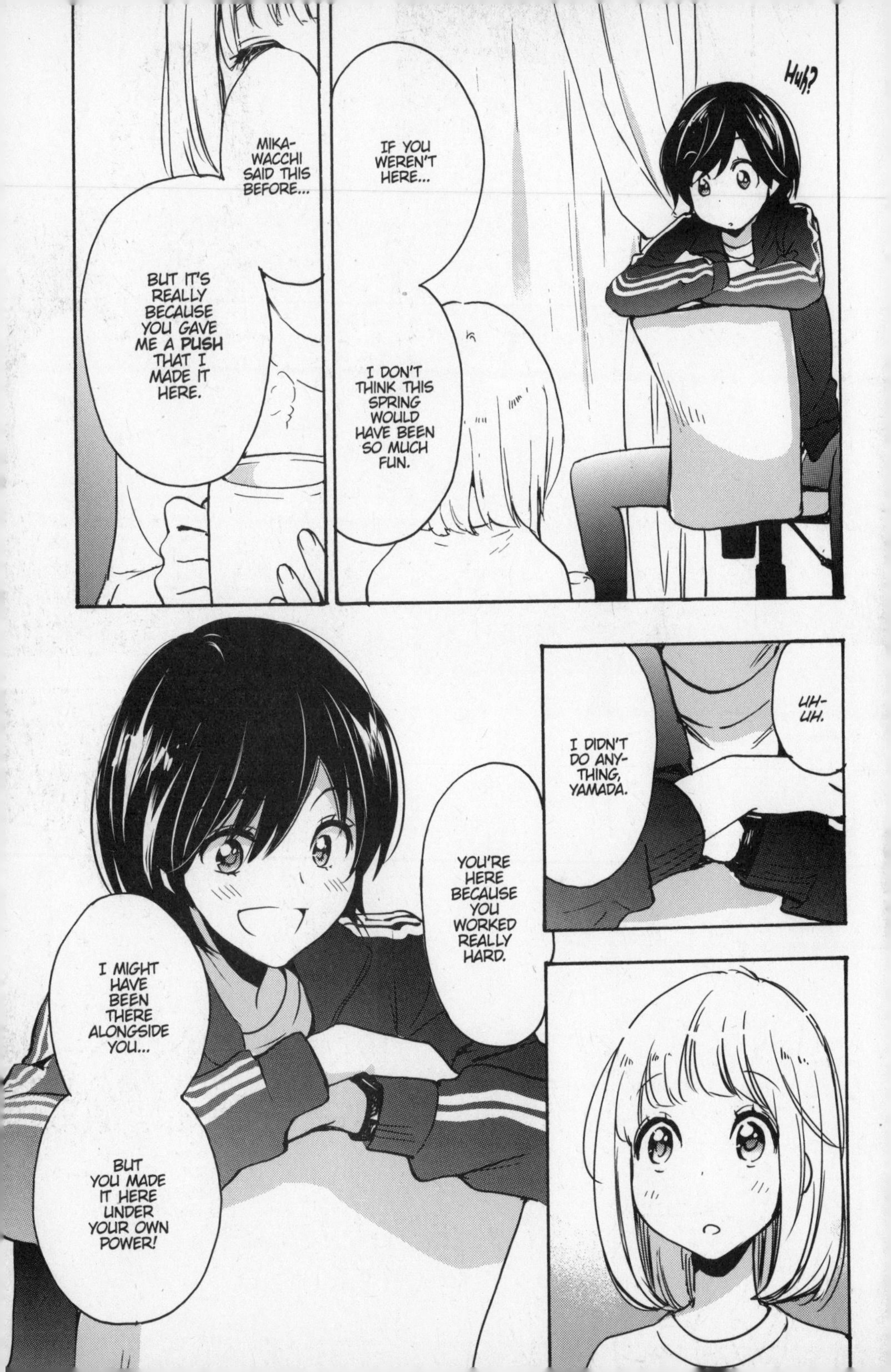
Huh?
IF YOU WEREN'T HERE...
I DON'T THINK THIS SPRING WOULD HAVE BEEN SO MUCH FUN.
MIKA-WACCHI SAID THIS BEFORE...
BUT IT'S REALLY BECAUSE YOU GAVE ME A PUSH THAT I MADE IT HERE.
UH-UH.
I DIDN'T DO ANY-THING, YAMADA.
YOU'RE HERE BECAUSE YOU WORKED REALLY HARD.
I MIGHT HAVE BEEN THERE ALONGSIDE YOU...
BUT YOU MADE IT HERE UNDER YOUR OWN POWER!

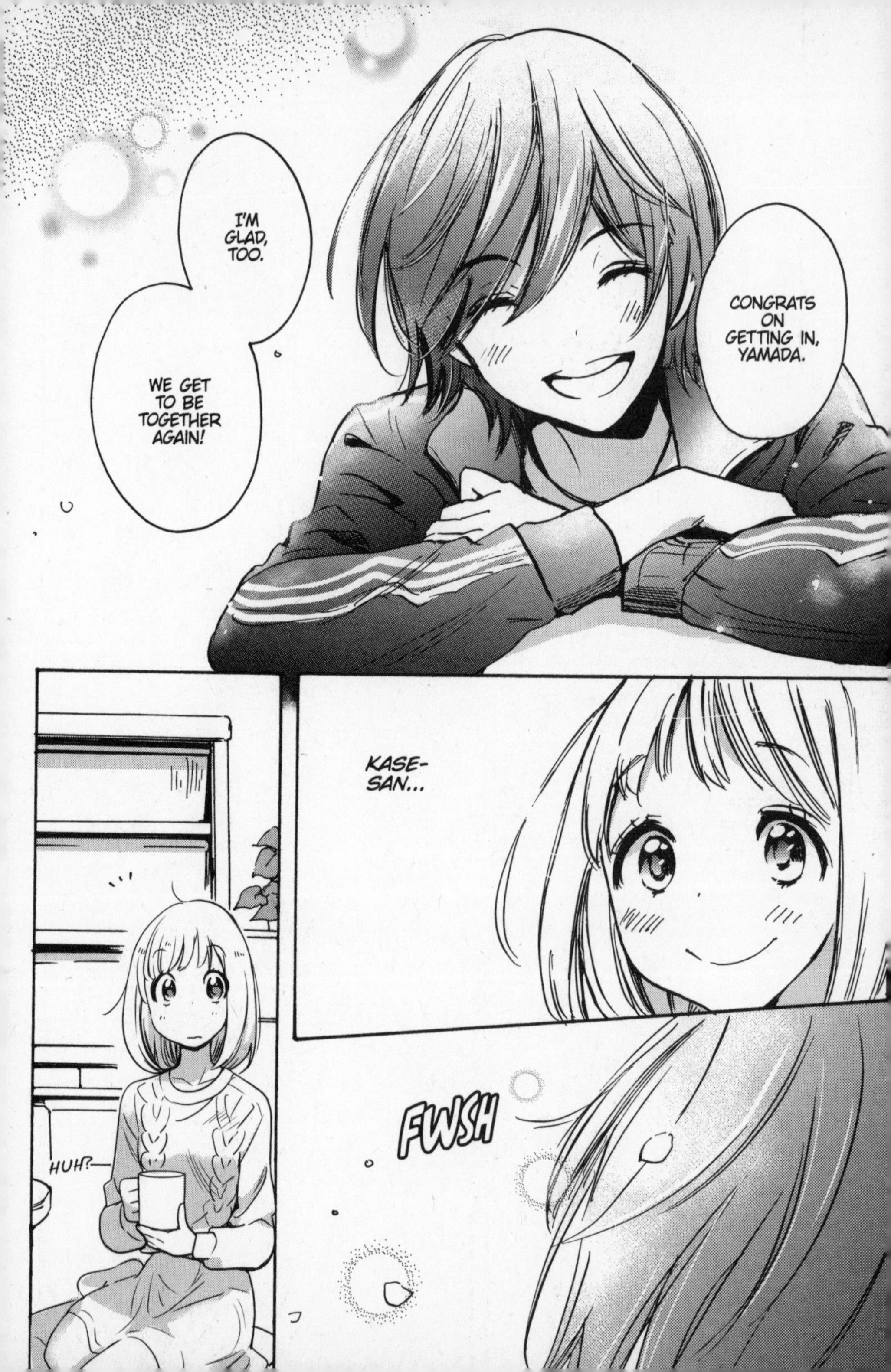
CONGRATS ON GETTING IN, YAMADA.
I'M GLAD, TOO.
WE GET TO BE TOGETHER AGAIN!
KASE-SAN...
FWSH
HUH?—

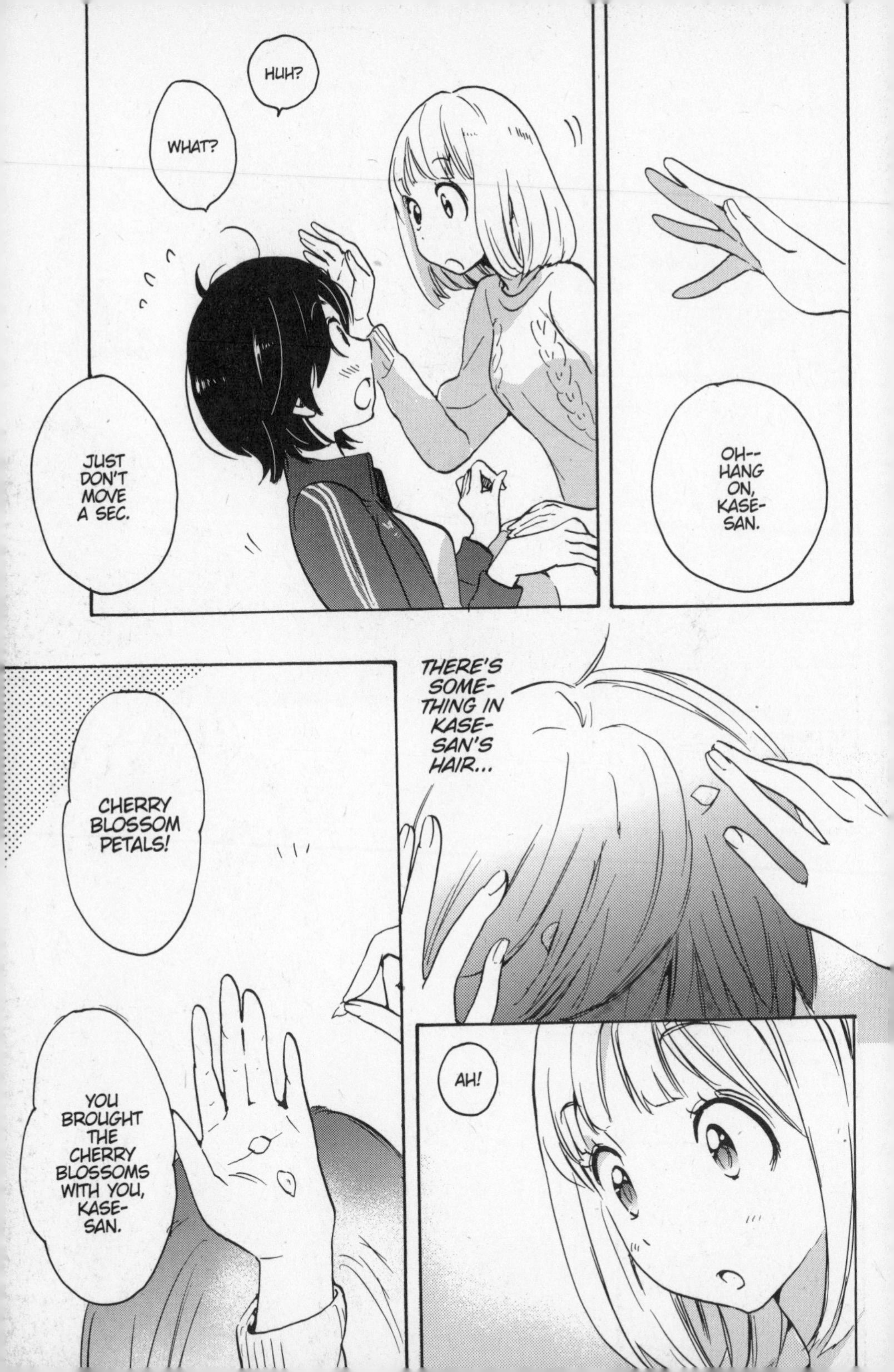
OH-- HANG ON, KASE-SAN.
HUH?
WHAT?
JUST DON'T MOVE A SEC.
THERE'S SOME-THING IN KASE-SAN'S HAIR...
CHERRY BLOSSOM PETALS!
AH!
YOU BROUGHT THE CHERRY BLOSSOMS WITH YOU, KASE-SAN.

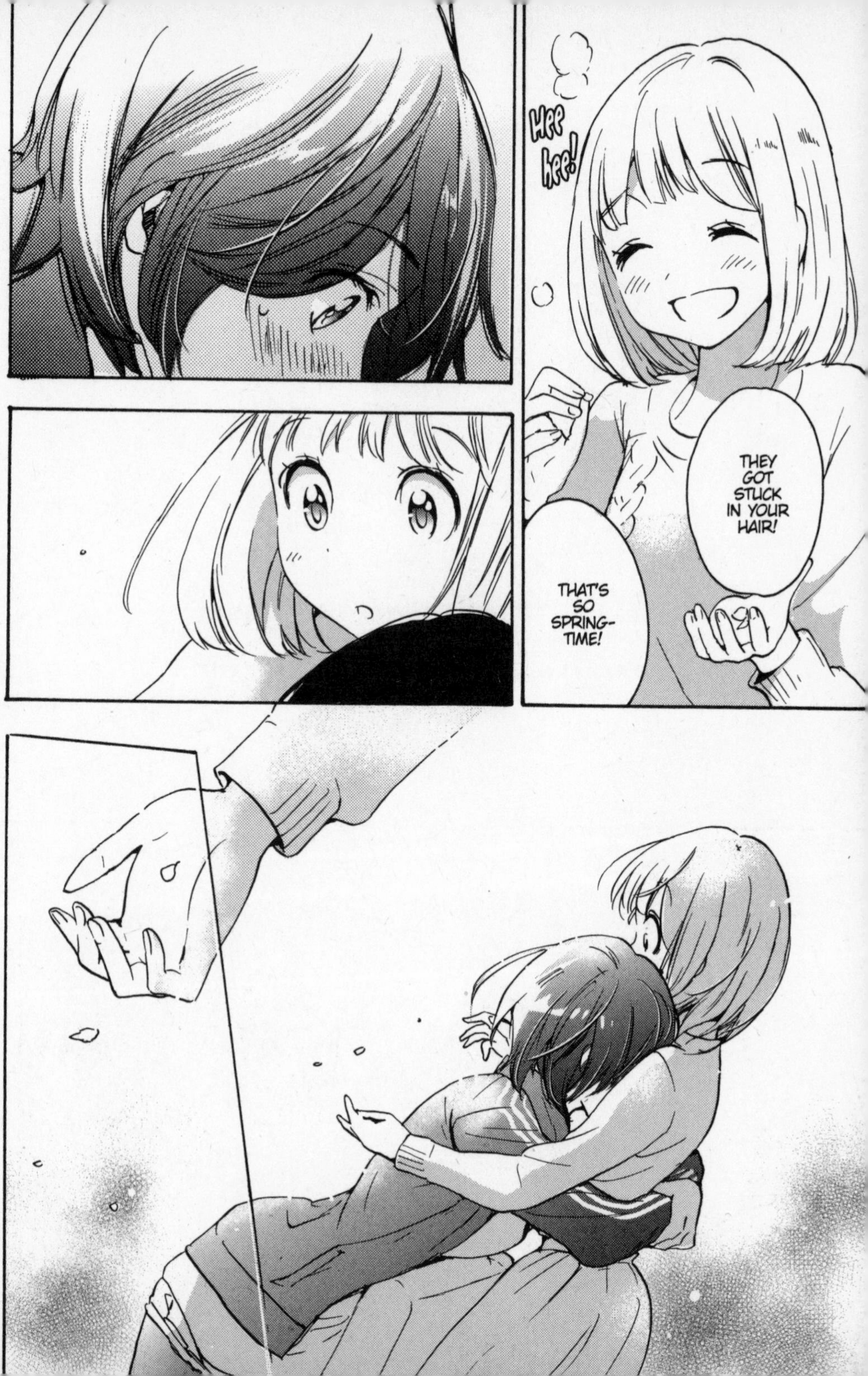
Hee hee!
THEY GOT STUCK IN YOUR HAIR!
THAT'S SO SPRING-TIME!

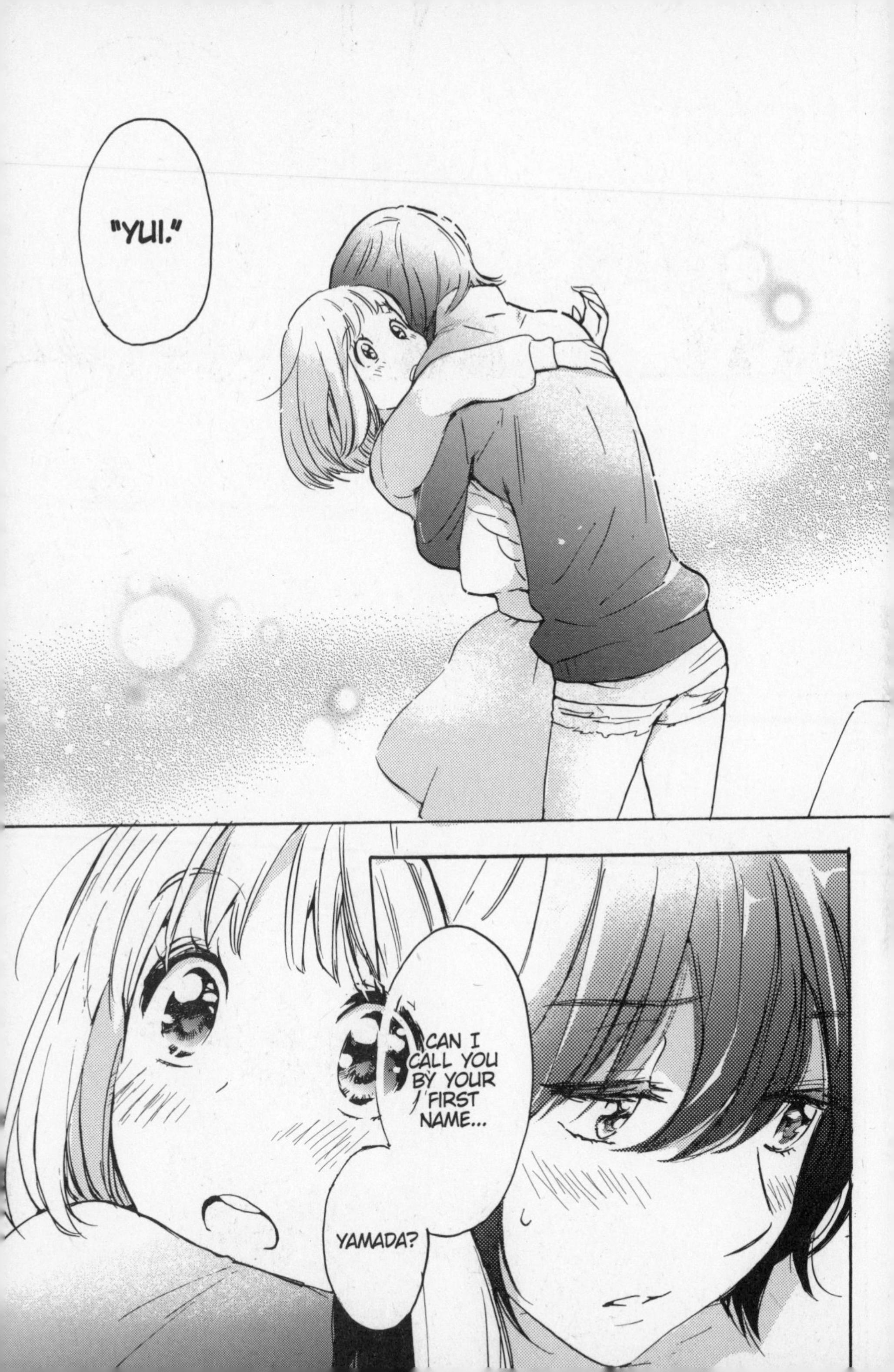
"YUI."
CAN I CALL YOU BY YOUR FIRST NAME...
YAMADA?

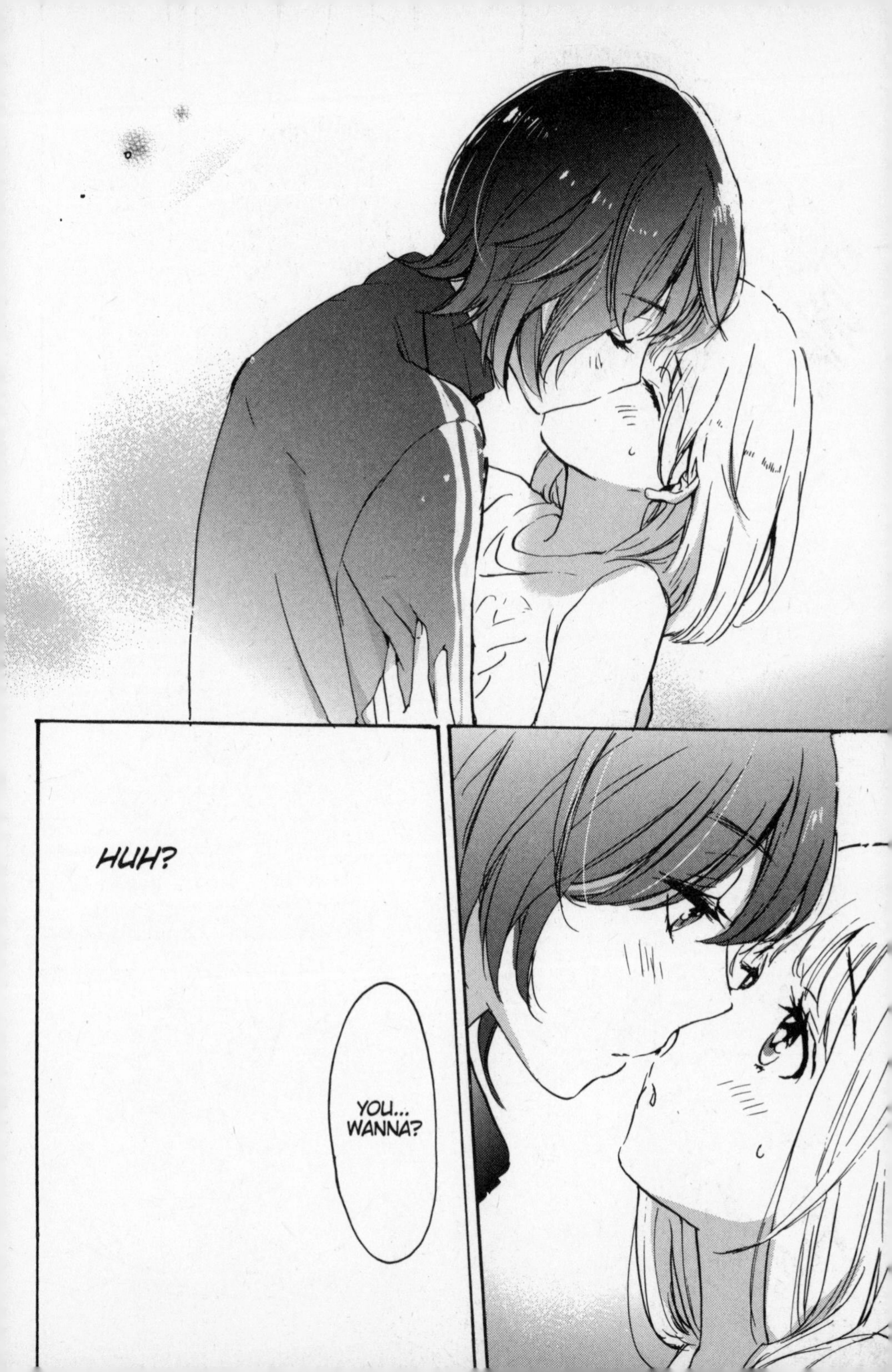
YOU... WANNA?
HUH?

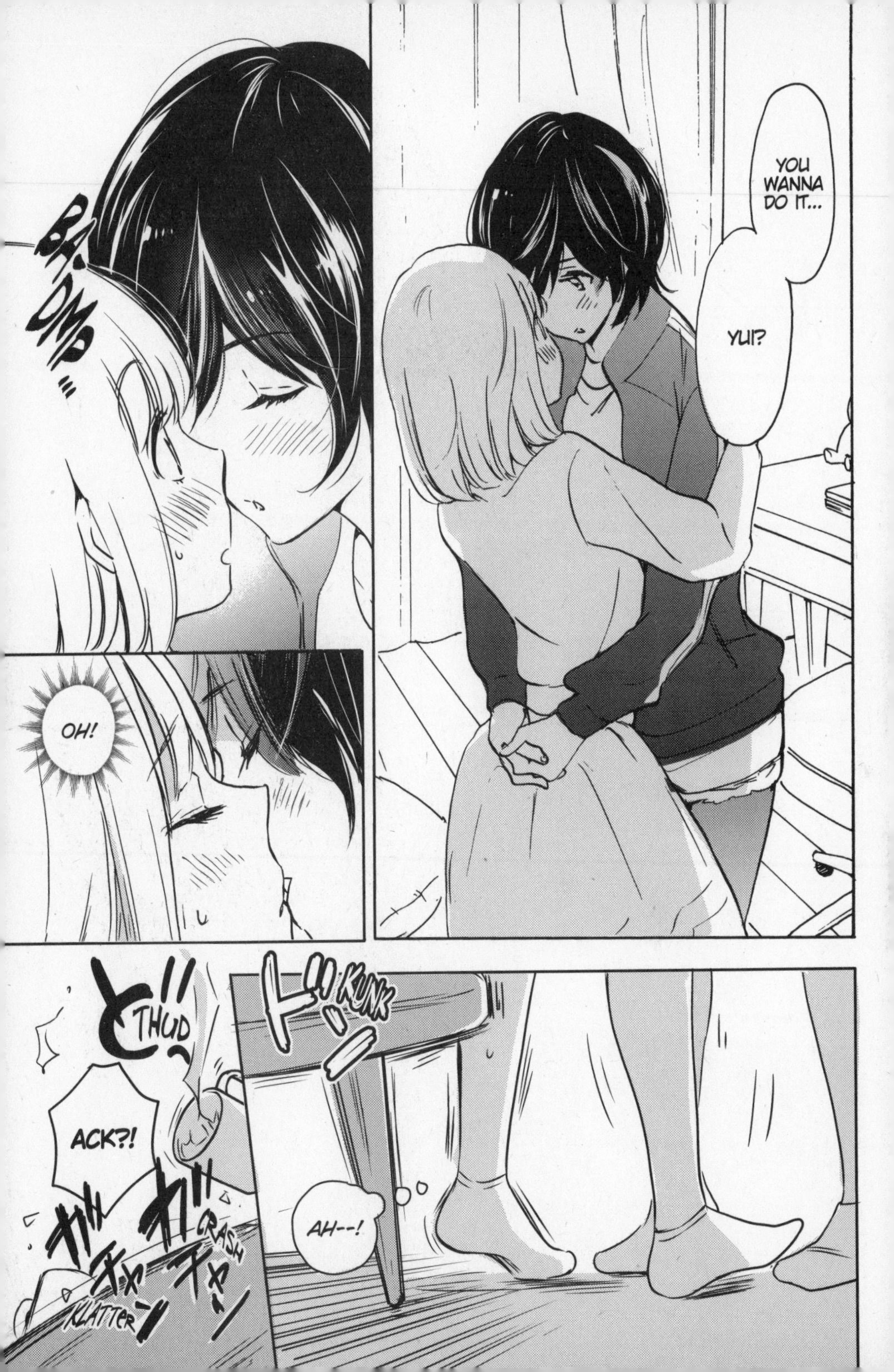
YOU WANNA DO IT...
YUI?
BA-DMP...
OH!
KUNK
THUD
ACK?!
AH--!
CRASH
KLATTER

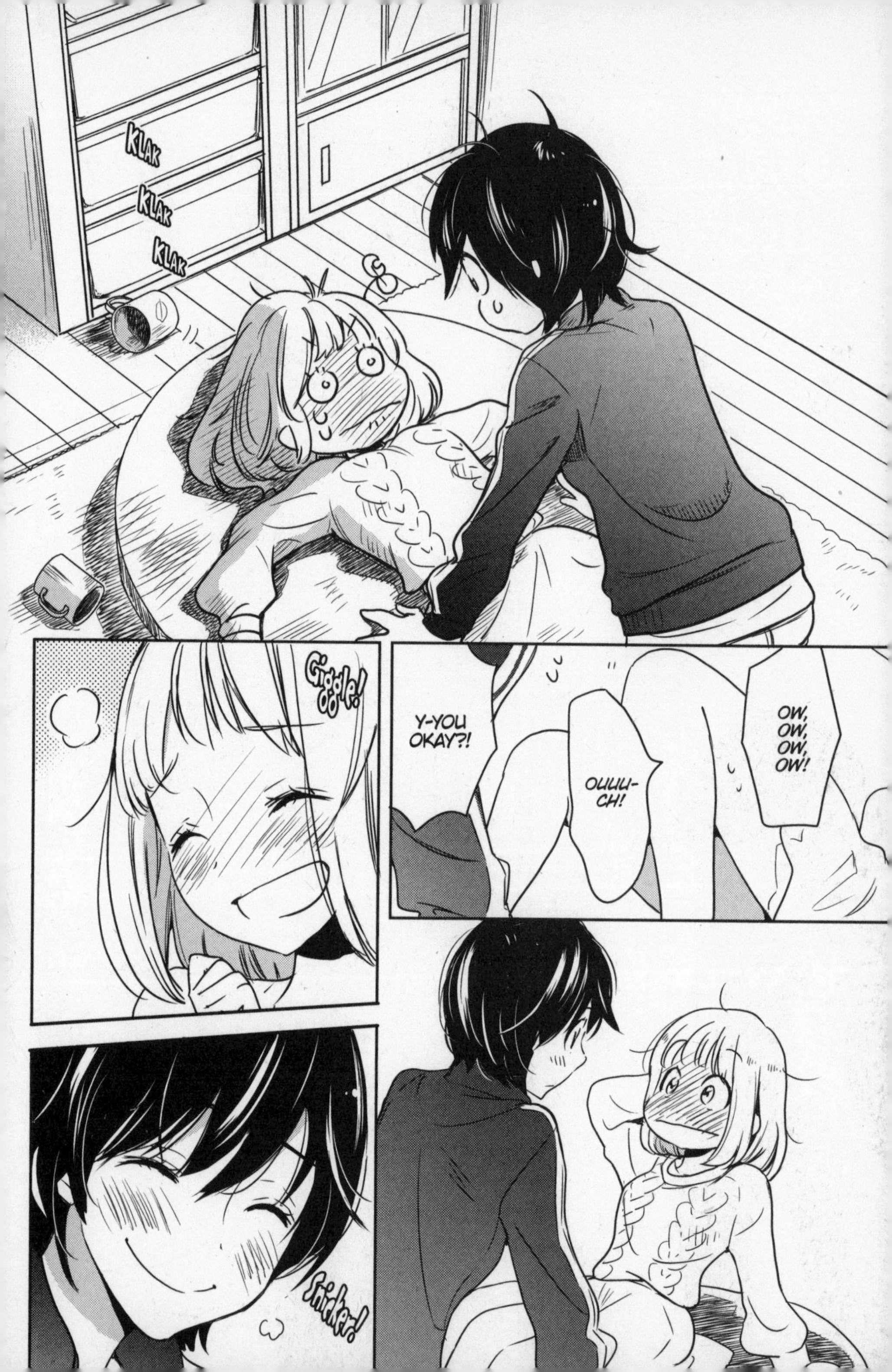
KLAK
KLAK
KLAK
OW, OW, OW, OW!
Y-YOU OKAY?!
OUUU-CH!
Giggle!
Snicker!

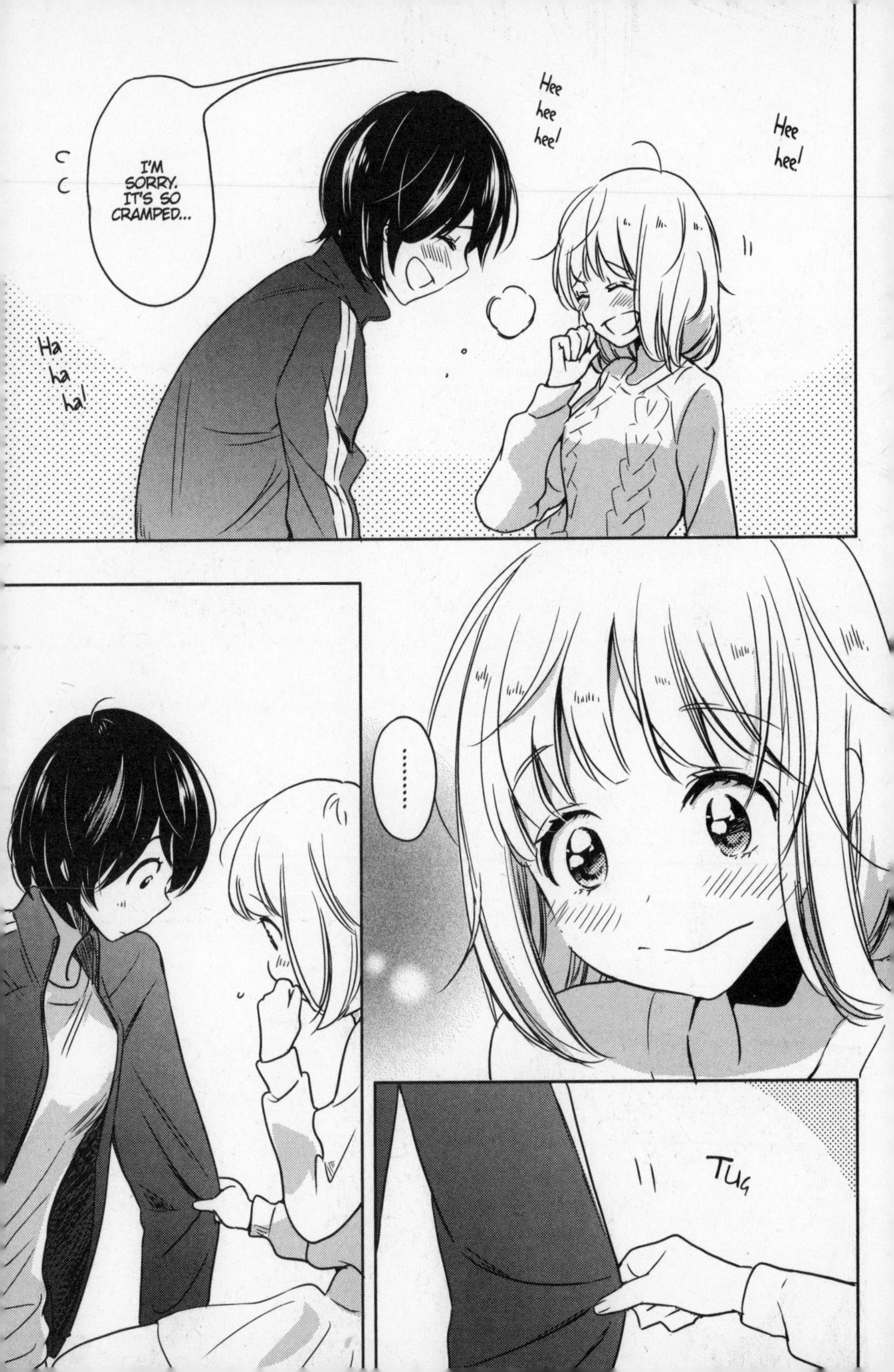
Hee hee!
Hee hee hee!
I'M SORRY. IT'S SO CRAMPED...
Ha ha ha!
......
TUG

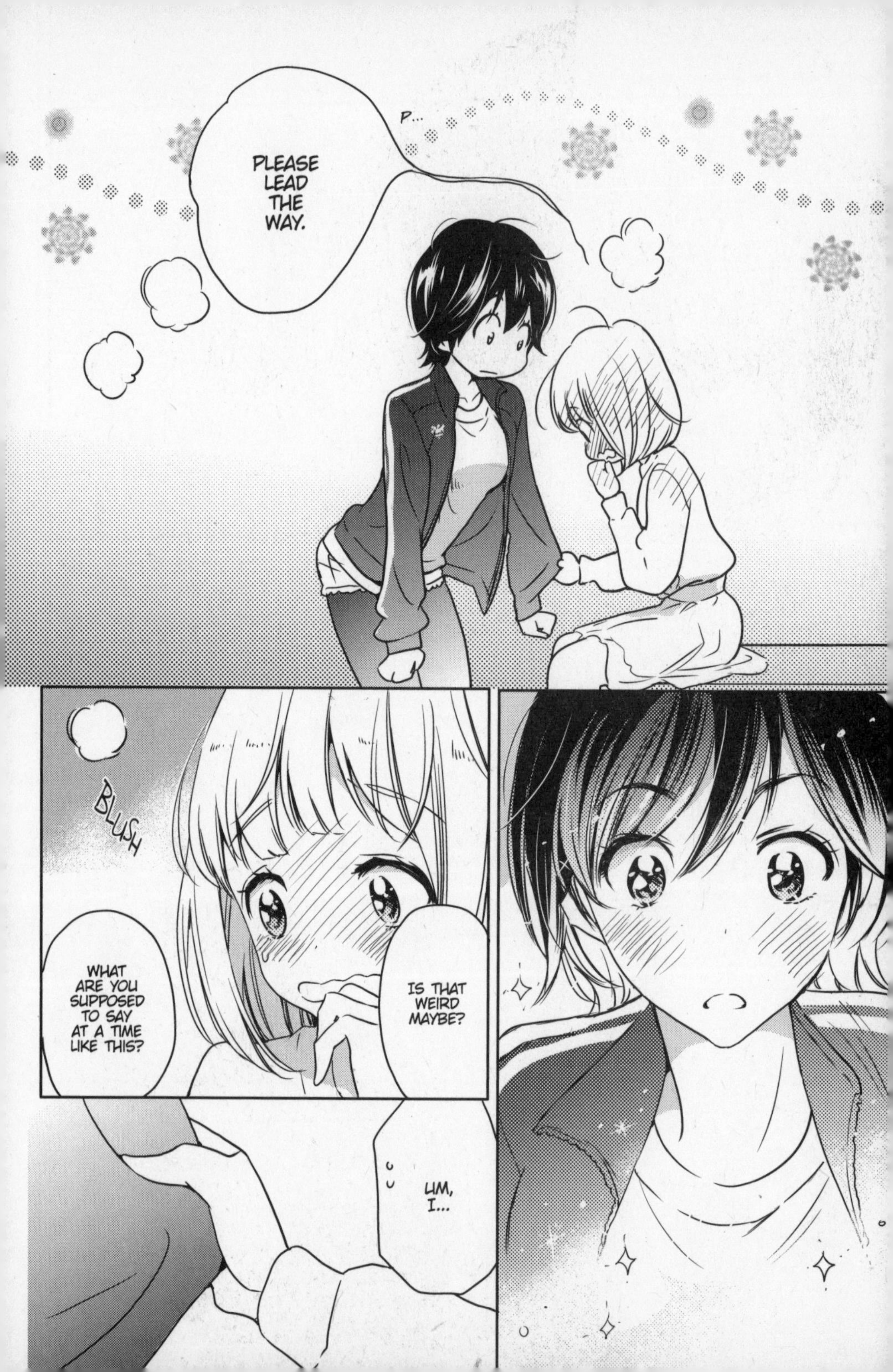
P...
PLEASE LEAD THE WAY.
BLUSH
IS THAT WEIRD MAYBE?
WHAT ARE YOU SUPPOSED TO SAY AT A TIME LIKE THIS?
UM, I...

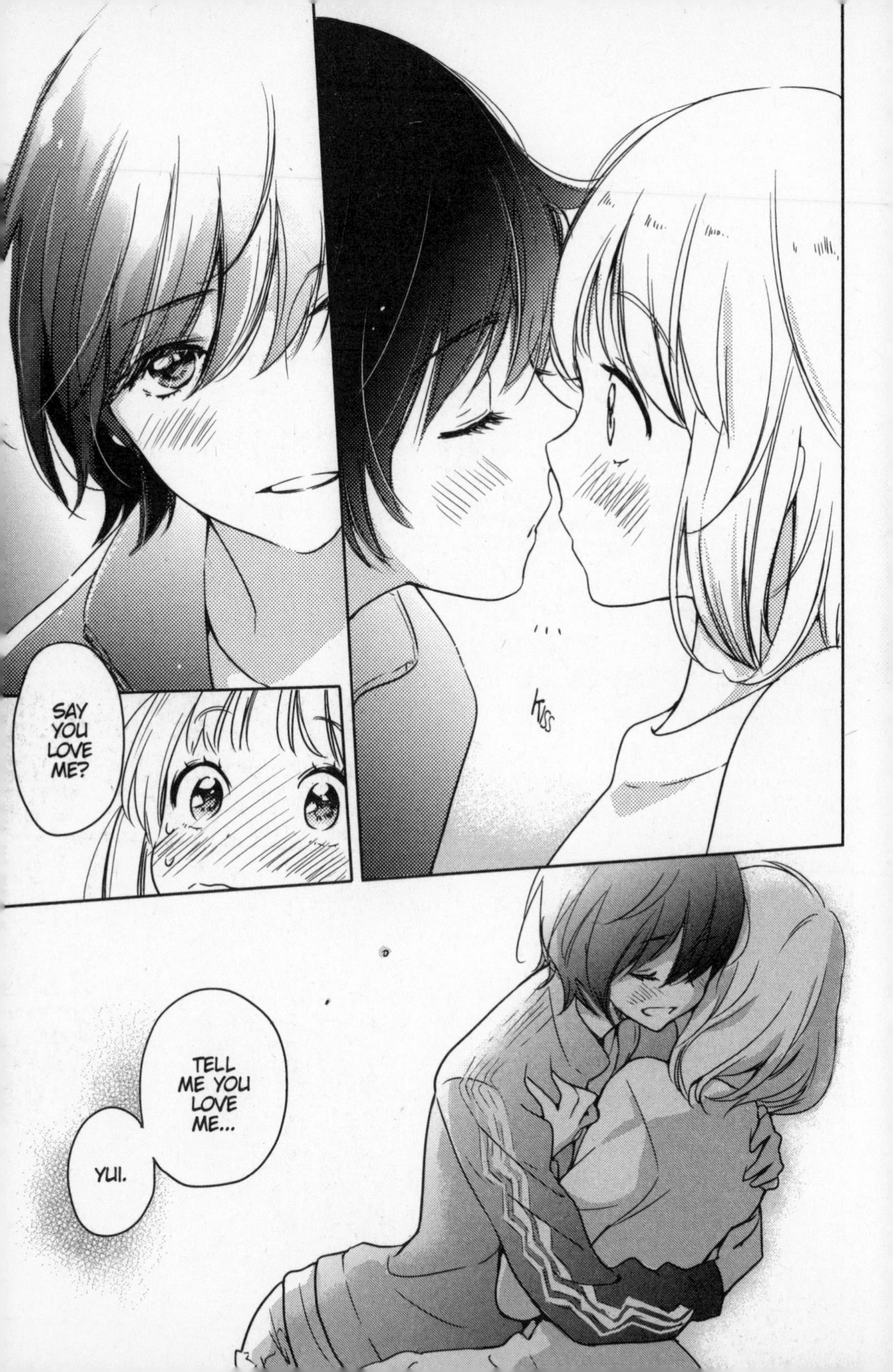
...
KISS
SAY YOU LOVE ME?
TELL ME YOU LOVE ME...
YUI.

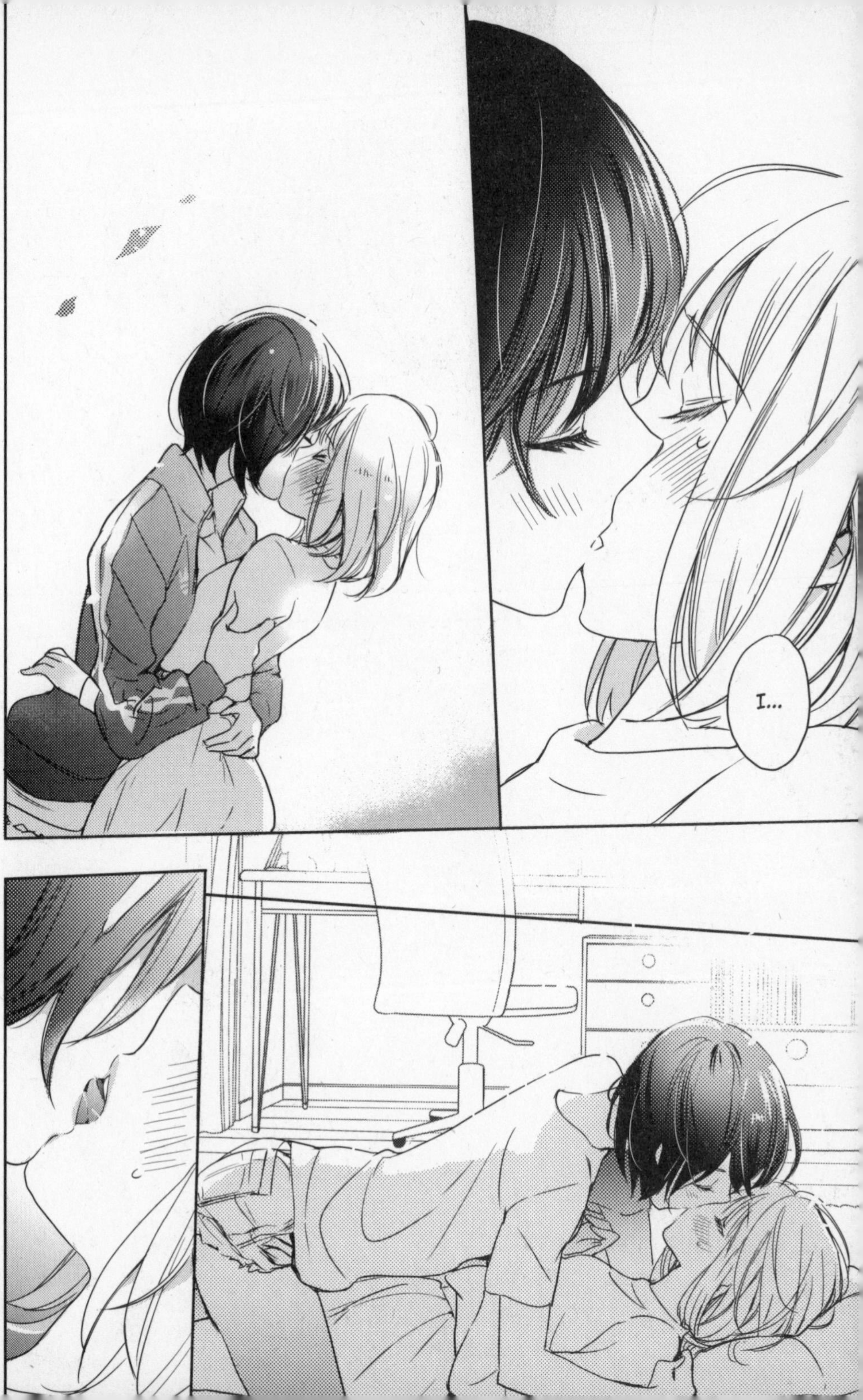
I...

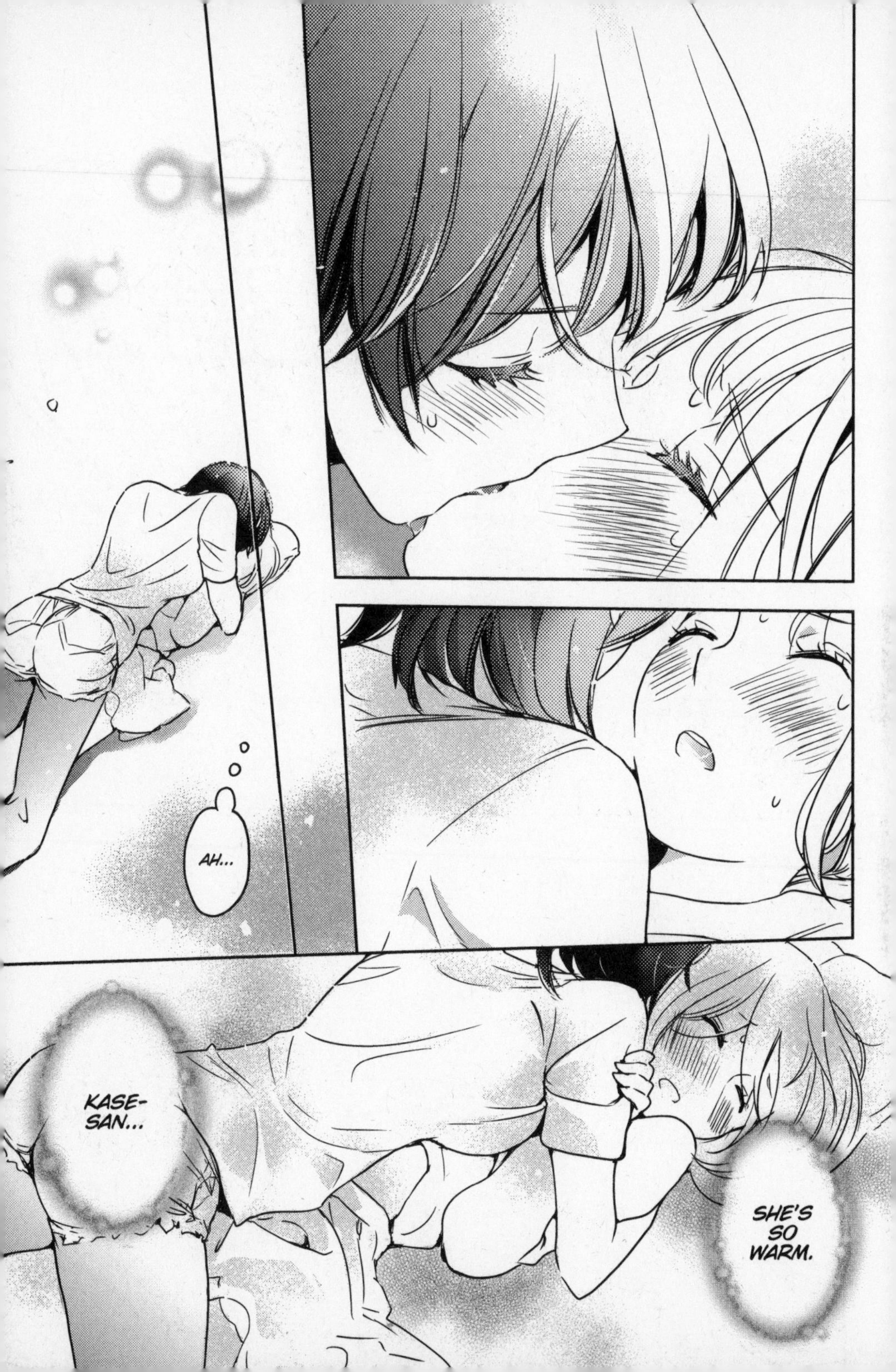
AH...
SHE'S SO WARM.
KASE-SAN...

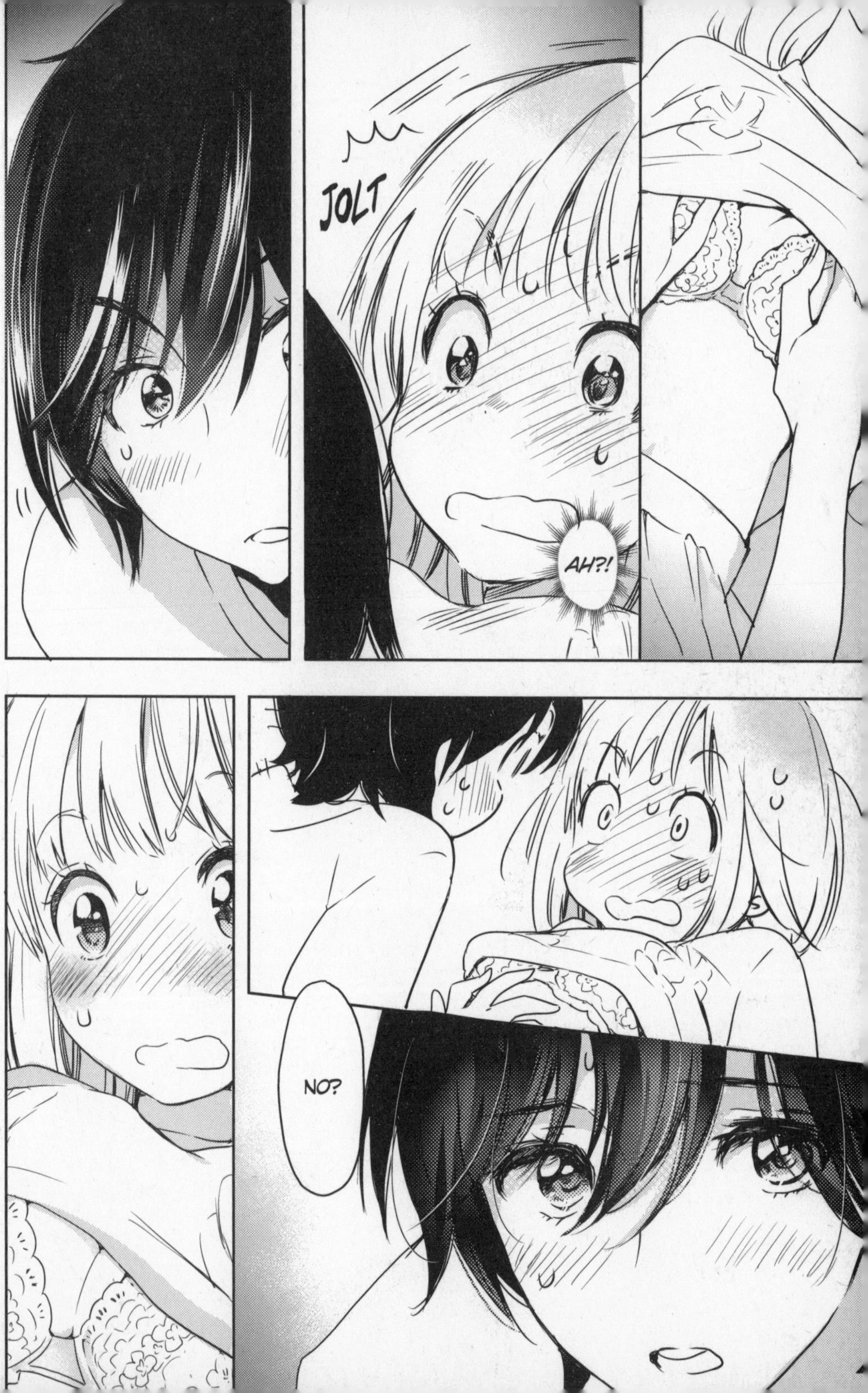
JOLT
AH?!
NO?

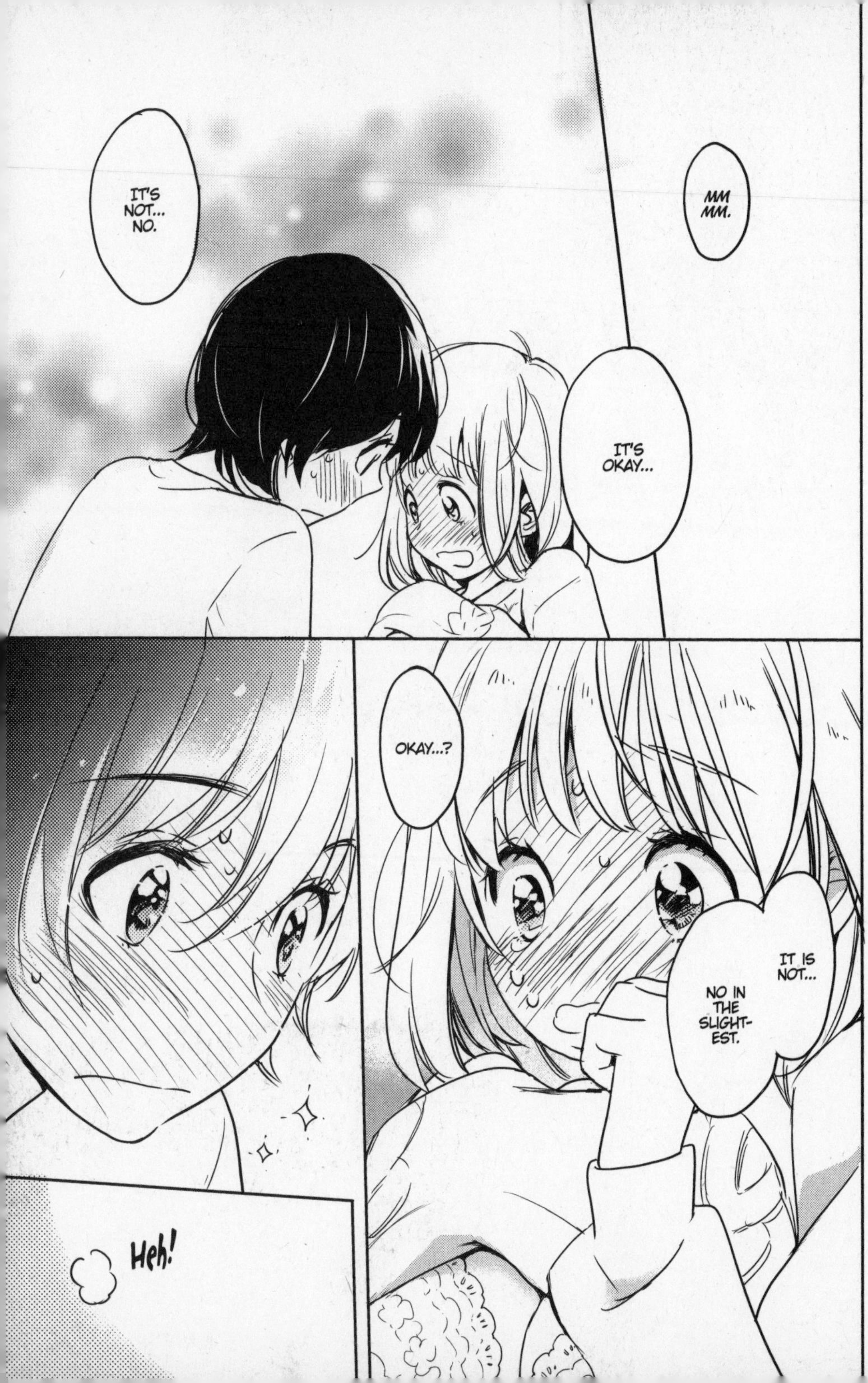
MM MM.
IT'S OKAY...
IT'S NOT... NO.
OKAY...?
IT IS NOT... NO IN THE SLIGHTEST.
Heh!

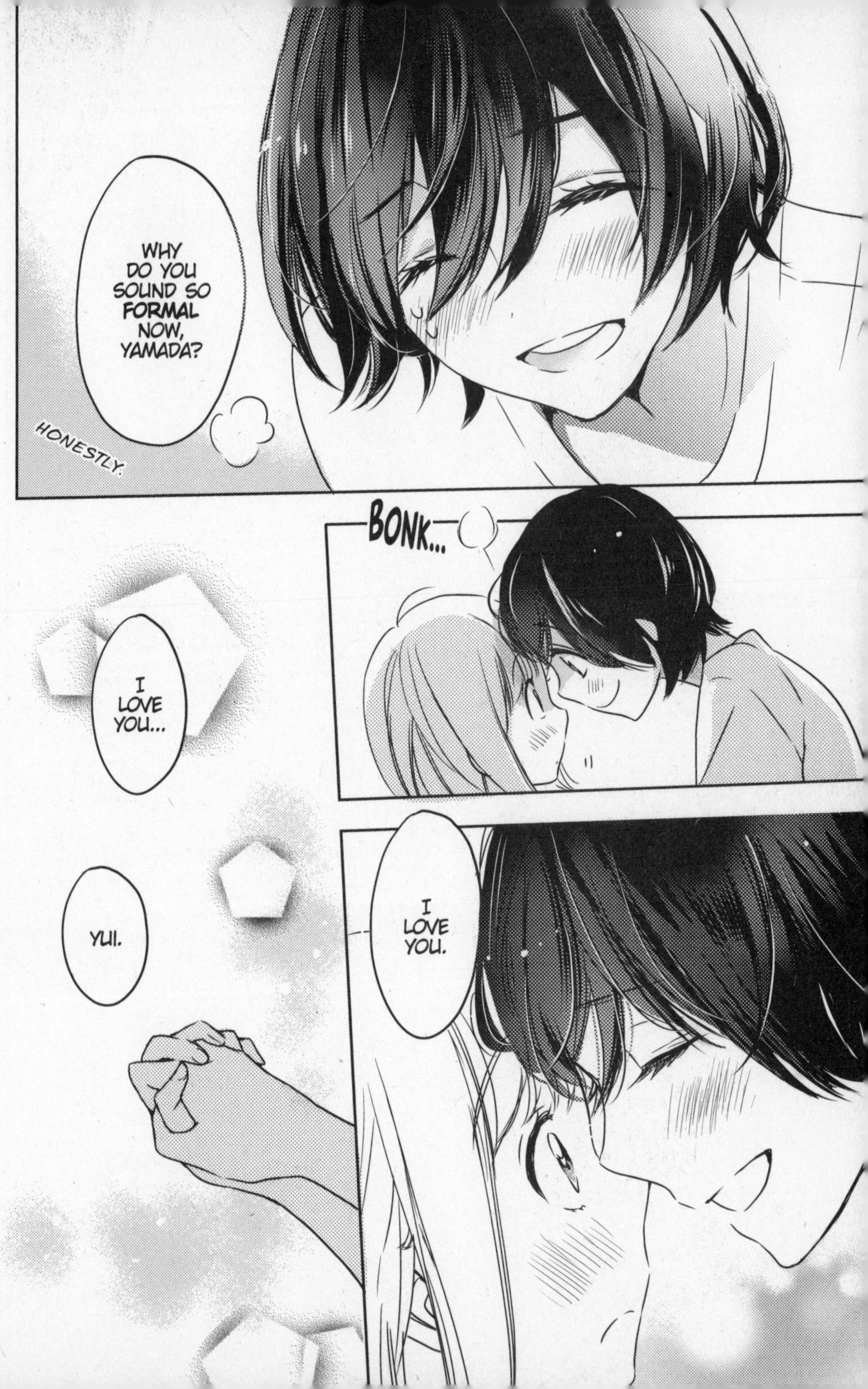
WHY DO YOU SOUND SO FORMAL NOW, YAMADA?
HONESTLY.
BONK...
I LOVE YOU...
I LOVE YOU.
YUI.

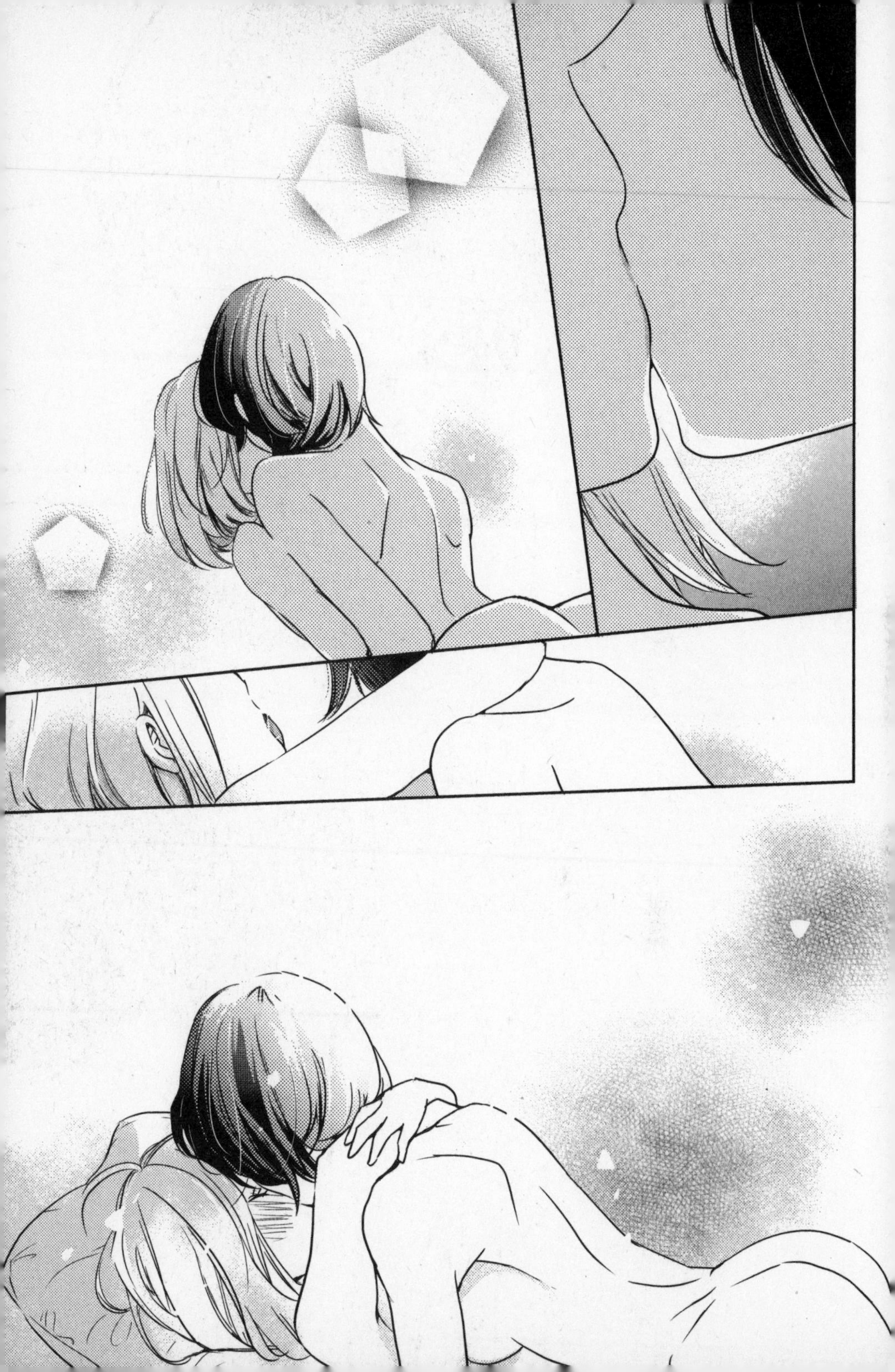

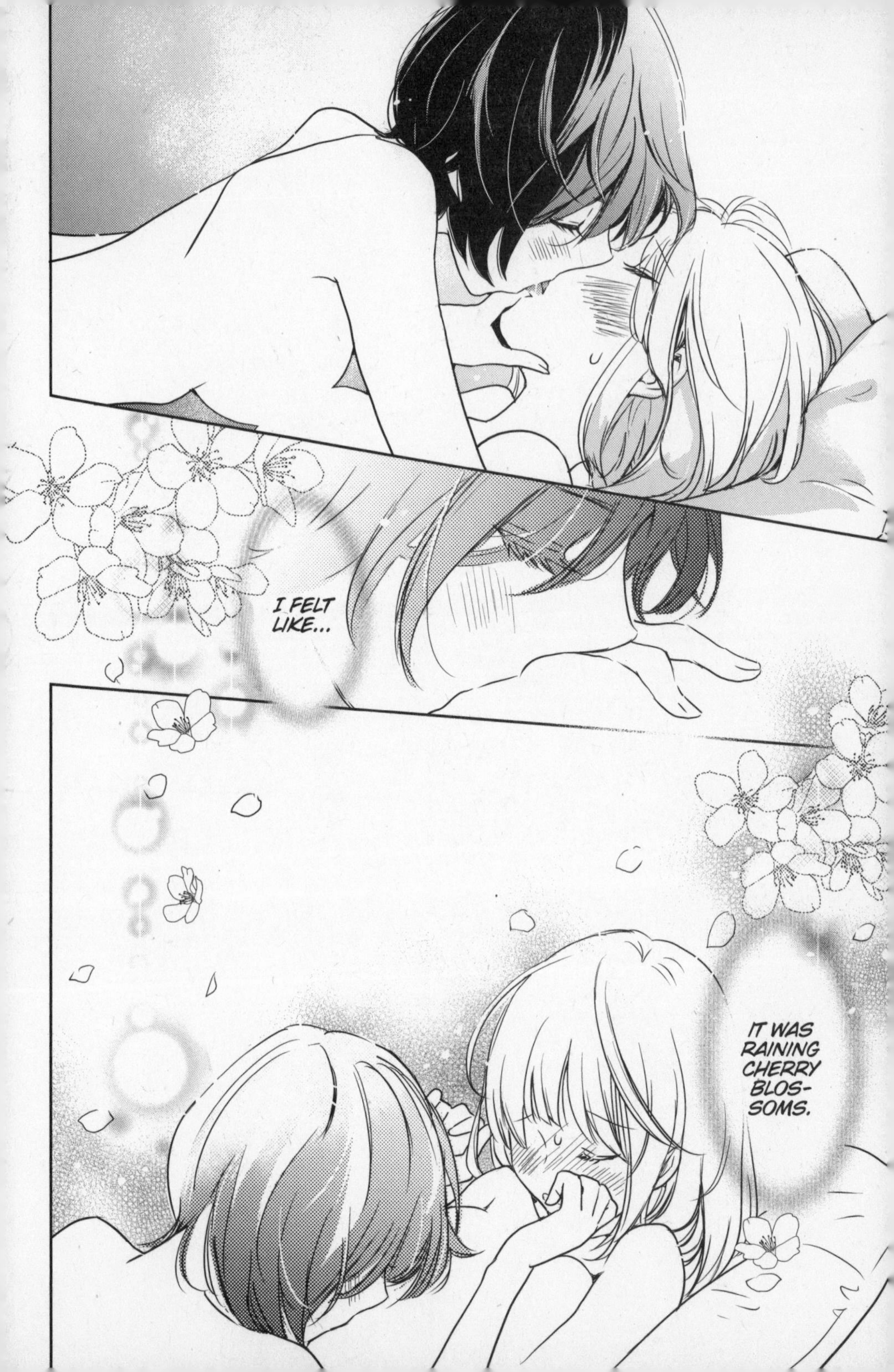
I FELT LIKE...
IT WAS RAINING CHERRY BLOS- SOMS.

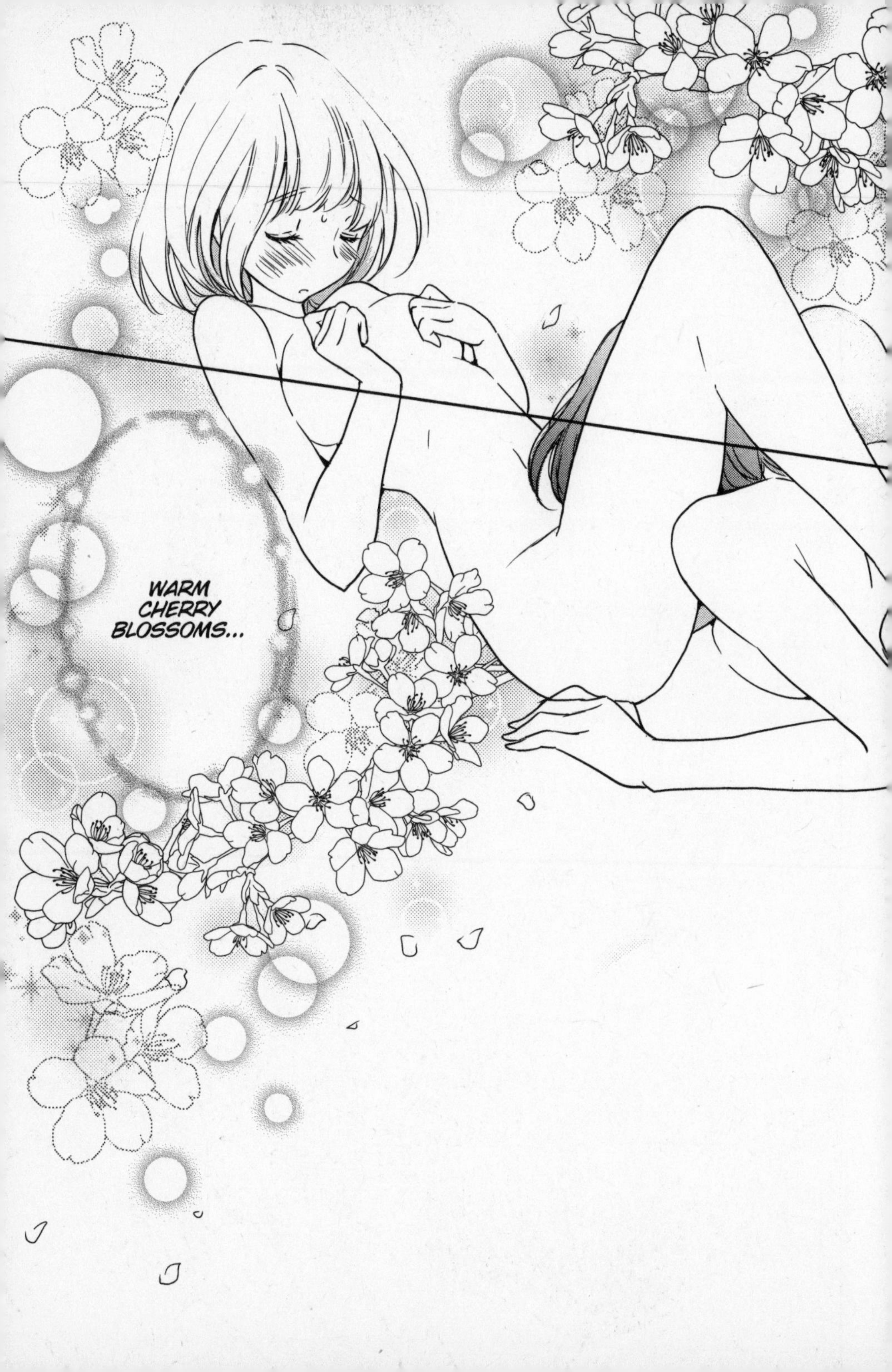
WARM CHERRY BLOSSOMS...

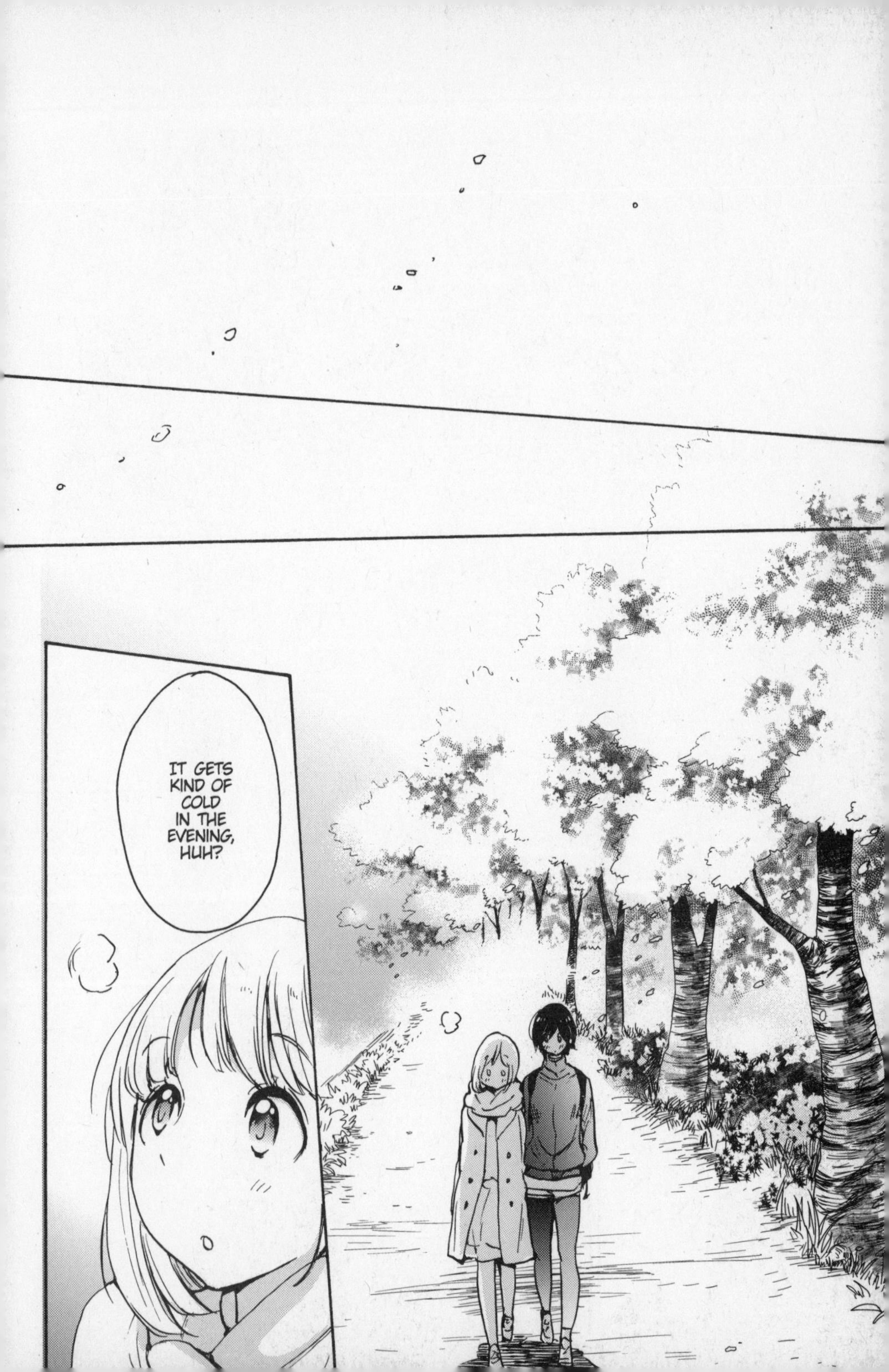
IT GETS KIND OF COLD IN THE EVENING, HUH?

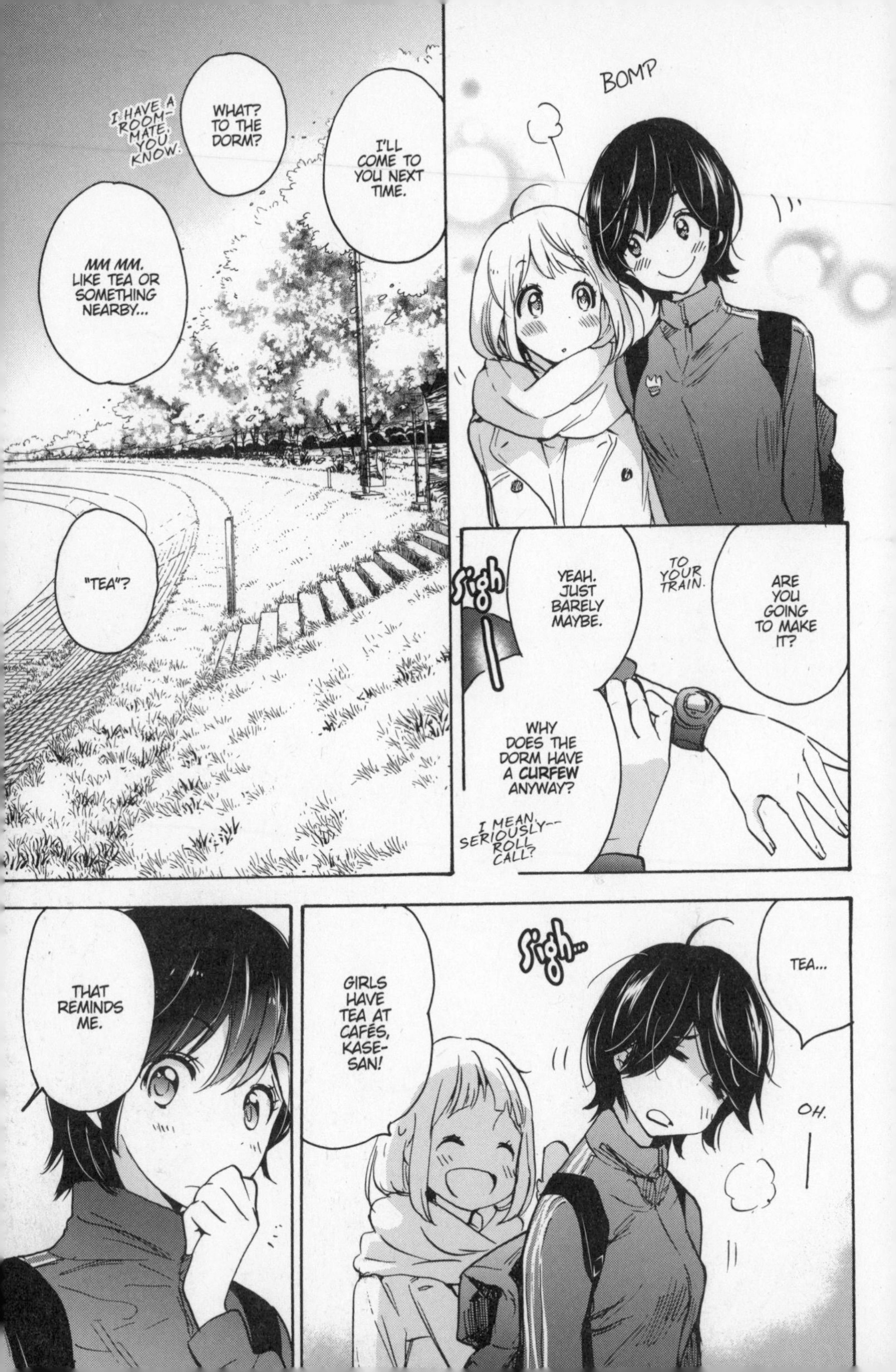
BOMP
ARE YOU GOING TO MAKE IT?
TO YOUR TRAIN.
YEAH. JUST BARELY MAYBE.
sigh
WHY DOES THE DORM HAVE A CURFEW ANYWAY?
I MEAN, SERIOUSLY-- ROLL CALL?
I'LL COME TO YOU NEXT TIME.
WHAT? TO THE DORM?
I HAVE A ROOM-MATE, YOU KNOW.
MM MM. LIKE TEA OR SOMETHING NEARBY...
"TEA"?
TEA...
OH.
sigh...
GIRLS HAVE TEA AT CAFÉS, KASE-SAN!
THAT REMINDS ME.

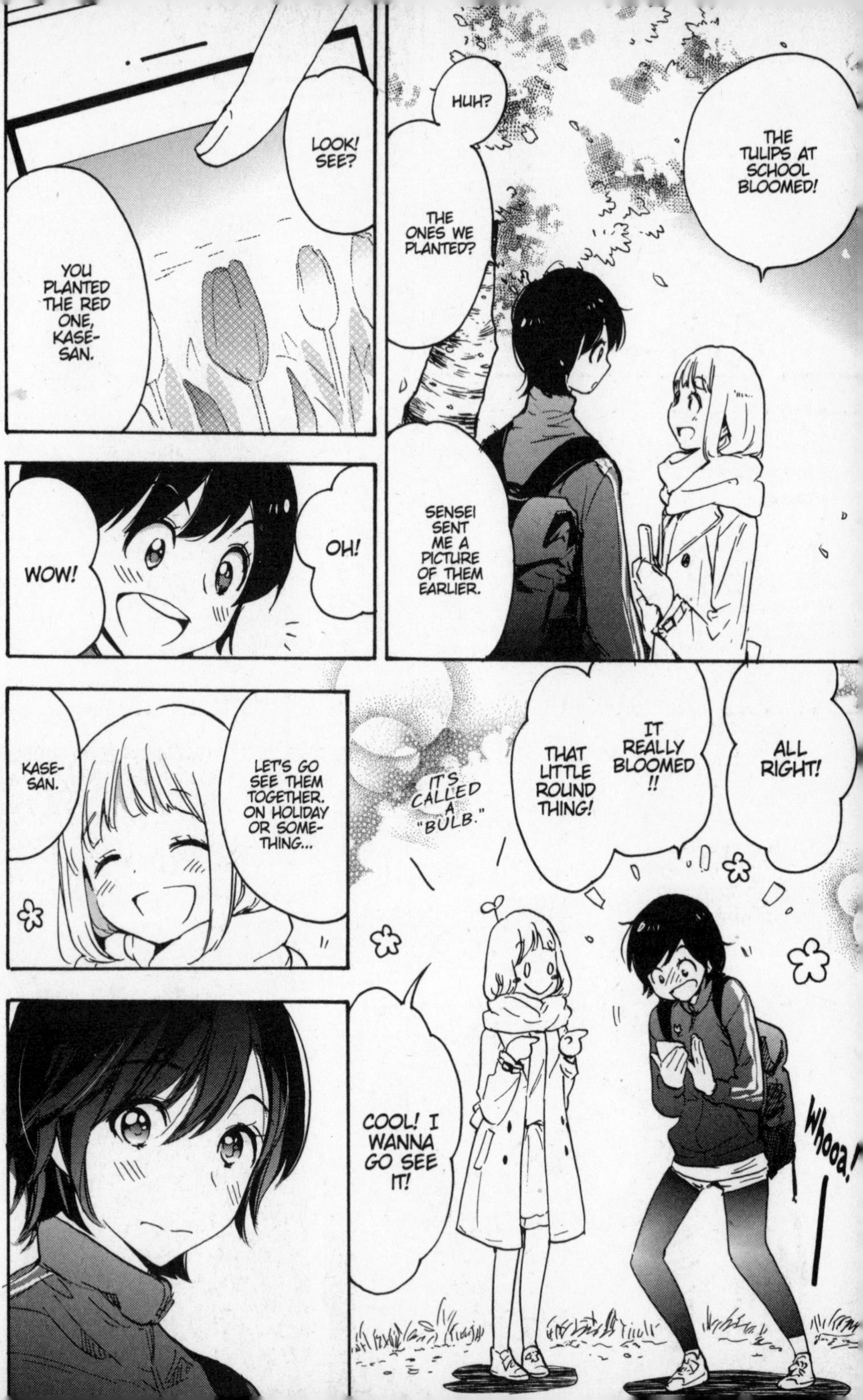

THE TULIPS AT SCHOOL BLOOMED!
HUH?
THE ONES WE PLANTED?
SENSEI SENT ME A PICTURE OF THEM EARLIER.
LOOK! SEE?
YOU PLANTED THE RED ONE, KASE-SAN.
OH!
WOW!
ALL RIGHT!
IT REALLY BLOOMED!!
THAT LITTLE ROUND THING!
IT'S CALLED A "BULB."
Whooa!
COOL! I WANNA GO SEE IT!
LET'S GO SEE THEM TOGETHER. ON HOLIDAY OR SOMETHING...
KASE-SAN.

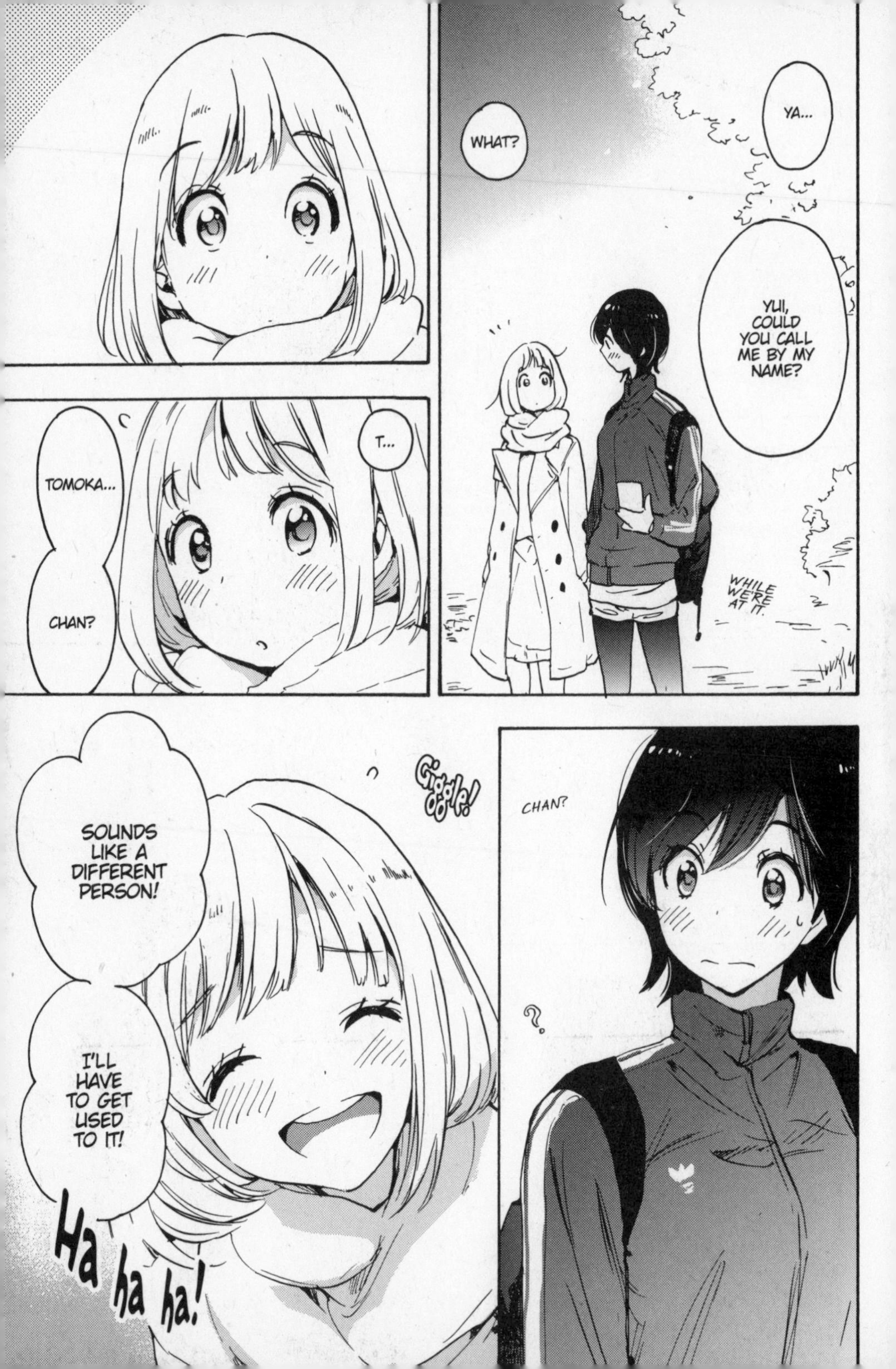
YA...
WHAT?
YUI, COULD YOU CALL ME BY MY NAME?
WHILE WE'RE AT IT.
T...
TOMOKA...
CHAN?
CHAN?
?
Giggle!
SOUNDS LIKE A DIFFERENT PERSON!
I'LL HAVE TO GET USED TO IT!
Ha ha ha!

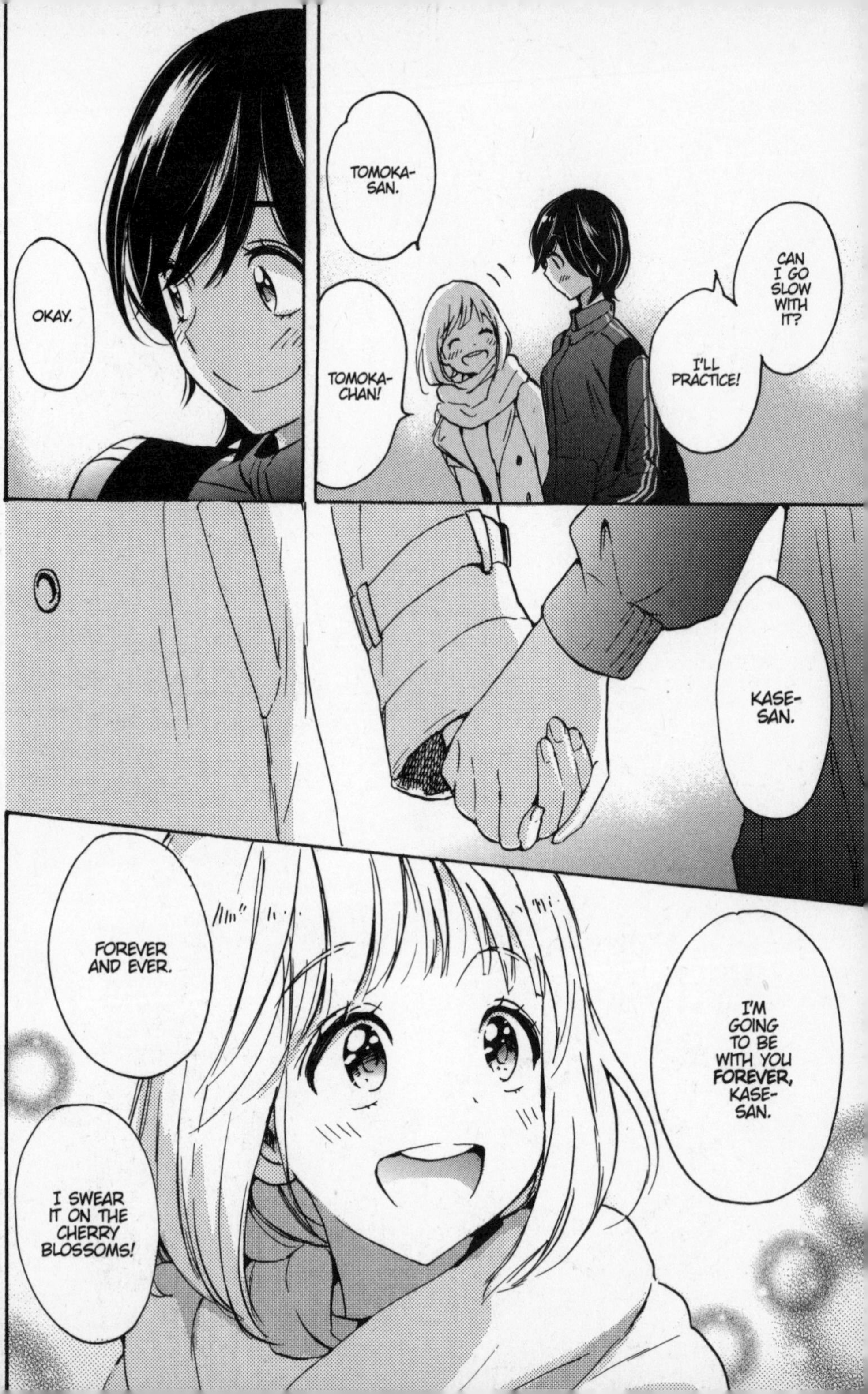
CAN I GO SLOW WITH IT?
I'LL PRACTICE!
TOMOKA-SAN.
TOMOKA-CHAN!
OKAY.
KASE-SAN.
I'M GOING TO BE WITH YOU **FOREVER**, KASE-SAN.
FOREVER AND EVER.
I SWEAR IT ON THE CHERRY BLOSSOMS!

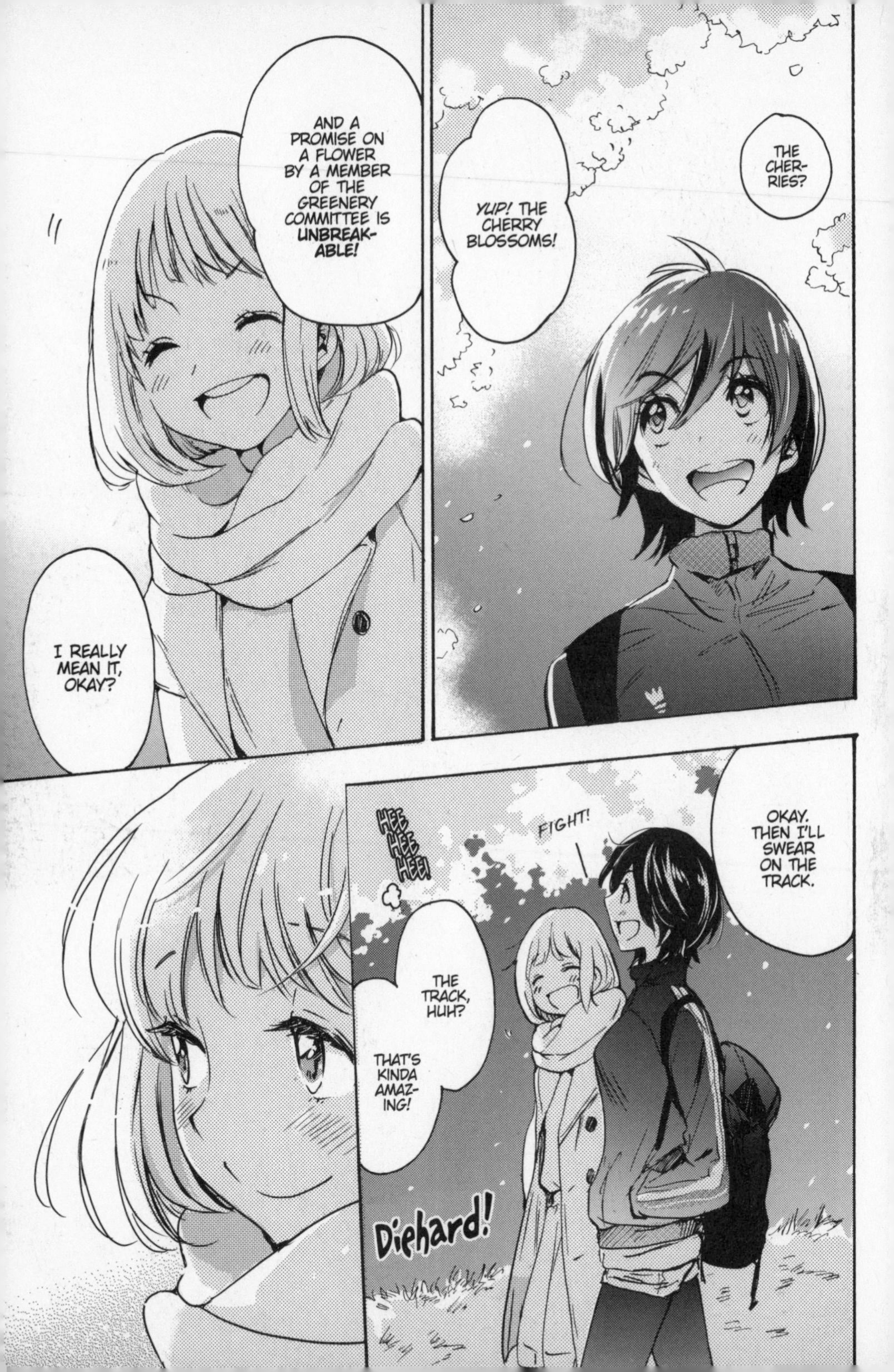
THE CHER-RIES?
YUP! THE CHERRY BLOSSOMS!
AND A PROMISE ON A FLOWER BY A MEMBER OF THE GREENERY COMMITTEE IS UNBREAK-ABLE!
I REALLY MEAN IT, OKAY?
OKAY. THEN I'LL SWEAR ON THE TRACK.
FIGHT!
HEE HEE HEE!
THE TRACK, HUH?
THAT'S KINDA AMAZ-ING!
Diehard!

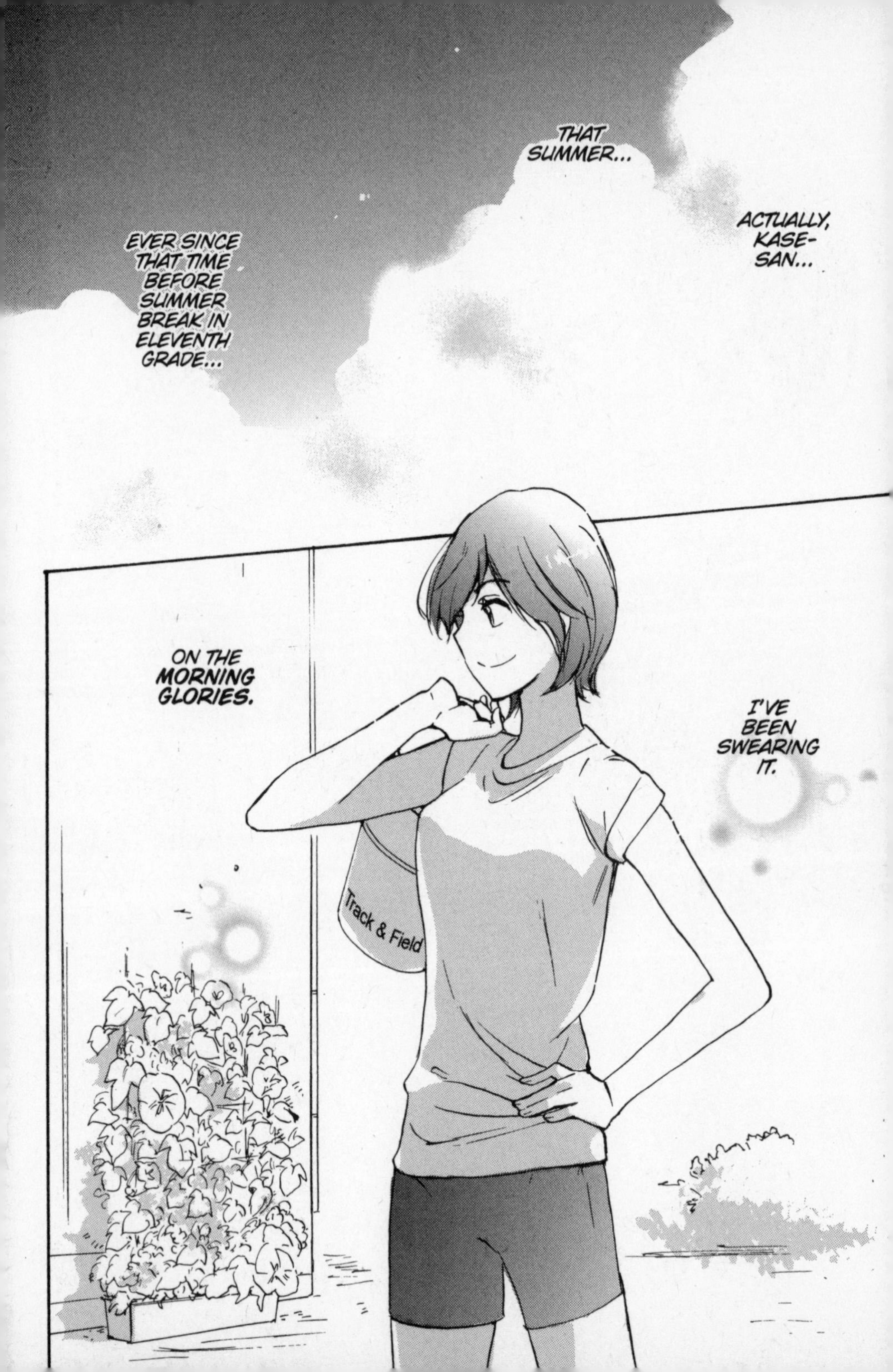
ACTUALLY, KASE-SAN...
THAT SUMMER...
EVER SINCE THAT TIME BEFORE SUMMER BREAK IN ELEVENTH GRADE...
I'VE BEEN SWEARING IT.
ON THE MORNING GLORIES.
Track & Field

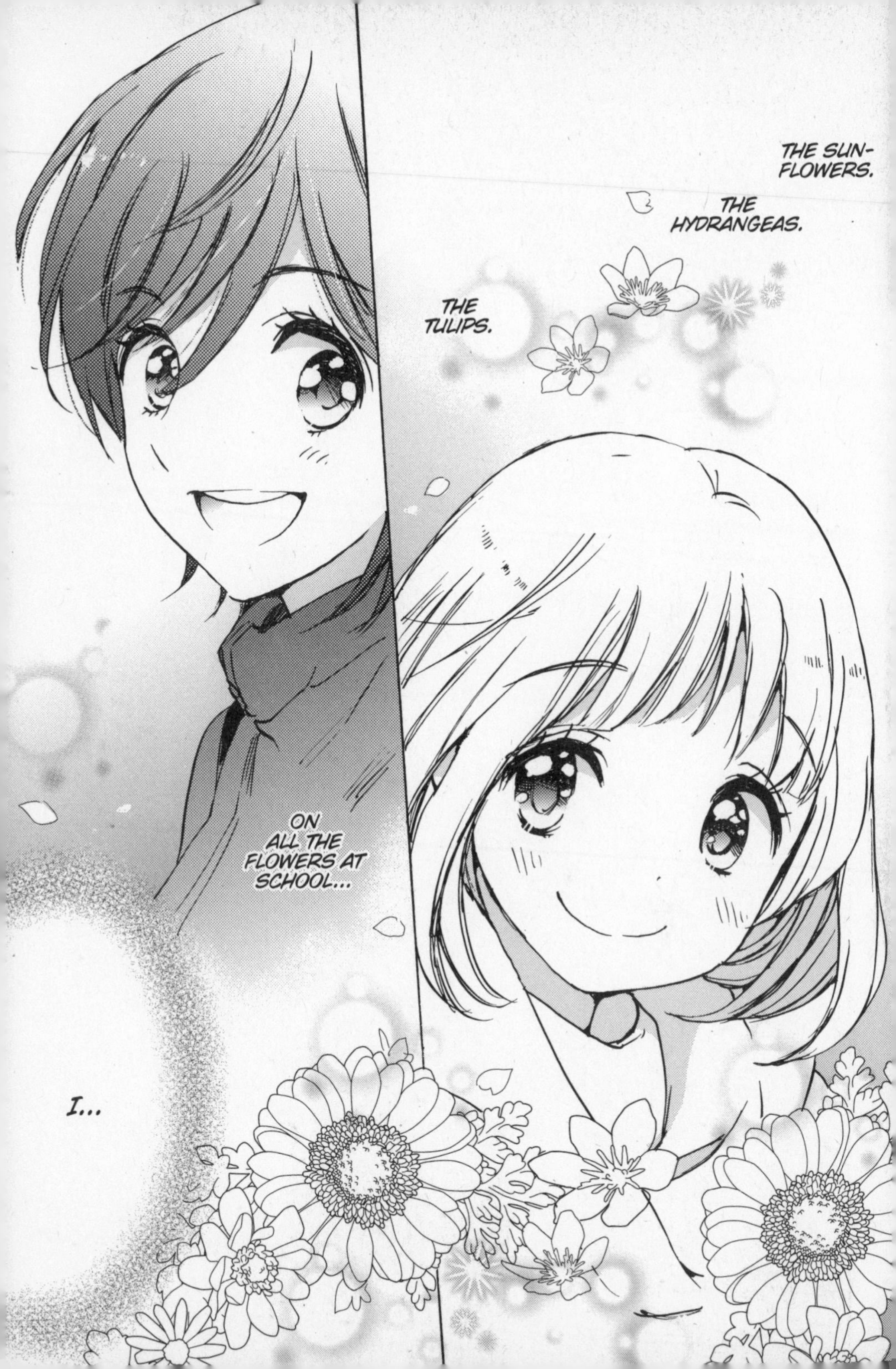
THE SUN-FLOWERS.
THE HYDRANGEAS.
THE TULIPS.
ON ALL THE FLOWERS AT SCHOOL...
I...

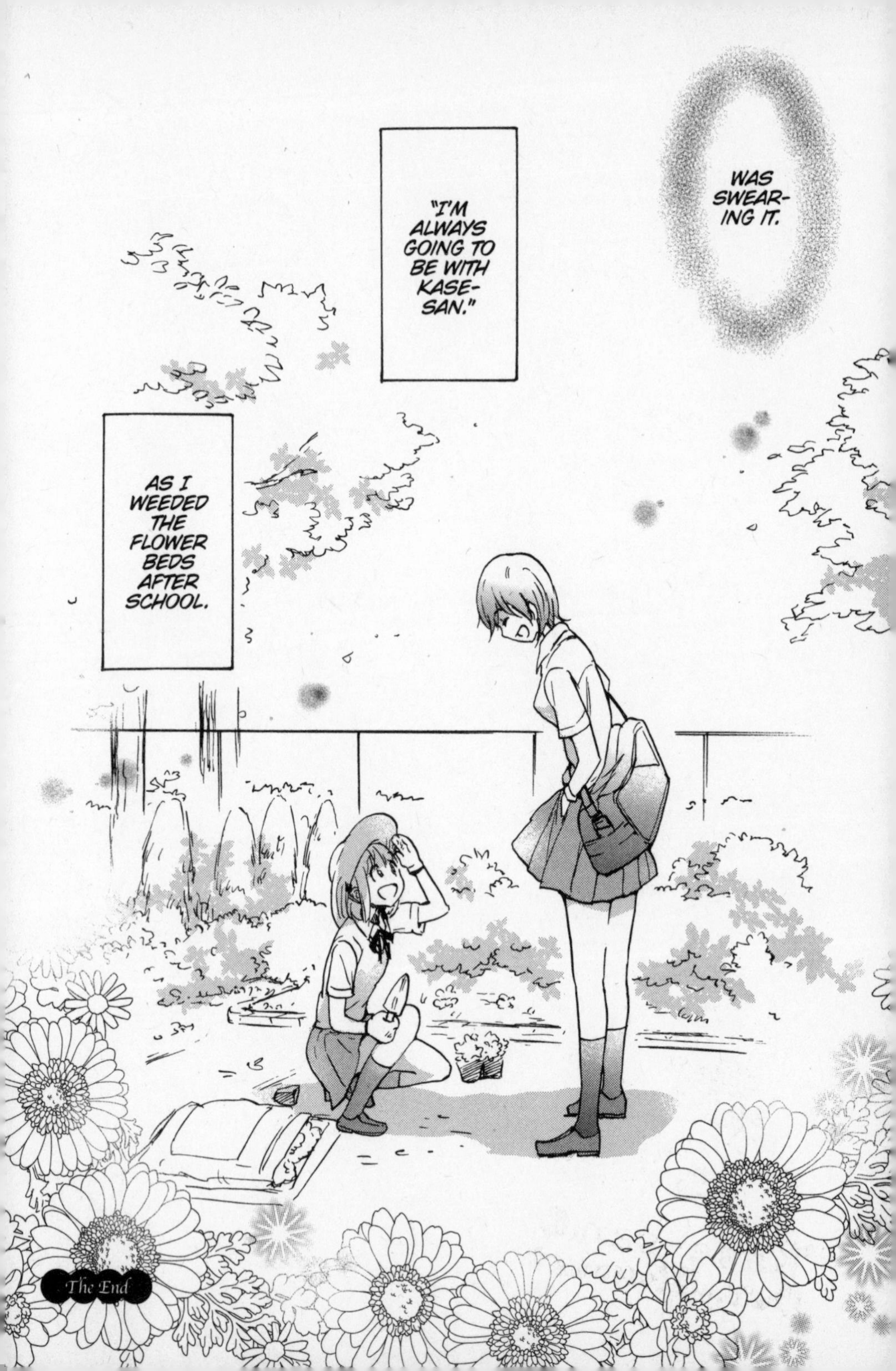
WAS SWEAR-ING IT.
"I'M ALWAYS GOING TO BE WITH KASE-SAN."
AS I WEEDED THE FLOWER BEDS AFTER SCHOOL.
The End

Kase-san and Cherry Blossoms ✿

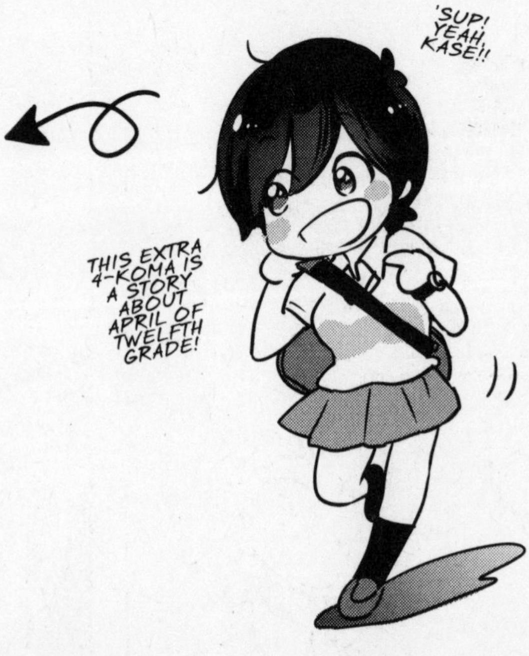
'SUP! YEAH, KASE!!
THIS EXTRA 4-KOMA IS A STORY ABOUT APRIL OF TWELFTH GRADE!

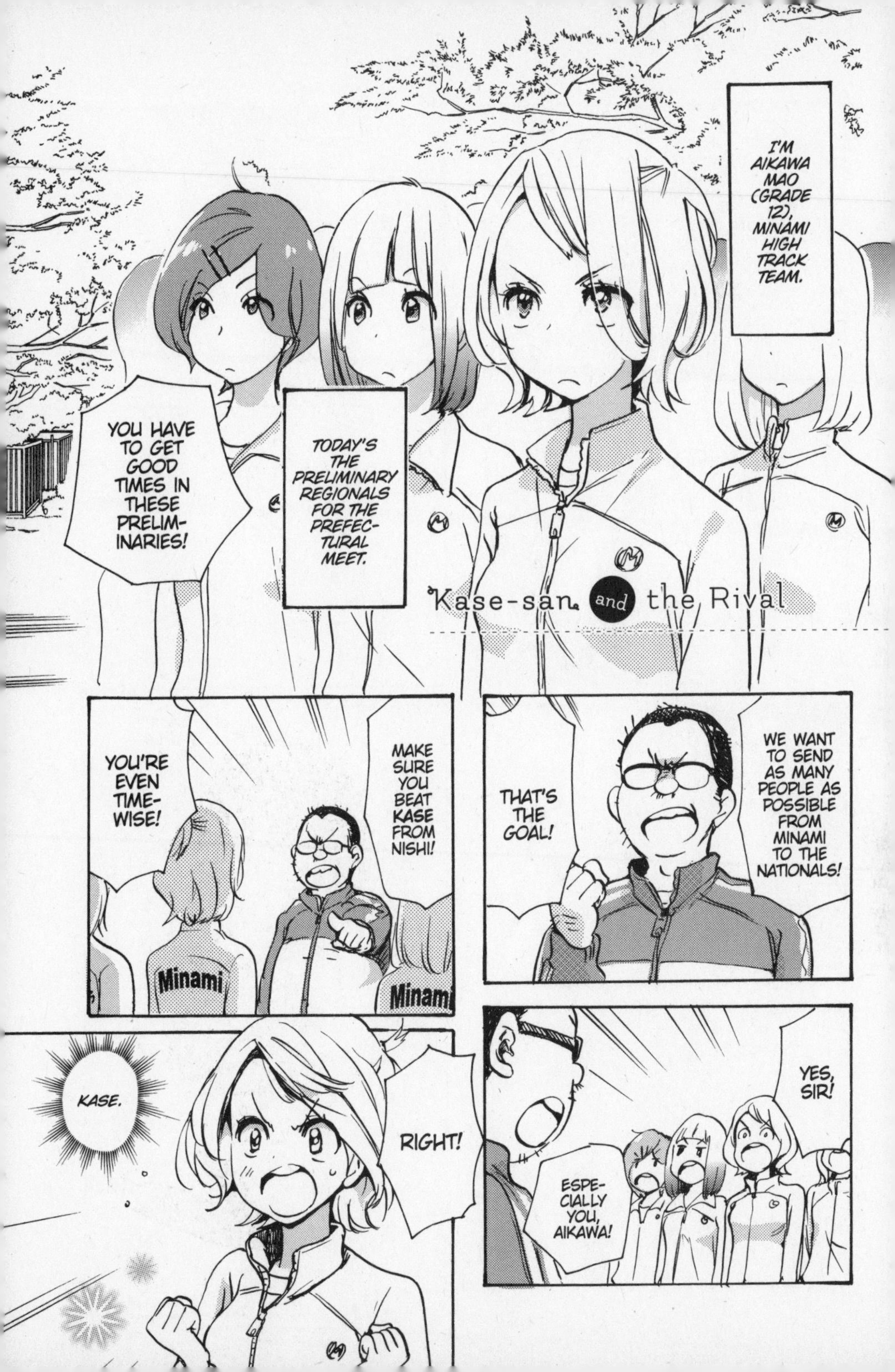
I'M AIKAWA MAO (GRADE 12), MINAMI HIGH TRACK TEAM.
TODAY'S THE PRELIMINARY REGIONALS FOR THE PREFECTURAL MEET.
YOU HAVE TO GET GOOD TIMES IN THESE PRELIMINARIES!
Kase-san and the Rival
WE WANT TO SEND AS MANY PEOPLE AS POSSIBLE FROM MINAMI TO THE NATIONALS!
THAT'S THE GOAL!
MAKE SURE YOU BEAT KASE FROM NISHI!
YOU'RE EVEN TIME-WISE!
Minami
Minami
YES, SIR!
ESPECIALLY YOU, AIKAWA!
RIGHT!
KASE.

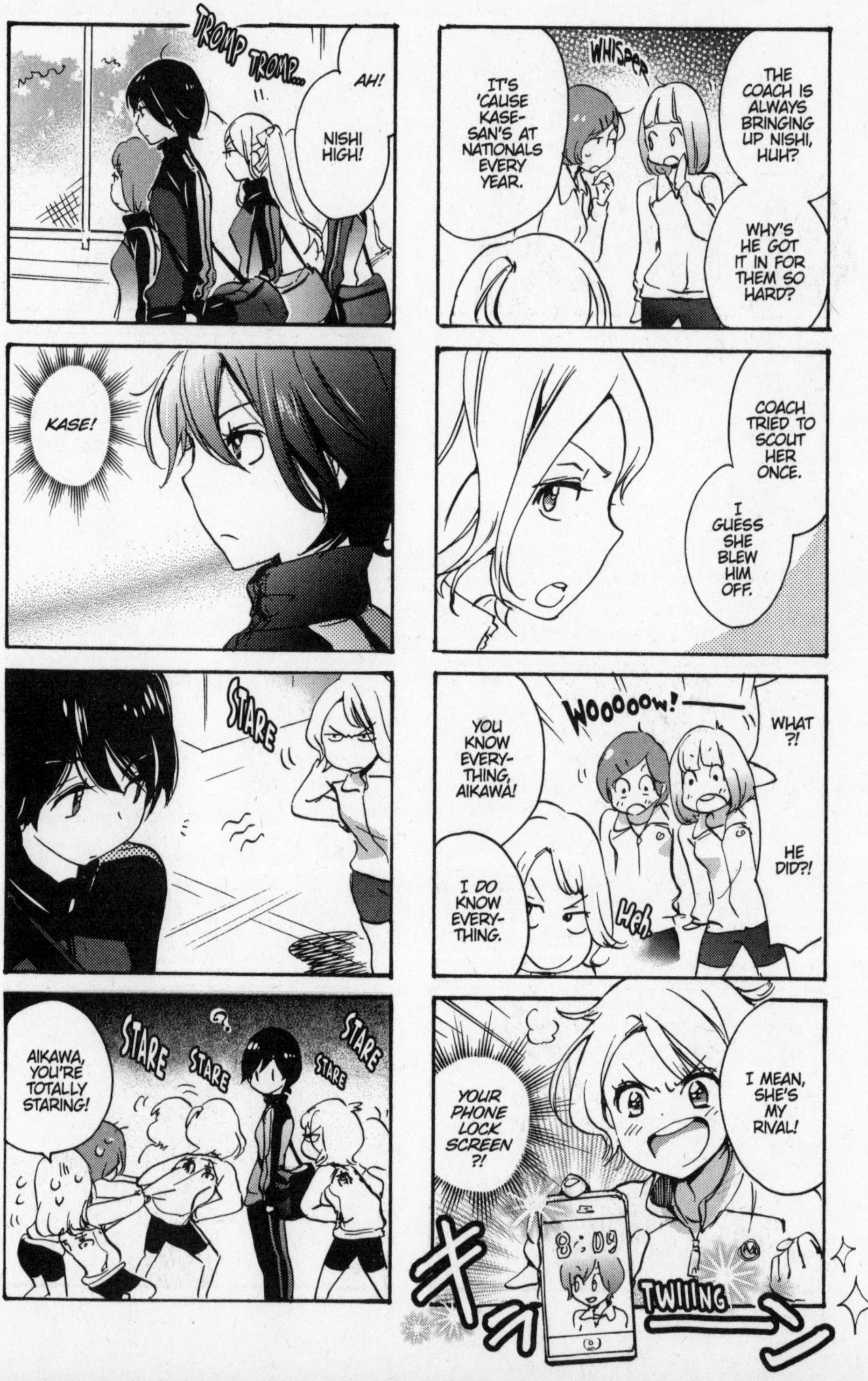
THE COACH IS ALWAYS BRINGING UP NISHI, HUH?
WHISPER
WHY'S HE GOT IT IN FOR THEM SO HARD?
IT'S 'CAUSE KASE-SAN'S AT NATIONALS EVERY YEAR.
COACH TRIED TO SCOUT HER ONCE.
I GUESS SHE BLEW HIM OFF.
WHAT?!
HE DID?!
WOOOOOW!
YOU KNOW EVERYTHING, AIKAWA!
I DO KNOW EVERYTHING.
Heh
I MEAN, SHE'S MY RIVAL!
YOUR PHONE LOCK SCREEN?!
8:09
TWIIING
TROMP TROMP...
AH!
NISHI HIGH!
KASE!
STARE
STARE
STARE
STARE
STARE
AIKAWA, YOU'RE TOTALLY STARING!

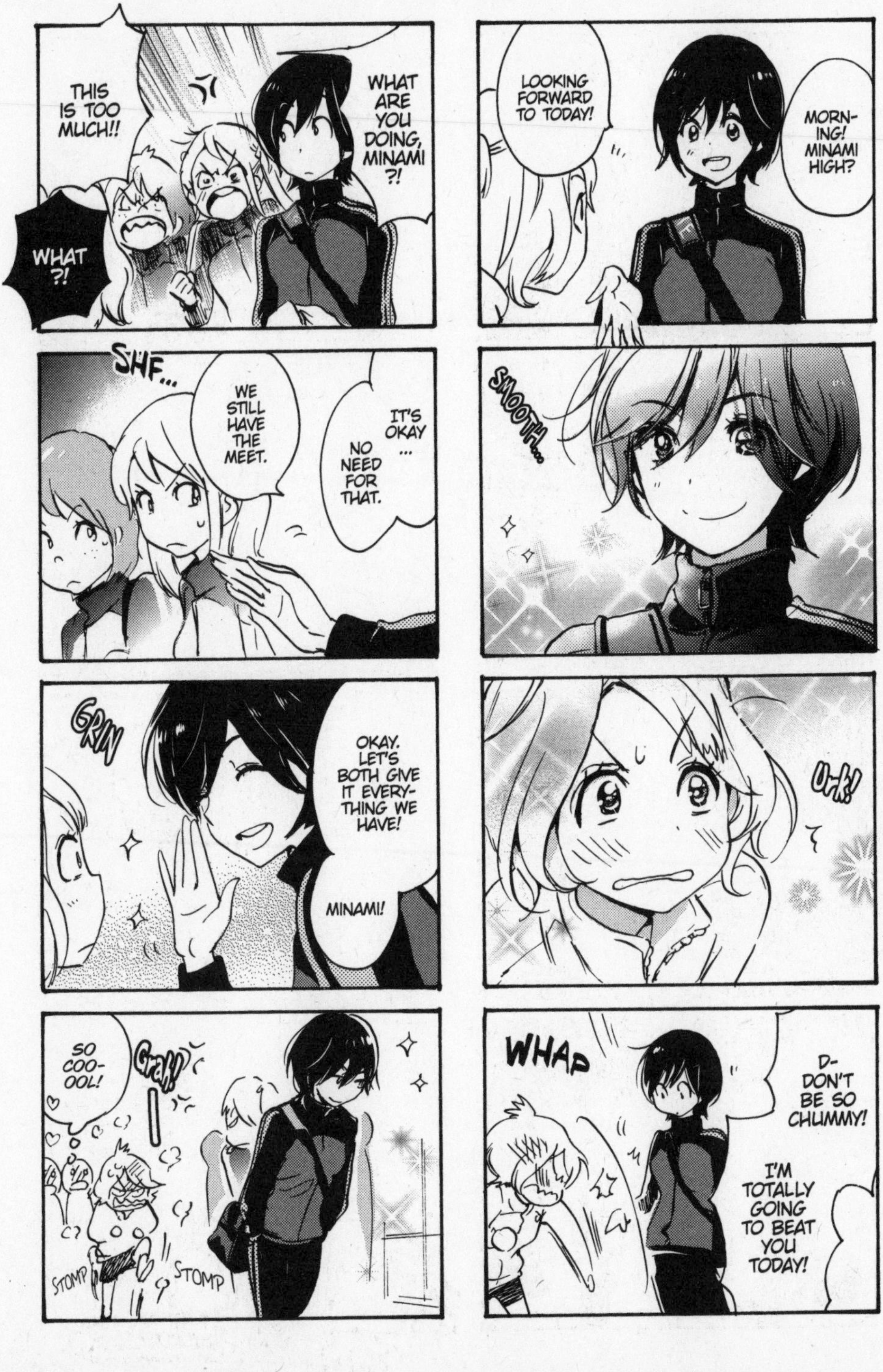
MORNING! MINAMI HIGH?
LOOKING FORWARD TO TODAY!
WHAT ARE YOU DOING, MINAMI?!
THIS IS TOO MUCH!!
WHAT?!
SMOOTH...
IT'S OKAY... NO NEED FOR THAT.
WE STILL HAVE THE MEET.
SHF...
Urk!
OKAY. LET'S BOTH GIVE IT EVERYTHING WE HAVE!
MINAMI!
GRIN
D-DON'T BE SO CHUMMY!
I'M TOTALLY GOING TO BEAT YOU TODAY!
WHAP
Grah!
SO COOOOL!
STOMP
STOMP

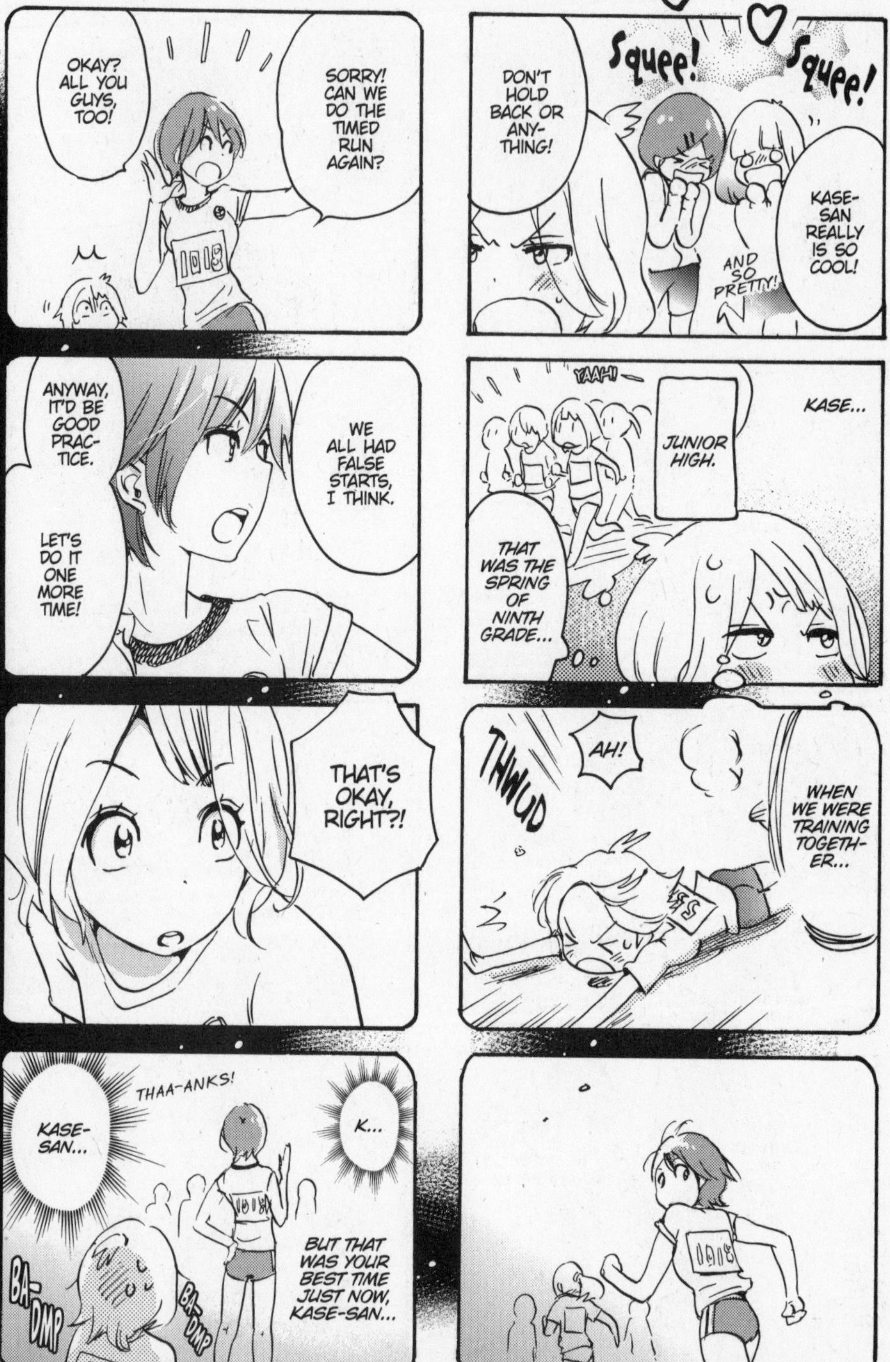
Squee!
Squee!
DON'T HOLD BACK OR ANY-THING!
KASE-SAN REALLY IS SO COOL!
AND SO PRETTY!
KASE...
YAAH!
JUNIOR HIGH.
THAT WAS THE SPRING OF NINTH GRADE...
AH!
THWUD
WHEN WE WERE TRAINING TOGETH-ER...
SORRY! CAN WE DO THE TIMED RUN AGAIN?
OKAY? ALL YOU GUYS, TOO!
WE ALL HAD FALSE STARTS, I THINK.
ANYWAY, IT'D BE GOOD PRAC-TICE.
LET'S DO IT ONE MORE TIME!
THAT'S OKAY, RIGHT?!
K...
THAA-ANKS!
KASE-SAN...
BUT THAT WAS YOUR BEST TIME JUST NOW, KASE-SAN...
BA-DMP
BA-DMP

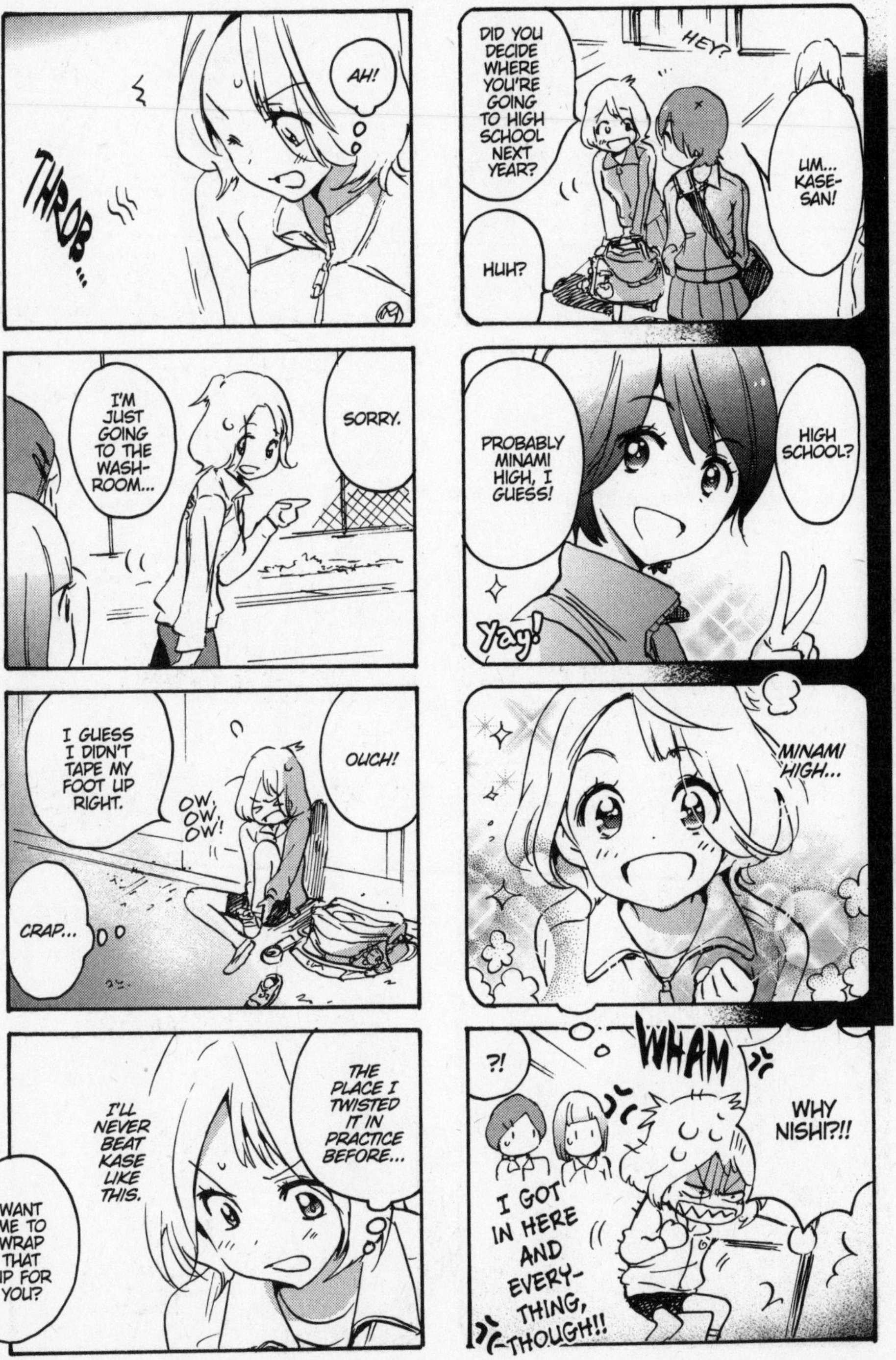
UM... KASE-SAN!
HEY?
DID YOU DECIDE WHERE YOU'RE GOING TO HIGH SCHOOL NEXT YEAR?
HUH?
HIGH SCHOOL?
PROBABLY MINAMI HIGH, I GUESS!
YAY!
MINAMI HIGH...
WHY NISHI?!!
WHAM
?!
I GOT IN HERE AND EVERYTHING, THOUGH!!
AH!
THROB...
SORRY.
I'M JUST GOING TO THE WASHROOM...
OUCH!
OW, OW, OW!
I GUESS I DIDN'T TAPE MY FOOT UP RIGHT.
CRAP...
THE PLACE I TWISTED IT IN PRACTICE BEFORE...
I'LL NEVER BEAT KASE LIKE THIS.
WANT ME TO WRAP THAT UP FOR YOU?

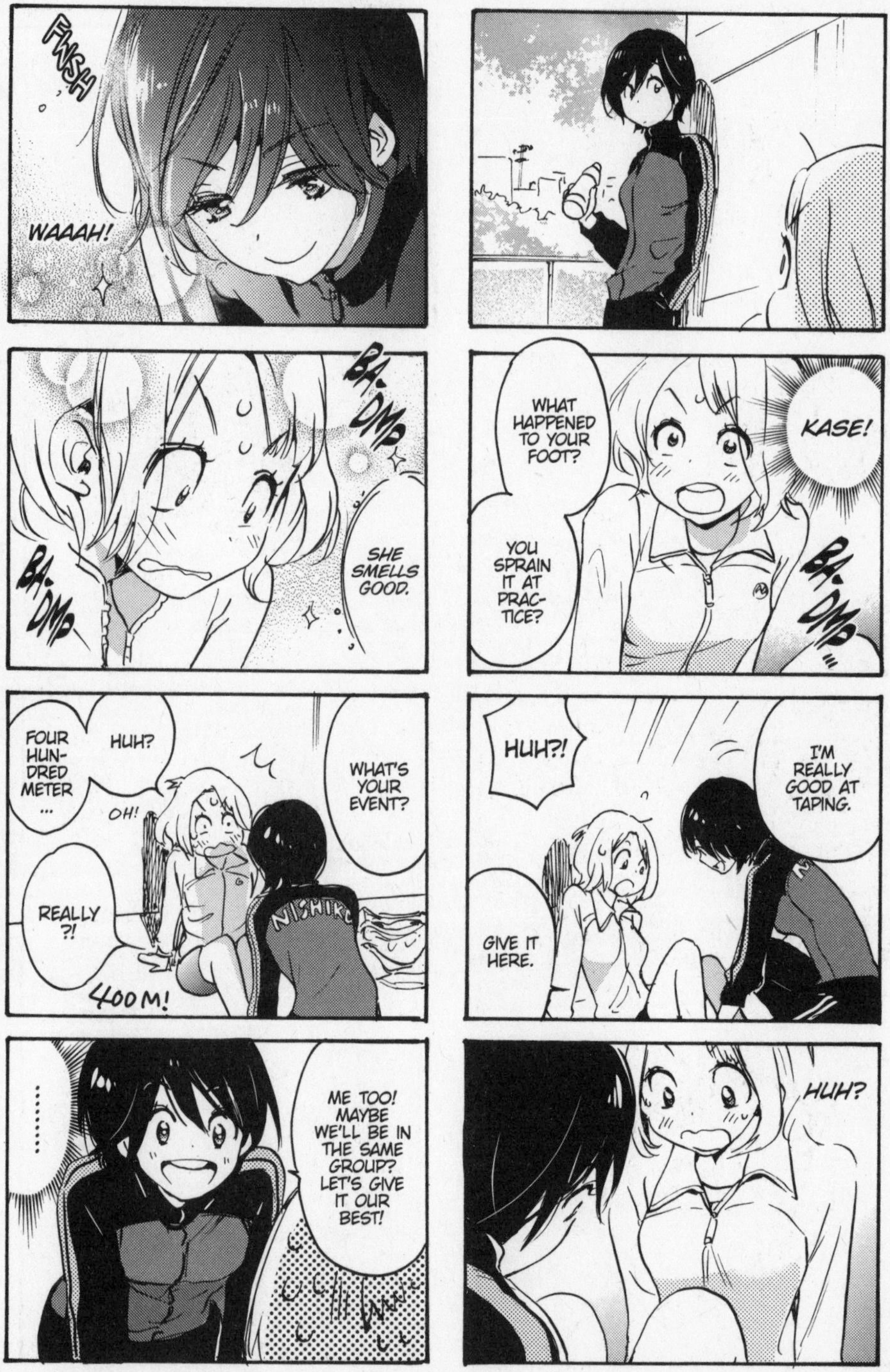
FWSH
WAAAH!
KASE!
WHAT HAPPENED TO YOUR FOOT?
YOU SPRAIN IT AT PRAC-TICE?
BA-DMP...
BA-DMP
SHE SMELLS GOOD.
BA-DMP
I'M REALLY GOOD AT TAPING.
HUH?!
GIVE IT HERE.
WHAT'S YOUR EVENT?
HUH?
FOUR HUN-DRED METER ...
OH!
REALLY ?!
400M!
HUH?
ME TOO! MAYBE WE'LL BE IN THE SAME GROUP? LET'S GIVE IT OUR BEST!
......

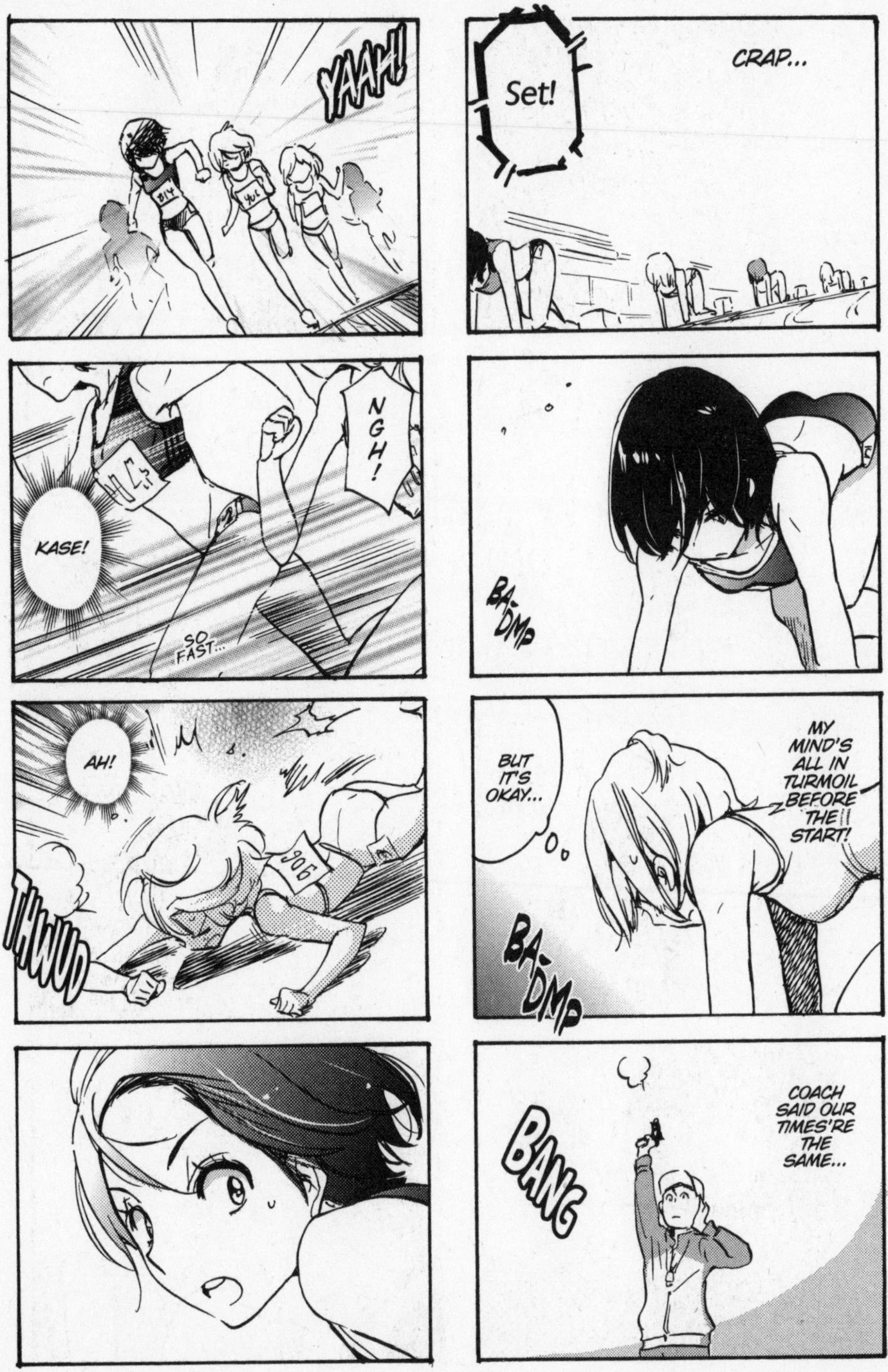
Set!
CRAP...
BA-DMP
MY MIND'S ALL IN TURMOIL BEFORE THE START!
BUT IT'S OKAY...
BA-DMP
COACH SAID OUR TIMES'RE THE SAME...
BANG
YAAH!
NGH!
KASE!
SO FAST...
AH!
THWUD

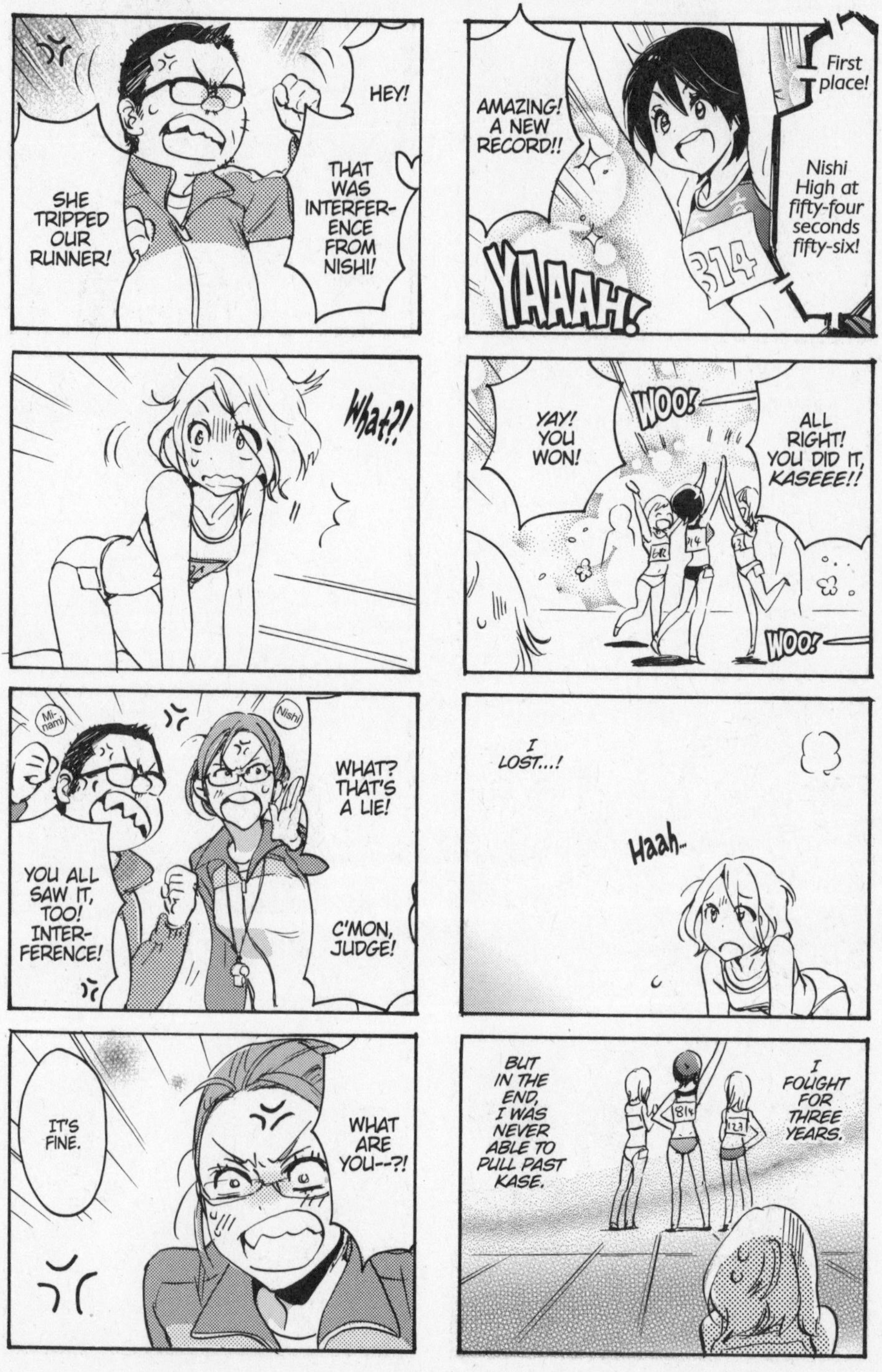
First place!
Nishi High at fifty-four seconds fifty-six!
AMAZING! A NEW RECORD!!
YAAAH!
HEY!
THAT WAS INTERFERENCE FROM NISHI!
SHE TRIPPED OUR RUNNER!
ALL RIGHT! YOU DID IT, KASEEE!!
WOO!
YAY! YOU WON!
WOO!
What?!
I LOST...!
Haah...
Nishi
Mi-nami
WHAT? THAT'S A LIE!
C'MON, JUDGE!
YOU ALL SAW IT, TOO! INTERFERENCE!
I FOUGHT FOR THREE YEARS.
BUT IN THE END, I WAS NEVER ABLE TO PULL PAST KASE.
WHAT ARE YOU--?!
IT'S FINE.

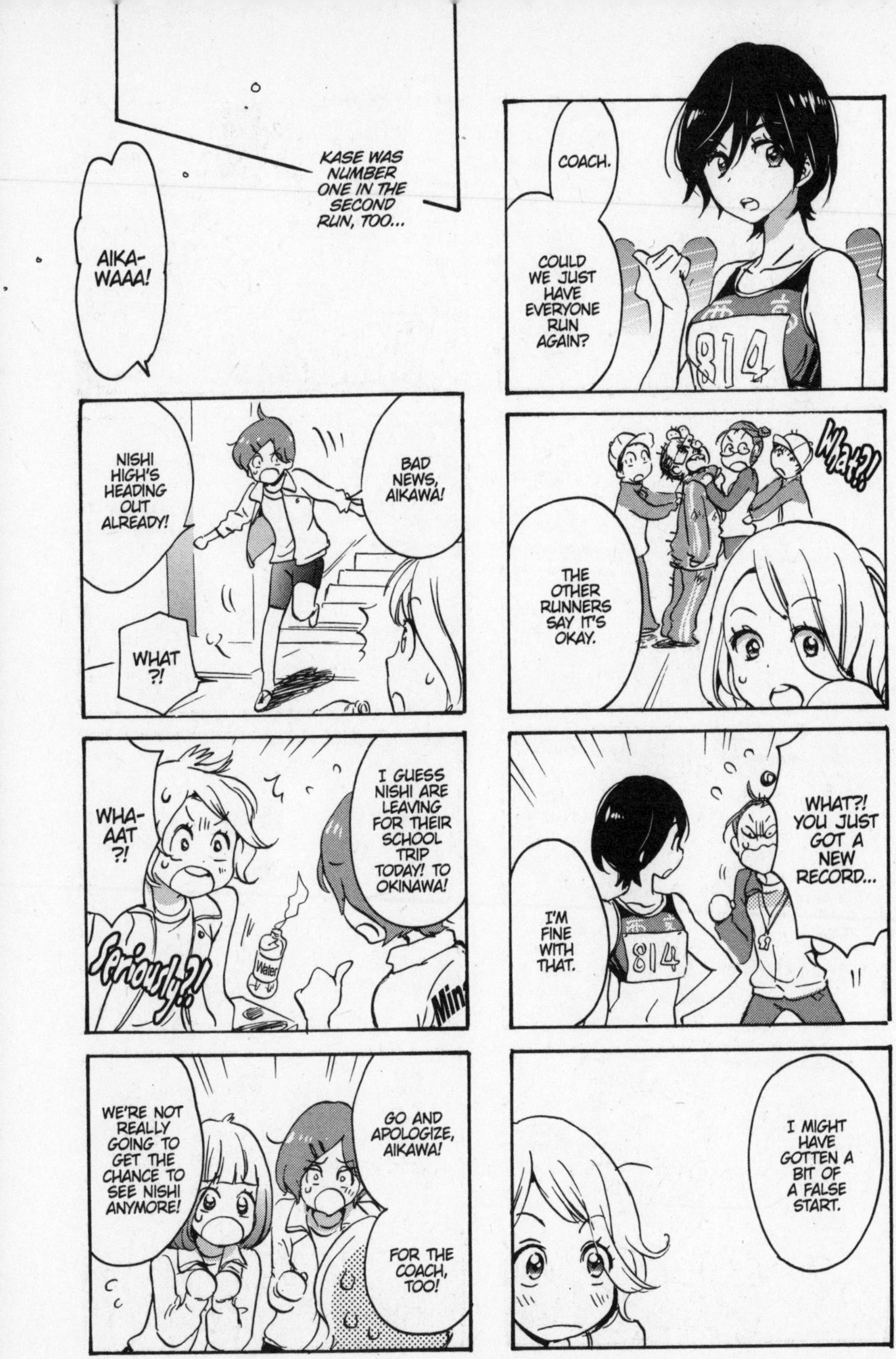
COACH.
COULD WE JUST HAVE EVERYONE RUN AGAIN?
KASE WAS NUMBER ONE IN THE SECOND RUN, TOO...
AIKA-WAAA!
What?!
THE OTHER RUNNERS SAY IT'S OKAY.
BAD NEWS, AIKAWA!
NISHI HIGH'S HEADING OUT ALREADY!
WHAT ?!
WHAT?! YOU JUST GOT A NEW RECORD...
I'M FINE WITH THAT.
I GUESS NISHI ARE LEAVING FOR THEIR SCHOOL TRIP TODAY! TO OKINAWA!
WHA-AAT ?!
Seriously?!
Water
I MIGHT HAVE GOTTEN A BIT OF A FALSE START.
GO AND APOLOGIZE, AIKAWA!
WE'RE NOT REALLY GOING TO GET THE CHANCE TO SEE NISHI ANYMORE!
FOR THE COACH, TOO!

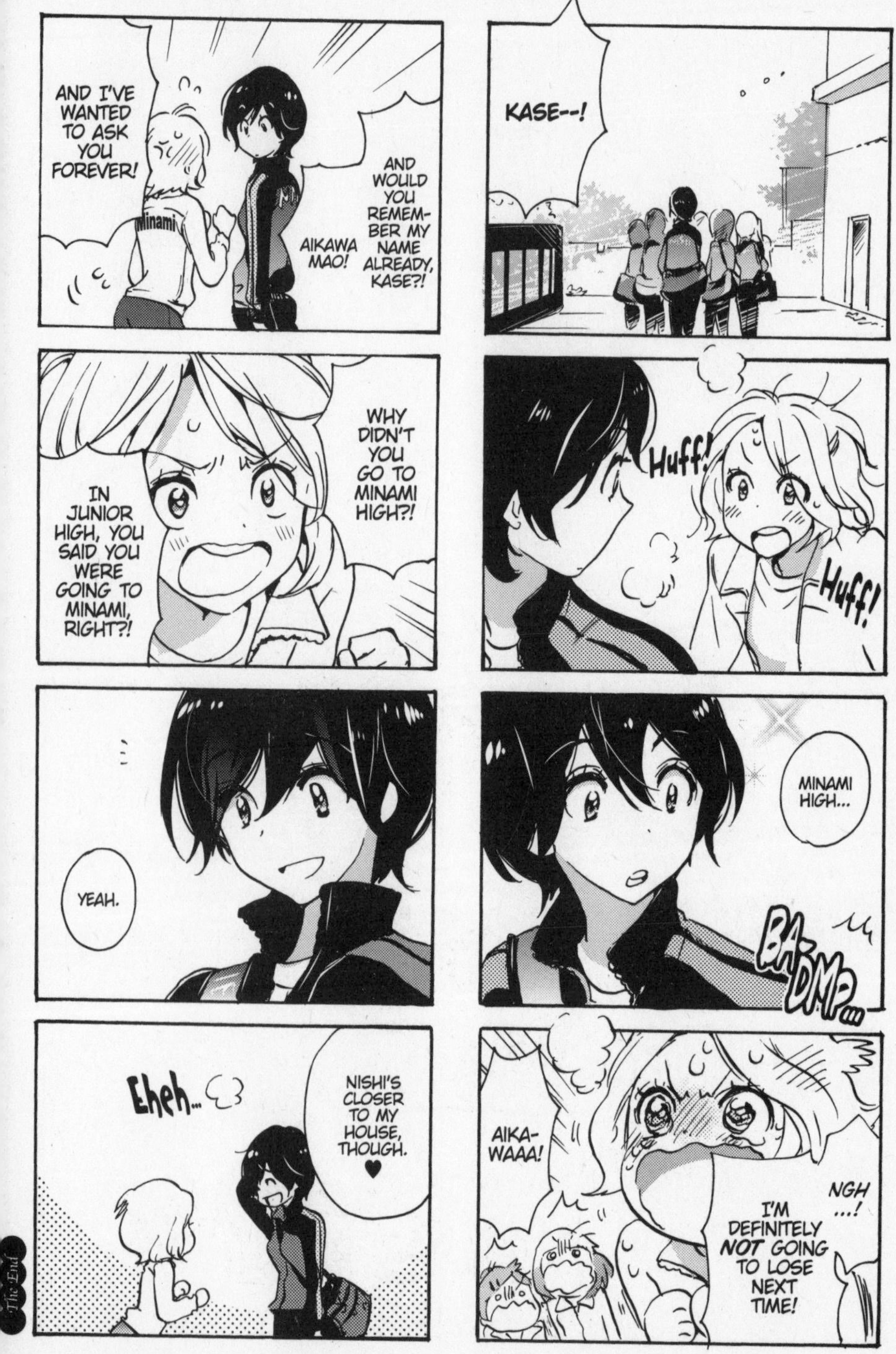
KASE--!
AND WOULD YOU REMEMBER MY NAME ALREADY, KASE?!
AIKAWA MAO!
AND I'VE WANTED TO ASK YOU FOREVER!
Huff!
Huff!
WHY DIDN'T YOU GO TO MINAMI HIGH?!
IN JUNIOR HIGH, YOU SAID YOU WERE GOING TO MINAMI, RIGHT?!
MINAMI HIGH...
BA-DMP...
YEAH.
AIKA-WAAA!
NGH ...!
I'M DEFINITELY NOT GOING TO LOSE NEXT TIME!
NISHI'S CLOSER TO MY HOUSE, THOUGH. ♥
Eheh...
The End

Kase-san and Anstagram

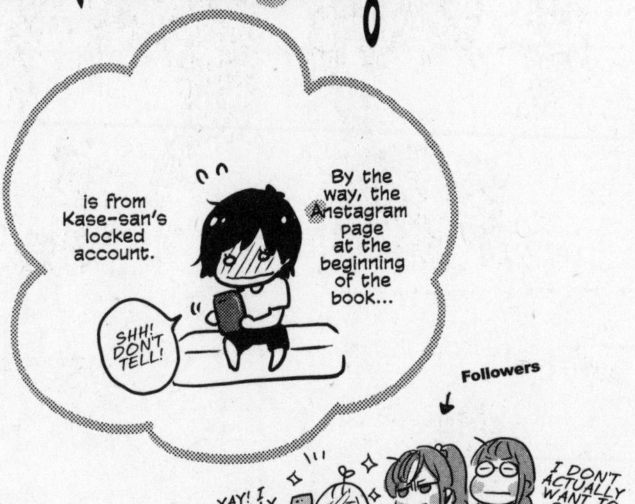
By the way, the Anstagram page at the beginning of the book...
is from Kase-san's locked account.
SHH! DON'T TELL!
Followers
I DON'T ACTUALLY WANT TO SEE IT.
YAY! I FINALLY GOT A SMART PHONE!

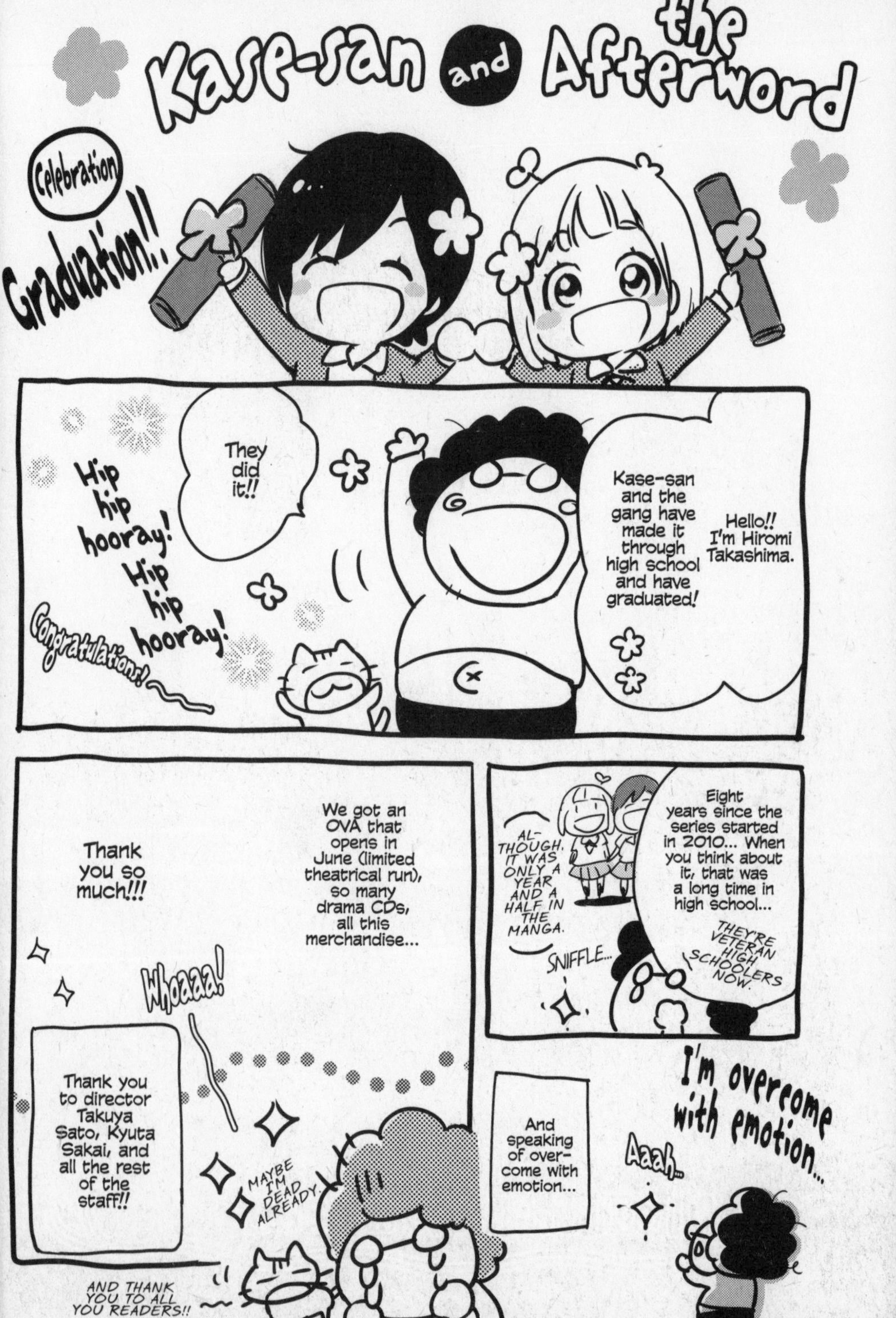
Kase-san and the Afterword
Celebration
Graduation!!
Hello!! I'm Hiromi Takashima.
Kase-san and the gang have made it through high school and have graduated!
They did it!!
Hip hip hooray! Hip hip hooray!
Congratulations!
Eight years since the series started in 2010... When you think about it, that was a long time in high school...
THEY'RE VETERAN HIGH SCHOOLERS NOW.
AL-THOUGH, IT WAS ONLY A YEAR AND A HALF IN THE MANGA.
SNIFFLE...
We got an OVA that opens in June (limited theatrical run), so many drama CDs, all this merchandise...
Thank you so much!!!
Whoaaa!
I'm overcome with emotion...
Aaah...
And speaking of over-come with emotion...
Thank you to director Takuya Sato, Kyuta Sakai, and all the rest of the staff!!
MAYBE I'M DEAD ALREADY.
AND THANK YOU TO ALL YOU READERS!!

🔍 Search

kase_tomo0501   [Follow]

56 posts   **3** followers   **10** following
I'm Kase Tomoka. I'm on the track team!

Kase-san and Cherry Blossoms ✿

Story and Art by Hiromi Takashima

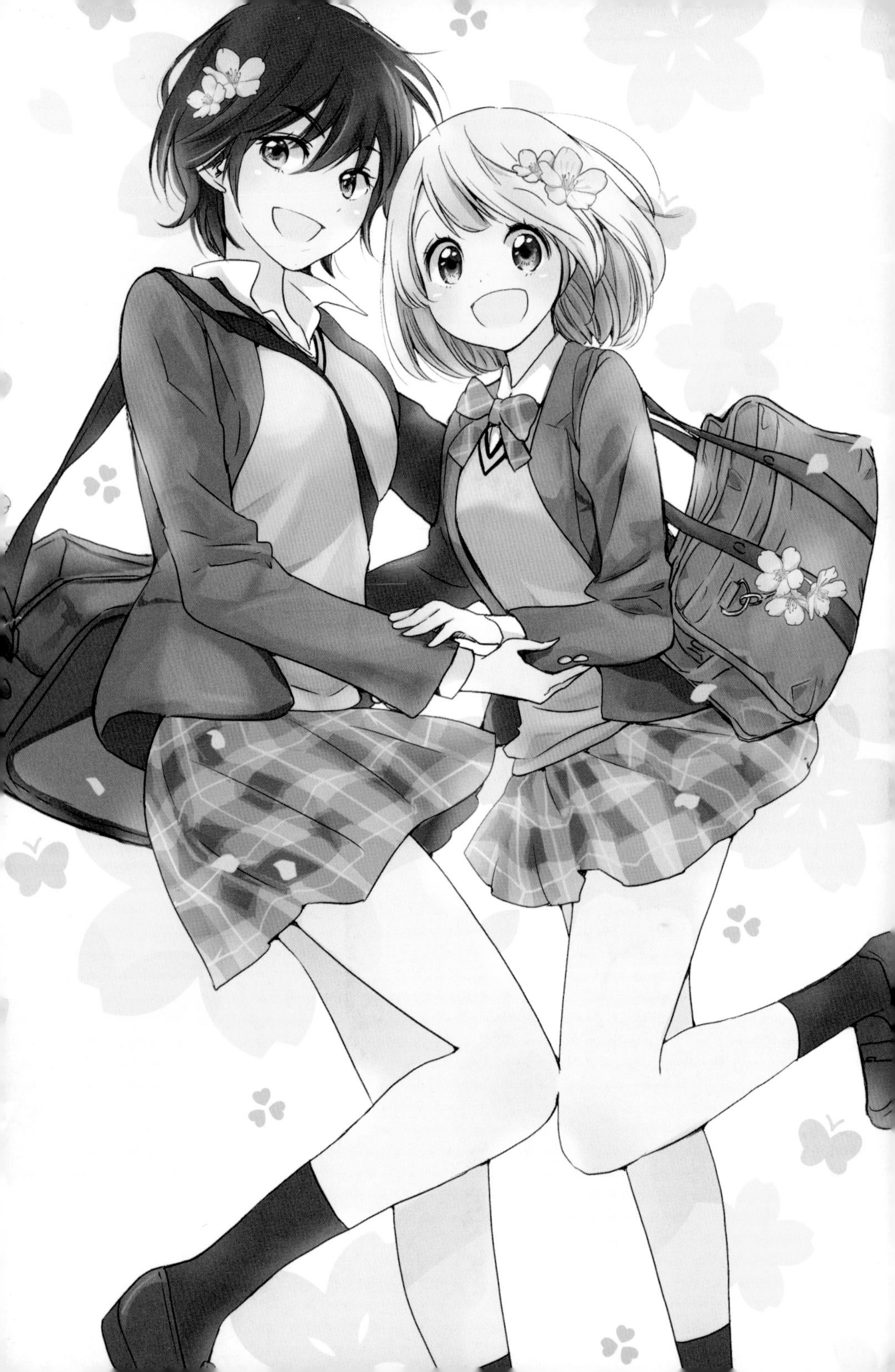